Lost Secrets of the Sacred Ark

Lost Secrets of the Sacred Ark

Amazing Revelations
of the Incredible Power of Gold

Laurence Gardner

Element
An Imprint of HarperCollins*Publishers*
77–85 Fulham Palace Road,
Hammersmith, London W6 8JB

The website address is: www.thorsonselement.com

and *Element* are trademarks of
HarperCollins*Publishers* Ltd

First published in Great Britain in 2003 by Element Books
This edition 2004

2

© 2003 Laurence Gardner

Laurence Gardner asserts the moral right
to be identified as the author of this work

A catalogue record of this book
is available from the British Library

ISBN 0 00 714296 X

Printed and bound in Great Britain by
Clays Ltd, St Ives plc

To my wife Angela
with love

"Our Stone is nothing but gold digested to the highest degree of purity and subtle fixation. It is fixed and incombustible like a stone, but its appearance is that of a very fine powder."
Eirenaeus Philalethes – The Philosophers' Stone, 1667

Contents

PART II

Genealogical Charts

Color Plates

Maps and Illustrations

Acknowledgements

For their invaluable assistance in the compilation of this work, I am indebted to those numerous archivists, librarians and curators who have facilitated my research, notably those at the British Library; the British Museum; the Bibliothèque Nationale de France; the Bibliothèque de Bordeaux; the Louvre Museum; the Oriental Institute Museum; University of Chicago; the Ashmolean Museum, Oxford; the Warburg Institute, London; the Royal Irish Academy, Dublin; the National Library of Scotland; Birmingham Central Library; and Devon County Library.

With regard to certain specialist and scientific areas, I am grateful for direct and indirect assistance from the World Gold Council, the Platinum Metals Congress, the Science of the Spirit Foundation, Argonne National Laboratories, the American Physical Society, the Patrick Foundation, and the Egypt Exploration Society. Express thanks in this regard are due to physicist Dr. Daniel Sewell Ward for his generous professional assistance.

My appreciation is due to HRH Prince Michael of Albany for affording me privileged access to Household and Chivalric papers of the Royal House of Stewart and the Knights Templars of St. Anthony. I am additionally thankful to my wife Angela, whose tireless effort has brought this work to fruition, and to my son James for his encouragement during my quest. Grateful thanks are also due to my agent Andrew Lownie, to my foreign rights agent Scarlett Nunn, editor Matthew Cory, and to all at Element and HarperCollins who have seen this edition through to its publication. I am indebted to Sir Peter Robson for his valued artistic liaison – particularly for his specially produced painting *Destiny of the House of Gold* – and likewise to the artist Andrew Jones for his enthusiastic collaboration.

To those many friends whose involvement has smoothed the path in one way or another I offer my appreciation – in particular to Chev. David Roy Stewart, Chev. Jack Robertson, Rev. David Cuthbert Stalker, Sandra Hamblett, Tony Skiens, Jaz Coleman, Shaun Pettigrew, Barry Carter of Subtle Energies, Nigel Blair of the Wessex Research Group, and Edmund Marriage of the Golden Age Project.

For their generous support in aiding my work internationally, my special thanks to Karen Lyster of Kiwis Graphics, to Eleanor Robson and Steve Robson of Peter Robson Studio, to Duncan Roads, Ruth Parnell, Marcus and Robyn Allen, Jeffrey Williams and Tom Bosco of *Nexus*, to Adriano Forgione of *Hera*, to J.Z. Knight and all at Ramtha's School of Enlightenment. Also to Christina Zohs of *The Golden Thread*, Nancy and Mike Simms of Entropic Fine Art, Laura Lee, Whitley and Ann Strieber, Nancy Lee, Dr. Robert Ghost Wolf and Shoshanna of the Wolf Lodge Foundation, and all at the International Association for New Science.

Finally, I must convey my gratitude to all those readers who have supported and encouraged my work over the years – especially to those many who have written to me with such a variety of useful comments and contributions.

Laurence Gardner

Introduction

Throughout the past century, and especially since the days of Albert Einstein, scientists have been searching for the *Holy Grail* of modern physics, which they classify as a "unified theory of everything." This has led to some amazing discoveries and the emergence of a whole new language, which includes superstrings, quarks, and superconductivity, along with an awareness of hitherto unknown planes of existence beyond our own familiar space-time.

In the field of quantum mechanics, scientists have recently confirmed that matter can indeed be in two places at once. It is now established that, through quantum entanglement, particles millions of light-years apart can be connected without physical contact. Space-time can now be manipulated; teleportation is becoming a reality; gravity-resistant material is heralded for air transport, and virtual science has led to a greater understanding of hyper-dimensional environments.

When discussing the attributes of monatomic gold and platinums in *Genesis of the Grail Kings*, I remarked that it would not be long before the potential of these noble metals was announced for environment-friendly fuel cells. These, I suggested, would supersede fossil fuels for transportation and other practical purposes. At the same time, I touched on their future use in the medical arena, particularly in the field of cancer treatment. More especially, we looked at the gravity-defying attributes of these exotic substances, and at their abilities to superconduct and literally bend space-time. These announcements, brief though they might have been, subsequently led to more reader interest and media interview enquiry than I have received for any other subject area of my writings. Consequently, the matter has now qualified for a book in its own right.

The truly astonishing fact about the enigmatic white powder of high-spin gold and platinum group metals is that it is not actually a new discovery. The ancient Mesopotamians called it *shem-an-na* and the Egyptians described it as *mfkzt*, while the Alexandrians and later chemists such as Nicolas Flamel venerated it as a gift from Paradise, calling it the Philosophers' Stone. At all stages of its history the sacred "powder of projection" was reckoned to have extraordinary powers of levitation, transmutation, and teleportation. It was said to produce brilliant light and deadly rays, while at the same time being a key to active physical longevity. In today's world, the Institute of Advanced Studies describes the substance as "exotic matter" and its superconductive powers have been claimed by the Center for Advanced Study as "the most remarkable physical property in the universe."

It is clear, however, from the documentary evidence of ancient times, that the attributes of superconductors and gravity defiance were known, if not understood, in a distant world of priestly levitation, godly communication, and the phenomenal power of the *electrikus*. In Greek mythology the quest for the secret of this substance was at the heart of the *Golden Fleece* legend, while in biblical terms it was the mystical realm of the Ark of the Covenant – the golden coffer which Moses brought out of Sinai, and was later housed in the Temple of Jerusalem.

For our present detailed investigation of the white-powder phenomenon, the Ark of the Covenant provides the best catalyst for relating the history, since its own adventurous story is intrinsically related. *Lost Secrets of the Sacred Ark* is not, however, limited to being a quest for the Ark – although it does indeed tread this ground to determine its likely whereabouts. More precisely, it is about the functions and workings

of the Ark from Mosaic to Templar times – moving to the
rediscovery of its sacred science in recent years, with related
commentary from the foremost scientific academies of the
world.

Laurence Gardner
Exeter, July 2002

PART I

House of Gold

The Holy Mountain

Our story begins early last century, in March 1904, with King Edward VII reigning in Britain and Theodore Roosevelt installed as President of the United States of America. The Great War (1914–18) was an unknown prospect of the future, and this was an enthusiastic time of adventure and exploration. Captain Robert Scott and his *Discovery* crew were returning to England from the Antarctic, while at the same time the British archaeologist Sir W.M. Flinders Petrie and his team stood upon a wind-torn rocky plateau in the Sinai desert.

The Petrie expedition had been sponsored by the lately established Egypt Exploration Fund (now the Egypt Exploration Society). Its purpose was to survey the old copper and turquoise mining region of the Sinai peninsula, between the Gulfs of Suez and Aqaba, above the Red Sea to the east of Egypt. This was the land of the biblical mountain of Moses, which the Old Testament book of Exodus (King James edition) refers to as Mount Horeb.[1] The place was more correctly represented as Mount Choreb in the ancient Septuagint Bible from the 3rd century BC.[2] Far from being straightforward nominal applications, the words *choreb* and *horeb* were of great significance in the days of Moses, as we shall discover.[3]

Prior to Petrie's undertaking, the difficulty in determining the exact position of Mount Horeb had been because the mountain range of Sinai is extensive and the local inhabitants (even if they cared about ancient history) were not too familiar with the high country. Back in the 4th century AD, an order of Christian monks had founded the mission of St. Catherine's Monastery on a mountain towards the south of Sinai, and had dubbed the place *Gebel Musa* (Mount of Moses). It was clear, however, that this was an inaccurate conclusion since it did not comply with the Bible's geographical references. The book of Exodus explains the route taken by Moses and the Israelites in around 1330 BC, when they departed from the Egyptian Delta region of Goshen, traveling beyond the Red Sea towards the land of Midian (north of present-day Jordan). Following this line of direction across the wilderness regions of Shur and Paran, the holy mountain of Moses is found soaring to over 2,600 feet within a high sandstone plateau above the Plain of Paran. Today it is known as *Serâbît el Khâdim* (the Prominence of the Khâdim), and it was this rugged outcrop which the Petrie expedition scaled. They had no particular expectation of the place, but it was part of the survey and they made their way to the summit where, to their astonishment, they made a monumental discovery.

Built over an expanse of some 230 feet (*c*. 70 m), extending from a great man-made cave, they found the ruin of an old temple, with inscriptions dating it back to the time of the 4th-dynasty pharaoh Sneferu, who reigned about 2600 BC.[4] Subsequently, Petrie wrote, "The whole of it was buried, and no one had any knowledge of it until we cleared the site."[5] It would perhaps not have surprised them to find a Semitic altar stone, or some other ritualistic landmark, but this was a vast Egyptian temple and clearly of some importance.

When I first discussed this expedition a few years ago,[6] I had no idea of the interest it would provoke for new venturers. Since that time, many readers have written to me after making the wearisome climb, recounting their visits and sending wonderful photographs of their exploits. In this regard, although no one has mentioned the fact in their correspondence, perhaps I should have clarified that, although the temple remains are still accessible and impressive by virtue of their unusual location, many of the specific artifacts, as portrayed in Petrie's photographs and writings, are no longer there.

It has been an unfortunate but standard practice for archaeologists to plunder ancient sites in other people's lands, bringing their trophies back to museums in the West. These include not just portable items, but great statues, obelisks, and even whole wall sections from places such as Egypt, Assyria, and Babylonia. The museums and vaults of Britain, Europe, and America are loaded with such items. It might seem logical that, in describing some of the more important Petrie findings at Mount Serâbît, I should have given details of where they might be seen today. The fact is, however, that the Serâbît hoard has not been easy to locate because, although some items made their way into public galleries, many were strategically concealed from open scrutiny. Nevertheless, I am pleased to say that I have now met with a certain amount of success, and a list of some museums where Serâbît items have been lodged is given in the Notes and References.[7] Although a good number of broken items recorded by Petrie were not removed by museum officials after the 1904 expedition, they were purloined by others once details of the site became known. Consequently, they were not there to be found by a subsequent Harvard University expedition in 1935.

The reason why many of the primary artifacts were secreted in storage is that Petrie's discovery was viewed with great displeasure at the time, and was reckoned to contradict the Exodus portrayal of events at the holy mountain. It was here that Moses was said to have seen the burning bush, where he talked with Jehovah, burned the golden calf, and received the Tables of Testimony. In practice, the Petrie report did not overturn the biblical account in any way; what it challenged was the Church's interpretation of the story and the manner in which it was being taught. Essentially, his discovery contravened the regulations of the Egypt Exploration Fund. The Fund's 1891 founding *Memorandum and Articles of Association* state that its objectives included the "promotion of surveys and excavations for the purpose of elucidating or illustrating the Old Testament narrative."[8] This, of course, meant the Old Testament as it was traditionally interpreted, not necessarily as it was written.

Following Queen Victoria's death in 1901, and with British Imperialism at a height of perceived glory, Victorian values were still paramount when Petrie made his 1904 discovery. These said values, imposed on society, might today be regarded as establishment intimidations rather than worthwhile concepts, and it took the brutal rigors of World War I (10 years later) to introduce some leveling of attitudes. But Petrie, despite being the most notable archaeologist of the era, felt the weight of authoritarian disapproval. Having decided to publish his findings once he returned, his hitherto unquestioned sponsorship by the Egypt Exploration Fund was terminated. He wrote in his report: "It has therefore been needful for me to trust for the future … in the Egyptian Research Account and British School of Archaeology in Egypt."

Petrie's logs were collated by him into a fairly substantial book entitled *Researches in Sinai*. This was published by John Murray of London in 1906, but it was not long-lived and copies are now very hard to find. Much later, in 1955, the newly styled and rather more inspired Egypt Exploration Society (in association with Oxford University Press) published their own edition concerning the Sinai reliefs and inscriptions.[9] This two-volume work dealt in the first instance with Petrie's findings, but the second part concentrated on the related manuscripts of prominent Egyptologists Alan H. Gardiner and T. Eric Peet. They had progressed Petrie's work

for the Society, transcribing, relating, and debating the hieroglyphs and carvings. But where were the original artifacts
from Serâbît el Khâdim? Where were all those items which
Petrie and the others described?

It transpires that since 1906 a great number have been kept
out of harm's way behind closed doors, with very few items
presented for public view. From what can now be ascertained,
some 463 items were officially removed from the mountain
temple – everything from large obelisks and stelae to small
wands and bowls. Fortunately, a whole new generation of
individuals is now responsible for the artifacts and, upon
being reminded of their existence (with the Victorian-style
constraints no longer applicable), the custodians are indeed
showing some enthusiasm in this regard.

Currently, I have access to a museum database list of some
114 specified items from Mount Serâbît. Although individually logged, numbered, and described, the relics have been
crated in storage for decades. Catalogued as being from the
"Findspot: Egypt, Sinai, Serâbît el Khâdim," these include
offering tables, statues, stelae, and an altar, along with vases,
amulets, plaques, wands, and tools. The various pharaonic
cartouches and inscriptions denote an extended time frame
from the 4th dynasty, through the Middle Kingdom (with a
particular emphasis on the 12th dynasty), the New Kingdom
(especially the 18th-dynasty time of Moses) to the Ramesside
era, culminating with the 20th dynasty. This represents an
operative use of the temple through about 1,500 years.

Dedicated to the goddess Hathor throughout its operative
life, the Serâbît temple appears to have ceased all function
during the 12th century BC, when Egypt fell into financial
decline and to outside influence, leading eventually to the
Greek rule of the Ptolemies. It was, however, fully operational
before the Giza pyramids were built, and continued in service
beyond the eras of Tutankhamun and Rameses the Great –
throughout the magnificent periods of the Lotus Eaters[10] and

the God-Kings. But why would there have been such an important Egyptian temple hundreds of miles away from the pharaonic centers, across the Red Sea gulfs at the top of a desolate mountain?

Field of the Blessed

At risk of being repetitive for those who have read *Genesis of the Grail Kings*, it is worth reiterating some of the key aspects of Petrie's discovery, while adding some extra details of the debate which later ensued back in the West.

The part of the temple above ground was constructed from sandstone quarried from the mountain. Its structure was a series of adjoining halls, shrines, courts, cubicles, and chambers, all set within a surrounding enclosure wall. Of these, the main features unearthed were the Hall of Hathor, the Sanctuary, the Shrine of Kings, and the Portico Court. All around were pillars and stelae denoting the Egyptian kings through the ages, while certain kings such as Tuthmosis III were depicted many times on standing stones and wall reliefs. After clearing the site, Petrie wrote: "There is no other such monument known which makes us regret the more that it is not in better preservation."[11]

The Cave of Hathor had been cut into the natural rock, with flat inner walls that were carefully smoothed. In the center was a large upright pillar of Amenemhet III (*c.* 1841–1797 BC). Also portrayed was his chief chamberlain, Khenemsu, and his seal-bearer, Ameny-senb. Deep within the cave Petrie found a limestone stela of pharaoh Rameses I – a slab upon which Rameses (traditionally reckoned by Egyptologists to be an opposer of the monotheistic Aten god cult of pharaoh Akhenaten) had surprisingly described himself as "The ruler of all that Aten embraces."[12] Also found was an Amarna statue-head of Akhenaten's mother, Queen Tiye, with her cartouche[13] set in the crown.

In the courts and halls of the outer temple were numerous stone-carved rectangular tanks and circular basins, along with a variety of curiously shaped bench-altars with recessed fronts and split-level surfaces. There were also round tables, trays, and saucers, together with alabaster vases and cups – many of which were shaped like lotus flowers. In addition, the rooms housed a good collection of glazed plaques, cartouches, scarabs, and sacred ornaments, designed with spirals, diagonal-squares, and basketwork. There were wands of an unidentified hard material, and in the portico were two conical stones of about 6 inches (15 cm) and 9 inches (22.5 cm) in height respectively. The explorers were baffled enough by these, but they were further confounded by the discovery of a metallurgist's crucible and a considerable amount of pure white powder concealed beneath carefully laid flagstones.

Subsequent to the event, Egyptologists began to argue over why a crucible would have been necessary in a temple, while at the same time debating a mysterious substance called *mfkzt* (sometimes pronounced "mufkuzt"), which had dozens of mentions in the Serâbît wall and stelae inscriptions.[14] Some claimed that *mfkzt* might have been copper, while many preferred the idea of turquoise, since both were known to have been mined in the lower country beyond the mountain. Others supposed it was perhaps malachite, but these were all unsubstantiated guesses, and there were no traces of any of these materials at the site. If turquoise mining had been a primary function of the temple masters through so many dynastic periods, then one would expect turquoise stones to have been found at the site, and in abundance within the tombs of Egypt – but such has not been the case.

In the course of the debate, it was ascertained that enquiries about *mfkzt* had been raised before by the German philologist Karl Richard Lepsius, who had discovered the word "*mfkzt*" in Egypt back in 1845. Indeed, the question was posed even earlier by the French scientist Jean François Champollion who, in 1822, found the key to deciphering the Rosetta Stone and pioneered the art of understanding Egyptian hieroglyphics.[15]

It had, in fact, been decided some time prior to the Petrie expedition that *mfkzt* was neither turquoise, copper, nor malachite. It was ascertained, however, that the word signified some form of "stone" which was extremely valuable and regarded as being in some way unstable. Numerous lists of substances considered precious by the Egyptians included *mfkzt*, but by virtue of the other gems, minerals, and metals in those same lists, it was known to be none of them. After more than a hundred years of research and investigation, when studying the lists in 1955, the best that the debating Egyptologists could determine was that "*mfkzt* was a valuable mineral product."[16]

Notwithstanding this, the earliest historical record of *mfkzt* outside of Sinai is probably the most telling of all. It appears in a very different and much more descriptive guise in the *Pyramid Texts* – sacred writings which adorn the 5th-dynasty pyramid tomb of King Unas at Saqqara, charting his resurrection into the Afterlife. Here is described the locality in which the dead king is said to live forever with the gods, and it is called the *Field of Mfkzt*. Another ethereal location named in the *Pyramid Texts* is the *Field of Iaru* – the Dimension of the Blessed – and there seems to be a commonality between the two. From this it is ascertained that *mfkzt* was not just a valuable earthly substance, sometimes classified as a "stone," it was also the key to an elusive Field – an alternative dimensional state of being. The word "field" is also used to describe regions where operative forces such as gravity and magnetism are active, and we shall return to this in due course.

The Great One

During the investigations, other causes of wonderment for the scientists were the innumerable inscribed references to "bread" found at Serâbît, and the traditional hieroglyph for "light" (a point within a circle) displayed in the Shrine of the Kings. Then, of course, there was the mysterious white powder to consider – many tons of it, by Petrie's reckoning.

On debating the powder, it was suggested that perhaps it was a remnant of copper smelting, but, as Petrie pointed out, smelting does not produce white powder; it leaves a dense black slag. Moreover, there was no supply of copper ore within miles of the temple. In any event, it was determined that smelting was conducted in the distant valleys. Others guessed that the powder was ash from the burning of plants to produce alkali, but there was no trace whatever of plant residue.

For want of any other explanation, it was considered that the white powder and the conical stones were probably associated with a form of sacrificial rite[17] – but this was an Egyptian temple and animal sacrifice was not an Egyptian practice until the later Ptolemaic era. Moreover, there were no remnants of bones or any other foreign matter within the powder which lay in the newly exposed storerooms – it was perfectly clean and quite unadulterated. Petrie stated in his report: "Though I carefully searched these ashes in dozens of instances, winnowing them in a breeze, I never found a fragment of bone or anything else."[18]

Since both the white powder and the *mfkzt* were equally indefinable and yet seemingly both of great importance, maybe they were one and the same. But how could a powder be described as a "stone," and how could either be a key to unlock a field of otherworldly dimension? Furthermore, what could they possibly have to do with bread and light?

At this stage of the research, another valuable substance associated with the Serâbît temple came into the equation: gold. On one of the rock tablets near to the Hathor cave entrance was found a representation of Tuthmosis IV in the presence of Hathor. Before him were two offering stands topped with lotus flowers and behind him a man bearing a conical object described as "white bread." Another stela details the mason Ankhib offering two conical bread-cakes to the king and there are similar portrayals elsewhere in the temple complex. One of the most significant representations is a depiction of Hathor and Amenhotep III. The goddess, complete with her customary cow horns and solar disc, holds a necklace in one hand, while offering the emblem of life and dominion to the pharaoh with the other.[19] Behind her is the treasurer Sobekhotep, who holds in readiness a conical loaf of "white bread." Importantly, treasurer Sobekhotep is described elsewhere in the temple inscriptions as the man who "brought the noble Precious Stone to his majesty."[20] Furthermore, he is said to be the "true royal acquaintance" and the "Great One over the secrets of the House of Gold."

Although difficult to comprehend, the 18th dynasty's royal treasurer was depicted presenting conical objects described as "white bread," while being the prestigious guardian of the

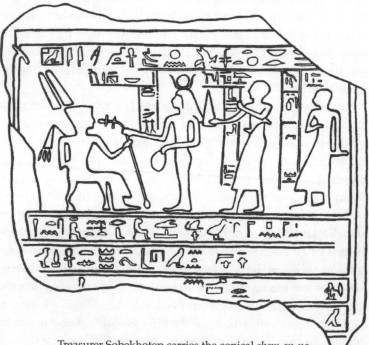

Treasurer Sobekhotep carries the conical *shem-an-na*.
He and Hathor make presentations to Amenhotep III.

House of Gold. But, according to the records, Petrie found no gold at the Serâbît temple on Mount Horeb. In fact, the Egypt Exploration Society writers made the specific point in their report that there is no evidence of gold ever being mined in Sinai – but that does not prove that gold was never taken there. Also, it is likely that any which might have been left at the temple in distant times was plundered by bedouin raiders centuries before Petrie arrived, just as many of the tombs of Egypt were vandalized and plundered before the days of archaeology.

What is interesting on this front is that the ancient Egyptians did not call Sinai by that name; they called the peninsula "Bia," and in this connection the puzzle begins to piece together. While remembering that the temple was dedicated to the goddess Hathor, and that the treasurer of the House of Gold was referred to as the "great one," we can now consider the British Museum's stela of the Middle Kingdom deputy treasurer Si-Hathor. The inscription on this stone relates, in the words of Si-Hathor, "I visited Bia as a child; I compelled the great ones to wash gold."[21] (There is a question mark after the word "wash," indicating that the translators were not wholly sure of the hieroglyph, or of quite what it was that the great ones did with the gold.)

The Ultimate Goal

Notwithstanding the fact that gold is not a traditional product of Sinai, there are important references to Sinai and gold in the Old Testament – events which specifically relate to Mount Horeb (the Prominence of the Khâdim). Moreover, one of the biblical accounts does indeed associate its gold with a mysterious powder, and it also mentions water – not for washing the gold as such, but for its immersion.

In the book of Exodus, Moses and the Israelites are at Mount Horeb, having journeyed beyond the Red Sea from Egypt. Moses climbs the rock to speak with El Shaddai, the

Lord of the Mountain (later called Jehovah), who instructs him that he is henceforth their God, and that they should no longer use their gold to make idols and deiform images.[22] Meanwhile, at the foot of the mountain, the Israelites become impatient and, believing that Moses must be lost – having been away for so long – they (apparently thousands of them) all remove their gold earrings and give them to Moses' brother Aaron. Without further ado, he melts down the rings and manufactures a golden calf to serve as a venerative idol for their onward journey. Soon afterwards, Moses comes down from the mountain and, becoming angry at their dancing around the idol, performs a most extraordinary transformation. Exodus 32:20 explains: "And he took the calf which they had made, and burnt it in the fire, and ground it to powder, and strawed it upon the water, and made the children of Israel drink of it."

In practice, this sounds rather more like a ritual than a punishment, even though the latter is how the story is conveyed. Aaron had previously melted the gold in the fire to mold the image, but what Moses did was plainly different because firing gold produces molten gold, not powder. The Septuagint is rather more explicit in stating that Moses "consumed the gold with fire," implying a more fragmentary process than heating and melting. The *Oxford English Dictionary* defines "to consume" as "to reduce to nothing or to tiny particles." So what is this process that, through the use of fire, can reduce gold to a powder? And why would Moses "straw it upon the water" and give it to his followers to drink? Here again the Septuagint differs slightly, but perhaps significantly, in saying that Moses "sowed" the powder in water. Either way, it is indicative of the baffling Si-Hathor translation which has settled upon "wash" for the ambiguous hieroglyph.

Since mysterious processes concerning gold have an alchemical ring about them, let us look at the writings of the 17th-century alchemist Eirenaeus Philalethes. This renowned British philosopher, revered by Isaac Newton, Robert Boyle,

Elias Ashmole, and others of his day, produced a work in 1667 entitled *Secrets Revealed*. In this treatise he discussed the nature of the Philosophers' Stone, which was commonly thought to transmute base metal into gold.[23] Setting the record straight, Philalethes made the point that the Stone was itself made of gold, and that the alchemical art was in perfecting this process. He stated: "Our Stone is nothing but gold digested to the highest degree of purity and subtle fixation ... Our gold, no longer vulgar, is the ultimate goal of Nature."

In another treatise entitled *A Brief Guide to the Celestial Ruby*,[24] Philalethes further pronounced: "It is called a Stone by virtue of its fixed nature; it resists the action of fire as successfully as any stone. In species it is gold, more purer than the purest; it is fixed and incombustible like a stone, but its appearance is that of a very fine powder."

In his writing, Philalethes described the gold as being "digested," a word closely associated with "consumed" (as in the Moses story) – both meaning to break down something into particles, or into some conveniently reduced form for physical, mental, or chemical assimilation. As stated, the Egyptian records identify *mfkzt* as a stone. Like the Philosophers' Stone of alchemy, Moses consumed the golden calf with fire and transformed it into a powder. The Horeb temple at Serâbît el Khâdim was established for the Great House[25] of the Kings: the dynasties of the royal House of Gold, but no gold in its metallic state was found there – only a preserved store of enigmatic white powder.

With regard to the *Pyramid Texts* and their references to the Field of Mfkzt as a dimension of the kingly Afterlife, it is pertinent to note that white bread-cakes were also associated with the jackal-god Anubis in Egypt. He was the one said to preside over funerary rites and lead the dead into the Afterlife. He was called the Guardian of the Secret[26] and a related 19th-dynasty relief at Abydos depicts Anubis sitting on an ark, while the pharaoh presents him with a conical loaf of the precious stone.

Pharaoh presents Anubis with a conical loaf of the precious stone.
From a 19th-dynasty relief at the Temple of Abydos.

Examples of Serâbît artifacts which are of special importance in respect of the Precious Stone (the *mfkzt*) are two
round-topped stelae from the 18th-dynasty reigns of Tuthmosis III and Amenhotep III. The first, which depicts Tuthmosis
presenting a conical loaf to the god Amun-re, is inscribed:
"The presenting of a white bread that he may be given life."
The second shows Amenhotep offering a conical loaf to the
god Sopdu, and states: "He gave the gold of reward; the
mouths rejoiced." From these, it is clarified that the white-
powder bread was perceived as a giver of life, and that it was
indeed made from gold.

The Paradise Stone

Giver of Life

From the earliest days of Egyptian dynastic history, Sinai was not a separate country, but an integral part of Egypt. Although it had no military garrison or resident governor, it fell directly under pharaonic control. During the 18th-dynasty time of Moses (the dynasty of Akhenaten and Tutankhamun) the Sinai peninsular was under the supervision of two officials: the Royal Chancellor and the Royal Messenger in Foreign Lands. In the time of Akhenaten's immediate forebears, Tuthmosis IV and Amenhotep III, the Royal Messenger was an official called Neby. He was also the mayor and troop commander of Zaru in the Delta region of Goshen (or Gesem, as given in the Septuagint), where the Israelites (descendants of Jacob-Israel, as against the Hebrews of Canaan) had lived for many generations since the time of Abraham. The position of Royal Chancellor was traditionally retained in the Hyksos family of Pa-Nehas,[1] and Akhenaten had appointed a descendant named Panahesy (Phinehas in Exodus) to the governorship of Sinai. Because of this, Moses knew that Sinai was a safe haven when he and the Israelites made their exodus from the Egyptian Delta – a haven where there was an operative Egyptian temple at Mount Horeb.

What Sir W.M. Flinders Petrie actually found in 1904 was the alchemical workshop of Akhenaten and the generations of pharaohs before him. Here the furnace would have roared and smoked in the production of the sacred *mfkzt*: the enigmatic white powder of gold. By way of ingestion (as conical bread-cakes or by water immersion) this was described as a "giver of life" for the kings of the House of Gold, while also affording entry to the mysterious super-dimensional field of the After-life. Under these circumstances, the appearance of a metallur-gist's crucible at Serâbît falls into a natural context. Now the words of Exodus begin to make sense as we read them again with a wholly new insight: "And mount Sinai was altogether on a smoke, because the Lord descended upon it in fire: and the smoke thereof ascended as the smoke of a furnace, and the whole mount quaked greatly." (Exodus 19:18).

Although seemingly anomalous that a temple should have been a type of laboratory workshop rather than a place of godly worship, it transpires that the anomaly does not exist in historical terms. In fact, it is our understanding of the word "worship" that has been wrongly interpreted through the ages. The original Semitic word which was eventually trans-lated to become "worship" was *avôd*, which meant quite simply "work."[2] The ancients did not just venerate their gods in the temples, they worked for them. In this regard, the Oxford Word Library explains the etymological base of "worship" (from the Old English *weorc*) as being *weorchipe* – in essence "'work-ship." Thus, for temples to have been work-shops of one sort or another was the norm in those days, and their tutorial governors were styled "craftsmen." The nature of their craft (as in The Craft of modern Freemasonry) was largely concerned with special esoteric knowledge referred to as *kynning*. Those who kept the secrets were referred to as being "crafty" or "cunning." In the New Testament, Jesus' father Joseph was described as a "craftsman" (Aramaic: *naggar*; and Greek: *ho tekton*) but, through a 17th-century misunderstanding of the old ways, this was mistranslated to become "carpenter."[3]

There were apparently two reasons why *mfkzt* was reckoned to be a "giver of life." First, because, as an ingested substance, it was of significance to the kings' active life spans. Second, because, after death, it was the route to their preservation in a field of the Afterlife. Clearly, it was not infallible in the first instance because the kings did die of natural causes, as well as in battle. However, the *mfkzt* plainly enhanced their lives in some way, and very likely extended their potential life spans beyond the norm. In this respect, it was akin to the enigmatic Fountain of Youth in popular Middle Ages romance.

With this concept to the fore, the logic of Hathor's association with the Serâbît temple becomes clear, for she was herself regarded as a life-giver. To the Egyptians, Hathor was representative of the Babylonian goddess Ishtar, and had attributes of nursing motherhood similar to those of Isis, the Great Mother. Hathor was defined as Queen of the West and Mistress of the Netherworld, to where she was said to carry those who knew the right spells.[4] She was the revered protectress of womanhood; the lady of the sycamore; the lady of turquoise; goddess of love, tombs, and song. It was from the milk of Hathor that the pharaohs were reckoned to gain their divinity, becoming gods in their own right. They were said to feed on the milk of Hathor just as the Babylonian kings had fed on the milk of Ishtar. It would appear that since natural mothers' milk contains the enzyme telomerase (the recently styled "enzyme of immortality"), then *mfkzt* (the symbolic milk of Hathor) must somehow have enhanced the production of this enzyme. Indeed, modern scientists have now described telomerase as being the "fountain of youth."[5]

As reported in the journal *Science*,[6] along with reports from corporate studies and those of the University of Texas Southwestern Medical Center, it has been determined that telomerase has unique anti-ageing properties. Healthy body cells are programmed to divide many times during a lifetime, but this process of division and replication is finite, so that a nondividing state is ultimately achieved. The division potential is controlled by caps at the end of DNA strands (rather like the plastic tips on shoelaces), and these caps are the telomeres. As each cell divides, a piece of telomere is lost, and the dividing process ceases when the telomeres have shortened to an optimum and critical length. There is then no new cell replication and all that follows is deterioration – ageing.

Laboratory experiments with tissue samples have shown that the application of the genetic enzyme telomerase can prevent the shortening of telomeres upon cell division and replication. Thereby, body cells can continue to divide far beyond their naturally restricted programming (just as do cancer cells, which achieve immortality through being rich in this substance). Telomerase is not usually expressed in normal body tissue, but, apart from being present in malignant tumors, it is also apparent in mature male and developing female reproductive cells.[7] It seems, then, that somewhere within our DNA structure (presumably in what is commonly termed "junk DNA") is the genetic ability to produce this anti-ageing enzyme, but the potential has somehow been switched off. As recently mentioned by Robert F. Newbold of the Department of Biology and Biochemistry at London's Brunel University, "Isolation (molecular cloning) of this gene will enable its fine structural integrity to be determined in a wide variety of human malignancies and, therefore, its role as an important target for inactivation in human cancer development to be established."[8]

It has already been suggested by scientists that, if telomerase can afford immortality to malignant tumors, then its introduction into normal human cells could well have the effect of extending lifespan. Numerous genetic researchers have agreed that "the ability to extend cellular lifespan (while maintaining the diploid status,[9] growth characteristics and gene expression pattern typical of young normal cells) has important implications for biological research, for the pharmaceutical industry, and for medicine."[10]

From all this, it can justifiably be assumed that if *mfkzt* is to live up to its expectations (as determined in the Egyptian records) then it should be capable of having: a) anti-cancerous attributes and the ability to combat cell deformation by repairing malformed DNA strands; b) the potential to stimulate certain hormonal functions of the endocrine system; and c) properties which can somehow activate a field of physical being beyond that of our familiar dimension. As we shall see, the white powder *mfkzt* has precisely these qualities.

Daily Bread

Later, we shall be looking at *mfkzt* in a modern laboratory environment — ascertaining what it is, how it is made, and how it works. Meanwhile, we need to consider its biblical representation to discover the particular significance of *mfkzt* to Moses, the Israelites, and the eventual Kings of Judah. They (as an offshoot of the Babylonian and Egyptian dynasties) succeeded as the continuing House of Gold.

Having now embarked on the trail of a magical substance – which: i) begins as gold; ii) transmutes with fire into white powder; iii) can be made into bread; and iv) is called a stone – we find that its references throughout the ages are numerous. In biblical terms it makes its first appearance about 600 years before the time of Moses in Genesis 14:18. Here we learn that Melchizedek, King of Salem and priest of the most high God, presented Abraham with bread and wine – the first Bible mention of a ritual act which became enveloped into later Communion ceremony.

At that time, Abraham had just completed his military campaign in Canaan, having led his army successfully against the troops of some troublesome kings. The God referred to is more specifically named in old texts as the mountain lord El Shaddai[11] – the same title alluded to again by the Lord who spoke with Moses at Mount Horeb in Sinai. It was only during the scribal recounting of events that the style Yahweh was introduced from the Hebrew stem *YHWH*: "I am who I am" (Exodus 3:14). This was apparently the response to Moses when he asked for confirmation of the Lord's identity, although it actually seems rather more like a refusal to give a name – "I am who I am," being akin to "My name is irrelevant." More important, however, was the statement made by this Lord to Moses (Exodus 6:3) that he was the God of Abraham. Early texts name Abraham's God as El Shaddai (Genesis 17:1), but in modern Bibles this has wrongly been translated as God Almighty. Used in Hebrew texts and retained in the Latin Vulgate Bible,[12] *El Shaddai* was a Semitic term, synonymous with the Mesopotamian god Enlil, who was called the *Ilu Kur-gal*: Great Mountain Lord. (Much later, in 1518, Yahweh was converted to the modern hybrid, Jehovah.)[13]

Melchizedek was therefore a priest of the Mountain Lord, and it was in his performance of this office that he presented the bread and wine to Abraham. On viewing the statue of Melchizedek at the northern Gate of the Initiates at Chartres Cathedral in France, however, we see him presenting a stone within a chalice, so that the bread-stone and the wine are portrayed in unison. The cathedral was designed by the Knights Templars and begun in 1194 by a guild of masons called the Children of Solomon.[14] They had acquired a unique masonic knowledge of ancient customs following the Templars' return in 1127 to Europe with treasures and documents from their excavations at the Temple of Solomon site in Jerusalem.

The name Melchizedek stems from two Hebrew words: *melek* (king) and *tsedeq* (righteousness). He was, therefore, the King of Righteousness or, as described in Genesis, King of Peace (Salem – *shalom*, as for Jerusalem: City of Peace). Fragments of the *Prince Melchizedek Document* found among the Dead Sea Scrolls indicate that Melchizedek and the Archangel

Michael were one and the same. The Scrolls (discovered in 1947 at Qumrân, Murabba'at, and Mird in the Wilderness of Judaea by the Dead Sea near Jericho) are now invaluable to our understanding of the Judaean culture of the pre-Gospel era. In these ancient parchments, Melchizedek (Michael-Zadok) is called the Heavenly One and the Prince of Light,[15] and it was he, with his early presentation of bread and wine, who is seen to have instigated the Eucharist sacrament.

Throughout the emergence of the Judaeo-Christian religions, bread retained a position of special prominence – from the story of Melchizedek to the familiar Lord's Prayer and its line, "Give us this day our daily bread." Even the birthplace of King David and Jesus was said to be Bethlehem (*Beth-le-hem* – House of Bread).[16] A pertinent fact about the Lord's Prayer is that, although it is defined in the New Testament (Matthew 6:9–13 and Luke 11:2–4, which are actually different versions), it was originally transposed from an Egyptian prayer to the State-god which began: "Amen, Amen, who art in heaven." Traditionally, the Christian rendition places the name of Amen at the very end of this prayer, a practice that was also adopted for other prayers and hymns.

Returning once again to Moses and the mountain, we discover the actual bread to which both the Lord's Prayer and *Beth-le-hem* refer. It appears in Exodus 25:30 and is called "shewbread."[17] The prefix "shew" is no more than an obsolete spelling of "show," and the bread's original description gained this rendering from the English 16th-century Bible translator William Tyndale. He noted that "It was shew-bread because it was in the presence and sight of the Lord." A better translation would have been "bread of the presence" or "presence loaves" as it is correctly given in the Septuagint (1 Kings/1 Samuel 21:6).[18]

In the Old Testament, Exodus 25:29–31 relates that the shewbread was made at Mount Horeb by Bezaleel, the son of Uri Ben Hur. He was said to have been filled with wisdom, understanding, and knowledge. We also learn that Bezaleel was a skilled goldsmith and a craftsman in all manner of "cunning" works (Exodus 35:31–33) who was placed in charge of building the Ark of the Covenant and the Tabernacle. In detailing how Bezaleel should manufacture various crowns, rings, bowls, and a candlestick, all of pure gold, the text adds shewbread to the list of precious items and, without further explanation, the process is seen to be completed (Exodus 39:37). This sequence is later recalled in the New Testament book of Hebrews (9:1–2), which states that at the Sinai covenant there were, within the holy confines of the Tabernacle, a candlestick and a table with the shewbread.

The book of Leviticus (24:5–7) returns to the subject of Bezaleel and the shewbread, stating that the loaves were wiped with frankincense. But, as astutely pointed out in the 1950s by the Russian Jewish psychiatrist Dr. Immanuel Velikovsky, "the shewbread was obviously not of flour, but of silver or gold."[19] In making this observation he drew particular attention to the Egyptian treasures of pharaoh Tuthmosis III, as reproduced in a bas-relief at the temple of Karnak. In the metals section (described as "cunning work") there are a number of cone-shaped items. They are explained as being made: one cone of silver and thirty of gold, and carry a description: "white bread."

Sacred Manna

Still at Mount Horeb with Moses and the Israelites, we discover more biblical references to a mysterious white substance. Exodus 16:15 states that "When the children of Israel saw it, they said to one another, It is *manna*, for they wist not what it was, And Moses said unto them, This is the bread which the Lord hath given you to eat." Subsequently, the manna is described as being white, resembling seed, and with a sweet taste like honey (Exodus 16:31).

Turning to the *Antiquities of the Jews*, as compiled by the Jewish historian Flavius Josephus in the 1st century AD, Josephus explains that the manna was first identified when it lay upon the ground and "the people knew not what it was, and thought it snowed." He continues, "So divine and wonderful a food was this ... Now the Hebrews call this food *manna*; for the particle *man*, in our language,[20] is the asking of a question: What is this?"[71] Some of the most important biblical and non-biblical records have been preserved in the writings of Flavius Josephus, whose *Antiquities of the Jews* and *Wars of the Jews* were written from a personal standpoint. He was the military commander in the defense of Galilee during the Jewish Revolt against the occupational forces of Imperial Rome in the AD 60s.

The sweet-tasting white substance which appeared around the mountain in the mornings and which Moses referred to as "bread" was, therefore, called *Manna* (What is this?) by virtue of its unknown origin.[22] The same question also appears in the Egyptian *Book of the Dead* – the oldest complete book in the world. Alternatively known as the *Papyrus of Ani* (a royal scribe), this 18th-dynasty scroll from Thebes (acquired by the British Museum in 1888) is extensively illustrated and around 76 feet (over 23 m) in length.[23] In this ancient ritualistic work, the "bread of the presence" is called "schefa food," and the pharaoh seeking the terminal enlightenment of the Afterlife asks, at every stage of his journey, the repetitive question, "What is it?"

Other *Books of the Dead* (though fragmented and incomplete) date back to the 3rd millennium BC, and it is clear from the Serâbît reliefs that the Egyptian kings were ingesting the white *manna* of gold from around 2180 BC. However, only the metallurgical adepts of the mystery schools (the cunning craftsmen) knew the secret of its manufacture. These adepts were operational priests, and the High Priest of Memphis held the title of Great Artificer.[24]

In life, as in death, the terminal enlightenment was a constant source of quest. As against the physical body, one was also reckoned to have a "light body," which similarly had to be fed so as to be nurtured and grow. It was called the *Ka* and, although essentially an intangible feature of life, it was said to remain active in the Afterlife. The food of the *Ka* was Light – which generated enlightenment, or as the Greeks called it, *gnosis* – the very hieroglyphic symbol found in the Shrine of the Kings at Serâbît el Khâdim. In the First Degree ritual of Freemasonry, the hoodwinked Entered Apprentice initiate is asked what he most desires – the ceremonial answer to which is "Light." In ancient Syro-Phoenicia, this realm of advanced enlightenment was called the *Plane of Shar-On* (the Dimension of the Orbit of Light) – a term later corrupted and misapplied to the coastal Plain of Sharon, extending between Haifa and Tel Aviv-Yafo, in Israel.

In the alchemical lore of the ancient Egyptian mystery schools, the process of achieving enlightened consciousness was of express importance. To aid the process, the temple philosophers prepared a miraculous "powder of projection" by which it was possible to transmute the base human ignorance into an ingot of spiritual gold.[25] This "powder of projection" was the *mfkzt*, the *manna*, the white-powder of gold – or as it became alchemically termed, the Philosophers' Stone.

To repeat Eirenaeus Philalethes' words: "Our Stone is nothing but gold digested to the highest degree of purity and subtle fixation … In species it is gold, more purer than the purest; it is fixed and incombustible like a stone, but its appearance is that of a very fine powder."[26]

In the New Testament (1 Corinthians 10:3) *manna* is referred to as a spiritual food, while also being established as the true bread of the Eucharist (John 6:31–41). Hence, the bread of the sacrament, which comes with the Communion wine, is the same Mass wafer served by the Holy Grail in the 12th-century romance, *Le Conte del Graal – The Story of Perceval*, by Chrétien de Troyes. This tale emerged in about 1180, just before the building of Chartres Cathedral was commenced, and it was born directly from a Templar environment. The Counts of Alsace, Champagne, and Léon (with whom Chrétien de Troyes was closely associated) all had affiliations with the Jerusalem knightly Order. The Melchizedek statue at Chartres, with its bread-stone in a chalice, was wholly representative of the Grail's service of the sacred *manna*.

It is explained by St. Paul in the New Testament that Jesus was himself raised to the high priesthood in the Order of Melchizedek (Hebrews 5:6, 6:20). This is how he gained the right to offer the bread and wine sacrament at the Last Supper. Paul explains that, since this was such a privilege, the law had formally to be changed to accommodate Jesus in this regard (Hebrews 7:11–17), for he was born into the Davidic House of Judah, which had rights to kingship, but not to priesthood.

In the New Testament book of The Revelation (2:17) it is said, "To him that overcometh will I give to eat of the hidden manna, and will give him a white stone, and in the stone a new name written, which no man knoweth saving he that receiveth it." Here then, having traveled from the near beginning of the Bible to the very end, the sacred *manna* retains its importance, while also being directly associated with a white stone.

A very similar portrayal appears in the much later Holy Grail tradition of the Middle Ages. In the romance of *Parzival* by the Bavarian knight Wolfram von Eschenbach, we read: "Around the end of the stone, an inscription in letters tells the name and lineage of those, be they maids or boys, who are called to make the journey to the Grail. No one needs to read the inscription, for as soon as it has been read it vanishes."[27] The stone being discussed here was said to be the "perfection of earthly paradise," with remarkable healing and anti-ageing properties. It was called *Lapis Elixis*, a variant of *Lapis Elixir*, the alchemical Philosophers' Stone. The text continues: "By the power of that stone the Phoenix burns to ashes, but the ashes speedily restore him to life again. Thus doth the Phoenix moult and change its plumage, after which he is bright and shining as before."

The key to the *Parzival* allegory lies in the ancient mythology of the Phoenix – likened in Egypt to the "benu bird," which was burned to ashes in the Temple at Heliopolis, but from whose ashes came the great enlightenment. Heliopolis (originally called On, relating to the light of the sun god) was a center of the Great White Brotherhood – the master craftsmen of Tuthmosis III (*c.* 1450 BC). There were 39 members on the High Council of Karnak,[28] and the Brotherhood's name derived from its preoccupation with a mysterious white powder.

Another such stone appears in the *Iter Alexandri ad Paradisium* – an old parable of Alexander the Great's journey to Paradise (the realm of *Pairi Daize* which, in the old Avestan language,[29] was the kingdom of Ahura Mazda the Persian god of Light). This tale features the enchanted Paradise Stone, which gave youth to the old[30] and was said to outweigh its own quantity of gold, although even a feather could tip the scales against it!

As we progress, we shall see that the Stone of Paradise (which is heavier than gold, but lighter than a feather) is no myth of the distant past. It now holds a primary position in the world of modern physics, with its baffling weight ratios fully explained as scientific fact. Similarly, the Phoenix also emerges in a laboratory environment, with the secret of its Light resurrection playing a major role in current technology. In fact, the Phoenix, when transposed to powder (ashes) is indeed the Paradise Stone – the Philosophers' Stone, which is both the *manna* of Moses and the *mfkzt* of the Serâbît temple craftsmen: the Great Ones of the House of Gold.

Light and Perfection

Mystery of the Jewels

Alongside the alchemical Paradise Stone in its Old and New Testament guises, other stones are similarly of great importance in the book of Exodus. The most obvious which spring to mind are the tablets which bore the Testimony and the Ten Commandments. These are often imagined as a couple of weighty slabs – customarily depicted by artists as barely portable by Moses, who had to bring them down from the mountain. Exodus, however, gives no indication whatever of the shape and size of these stones, whereas in the strict Jewish tradition of the Qabala, the Tablet of Testimony was said to be of a divine sapphire called the *Schethiyâ*,[1] which Moses held in the palm of his hand.

The Qabala tradition of light and knowledge emanates from the time of Abraham (around 600 years before Moses), who was said to have received the "testament of a lost civilization." His birthplace is given in Genesis[2] as Ur of the Chaldees (an ancient city of Sumerian Mesopotamia), but Qabalists additionally cite his cultural heritage as being of the *Aur Kasdeems*, which meant Light of the Magicians.[3] Abraham's tablet was said to have contained "all that man had ever known" and "all that man would ever know." To the ancient Sumerians this composition was known as the Table of

Destiny. It was said to have been handed down by the gods Enlil and Enki (sons of the great Anunnaki sky-god Anu),[4] and was depicted in pre-biblical writings concerning the Babylonian god Marduk as being worn against his breast.[5]

Qabalistic doctrine relates that the Table of Destiny was a sapphire, later inherited by Moses and subsequently passed to the guardianship of King Solomon of Judah. Hence it follows that, when the interpreted portrayals of latter-day artists are dismissed, the Exodus Tablet of Testimony appears not to be a slab of common stone, but something far more precious.[6] Notwithstanding the English translations of the Qabala, the term originally used in old texts was *sappir*, whereas the word generally related to "sapphire" in biblical writings was *leshem*.[7]

The principal work of the Qabala is *Sefer ha Zohar* (Book of Radiance)[8] – close to a million words of applied scriptural philosophy based on ancient Jewish traditions, and mostly written in a form of Aramaic.[9] This was a language of the Aramaeans, who were established in Mesopotamia in the 13th century BC and later spread into Syria and Palestine. From around 500 BC, Aramaic was the official language of the Persian Empire and it overshadowed Hebrew as a language of the Jews for about 1,000 years. The content of the *Zohar* is attributed to the 2nd-century Palestinian rabbi Shimeon ben Yohai,[10] and was collated in 1286 by Moses ben Shem Tov de Léon in Castile, Spain. In essence, it is an investigative commentary on the Torah – the five books of Moses (also called the Pentateuch), which constitute the Jewish Law. Along with the Talmud it has remained a venerated work in the Asian, African, and European countries of the Diaspora.[11]

The *Schethiyâ* stone of King Solomon features not just in Qabalistic tradition, but also in the tenets of Royal Arch Freemasonry. The Jewish Talmud (a commentary on philosophical Hebrew texts)[12] relates that the *Schethiyâ* was called the "stone of foundation." It seemingly functioned as a levitational device in the Holy of Holies (the *Sanctum Sanctorum*) of the Temple in

Jerusalem, enabling the Ark of the Covenant to remain out of contact with the earth – hovering three-fingers' distance above ground.[13] By virtue of maintaining the Ark in a perfectly poised attitude, it was also called the "stone of perfection."

Another stone associated with Solomon was called the *Schamir* – known as the "lightning stone." The Talmud tells of how the King used this to make true the stones of his Temple.[14] The *Schamir* was said to cut through rock, silently and with precision from its own magnificent spear of light. As with the *Schethiyâ*, Moses was also reckoned to have previously held the awesome, light-radiating *Schamir*, which Solomon was said to have placed in his ring.[15]

Having established the esoteric attributes of the Stone of Perfection and the Lightning Stone, we can now return to the Bible to find them mentioned on a number of occasions. Their first appearance is indeed with Moses at Mount Horeb in the book of Exodus. The sequence describes the making of a gold breastplate (the *essen*) for Moses' brother Aaron to wear in his capacity as the first High Priest to guard the Ark of the Covenant. Exodus 28:30 relates: "And thou shalt put in the breastplate of judgment the *Urim* and the *Thummim*: and they shall be upon Aaron's heart, when he goeth before the Lord." The words *U'rim* and *Thum'mim* meant Light and Perfection.[16] Hence, the *Schamir* ("lightning stone") and *Schethiyâ* ("stone of perfection") of the Talmud are synonymous with the *Urim* and *Thummim* of Exodus.

At no time in the Old Testament is there any question concerning the nature of the *Urim* and *Thummim*. Neither their shape, size, color, nor weight is discussed. They are simply accepted as something with which Moses was familiar. What we have here, nevertheless, are two magical stones. One is a radiating jewel, which emits a charge of lightning that cuts through stone, while the other has the power of levitation.

The jewels subsequently passed from Aaron to his son Eleazar, who succeeded as High Priest (Numbers 20:28). They were considered to be so energetic that it was said they represented the very presence of God himself – referred to in the Fellowcraft (2nd-degree) ceremony of Freemasonry as the "Great Luminary." The Old Testament books of Ezra 2:63 and Nehemiah 7:75 confirm that the stones remained the prerogative of the Levite high priests, and it was they who guarded the stones and the Ark from their Tabernacle abode in Sinai to a permanent residence in the Temple of Jerusalem.

Apart from the *essen* (breastplate), another garment worn by the High Priest was a sleeveless, bibbed and girdled tunic called the *ephod*.[17] In later times this garment became a badge of the Levite guardians of the Ark, with its bib folded down over the girdle to form a small flapped apron.[18] Then made of white linen, it is represented today by the short apron of masonic regalia. In 2 Samuel 6:13–15, King David was "girded with a linen *ephod*" when he danced before the Ark.

The Curious Spiral

Numbers 27:21 tells that the *Urim* was used by the High Priest when he sought council with the Lord, and this divine wisdom was obtained from between the golden cherubim which surmounted the Ark of the Covenant (Exodus 25:22). Then Judges 20:27–28 explains that standing before the Ark was indeed considered to be standing before God. Since the *Urim* and *Thummim* had to be present for the Ark to convey the word of God, some have suggested that they were like dice or oracular lots. But the key attribute of the *Urim*, when in the presence of the Ark, was its radiating light, and the Bible says that "God is Light."[19] In accordance with this precept, therefore, the Ark-light of the *Urim* was a perceived manifestation of God.

What then was this *Urim-Schamir* that was so fundamental to summoning the power of the Ark? Thus far we have ascertained that it was a precious stone: a crystal gem with the ability, under certain conditions, to emit a spear of light that could cut through stone with precision. This may seem a little implausible for those apparently non-technological times in the ancient Egyptian empire. However, as we shall see in relation to the Paradise Stone of the *mfkzt*, recent science has proven much that would have been quite incomprehensible to researchers even 50 years ago.

Whether related to the *Urim-Schamir* or other sources of divine judgment, the graphic symbol for wisdom remained constant from the earliest times in Mesopotamia (now Iraq). It was the emblem of the Sumerian god Enki, Lord of the Sacred Eye[20] – a serpent spiraling around a central rod or stem. In Egypt, the White Brotherhood of Karnak were priestly craftsmen of the Therapeutate, whose work with the *mfkzt* also

The serpent of wisdom and healing.

involved them with healing, so that wisdom and healing became synonymous and the same serpentine emblem was adopted.

In the ancient Greek tradition, the influential Father of Medicine was Asklepios of Thessaly (*c.* 1200 BC), whom the Romans called Aesculapius. His statue[21] at the Capodimonte Museum, Rome, also portrays the staff and coiled serpent. In the footsteps of Asklepios came the Greek physician Hippocrates (born in 460 BC), whose Hippocratic Oath is sworn by physicians to this day. Even now, the spiraling serpent remains the emblem of the British, American, and Australian Medical Associations, along with the confederate World Medical Association. The question is: why? What had a spiraling serpent to do with medicine and wisdom gleaned from sacred stones? Another constant to be addressed is the fact that Wisdom has long been associated with Light, so that the acquisition of knowledge became defined as enlightenment or illumination.

Even in the Sinai story, this emblem is directly related to healing the Israelites, when the Lord said to Moses "Make thee a serpent and put it on a staff." (The descriptions "brazen serpent" and "pole" are generally used in English-language Bibles, but it was not so in the original Greek Septuagint, which described only a "serpent" and a "staff.") The intriguing anomaly here is the same irregularity that exists in respect of the golden cherubim on the Ark of the Covenant. The instructions to make both the serpent and the cherubim were claimed as being directives from God, and yet God was said to have issued the dictate: "Thou shalt not make unto thee any graven image, or any likeness of any thing that is in heaven above, or that is in the earth beneath, or that is in the water under the earth." (Exodus 20:4). One moment we have Moses admonishing Aaron and the Israelites for making a golden calf, and the next he is busy making a serpent and cherubim! In the wake of such an inviolable proscription, it is not feasible that Moses would be divinely required to manufacture figurative life forms. Hence, it is likely that the serpent was not a snake as such, and the cherubim were not angels.[22]

When discussing the Essenes of Qumrân in the 1st century AD, Josephus explained that these white-garbed inheritors of the Egyptian Therapeutate acquired their knowledge of medicinal stones from the ancients.[23] We shall discover that *mfkzt* was indeed medicinal – but for now we are concerned with the rock-cutting gem of the *Urim-Schamir* – the "lightning stone."

The High Priest's breastplate (in the pouch of which the *Urim* and *Thummim* were ceremonially placed) is described in Exodus 28:17–20 as being ornamented with 12 precious stones. They are given as sardius (carnelian), topaz, carbuncle (garnet), emerald, sapphire, diamond, ligure (amber), agate, amethyst, beryl, onyx, and jasper. Noticeably missing from this list is ruby, but both Job 28:18 and Proverbs 8:11 compare wisdom with rubies.

The Remarkable Ruby

Traveling forward in time to California, just a few decades ago in 1960. Physicist Theodore Maiman was then working at Hughes Aircraft Research in Malibu, having read an interesting article in the *Physical Review*[24] – the journal of the American Physical Society. It related that a professor and a research associate from Columbia University were jointly investigating light amplification at the Bell Laboratories. Their names were Charles Townes and Arthur Schawlow, and they were specialists in the field of microwave spectroscopy, which dealt with the puzzling characteristics of various molecules. They knew that as the wavelength of microwave radiation grew shorter, its interactions with molecules became stronger, thereby making it a powerful spectroscopic tool for examining the component degrees of light refraction. What they wanted to achieve was a control of wavelengths shorter than microwaves – the wavelengths of infrared and optical light. They began to bounce light back and forth with mirrors and subsequently published their *Physical Review* paper, explaining how they had perfected an amplified single frequency in the visible spectrum. What they did not have, though, was an application for the discovery, and it was booked as "an invention looking for a job."

Fascinated by this, Theodore Maiman, working independently of Townes and Schawlow, looked into the wavelengths of colors and their relative energy levels. Chromium atoms, he discovered, absorb green and blue light, giving off only red, which is penetratively very powerful. The pulsing crystal with its red color created by chromium atoms is the ruby, and Maiman found that the electrons in these atoms could be excited to higher energy levels with intense white light. Taking a rod-shaped ruby, he coated the parallel ends with evaporated silver (one a little less reflective than the other). Then he wrapped a quartz flash-tube coil around the stone. Photo-pumped by fast-action light flashes, the ruby rod emitted a powerful beam of red light, and in August 1960, Maiman published his experiment in the journal *Nature*.[25] Subsequently, Bell Laboratories replaced the flash with an arc lamp, to produce a continuous spear of high-energy light – a coherent beam more than a million times brighter than the sun. This beam was so intensely narrow that, on being perfected, it could cut with precision through steel, like a knife through butter. The process was called Light Amplification by Stimulated Emission of Radiation – soon abbreviated to "Laser."[26]

So, what did the world's supposedly first ruby laser, a little over 40 years ago, look like? It looked precisely like a serpent coiled around a central stem – just as in the emblems of Enki and Asklepios. Not surprisingly, lasers were soon adapted for use in the world of medicine, taking over from scalpels in the field of microsurgery. If the *Urim-Schamir* were indeed a cylin-

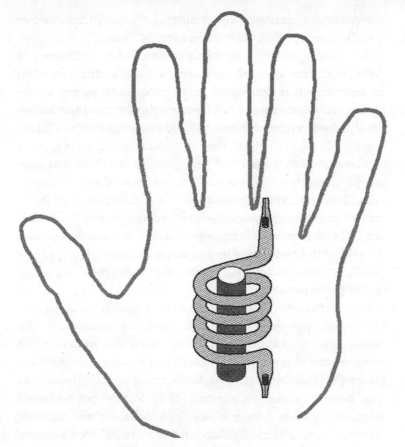

Maiman's first ruby laser (to scale).

drical ruby, with a suitable helicoidal crystal sleeve to hand, then all it would have needed to become operative was a connective power supply.

Ring of the Testimony

Artists of the past have depicted Moses with tablets like tombstones, up to three-feet apiece, just to carry the Ten Commandments. In contrast, the unearthed tablets of ancient

Mesopotamia carry proportionately large amounts of inscribed information within a few inches of clay.

The nature of the original Sumerian Table of Destiny is difficult to determine, but its history is far older than any biblical reference. It is first mentioned in the seven tablets of the *Enûma elish* (meaning "When on high"): a pre-Genesis Creation epic composed around 3,500 years ago.[27] When inherited by Abraham in about 1960 BC, the Table was said to have contained "all that man had ever known" and "all that man would ever know." (There was no mention of any writing – only that the tablet "contained" this information.) If, as explained in the Qabala, Moses inherited the very same artifact, then it is probably this stone which the Exodus scribes dubbed as the Testimony. It was, however, quite distinct from the Ten Commandments, as the Old Testament narrative makes perfectly clear.

It is explained in Exodus (chapters 20–23) that the Ten Commandments were delivered by the Lord to Moses and the people at Mount Horeb, and that these were accompanied by a series of verbal ordinances. Moses then wrote down all these things (Exodus 24:4), reading them again to the Israelites as their new Book of the Covenant (24:7). We are not told with what, or on what, Moses transcribed these ordinances, only that they were said to be in the form of a "book" (not a tablet). After the book had been read, the Lord said to Moses: "Come up to me into the mount, and be there: and I will give thee tables of stone, and a law, and commandments which I have written; that thou mayest teach them." (24:12).

Later, it is related that the Lord said, "And thou shalt put into the ark the testimony which I shall give thee." (25:16). Then follows, "He gave unto Moses … two tables of testimony, tables of stone, written with the finger of God." (31:18). But then, on bringing the tablets down from the mountain, Moses saw the Israelites dancing and promptly "cast the tables out of his hands, and brake them …" (32:19). What we learn from this is that these tablets were breakable, so they were clearly not of the magical *sappir* on that occasion.

Then the story changes to portray a different picture of the subsequent tablets than is normally conveyed in scriptural teaching. The Lord said to Moses, "Hew thee two tables of stone like unto the first: and I will write upon these tables the words that were in the first tables, which thou brakest." (34:1). But nothing further is mentioned in this regard. What happens is that the Lord verbally reiterates various civil regulations, and then gives Moses a further instruction: "Write thou these words" – whereupon Moses "wrote ... the words of the covenant, the ten commandments," (34:27–28) and brought his personally written tablets back down the mountain (34:29).

No matter how one reads this Old Testament sequence (whether in the Greek Septuagint, the Hebrew Masoretic text, or the King James edition), there is no variation in the fact that Moses did not end up with anything written by God, as is so commonly portrayed. He is depicted only with the Book of the Covenant (written by himself) and the Ten Commandments (similarly written by himself). So, what happened to the Testimony from the hand of God, which was supposed to be placed in the Ark of the Covenant?

In this connection, Exodus 40:20 does later relate that Moses "put the testimony into the ark," and it is generally reckoned that this represented the tablets with the Ten Commandments. But there was nothing special about these – they were just a set of brief regulations, written down by Moses himself. They certainly did not warrant the construction of a richly adorned 4-foot (*c.* 1.22 m) gold coffer. They were not even secret; they were known by all then present, and they are known to many people today. Neither was it the Book of the Covenant which Moses placed in the Ark, for this was merely a series of judicial decisions and commands – a reference work for those administering civil law.[28] Its very objective was to remain accessible, not to be hidden away. For whatever reason, however, the Ark was closely guarded by the Levite priests and, once transported to Jerusalem, it was kept in a solitary and sanctified environment.

Adding weight to the perceived value of the Ark's contents in a modern Church environment, it is commonly taught that, along with the Ten Commandments, the Ark also contained a pot of *manna* and Aaron's budding almond rod. But there is no Old Testament mention of these items in this context. Their association with the Ark was a much later Christian notion of the New Testament, appearing for the first time in St. Paul's Epistle to the Hebrews 9:4.[29] What, then, was the so-called "testimony" that Moses placed in the Ark?

The answer is found in 2 Kings 11:12, which deals with the priestly installation of King Joash of Judah (*c.* 839 BC): "And he brought forth the king's son, and put the crown upon him, and gave him the testimony; and they made him king, and anointed him." This "testimony" was an important royal insignia of the era[30] – a treasured talisman of kingship, being a coiled ring of attestation and witness.

Exodus 35:22 lists some of the items of jewelry brought to Moses by the Israelites to provide gold for the Tabernacle furnishings. The verse (in the 1611 King James Authorized Bible) reads: "And they came, both men and women … and brought bracelets and earrings and rings and tablets, and all jewels of gold." The 1885 Revised Old Testament renders these "tablets" more directly as "armlets," whereas the Masoretic Bible gives them as "signets." The original Semitic word, however, was *tabba'ats* which, as correctly specified in the Septuagint denotes "finger rings." Hence, the talismanic ring of King Joash was itself a "tablet (*tabba'at*) of testimony," previously identified as a *sappir*.

Earlier, we saw that King Solomon had placed his "lightning stone" (the *Schamir*) into his ring so as to cut the stones for the Temple, and it was this item of regalia – the tablet-ring of the Testimony – that was inherited by the kings of his line, down to his seventh generational successor, King Joash. But Solomon's ring was said to have been of precious metal (as were the gold rings at Sinai), whereas the *sappir* tablet was identified as a stone! As we have ascertained, the *mfkzt* was of gold, but was alchemically termed a stone. In the same way, so was the *Schethiyâ* – a magnificent helicoidal crystal – made, as we shall see, from iridium by the master craftsmen. This remarkable glass-like substance had been known to the ancient temple vulcans of Mesopotamia, and they called it *an-na*: fire-stone; while the powder of the *mfkzt* was called *shem-an-na*: highward fire-stone.

Whereas the *Urim* (the male stone) was perceived as a godly manifestation, the female *Thummim* represented the Queen of the Heavens, whom the Canaanites called Anath. In Phoenicia she was known as Barat An-na (Royal Anna), and her culture eventually entered tribal Britain, where she became known as Britannia.[31]

The "testimony" which Moses brought down from the mountain and lodged in the Ark (Exodus 40:20) was very likely the noble crystal coil in which the *Urim-Schamir* was inserted – the very jewel for which Solomon built the Temple of Jerusalem as a sacred abode. Moses had acquired it from the El Shaddai (Lord of the Mountain), and in this regard the Qabalistic doctrine that the tablet was a *sappir* which Moses held in the palm of his hand makes a good deal more sense. What he had was the other part of the light-spear equation – the spiraling *Schethiyâ*, or, as it was known to the high priests Aaron and Eleazar, the *Thummim*. It is of particular relevance to note that, throughout the book of Exodus, the Ark is referred to as the Ark of Testimony. Only from the book of Numbers 10:33 (when the Israelites began their onward journey from Sinai) was it restyled, as a mark of godly allegiance, to become the Ark of the Covenant.

Since the *Urim* and *Thummim* (as separately identified in the Bible) were mutually supportive devices, it is not entirely through misapplication that the Mormon tradition often portrays them in operation as a single object: the *Urim-Thummim*.[32] They constituted the male and female, and when brought together at the Ark they did indeed manifest their unified Light and Perfection. Alone, however, the *Thummim-Schethiyâ* was a uniquely empowered substance with levitational attributes, just as described in the Qabalistic doctrine.

A New Dynasty

The scenario that we have so far is that, from around 2600 BC and the 4th Egyptian dynasty of Sneferu, the temple of Serâbît el Khâdim was operative at Mount Horeb in Sinai. This was the dynasty of Khufu (Cheops), Khafre (Chepren), and Menkaure, to each of whom the three pyramids of Giza are attributed. Here at Serâbît the Great Ones manufactured from gold a mysterious white "powder of projection" called *mfkzt*, which the Israelites questioned as being *manna* (what is it?). The *mfkzt* was formed into conical cakes (referred to as "white bread") and fed to the kings of the royal House of Gold. It seemingly enhanced their qualities of kingship and was also connected with an enigmatic "field" of the Afterlife into which the dead kings were transported – the *Field of Mfkzt*.

The Serâbît temple ceased to function as a place of alchemical workship in the Ramesside era (*c.* 1330 BC), when the Lord of the Mountain passed the secrets of the House of Gold to a new order of Aaronite priests. The days of the legitimate dynasties in Egypt were done, and new influences were pressing from outside. Rameses I (from *c.* 1335 BC) was not of royal descent and, although his wife Sitre was of a pharaonic cousin line, she was too far removed for consideration as an hereditary heiress. Following the earlier death of the boy-king Tutankhamun and the wind-down of the 18th dynasty, it was time for the kingly bloodline to move on. Meanwhile, Tutankhamun's sister had married into the Israelite family line. Since Egyptian kingship was strictly concerned with matrilinear heritage, she was the true heiress of the old dynasties and was present in Sinai with her husband and Moses.

The treasures of the House of Gold (the *Urim-Schamir* and the *Thummim-Schethiyâ*) were placed in the care of Moses and the new Israelite priests, who were charged in Sinai to establish a reigning dynasty in the Promised Land. In time, these kings (in descent from the 18th dynasty of Egypt) were to become the Royal House of Judah – the line of David, Solomon, and, eventually, Jesus. First, however, the land of Canaan (later Palestine) had to be entered, traversed, and conquered before the new monarchy could be established in Jerusalem.

4

Out of Egypt

Children of Israel

In the days of Moses there was a distinct difference between the Israelites and the Hebrews – something that is not made clear in the scriptures. The designation "Hebrew" derives from the Mesopotamian patriarch Eber (Heber/Abhâr, *c.* 2480 BC), six generations before Abraham.[1] The term "Israelite" comes from the renaming of Abraham's grandson Jacob, who became known as Israel (Genesis 35:10–12). His descendants, during their Egyptian sojourn from around 1790 BC, became known as Israelites or Children of Israel. By way of varied translations, *Is-ra-el* means "soldier of El," while some say that *Ysra-el* means "El rules," and others prefer "El strives." The place called Lûz, where Jacob received his new name, was itself renamed *Beth-el* (Genesis 28:19), meaning "House of El."

The ancient Canaanite term *El* was used to identify a great Lord or Lofty One – as in El Shaddai, the Lord of the Mountain from whom Moses received the tablets in Sinai. The old Hebrew text of Exodus 6:3 explains that El Shaddai was a term also used in Abraham's day. Retained in the Vulgate Bible from *c.* AD 385,[2] the description "El Shaddai" is found 48 times in the canon, but in every case has been rendered in Authorized English-language Bibles since 1611 as "Almighty." In the earlier Mesopotamian tradition, the equivalent was *Ilu Kur-*

gal, meaning "Great Mountain Lord,"[3] while in the Sumerian tongue *El* related more specifically to a "Shining One."[4]

As for the term "Jew," this comes from the style "Judaean" – Jews being the ultimately conjoined Israelites and Hebrews of Judaea in southern Canaan. It subsequently became an all-embracing style for the Israelite–Hebrew nation. (Judaea was the Romanized form of Judah). To the north of Judaea was Samaria, and above that was Galilee.

While the generations of original Israelites were in Egypt prior to the Mosaic exodus, they had little to do with their ancestral Hebrew cousins in Canaan: a tribe which the Egyptians called the *Habiru*. However, in *c*. 1330 BC, the Israelites were in Sinai, en route to encounter the Hebrews – eventually to become interconnected after many centuries. It was for this reason that the El Shaddai was forthcoming with the laws, customs, and obligations of the Israelites' new environment. In effect, they learned the Hebrew culture by way of decrees (ordinances) at Mount Horeb – cementing their allegiance to a type of constitutional document called the Book of the Covenant.

The Ten Commandments were another matter. They were enforced reminders of the valued precepts of the Israelites' Egyptian tradition. Given in Exodus 20, they were not newly invented codes of conduct, but newly stated versions of the ancient pharaonic confessions from Spell Number 125 in the Egyptian *Book of the Dead*. For example, the confession "I have not killed" was translated to the decree: "Thou shalt not kill;" "I have not stolen" became "Thou shalt not steal;" "I have not told lies" became "Thou shalt not bear false witness" – and so on.[5]

So, what of Moses? He is generally perceived as a Jew at a time when there were no Jews. He is often imagined as a Hebrew, when in fact he emerged from Egypt with the Israelites. Some consider him to have been a senior Israelite. But, despite all these popularly conceived notions, the Old Testament makes it perfectly clear that Moses was neither a

Hebrew nor an Israelite. Exodus 2:19 specifically refers to Moses as "an Egyptian." It is even stated in Exodus 4:10 that Moses was concerned about his ability to address the Israelites in Egypt (as previously required of him in Exodus 3:12), confessing that he was "not eloquent," being "slow of speech, and of a slow tongue" – not being well-versed in the Israelite language.

The Burning Bush

In *The Aegyptiaca* by Manetho (an adviser to pharaoh Ptolemy I around 300 BC) Moses is recorded as having been an Egyptian priest at Heliopolis.[6] The later 1st-century Jewish historian, Flavius Josephus, took exception to this assertion of Egyptian priesthood by Manetho,[7] but then in his *Antiquities of the Jews* he himself alleged that Moses was a commander of the Egyptian army in the war against Ethiopia.[8]

The route to discovering the identity of Moses lies in his name which, although converted to Mosheh in Hebrew, is not of Israelite or Hebrew origin. This, coupled with the fact that Exodus 11:3 informs us that "Moses was very great in the land of Egypt," leads to an awareness that the name Moses had an Egyptian root. As cited by Sigmund Freud, James Henry Breasted, Ahmed Osman, and others who have researched the etymology, the name Moses actually derived from the Egyptian word *mose* (Greek: *mosis*), which related to an "offspring" or "heir,"[9] as in Tuthmose (Tuthmosis): "born of Thoth;" and Amenmose (Amenmosis): "born of Amen."

The Hebrew name Mosheh is said to derive from the word *mosche*, which means "the drawer out,"[10] or "one who draws out." This is claimed to stem from the baby Moses being named by the pharaoh's daughter, who drew his reed basket out of the river.[11] It is most unlikely, however, that an Egyptian princess would have been aware of Hebrew etymology, especially since Hebrew would not have been the language of the

Egyptian Israelites after more than 400 years of settlement in the Delta. She would plainly have used an Egyptian name for the boy she adopted. Secondly, Moses was not the "drawer out" (the *mosche*), he was the one "drawn out," for which the Hebrew was *moshiu*.[12]

The root story of the boy in the basket or rushes is not difficult to trace. It appears in records that the later Israelites, who were held captive by Nebuchadnezzar in Babylon (*c.* 586–536 BC), would doubtless have perused with ancestral interest. In the libraries of Mesopotamia there would have been the original Creation story, the *Enûma elish*, along with the *Epic of Gilgamesh*, which described the great Flood, and the *Adapa Tablet*, detailing the first kingly man, the *Adâma*.[13] Within those clay-tablet archives (ancient even in the 6th-century BC) was the ark of rushes prototype in the *Legend of Sharru-kîn*, who became Sargon the Great, King of Akkad (2371–2316 BC). An Assyrian text relating to Sargon reads: "My changeling mother conceived me; in secret she bare me. She set me in a basket of rushes, and with pitch she sealed my lid. She cast me into the river, which rose not over me. The river bore me up, and carried me to Akki, the drawer of the water."[14]

Who then was the Egyptian baby (ultimately the man) called Moses – the legendary character who established his famous mission at Mount Horeb and found his destiny as the patriarch of eventual Jewish Law? In preparation for this book, I have discussed the heritage of Moses before in both *Bloodline of the Holy Grail* and *Genesis of the Grail Kings*. The time has now come to put the key pieces together as we prepare to embark on our journey from Sinai with the Ark of the Covenant – a journey that will take us through more than 1,300 years to the Gospel era and into the centuries beyond. Here, we shall cover some elements of familiar ground, but this is necessary in order to set the emergent scene – especially for those who have not read other works in this series.

An Oxford University theologian remarked to me during a BBC radio debate that there is no historical evidence that characters such as Abraham, Moses, David, or Solomon ever existed. They appear, he said, only in foreign Hebrew writings! So let us clarify the nature of "history" which, by all legitimate definition, is "a chronological record of important or public events, past events and affairs." History is the record of events, not the events themselves. There is no rule anywhere which states that only the records of Britain or other Christian nations can be considered as history, as the professor implied. In this respect, ancient Hebrew literature coming out of a Middle Eastern environment is just as valid historically as the record of any other race from any other place. All must be taken into consideration in order to quantify the bigger picture. Of course, these distant characters of Jewish record do not appear in the history of nations outside their own environment (no more than Boudicca and Caractacus of the Britons appear in the Middle Eastern chronicles) – but neither do they solely appear in the Bible.

Prior to the 20th century, little was known of the ancient Canaanite traditions, but from 1929 a large number of texts, dating from around 1400 BC, were found at Ras Shamra (the old city of Ugarit) in north-west Syria.[15] Also, as recently as 1975, more tablets were discovered at nearby Tel Mardikh (the old city of Elba). Characters hitherto considered only to be biblical have now been brought to life archeologically, including E-sa-um (Esau), Ab-ra-mu (Abraham), Is-ra-ilu (Israel), and Ib-num (Eber). These discoveries, partnered with similar ones in Mesopotamia, Egypt, and elsewhere, prove beyond doubt that we cannot limit history to material available in archives at any given time. There is more history asleep beneath the oceans and windswept sands than will ever be found.

The book of Exodus relates that the baby Moses' life was under threat because the pharaoh had decreed death to all newborn Israelite males. The supposed reason for this sentence was that the Israelites had "multiplied, and waxed exceeding mighty: and the land was filled with them" (Exodus 1:7). It was pronounced that "every son that is born ye shall cast into the river" – and so a woman of the house of Levi placed her three-month-old boy in a basket of rushes and pitch, setting him down among the water reeds.

The story then becomes somewhat implausible, for along came the pharaoh's daughter, seeming to care nothing for her father's dictate. She discovered the baby and began conversing with his sister, who just happened to be nearby. The baby was then returned to his mother, who was paid by the princess to nurse him. Within no time, the boy was back where he started and all fear of the pharaonic persecution appears to have been forgotten! Eventually, the princess adopted the boy as her own and called him Moses, with no one thinking to ask about his natural parents. That is the extent of the biblical story of Moses' childhood, and in the very next verse (Exodus 2:11) he is portrayed as a grown man.

The Cairo-born historical linguist Ahmed Osman has conducted in-depth research into the identity of Moses and the customs of the era. Quite apart from the obvious grafting of the *Legend of Sharru-kîn*, Osman makes the point that, under prevailing custom, it would have been improbable for an unmarried Egyptian princess to have been allowed to adopt a child.[16] From Egyptian records, he also explains that there was a factual base for the ark of rushes tale, although with a rather more understandable cast and plot.

An influential Israelite named Yusuf-Yuya (Joseph) had been chief minister (vizier) to the pharaohs Tuthmosis IV and his son Amenhotep III. When Tuthmosis died, Amenhotep married his young sister Sitamun (as was the kingly tradition) so that he could inherit the throne in the matrilinear succession.[17] Shortly afterwards, in order to have an adult wife as well, Amenhotep also married Tiye, the daughter of Yusuf-

Yuya. It was decreed, however, that no son born to Tiye could inherit the throne and, because of the length of her father's governorship, there was a general fear that his Israelite relatives were gaining too much power in Egypt. In addition, since Tiye was not the legitimate heiress, she could not represent the State god Amen (Amun).[18] So, when Tiye became pregnant, certain palace officials thought that her child should be killed at birth if a son.[19] In the light of this, arrangements were made with her Israelite relatives, who lived at Goshen in the Nile Delta country. Nearby, at Zaru,[20] Tiye had a summer palace, where she went to have her baby son. In the course of this, the midwives arranged to have the boy nursed by Tiye's sister-in-law Tey of the house of Levi.

The boy, Amenhotep (born c. 1394 BC) was later educated at Heliopolis by the Egyptian priests of Ra (as explained by Manetho in respect of Moses) and in his teenage years he went to live at Thebes. By that time, his mother had become more influential than the senior queen, Sitamun, who had never borne a son and heir to the pharaoh, only a daughter, Nefertiti.[21] Pharaoh Amenhotep III then suffered a period of ill-health and, because there was no direct male heir to the royal house, young Amenhotep was brought to the fore. He married his half-sister Nefertiti in order to reign as co-regent during this difficult time – and when their father died, he succeeded as Amenhotep IV.

In ancient Egypt it was common practice for the pharaohs to marry their sisters in order to progress their kingship through the female line. These wives were often the pharaohs' half-sisters, born of their mothers by different fathers.[22] It can be seen from genealogical charts of the era that, although Egypt had many successive kingly dynasties, these houses were only renamed and renumbered when a pharaoh died without a male heir. The important thing was that his queen had a female heiress, and it was upon that daughter's marriage into another male line that a new dynasty began.

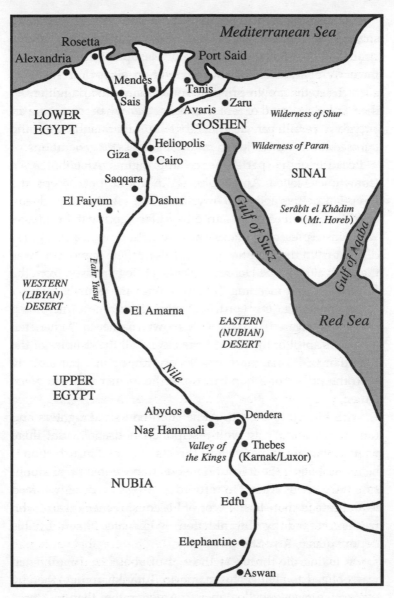

Egypt and Sinai – lands of the Exodus.

It is also apparent that many pharaohs had a number of strategically chosen wives and often married into various strains of the original royal blood of Mesopotamia from which the early pharaonic dynasties were themselves descended. In such cases, the crown princes would marry the daughters of their fathers' second or junior queens, thereby perpetuating an apparent patrilinear descent, but in fact heightening the female blood of their line in favor of successive generations.

Because of his part-Israelite upbringing, Amenhotep IV (sometimes called Amenophis IV)[23] could not accept the Egyptian deities and their myriad idols. He therefore developed the notion of Aten – an omnipotent god with no image, who was represented by a solar disc with downward rays (as distinct from the Egyptian sun god Ra).[24] The name Aten was the equivalent of the Hebrew *Adon* – a title borrowed from the Phoenician and meaning "Lord" – with the equally familiar *Adonai* meaning "my Lord."[25] At the same time, Amenhotep (Amen is pleased) changed his own name to Akhenaten (Glorious spirit of the Aten).[26] He closed all the temples of the Egyptian gods, making himself very unpopular, particularly with the priests of Ra and those of the former national deity, Amen.

With his wife Nefertiti, Akhenaten had six daughters and ran an extraordinarily well-disciplined household. But there were plots against his life and threats of armed insurrection if he did not allow the traditional gods to be worshipped alongside the faceless Aten. He refused and was eventually forced to abdicate in short-term favor of his cousin Smenkhkare, who was succeeded by Tutankhaten (Akhenaten's son by his deputy queen, Kiya).

On taking the throne at the age of about 11, Tutankhaten was obliged to change his name to Tutankhamun – thereby denoting a renewed allegiance to Amen, rather than to Aten – but he was only to live for a further nine or ten years.[27] Akhenaten, meanwhile, was banished from Egypt in about 1361 BC,[28] but his supporters still considered him to be the rightful monarch. To them, he was the living heir to his father's throne, and they regarded him still as the royal *Mose* (Greek: *Mosis*).[29]

From the moment of his exile, Akhenaten (henceforth to be equated with Moses) made two journeys into Sinai, returning briefly to Egypt in between, as the book of Exodus explains. The general Israelite exodus, which he led, occurred on the second occasion in about 1330 BC. The Aten cult continued for a while after Tutankhamun's death, at which time the crown was transferred to his great-uncle Aye, the husband of Tey who had nursed both Akhenaten and his half-sister Nefertiti. Tey was the Glorious One – the *Yokâbar*, whom the Bible calls Jochebed. Aye was succeeded by his son-in-law General Horemheb, who dispensed with Aten, forbade the mention of Akhenaten's name, and excised the Amarna Kings from the official King List. He also destroyed numerous monuments of the era,[30] and it was for this reason that the discovery of Tutankhamun's tomb in November 1922 came as such a welcome surprise, for so little was known about him before-hand.[31]

Initially, as explained in Exodus 2:15–3:1, Moses fled to the land of Midian, east of the Sinai peninsular. His senior queen, Nefertiti, appears to have died a short while before this, and although her remains have not been discovered, a cartouche bearing her name was found in the 1930s in the royal tomb at Amarna.[32]

In Midian, Moses took yet another wife, Zipporah, the daughter of Lord Jethro, and she bore him two sons, Gershom and Eliezer (Exodus 2:22, 18:4). The story then moves to the "burning bush" sequence at Mount Horeb in Sinai. The bush was enveloped in a fiery light, but it was not consumed (Exodus 3:2–4) and from its midst came an angel. The Lord, El Shaddai, then appeared in person, announcing to Moses that he was to be called "I am that I am'"(3:14) – *YHWH*: Yahweh or Jehovah. After this, arrangements were made for Moses to return to Egypt and retrieve the Israelites, who had been placed in bondage by the harsh new authorities.

By that time, Horemheb's reign had concluded, and a whole new regime had begun in Egypt: the 19th dynasty, whose founding pharaoh was Rameses I. Having been away from Egypt for many years, Moses evidently asked the Lord how he could prove his identity to the Israelites, whereupon three instructions were given. These have puzzled theologians for the longest time because, although the Bible opposes all forms of magic, Moses was advised to perform three magical feats. Generally, when such deeds are discussed, they are referred to as "miracles," so that the achievements of man are always superseded by the supreme abilities of God. But in this instance Moses was seemingly granted divine powers to enable him to convince the Egyptian Israelites that he was indeed their deposed king (Exodus 4:1-9).

He was first advised to cast his rod to the ground, where it would become a serpent, but would be reinstated as a rod when lifted. Secondly, he was to place his hand on his breast, from where it would emerge white and leprous, but would return to normal when the act was repeated. Then he was to pour river water onto the land, at which it would turn to blood.

Right of Succession

Until this point in the story, only an unnamed sister of Moses has been introduced (the sister who talked with the pharaoh's daughter by the river), but now a brother called Aaron makes his appearance (Exodus 4:14), and with a somewhat baffling aftermath. Moses and Aaron journeyed back to Egypt and made themselves known to the Israelites – but it was before the pharaoh, not before the Israelites, that the magic of the rod and serpent was performed. Moreover, it was not performed by Moses as planned, but by Aaron (Exodus 7:10-12).

This sequence is of particular importance because it serves to indicate that, along with Moses, Aaron held his own pharaonic status. The rituals of the serpent-rod and the withered hand (though described as if magic in the Bible) were both aspects of the rejuvenation festivals of the Egyptian kings – ceremonies wherein their divine powers were heightened. The pharaohs had a number of scepters (rods) for different occasions, and the scepter of rejuvenation was a rod topped with a bronze serpent. It was also customary for the king to place his right arm limply across his chest, while supporting it with his left hand.[33] A preparation for this ceremony is pictorially shown in the tomb of Kherof, one of Queen Tiye's stewards, and the scene depicts her husband (Moses' father) Amenhotep III.

So, did Moses (Akhenaten) have a brother who was himself a pharaoh, whose fate is unknown and who is similarly recorded as having disappeared rather than dying? Indeed he did – at least, he had a feeding-brother, whose own mother was Tey the *Yokâbar*, the Israelite wet-nurse of Akhenaten and Nefertiti. As a pharaoh, this man had succeeded for just a short while after the deposition of Akhenaten, and his name was Smenkhkare. He was the grandson of Yusuf-Yuya the vizier, and the son of Aye (the brother of Akhenaten's birth-mother, Tiye). Correctly stated, this pharaoh's name was Smenkh-ka-ra (Vigorous is the Soul of Ra).[34] Alternatively, since Ra was the sun-god of the Heliopolis House of Light, called On,[35] pharaoh Smenkh-ka-ra was also Smenkh-ka-ra-on, from the phonetic ending of which derives the name Aaron.[36] In parallel, the name also derives from the Semitic word for "ark," which was *ãron*. (For further notes concerning Smenkhkare, *see* Appendix I: Enigma of the Tombs.)

Having been in Sinai and Midian from his exile in about 1361 BC, Moses returned to Egypt with Aaron to take up the Israelite cause against the incoming pharaoh Rameses I, who was apparently holding many of the families in bonded service. Given that their own 18th dynasty had terminated with pharaoh Horemheb, who had no legitimate heir, a new dynasty had commenced (c. 1335 BC) under Horemheb's erstwhile vizier Rameses, the son of a troop commander called Seti.[37] By performing the secret rituals of the serpent-rod and withered hand, Aaron was clearly challenging Rameses' right of succession – but Rameses controlled the Egyptian army and this proved a decisive factor in the power struggle.[38] Plainly, the Amarna cousins were not about to have any kingly rights reinstated, but they did manage to persuade Rameses to allow the Israelites of Goshen to leave the country.

Rameses I did not survive his second regnal year, which might equate with the Bible's implied death of the pharaoh in pursuit of the Israelites (Exodus 15:19). However, immediately after the event (even before the mummification of Rameses),[39] his son Seti I launched a campaign into Sinai and Syria, taking his troops in a swift military assault into Canaan.[40] The very fact that the people of Israel are mentioned by name in a documented account of this campaign proves that the Israelites were in Canaan at that time – for the Israelites (Children of Israel) were specifically the Egyptian-born descendants of Jacob-Israel. Outside Egypt, prior to the exodus, there were plenty of Hebrews, but there were few (if any) Israelites, and there was no land of Israel.[41]

The information concerning Seti's campaign comes from a large granite stela discovered in 1896 by Sir W.M. Flinders Petrie. It was found in the Theban funerary temple of pharaoh Merneptah (c. 1236–1202 BC), and its inscribed record had been commenced in the reign of Moses' father, Amenhotep III. Merneptah (the grandson of Seti I) had brought the history down to date on the reverse of the stela, and in year five of his reign he spoke of the Israelite residents of Canaan. Not only had the Israelites completed their period in the wilderness of Sinai, but they had been in Canaan long enough to pose a significant threat to the pharaoh. The *Israel Stela*, as it is called, is now in the Cairo Museum, and within the context of Merneptah's record are details of anti-Israeli campaigns. Egyptologists have dated these to the reigns of his predecessors, Rameses II and Seti I.[42] "Israel is devastated," recounts the stela. "Her seed is no more; Palestine has become a widow of Egypt."[43] It can therefore be deduced that the Israelite exodus from Egypt occurred early in the reign of of Rameses I (c. 1335 BC).[44] (For additional notes concerning this date, see Appendix II: The Exodus.)

Beloved of Khiba

Having identified Moses and Aaron, we still have another of the immediate family to discover, their sister Miriam. An elder sister first appears in the story of the ark of rushes (Exodus 2:7), but she is not named at that stage. Much later (Exodus 15:20) we are introduced to a woman called Miriam, who is described as being the sister of Aaron. Then, eventually (Numbers 26:59), it is said that she was the sister of both Moses and Aaron.

The Hebrew name Miriam has its equivalent in the Greek form of Maria/Mary, and derived from the Egyptian name Mery, meaning "beloved."[45] It comes as no surprise to discover in the family records of Akhenaten, two princesses called Merytaten (Beloved of Aten) – one being his daughter and the other his granddaughter. The *Mery* epithet was also applied to Queen Nefertiti herself. She too was a feeding-sister of Smenkhkare (Aaron), for her wet-nurse was Aaron's mother Tey of the house of Levi. An inscription at Tey's Amarna tomb describes her as "nurse and tutor of the queen." Similarly (with regard to Moses), Tey is described as being "The great nurse, nourisher of the god, adorner of the king."[46] In view of this, Nefertiti was identified some years ago as the possible sister of Moses who appeared at the water's edge when he was a baby.[47] In theory, such a deduction would appear logical, but since the story of the ark of rushes has a partly fictional base, the identity of the sister portrayed in this episode is of little relevance.

More important is the later Miriam, who first appears with Moses and Aaron in Sinai. In this regard we find the *Mery* epithet applied to another half-sister and wife of Akhenaten. This junior queen was called "the Royal Favorite; the Child of the Living Aten."[48] She was the deputy of Queen Nefertiti, whom she outrivaled in many respects. Better known these days as Queen Kiya, this prominent royal was the greatly beloved Mery-khiba[49] – a daughter of Amenhotep III and his third wife Gilukhipa. One of the reasons for Kiya's prestige was that (unlike the senior queen, Nefertiti) she bore a son to Akhenaten – the future pharaoh Tutankhamun.

Another cause of Kiya's high station was that her mother was a Mesopotamian princess, whose father was King Shutarna of Mitanni. The name Kiya derives from the Mitannian goddess Khiba (pronounced *kiya*). Indeed, Abda-khiba (Servant of Khiba), a regional governor in Canaan, appealed for Akhenaten's assistance against invading Hebrews. At that time, the Mitannian dynasts were powerful throughout Canaan, and their Mesopotamian heritage (from the same root stock as the 2nd dynasty of Egypt) was held in the highest esteem.

Records indicate that towards the end of Akhenaten's reign, Mery-khiba (Beloved of Khiba) had become the dominant queen as Mery-amon (Beloved of Amon), carrying a dual royal legacy from the kings of Mesopotamia and Egypt. It was she who moved into exile with the deposed Moses, to become known to the Israelites as Miriam (Mery-amon), and it was her matriarchal blood which, through her daughter (the sister of Tutankhamun), cemented the succession for the eventual Royal House of Judah. During the strategic destruction of Amarna records by pharaoh Horemheb, the name of her daughter was expunged wherever it appeared in Egypt.[50]

Hence, the daughter can now only be identified as Kiya junior (Khiba-tasherit).

Despite the sovereign legacy of Miriam, the Old Testament affords her very little space. In Exodus 15:20 she is said to have led the Israelite women in Sinai with her timbrel (tambourine). She and Aaron are seen to admonish Moses because of his marriage to an Ethiopian woman (Numbers 12:1), and this appears to relate to Princess Tharbis of Ethiopia. She (as stated in the *Antiquities of the Jews*) had been married to Moses during his early Egyptian military campaign,[51] and made her presence known again in Sinai. Subsequently, Miriam is said to have died at Kadesh (Numbers 12:10, 20:1), and that is the extent of her portrayal in the Bible. Outside the authorized scripture, however, her story is told at some length in the Book of Jasher, a work not selected for inclusion in the canonical Old Testament.

It was not until after the time of Jesus that the separate Old Testament scriptures were collated into a single volume, and it was then that certain books were excluded because they were at variance with the compositional strategy. One of these was the Book of Jasher – a work previously considered important enough to be mentioned twice in the canonical Bible.[52] The very fact that these references are to be found in Joshua 10:13 and 2 Samuel 1:18 indicates that Jasher was around before these books were written – and they each claim that it was a repository of essential knowledge. Although not promoted by the mainstream establishment, the Book of Jasher has not been as much of an historical secret as might be imagined. The 9-foot (*c*. 3-m) Hebrew scroll was a prize of the Frankish Court of Emperor Charlemagne (AD 800–814), having been discovered in Persia by the monk Alcuin, who later founded the University of Paris.[53] As a reward for his discovery, Alcuin was awarded three abbeys and also became England's Archbishop of Canterbury.[54]

Jasher was the Egyptian-born son of Caleb. He was brother-in-law to the first Israelite judge Othneil (Judges 1:13) and was the appointed royal staff-bearer to Moses. Consequently, the Book of Jasher does not make the biblical error of first calling Moses' Midianite father-in-law Reuel (as does Exodus 2:18–21; corrected in Exodus 3:1), but calls him Jethro from the outset.[55] Another difference, which becomes increasingly apparent, is the ultimate significance of Miriam, who is a constant adviser to Moses and Aaron, and is greatly revered by the Israelites, to whom she is clearly a cultural leader. In this we find another reason for the biblical exclusion of the Book of Jasher, for it is quite unlike the familiar biblical books in its portrayal of a woman who issues instructions that are generally obeyed by all who take counsel from her. Indeed, the reader is left in little doubt of Miriam's supreme royal heritage.

The main contrast between Jasher and the biblical account begins when the Lord issues his laws and ordinances to Moses at Mount Horeb. These are the commonly known directives that accompany the Ten Commandments, which are left quite unstated in Jasher. Exodus 21:1–36 explains that the Lord issued instructions to Moses concerning masters and servants, covetousness, neighborly behavior, crime, marriage, morality, and many other issues, including the all-important rule of the Sabbath. But, in Jasher, these laws and ordinances are not conveyed to Moses by God; they are directly communicated by Jethro, Sheikh of Midian, at the foot of Mount Horeb.[56] As the senior priest of Sinai, it was he who told Moses he was the El Shaddai: Lord of the Mountain. Jethro was, therefore, the prevailing Great One of the Horeb temple, the overseer of the House of Gold.

At that point in the story, Jasher explains that Miriam took up the challenge. She enquired why the Israelites should abandon all their customs for the laws of a foreign nation, asking, "Are the children of Jacob without understanding?" But in the ensuing debate, there is no talk whatever of God – only of the Lord Jethro. Contrary to the Exodus portrayal of the Israelites' allegiance to Moses, Jasher relates that "the voice of the tribes of the congregation were on the side of Miriam." Moses became so angry that he had Miriam imprisoned, "and the people of Israel gathered themselves together unto Moses and said, Bring forth unto us Miriam our counselor,"[57] whereupon Moses was compelled to release her after seven days.

Clearly, Miriam was rather more popular than her half-brother, and the Book of Jasher makes much of her standing, while detailing the Israelites' great sorrow when she died in Kadesh: "The children of Israel mourned for Miriam forty days; neither did any man go forth of his dwelling. And the lamentation was great, for after Miriam arose up no one like unto her ... And the flame thereof went out into all the lands ... yea, throughout all Canaan, and the nations feared greatly."[58]

A scholar named Tobias wrote in the testimonies appended to the Book of Jasher that Miriam "brought a grain out of Egypt, and sowed it in the field" – but this was totally ignored by the Bible compilers who promoted only the legacy of the Hebrew patriarchs in their attempt to forge a male-dominated succession. As the scriptural account progresses, we are led to believe that the eventual Royal House of David and Solomon gained its office because an Israelite shepherd boy slew a giant Philistine with a stone. The Bible tells absolutely nothing about David's sovereign descent from Miriam and the mighty dynasties of Mesopotamia and Egypt.

There is no doubt that, for all the scribal manipulation of old texts, Miriam (Mery-amon) and her daughter, Kiya-tasherit (espoused to Rama of Judah), emerge as key figures in the Grail bloodline of the House of Gold. But they have been ignored and forgotten by religious establishments founded as patriarchal institutions. Consequently, Moses (the royal husband of Mery-amon) was sidestepped altogether as a progenitor of the Davidic ancestral family. Instead, he has been remembered as a redeemer of the Israelites and guardian of the Law, but without any thought as to why he was such a prominent and respected figure in his day. Meanwhile, the authorized published line from Abraham to David entered the scriptures with many of its generations completely excluded (400 years missing in all), so as to avoid citing the Egyptian connection, which was anathema to the eventual Israelite scribes of Genesis and Exodus.[59]

Of Miriam, the Book of Aaron – credited to Moses' confederate Hur (who appears in Exodus 24:14) – relates: "Miriam from hence became the admired of the Hebrews; every tongue sang of her praise. She taught Israel; she tutored the children of Jacob – and the people called her, by way of eminence, the Teacher. She studied the good of the nation, and Aaron and the people hearkened unto her. To her the people bowed; to her the afflicted came." Hur was the father of Uri Ben Hur, whose son built the Ark of the Covenant (Exodus 35:30–31), and it is to this subject that we now turn.

The Ark of the Covenant

Conflict of Deuteronomy

Like the Holy Grail and the Golden Fleece, the Ark of the Covenant is a primary relic of sacred quest. But in contrast to the intangible characteristics of the others, the Ark maintains a physical status, with its material construction related in the Bible. The Ark is, nevertheless, just as much an enigma as the Grail or the Fleece. Its purpose as a repository is described, but with no reason given as to why it was so richly adorned. It is portrayed as having awesome and deadly powers, but these are not satisfactorily detailed. We are left in no doubt that it was the most valued possession of the Israelites – and yet, after some four centuries of adventurous history, it drifts without explanation from biblical record.

As defined by the Oxford Word Library, "ark" is an obsolete form of the modern word "arc," and was equivalent to the Latin *arca*: a chest, box or coffer. Something hidden or secreted in such a box is called "arcane," while a profound mystery is an *arcanum* (plural *arcana*) as in alchemy and the Tarot. A repository for preserving documents is an "archive," and an item of great antiquity is "archaic" or "archaean." Hence, the study of such items through excavation and analysis becomes "archaeology."

Arks have also been identified with enclosed vessels, such as Noah's Ark and Moses' ark of rushes. The word "ark," as conveyed in the Bible and rendered from the old Greek of the Septuagint, had its Hebrew parallel in *ãron* – a box or container, as used to describe a coffin in Genesis 50:26 and a cash box in 2 Kings 12:10.[1]

Onwards from the book of Exodus, and through much of the Old Testament, the Ark of the Covenant is prominently featured, playing an important role in the Israelites' conquest of Canaan.[2] In the course of its history, the Ark killed without warning if the rules of its handling were not obeyed,[3] and the fury of its unleashed power caused tumors on a plague-like scale.[4] As for providing storage for the Ten Commandments, there is nothing further from the original portrayal. As we have seen, Exodus 40:20 states that Moses put the Testimony into the Ark, but the reference relating to the Commandments comes from a later retrospective in Deuteronomy. Here, before the Israelites carry the Ark into Jordan, Moses reminds them of its great power, and of the earlier events at Mount Horeb. He recounts that the tables of stone, written with the finger of God, were those which he had cast to the ground and broken before their eyes.[5] Then, he tells of how he was instructed to hew two more tablets, on which would be written what was on the former stones, and that these were the "commandments" which he placed in the Ark.

The fact that the original tablets (said to have been written with the finger of God) had nothing to do with what might have been placed in the Ark, has caused much consternation over the centuries. In religious terms, the whole lore of the Ark has been based on this ideal, but it is known by Judaic scholars to be an historical fallacy. In an attempt to reconcile the matter and appease clerical teaching, a compromise concept was born in the Middle Ages, when it was determined by theologians that there must have been two Arks! The one built by Bezaleel housed the Testimony stone, as explained in Exodus 40:20, while the other (a copy) contained the tables which had been broken by Moses![6] It was stressed, however, that it was the real

Bezaleel Ark which found its eventual residence in King Solomon's Temple. As to the fate or fortune of the supposed duplicate with the Commandments, this was never discussed – at least not by Jewish historians.

The notion of a "second" Ark was grasped with enthusiasm by the Christian fraternity in Ethiopia. If the Jews were not inclined to capitalize on the fable, then the Christians could surely build a new tradition around it. So it was that, in the 1300s, an anonymous Ethiopic book appeared, entitled *Kebra Nagast* (Glory of the Kings.)[7] During this era of European infiltration into African countries, the object of the book was to establish the pretence of a long-standing Judaeo-Christian culture in old Abyssinia. It claimed that the kings of that country had descended from a certain Menyelek, who was the hitherto secret son of King Solomon of Judah and the Queen of Sheba. Not only that, but Menyelek had brought the Ark with the Commandments to Ethiopia. Amazingly, the legend lives on to this day – encouraged by the Ethiopian Orthodox Church and the Axum tourist industry. The relic is said to be kept in a crudely erected 1960s chapel to which entry is, not surprisingly, prohibited. According to a suitably briefed doorkeeper, who refuses to discuss the Ark, no one (not even the Patriarch) has ever seen it![8]

The discrepancies between the Deuteronomy passage and the older Exodus account are considerable – even to the extent that Moses is said in the Deuteronomy review to have made the Ark himself (Deuteronomy 10:5). This is in complete contrast to the original detailed accounts of how the craftsman Bezaleel made the Ark, culminating in, "And Bezaleel made the ark of shittim wood; two cubits and a half was the length of it, and a cubit and a half was the breadth of it, and a cubit and a half the height of it.[9] And he overlaid it with pure gold, within and without ..." (Exodus 37:1–2). Prior to that, it was explained that Bezaleel (assisted by Aholiab) was specially chosen by the Lord for the commission.[10] So, why is there a conflict between the Exodus account and the later retrospective analysis in Deuteronomy?

From the very beginning of the Old Testament, it is now generally accepted by scholars that there was more than one writer of the Pentateuch (Genesis, Exodus, Leviticus, Numbers, and Deuteronomy). There were not only different hands for penning these books and the Old Testament in general, but the individual books emanate from different scribal time frames. In short, the Old Testament is a hotchpotch of glued together accounts, which make their competitive presence felt right from the outset. In Genesis 1:27 it is related that God created Adam. Then, in Genesis 2:7, Adam is seen to be created again, thereby determining that the same story is being told by two different writers. In fact, there are two quite distinct Creation stories in Genesis.[11] The first (Genesis 1:1–2:4) is considered to be the work of a priestly writer of the 6th century BC (academically referred to as "P"), and its purpose was the glorification of God by way of his bringing the Earth out of the darkness of Chaos. The second Creation account (Genesis 2:5–25) has a somewhat older tradition, and its author is often called the Jahvist (known as "J") because he introduced the godly name of Jehovah (Yahweh). Among the other Pentateuch writers were those classified as the Elohist ("E") and the Deuteronomist ("D").

The books of the Old Testament were compiled between the 6th and 2nd centuries BC. They were commenced during the Babylonian captivity of the Israelites, and concluded by subsequent generations back in Judaea. It was, therefore, not a cohesive composition as such, but a series of separate accounts from Mesopotamian and Jewish sources. Hence, there is massive replication in certain areas: the books of Kings and Chronicles, for example. Some of the Old Testament is prophetic, some is historic, and some is straightforward religious scripture. Within these categories, the book of Deuteronomy has a very Judaean religious base, with its writers deeply committed to unifying people into a common belief structure in a time of severe hardship and oppression.

Some 800 years or so after the time of Moses, Deuteronomy was purposefully shaped as if it were coming directly from the mouth of Moses. It was not so much about ancestral record (as was more the case with Exodus), but about creating a framework of lore which was to become Law. Its use of history was wholly manipulative in that a primary requirement was to justify the Israelites' violent invasion of Canaan by promoting it as having been God's will. In this regard, we have Moses stating that God is going to "destroy these nations from before thee, and thou shalt possess them" (Deuteronomy 31:3). Other similar announcements include: "Thou shalt utterly destroy them" (20:17) and "Thou shalt make no covenant with them, nor show mercy unto them" (7:2). There is, of course, no record that Moses ever said such things, while prior to that (in Exodus) we have him delivering the thoroughly contrasting commandment, "Thou shalt not kill."

These historically adjusted aspects of Deuteronomy are presented as a script might be written for a play, and it is within this framework that we find the spurious references to the Commandments and the Ark. In practice, Deuteronomy is a wholly reflective account. It looks back to the time of Moses, when the Israelites were the invaders, but expresses the concerns applicable when they were themselves being invaded by Nebuchadnezzar's Babylonian army in a much later era.

Origin of the Bible

It is worth remembering that even by the 1st-century Gospel era there was no single composite text available to the Jews at large. The various books existed only as individual texts, as indicated by the 38 scrolls of 19 Old Testament books found at Qumrân, Judaea, between 1947 and 1951. These include a

23-foot (c. 7-m) Hebrew scroll of the book of Isaiah,[12] the longest of all the Dead Sea Scrolls. Dated to about 100 BC, it is the oldest biblical text discovered to date. Such scrolls were held for use in synagogues, but were not generally available to people at large. The first set of amalgamated books to be approved as the Hebrew Bible appeared after the fall of Jerusalem to the Roman general Titus in AD 70. It was compiled in an endeavor to restore faith in Judaism at a time of social turmoil. (The word Bible comes from the Greek plural noun *biblia*, meaning "a collection of books".)

In its composite 1st-century form, the Old Testament was written in a Hebrew style consisting only of consonants. In parallel with this, a Greek translation emerged for the benefit of the growing number of Greek-speaking Hellenist Jews. This has since become known as the Septuagint (from the Latin *septuaginta*: seventy) because 72 scholars were employed in the translation. Later, in the 4th century AD, St. Jerome made a Latin translation from the Hebrew for subsequent Christian usage; this was called the Vulgate because of its "vulgar" (general) application.

In about 900 AD, the old Hebrew text emerged in a new form, produced by Jewish scholars known as the Masoretes because they appended the *Masorah* (a body of traditional notes) to the text. Known as the *Codex Petropolitanus*, the oldest existing copy of this comes from less than 1,100 years ago, in AD 916.

These days, we may work from the Masoretic text, from the Latin Vulgate, or from English, and other language translations. But, whatever the case, the fact remains that these books are all from our present era, and have each been subjected to translatory and interpretational amendment. The Greek Septuagint is somewhat more reliable (being based on texts from the 3rd century BC), but 1st-century and subsequent adjustments, along with translatory variations, have divorced even this from its true original.

The Dwelling Place

The Tabernacle of the Congregation is customarily regarded as the elaborate sanctuary erected in Sinai to house the Ark of the Covenant. This extravagant construction is, however, confined to the Priestly ("P") aspects of the Pentateuch, and does not conform to the much simpler Tent of Meeting described elsewhere in the text.[13] In this regard, the Elohist ("E") entries make such statements as, "Now Moses took the tabernacle and pitched it without the camp, afar off from the camp" (Exodus 33:7-11). Subsequent to this is a most interesting entry, which bears close resemblance to the item in Genesis 3:8-9, when the Lord walked in the Garden of Eden, having lost sight of Adam. In Exodus we are reminded again, quite abruptly, that there was a distinct difference between the mysterious God whose presence emanated from the radiance of the Ark, and the Mountain Lord El Shaddai, who is portrayed as behaving in a very down-to-earth fashion. Exodus 33:11 relates that, at the entrance to the Tent of Meeting, "The Lord spake unto Moses face to face, as a man speaketh to his friend." Similar references are found in Numbers 11:16-30 and 12:4-9.

There is no apparent similarity between the straightforward tent of the Elohist, pitched outside the camp, and the mighty Tabernacle of the Priest, situated in the center of the camp with its army of attendants and Levite guardians. It is, however, this hugely burdensome Tabernacle, with its great brazen altar, that is best remembered as the prototype ultimately replicated by Solomon's proportionally constructed Temple in Jerusalem.

Apart from all its richly described furnishings, hangings, rings, and adornments,[14] the Tabernacle walls were constructed of upright boards 13.5 feet high and 27 inches wide (c. 4 m x 69 cms). There were more than four dozen wide planks, with additional corner pieces, in an overall 3:1 ground ratio of 45 feet x 15 feet (c. 13.7 x 4.6 m) and 15 feet in height.[15] This was all covered and draped in heavy linen and goat skins, while curtained within was the Sanctuary of the Ark, contrived as a 15-foot cubic space. It has been suggested that the said definition of "boards" is perhaps a mistranslation for "frames," but the old technical terms are obscure, so it is difficult to tell which is the more accurate.[16] Either way, we have something here which was far from portable – as it was supposed to be. But there is more. This construction (a covered timber building rather than a tent) was set within a 150 foot by 75 foot enclosure: the Court of the Dwelling (c. 45.6 x 22.8 m) – about the size of an Olympic swimming pool. This was boundaried by 60 pegged wooden poles with bronze bases, and some 450 feet (137 m) of weighty curtaining, to a height of 7.5 feet (c. 2.28 m). For transportation, the dimensions, volume, and weight of all this would have been enormous, if indeed factual as portrayed. It is not surprising that the Tabernacle (Hebrew: *Mishkan*, Dwelling Place) is diminished in the narrative reckoning soon after the Israelites' onward journey from Sinai is under way. It is further mentioned in Joshua 18:1 as being erected at Shiloh after the battle of Jericho and, according to 1 Kings 18:4, it was eventually in Jerusalem when Solomon dedicated the Temple. In the interim, 1 Chronicles 15:1 explains that David had pitched a new tent for the Ark.

Chariots and Cherubim

The Ark receives its first biblical mention in Exodus 25:10–22, when the Lord laid down the specifications for its manufacture. With the measurements of the main coffer given in cubits, and using 18 inches as a cubit standard, it resolves at 45 inches in length, 27 inches in width, and 27 inches in height (c. 113 x 68 x 68 cm). Since the cubit was a variable measurement, often given as 22 inches,[17] it could have been 55 inches long, by 33 inches in height and width (c. 140 x 84 x 84 cm), or anywhere in between. Whatever the case, the precise width/height-to-length ratio is given as 1:1.666.

The box construction was of "shittim wood" (generally reckoned to be acacia, but translated directly from the old Greek of the Septuagint as "incorruptible wood"),[18] plated on the inside and outside with pure gold. Around the upper perimeter it was adorned with a rectangular crown. At each end of the long sides was a permanently fixed gold ring – four rings in all, to house the two carrying staves which were also made of shittim wood, overlaid with gold.

At this stage of the description, a device called a "mercy seat" is said to be placed on top of the Ark – its dimensions being precisely the same as the outside edges of the open box: 2.5 x 1.5 cubits (1.1.666). It was, in effect, a lid which was prevented from slipping by the coffer's crowned outer rim. There was, however, no wood in the lid – it was a slab of pure gold, which must have been quite thick to avoid bowing. The relevant Hebrew word for the "mercy seat" (*kapporeth*) trans-lates better to "cover," while the Septuagint specifies it as a "lid," defining it as a "propitiatory" – a place of appeasement. At each end of this lid was a solid gold cherub, and they faced each other, with wings that stretched inwards over and above

The Ark of the Covenant.

the mercy seat. Finally, it is related that God would commune with Moses from the space above the lid, between the cherubims. (These descriptions are all repeated in Exodus 37:1–9, which tells of Bezaleel making the Ark in accordance with this specification.)

The main difficulty in envisaging the Ark is the nature of the cherubims, because the Lord had previously issued the directive, "Thou shalt not make unto thee any graven image, or any likeness of any thing that is in heaven above, or that is in the earth beneath, or that is in the water under the earth" (Exodus 20:4). If the cherubims were angelic representations, as is the popular artistic portrayal, then the divine regulation would have been broken at its outset. Not long before this manufacturing project, Moses (upholding the dictate) admonished Aaron for making a golden calf (Exodus 32:20–21). It is therefore inconceivable that he would then have asked Bezaleel to make a couple of golden angels.

In this regard, we should not be automatically lulled into a sense of the cherubims being life-form representations just because (like birds, bats, and insects) they had wings. Hospitals have wings, aircraft have wings, shirt collars have wings, ploughs have wings. A "wing" is simply a lateral projection which extends from the main body of an object. Neither should we be sidetracked by the winged creatures found in Mesopotamian and Egyptian artwork. That is not to say that the compilers of Exodus in the 6th century BC were not swayed by such images when describing the Ark, which appears to have been lost to them by that time (around 400 years after it was installed in the Temple of Solomon). If it had been in the Temple immediately prior to Nebuchadnezzar's invasion and the 70 years of Babylonian captivity from 586 BC, then the last Israelite priest to have seen the Ark might well have died in the interim, leaving the cherubims open to interpretation. Even excepting that possibility, the fact is that (at any stage of its Temple residence) only the High Priest ever saw the Ark.

The Exodus scribes would have had no personal insight and could only have based their description on tradition and hearsay.

The popular angelic use of the word *cherubim* was developed by the Judaeo-Christian establishment as a plural form of *cherub*. This means that "cherubims" (according to the Old Testament translations) constitutes a double plural, which is impossible. The error is partly corrected in places – as in Exodus 25:18–19, which refers to "two cherubims" with "one cherub" at each end. The same is said in Exodus 37:8. However, the Septuagint and other old texts do not make the error, referring generally to cherubs rather than cherubims.

For the best clue as to the nature of the cherubim, we should consider the early use of the word. In biblical terms, we first encounter it in Genesis 3:24, when (seeming more like armed chariots than angels) cherubims and a flaming sword, which turned every way, were used to protect the Tree of Life. Quite unrelated to the Bible is a tractate from 3rd-century Alexandria, entitled *The Origin*. It tells of the immortal Sophia, goddess of wisdom, and of the ruler Saboath who "created a great throne on a four-faced chariot of cherubim."[19]

The term "cherub" evolved from the old Semitic *kerûb*, meaning "to ride."[20] Hence, "cherub" is a noun rendered from a verb, and is correctly pronounced "qerub." It is consequently of some significance that, wherever forms of identification for cherubs or cherubim appear (in the Bible or elsewhere), they are in all cases depicted as types of mobile throne, regarded as heavenly and associated with flight. They are certainly not portrayed as creatures in their own right. Such particular identification occurs many times in the Old Testament. In their accounts of the Lord on a rescue mission, both 2 Samuel 22:11 and Psalm 18:10, state: "He rode upon a cherub and did fly: and he was seen upon the wings of the wind." Also, Ezekiel 9:3 refers to God on a cherub, stating, "[He] was gone up from the cherub whereupon he was, to the threshold of the house."

Likewise, 1 Chronicles 28:18 directly associates the cherub guardians of the Ark in Solomon's Temple with "chariots."[21] Knowing that these cherubs were not of the popularized angelic variety, Josephus maintained in his 1st-century *Antiquities of the Jews*, "Nobody can tell, or even conjecture, what was the shape of these cherubims."[22] At much the same time, the Jewish philosopher Philo (30 BC–AD 45) wrote that, whatever the Ark's cherubim might have looked like, he rather felt they were in some way symbolic of knowledge.[23]

The Oxford Word Library[24] specifies that the fundamental root of "cherub" is obscure. It was, nevertheless, rooted in a notion of transport, and an ancient alternative to *kerûb* (to ride) was *erûb*. In this we have a direct association with the variant forms *Choreb* and *Horeb*, as the holy mountain of Moses was called.[25] It was, therefore, the Mount of the Cherub, or Cherub Mountain.

As for the association of cherubs with thrones, the Bible certainly relates that, on occasions, the Lord sat on the mercy seat of the Ark: "He sitteth between the cherubims."[26] It is also confirmed that he communed with Moses from this throne: "He heard the voice of one speaking unto him from off the mercy seat."[27] In these respects, there is no doubt from the text that we are in the physical world of the El Shaddai. But there was also the metaphysical aspect of the Ark-light (the perceived presence of the omnipotent God), which dwelt permanently between the cherubim[28] and was classified as a "dangerous trust" for the Levites.[29] Philosophical Judaism has long perceived the Ark as representing a celestial throne – but has centered its awe on the "tube of fire" and the "sparks that issued from the cherubim," rather than on what the box beneath might have contained.[30] The point is made in the Talmud, however, that two sapphires (*sappir* stones) had been placed in the Ark by Moses.[31] These were of the same *Schethiyâ* crystal from which Moses' own wand was made. (Listed in the 1906 Petrie Report of items discovered at the Serâbît temple on

Mount Horeb were wands of a pale blue-green, unidentified hard material.)[32]

The most explicit of all biblical stories concerning cherubim as chariots or mobile thrones comes from the book of Ezekiel – the prophet whose haunting visions are among the Old Testament's most stirring episodes. Notwithstanding all we have discovered about mobile thrones and the riding of *kerûbs* on the wind, Ezekiel added an intriguing extra dimension, for his cherubs had wheels.

Ezekiel was one of the Jerusalem priests who, in 598 BC, were deported to Babylonia, along with King Joachim of Judah (2 Kings 24:12–16). Together with other exiles, he settled in Tell-Abib (Iraq) and seems to have spent the rest of his life there. It is not important to debate whether Ezekiel's recountings are true or otherwise; in any event, he calls them visions. What is important is that they serve, better than any other biblical story, to identify the nature of cherubim as they were perceived in those times – not as celestial putti, but as formidable contraptions which rose into the air by mechanical means.

Ezekiel explained: "And when I looked, behold the four wheels by the cherubims ... and the appearance of the wheels was the color of beryl stone. As for their appearances, they four had one likeness, as if a wheel had been in the midst of a wheel. When they went, they went upon their four sides; they turned not as they went, but to the place whither the head looked they followed it ... And when the cherubims went, the wheels went by them; and when the cherubims lifted up their wings to mount up from the earth, the same wheels also turned not from beside them."[33]

On another occasion, Ezekiel adds even more information concerning lights and noisy rotating rings. He tells that a great whirlwind came out of the north, spouting fire. Out of the brightness flew what appeared at first to be four living creatures, each with four wings and straight feet, shining like burnished brass. Their wing sets were joined together and they displayed on their sides the faces of a man, an ox, a lion, and an eagle. They all flew straight forwards, gleaming like lamps and issuing bolts of lightning. (This intriguing and mysterious scene is strikingly portrayed in the dramatic painting *Ezekiel's Vision* by Sir Peter Robson; *see* Plate 5.)

There were dreadful rings above them, noisy like rushing waters – while the flying phenomena were as green as beryl and appeared to be full of eyes. They also had wheels which folded against them when flying, and each had a crystal firmament above. But when they stood and let down their wings, there was a throne with the appearance of a man upon it within each lighted firmament.[34]

Blazing spectacles with wheels appear again in Daniel 7:9: "His throne was like the fiery flame, and his wheels as burning fire." There is mention of a similar vehicle in 2 Kings 2:11, which relates how a chariot of fire conveyed Elijah in a whirlwind to heaven. Then, in the book of Isaiah (6:1–2) there is a further account of an airborne cherub, which introduces yet another daunting Old Testament phenomena. Isaiah describes the soaring throne, and continues: "Above it stood the seraphims: each one had six wings."

Flaming seraphims appear with great regularity in ancient documents. That they are fiery is consistent with the etymology of the word *seraph*, which is related to an old Hebrew stem meaning "flame." Sometimes they have awesome destructive properties, as in Numbers 21:16 when a large proportion of Israel died after the Lord sent fiery serpents (seraphim) among them. Such stories are not confined to the countries of the Middle East. From that same period similar accounts come from Tibet, India, Scandinavia, and elsewhere. The writings all tell of heavenly chariots that spout fire and quicksilver, and of thunderbirds with brazen wings.[35]

Without a good deal of speculation, it is impossible to examine the precise whys and wherefores of such seemingly automated devices, with their noisy rotating wings, folding wheels, illuminated glazed compartments, and men within. One can only present them as they are depicted in the ancient texts. What is certain is that these flying chariots (*cherubim*) with their accompanying *seraphim* (fiery, dragon-shaped auxiliaries) were never at any time classified as angels, whose status in the Bible and elsewhere was quite different.[36]

An interesting, and possibly related, fact is that the notion of flying devices did not disappear with ancient mythology. The world of pictorial art, from early times, through the European Renaissance and beyond, provides a variety of images with UFOs sending out spears of light that are somehow related to important religious events on the ground. A 17th-century example by the Dutch artist Aert de Gelder, is *The Baptism of Jesus*, found in the Fitzwilliam Museum, Cambridge (*see* Plate 9).

A Divine Essence

Despite all this, it must be concluded that the topmost cherubim of the Ark of the Covenant were not mobile thrones of the gods. They are presented as functional extensions of the golden lid, and there are no references anywhere to the Ark's ability to fly as such – only to levitate and move of its own accord.[37] These cherubs cannot have been very large but, whatever their shape and size, their significance appears to have been concerned with the deadly force that was said to dwell between them, above the great slab of gold. They were, nevertheless, called *kerûbs* and must therefore have had some connection with the phenomena of Ezekiel, Isaiah, Elijah, and Daniel. In this regard, the Ark and the soaring thrones were spectacular power devices, which blazed fire and light of a kind that was clearly no ordinary flame. They were equally awesome in their destructive abilities, which again were not the norm during that period. If the word *kerûb* denoted a driving source, then a comparative word today might be "engine" (from *ingeny*: a clever contrivance),[38] equally applicable to powering a stationary machine or a traveling aircraft.

In addition to the *Urim* and *Thummim* becoming active in the presence of the Ark, the Bible also explains that the power of the Ark was deadly. Two of Aaron's sons, Nadab and Abihu, were killed by the fire which leapt from the Ark (Leviticus 10:1–2), given in the Talmud as bolts "as thin as threads."[39] And when Uzzah the carter attempted to stay the Ark when its conveyance swayed, he was struck dead the moment he touched it (1 Chronicles 13:10–11). When not on its cart, the Ark had to be carried with independent staves, which were slipped through fixed rings, and close proximity was afforded only to the Levite High Priests (Aaron, Eleazar, and their successors), who were garbed in a very particular fashion. They had large amounts of gold in their specially designed apparel – a golden breastplate, attached to golden rings, chains, and various other fixtures around their bodies (Exodus 28:4–38). And they were instructed to remove their shoes and wash their feet "that they die not" when approaching the Ark (Exodus 30:21). Similarly, those who bore the Ark on its staves were instructed to walk barefoot.[40]

The descriptions of special clothing and procedures for approaching the Ark, although seeming very precise in the text, are actually vague and confused. This is hardly surprising, for the Old Testament scribes of a later era were not working from any practical knowledge. Their approach was from a base of tradition while, at the same time, they thoroughly confused the whole Sinai experience with a resultant religion that had developed in the interim (worship, as against workship). All things considered, however, there is enough information to determine that, whether on the ground or in the air, the extraordinary arcane power of the *kerûbs* was high-voltage electricity.

We can now return to the arkite etymology with which this chapter began, continuing from the Greek word *ark*, with its equivalent being the Latin *arca*: a box or chest.

In old France *arca* became *arche*, which moved into English use in the early Middle Ages. William Caxton's 1483 printing of *The Golden Legend*, by Jacobus de Voragine, refers to the Ark of the Covenant as the "Arche of the Testaments." Subsequently, the word *arche* became *arch*, and then *arc*, which is the proper English form of *ark* today.[41] Meanwhile, a direct association was made in Gothic times with an arch as in "architecture," "arcade," and "architrave." Given that "to arch" meant to overreach or span, the word then fell into use as relating to "above" or "chief'" as in "archduke," "archangel," and "archbishop."

Pulling aspects of this morphology together is the emblematic depiction of Royal Arch Freemasonry, devised in about 1783 by Laurence Dermott, Secretary of the Ancient Grand Lodge of England. His image portrays an architectural arch housing the Ark of the Covenant – an arc within an arch. In this respect, the point is made that *ark* and *arc* (or *arche* and *arch*) are mutually reliant, for they each relate to a state of protective enclosure (Latin: *archeo*). If the Old Testament were being written from scratch today, the Ark of the Covenant would be correctly given as the Arc of Testimony.

As a protective enclosure, the Arc of Testimony was considered to embody the very essence of light and energy; it was a manifestation of the supreme power of God. But since it was a manufactured device, from where did this electrical essence derive? A clue is immediately found in the original use of the Hebrew word *ãron* which, as we have seen (like *arca*), defined a box. However, it was more specifically a collecting-box, and the older root meaning of *ãron* was the verb "to gather" or "gathering."[42] The power was gathered and stored by the box itself, while the most fearful discharge (when the *Urim* and *Thummim* were present) was regarded as an ultimate judgment. It was perceived as the Light and Perfection – a divine oracular inspiration of the great Archon (an ancient Greek word meaning a "bow" or "arc").[43] The

Archons who delivered their mighty judgments were said to be the Rulers of Entirety, and an ancient Greek text entitled *The Hypostasis of the Archons*[44] relates to the chariot of the Foundation, which rose above the forces of Chaos – a chariot called *Cherubim*.

6

The Power of Gold

The Abundance

The mercy seat of the Ark of the Covenant is given as covering the whole coffer, from corner to corner within the perimeter crown. At the lowest estimate of cubit conversion[1] it was 45 inches in length and 27 inches in width (*c.* 113 x 68 cm). To avoid sagging beneath the cherubim, it would need to have been relatively thick, and it was said to have been 100% gold (24 carat).[2] Jewish tradition relates that the mercy seat was a palm-span in depth,[3] which is recorded at 3.5 inches (*c.* 8.25 cm). This would seem about right to support the slab over an empty space on a rigid box-frame, but it is worth getting this volume of gold into a physical perspective.

The weight of gold is expressed in troy ounces, with a troy ounce equivalent to 1.097 *avoirdupois* ounces (*c.* 31.10 gms). According to Argonne National Laboratory (United States Department of Energy), gold atoms form tighter bonds to their neighbors than do the atoms of lead, so gold is denser than lead and comparatively heavy. A cube of gold with a 11.7 mm edge weighs 1 troy ounce, and the Ark lid contained around 39,581 such cubes. Its total weight was around 2,714 pounds (1,231 kgs). This is an astonishing amount of gold, with a current market value of about US $10.5 million. The World Gold Council[4] advises that 24-carat gold has a specific density

of 19.32 gm/cm³. So, by applying this for a more precise calculation, a marginally lower weight of 2,700 pounds (c. 1,224
kgs) is ascertained. Hence, the Ark lid weighed over a ton.[5]
Since the Ark was said to be lifted by wooden shafts onto its
transport by four (or even eight) men, it would need to have
been far lighter than this unless levitational powers were
employed. But even at a quarter of the reckoned lid thickness,
it still constitutes an extraordinary volume.

We shall investigate matters of levitation in due course, but
for now it is worth giving the subject some small initial
consideration. Levitation is the raising and suspension of a
material substance in defiance of gravity. The word "levitate"
stems immediately from the Latin *levis*: "light," as against
gravis: "heavy." However, the term *levis* has an older association with the priests of Levi (the Levites), who were the designated guardians of the Ark of the Covenant. Feats of natural
levitation are difficult to comprehend because material objects
are, of course, subject to the downward thrust of gravity.
Nevertheless, this thrust can be defied by an opposing force
which is seemingly of no comparative consequence. The very
smallest magnet can lift pins and paper clips with a greater
force than the Earth's entire gravitational thrust can muster in
opposition. Notwithstanding this, the magnet would itself
drop to the ground if let go. Hence it is the motive energy
applied to an object, rather than the object itself, which is
crucial to levitation.

Looking at the overall quantity of gold for the Ark and the
Tabernacle, the Exodus list (along with the Ark's double-
plating, rings, and cherubim) includes a crowned table, an
incense altar, a large plate, a seven-branched candlestick, bells,
a breastplate with chains and fittings, plating for the Tabernacle boards, tapestry rods, rings and fixings, dishes, spoons,
tongs, snuffers, bowls, curtain fastenings, and a variety of inci-
dental items. The sum total of necessary gold is staggering and,
if taken as read, begs the question: Where did it all come from?

Previously, we saw how the Israelites parted with their earrings and small items to provide the gold with which Aaron made the calf (Exodus 32:2–3, 24). But Moses subsequently transmuted this to powder and fed it to the Israelites. Later, we are informed that they supplied bracelets, rings, armlets, and other personal items to aid the Ark and Tabernacle projects (Exodus 35:22), but these trinkets would have comprised a fraction of the total requirement. So, how did they acquire such a quantity in the midst of the Sinai plateau? There were no gold mines in the region – only copper and turquoise. The answer must be that it came from the Horeb mountain temple, where the white-powder *mfkzt* was already being made with Egyptian gold.

In those times Egypt had what amounted to a monopoly of gold, with the most important mines located in the Eastern Desert between the Nile and the Red Sea. There was also extensive mining in the Nubian Desert east of Wadi Halfa, and south towards the Third Cataract. A 20th-dynasty papyrus map (*c.* 1200 BC) of the ancient gold mines of Wadi Hammamat is presently held by the Museo Egizio, Turin. Administration and overall control of gold mining was in the hands of high-ranking court officials, and the king received all resultant income, being the outright owner of the land. These vast gold resources were further enhanced by imports and tribute payments from places such as Syria and Babylonia.

The gold served to decorate temples and other pharaonic dedications. It was used lavishly for doors, doorsteps, floors, and reliefs, as well as for an assortment of other decorative purposes. It was also used for the funerary equipment of the kings, and to provide stocks for their time in the Afterlife. Tutankhamun's inner gold sarcophagus alone weighs over 728 pounds (*c.* 330 kgs). Priests, generals, and court officials were rewarded with gold chains presented by the king, and gold was used in abundance for statuettes, masks, mirrors, harps, vessels, and all manner of richly adorned items.

A Brief History of Gold

Throughout history, gold has always held a special place among metals because of its soft yellow luster and comforting appeal. Even above rarer metals, it has constantly been the badge of wealth and supremacy but, according to the World Gold Council, only 10% of all the gold ever mined was extracted before 1848. An estimated 90% of all gold mined from the beginning of recorded time has been brought up in the past 154 years!

In the days of the ancient empires (Sumerian, Babylonian, Egyptian, Persian, Macedonian, and Roman), gold played a major role in the traditions of ruling cultures. Following the 5th-century fall of the Roman Empire, Western European interest in gold declined, and was not revived until the Spanish conquistadors arrived in 16th-century Peru. The goldsmith's art had flourished there for centuries and had become very sophisticated. From the ancient Chavin artisans and the Nazca society of the 6th century BC, gold had been worked and molded. The later Chimu Empire developed the craft from around 1150, with their knowledge subsequently inherited and maintained by the Incas. They knew about lost-wax casting, filigree, fine gold thread-work, and were masters in plating and gilding. Most astonishing to behold was the Inca's Temple of the Sun, with almost every inch of its walls covered in gold, while the gardens of the capital included ornamental animals, plants, birds, and trees all made from gold.[6]

Hernando Cortes entered Mexico in 1519, where he found a similar culture among the Aztecs. Emperor Montezuma offered him priceless gifts but, not content with these, the Spaniard ruthlessly seized their extensive golden treasures. Francisco Pizarro likewise plundered in Peru, destroying the Inca heritage by melting down all the gold in sight, with the majority being shipped back to the courts of Europe.

Following the decimation of at least 3,000 years of cultural achievement in Mexico and Peru, the problem was that neither the Spaniards nor anyone else in Western Europe knew the first thing about gold mining. By then, gold had also been discovered in Brazil, but the mines were not worked beyond superficial extraction. Having regained a taste for gold, Western Europeans turned their attentions to Africa, where mines had long been operated in what became known as the Gold Coast (now Ghana). Also, Transylvanian gold became important to the countries of Central Europe, while gold for the home market was being mined in Scotland. Russia then discovered her own gold, with Tsar Peter the Great (1672–1725) moving its use into architectural design and furnishing, just as it had been used in ancient Egypt.

More than 100 years after Peter's death, the great discoveries which rocked the market occurred in America and South Africa. The crucial turning point was the find at Sutter's Mill on the American River in January 1848, when the Californian gold rush began. Three years later the same happened in Australia. The ultimate discoveries were then made at Witwatersrand in 1886, and South Africa ousted America as the world's largest producer. Another gold rush occurred in Kalgoorlie, Western Australia, in 1893, and in 1896 deposits were found in the Yukon territories of Canada, initiating the Klondike rush. Through all this, however, South Africa has remained the primary source, delivering some 40% of the world's gold, with its highest year of production being 1970. Gold fever reached its zenith in the 1980s, when interests expanded into Brazil, Venezuela, and the Philippines. The application of new technologies was of considerable assistance to this recent gold boom, and new techniques were developed, especially in Western Australia, and in Nevada (accounting for over 60% of United States production).

Day of the Ark

An astonishing fact which emerges from all this is that, in the days of Moses and ancient Egypt, gold was clearly in large-scale use, as replicated for a while in Imperial Rome and Russia. Today, however, we are comparatively swamped with gold, but it is barely noticeable. Where is it all? As a symbol of wealth and success, it is mainly confined to jewelry, commemorative coins, watches, trinkets, and the like – a few ounces here and a few ounces there. But it would perhaps take all the golden baubles in Britain just to make a lid for the Ark of the Covenant!

What has happened is that we have become hoarders of gold, worshippers of bullion, rather than aesthetic users of gold. Today, some 900-million ounces of gold (against the 40,000 ounces for the mercy seat – which suddenly looks small in comparison) are held by monetary authorities as national currency reserves. Why? Gold is not especially rare when compared to some precious metals and gems. It is extremely heavy, like lead, and requires a lot of storage space. Surely there would be substances better suited for such a purpose.

The fact is that gold has always held a peculiar magic and fascination quite unlike any other substance. It is a deeply rooted notion of our psyche that gold is not just a noble and functional metal, it is also warm and beguiling like no other. We have always known that gold is especially important. The vulcans of Mesopotamia knew it, the craftsmen of Karnak knew it, the Lord of Mount Horeb knew it, as did Moses, King Solomon, and many others of the distant past. The difference was that they knew "why" gold was important, whereas for centuries since (like so many wisdoms of olden times) the nature of this importance was lost and forgotten. We have craved gold, killed for it, dug for it, and died for it, but when all is said and done, we took thousands of tons of the world's most enchanting substance, molded it into bars and locked it out of sight in barricaded vaults as if it had never been brought out of the earth!

In times past, gold (along with silver and electrum – a mixture of gold and silver) was made into functional coins, or was directly transferable, by weight, as a means of trading exchange. The Greek historian Herodotus[7] related that the oldest coins were those issued from the Sardis refinery of King Croesus of Lydia (Western Turkey) in the 6th century BC.[8] As modern economies evolved, gold was removed from our pockets, to be held as bullion by the central banks. It was replaced during the Industrial Revolution by token notes and coins with intrinsic values far lower than their face values. At first, the promissory items were redeemable for gold under the development of the International Gold Standard in the 19th century, but the practice ceased as gold became its own commodity device in the financial trading markets. Gold was, of course, bulky and uneconomic to ship between buyers and sellers – so more promissory papers were issued for the dealers. Hence, there are those who own volumes of gold on paper, but have never seen it and have certainly never touched it.

Today, most countries hold some of their reserves in the form of gold, in conjunction with short-term securities such as Treasury Bills. Around 70% of national Treasuries report their holdings to the International Monetary Fund (IMF). Gold is said to be the Asset of Last Resort – when all else fails, it will still be there, and marketable. Although this means that we have been divested of our right to experience the daily magic of gold (unless buying jewelry at exorbitant prices: paying for artistry and manufacture above the gold value), we have at least known that our national assets were secure. But this protective aspect is now changing and, with the approval and involvement of the IMF, Western Treasuries are swapping our gold for fickle currencies, while appearing content to suffer huge compensational losses that threaten economic security. Why are they doing this? And who are the mysterious buyers, whose identities are so well guarded by the vendor Governments?

Details of these auctions are given in Appendix III: Gold for Sale, but for now it is sufficient to suggest that these Treasury exchanges have arisen because it has recently been rediscovered "why" gold is important, just as it was known thousands of years ago. Those doing the buying are acquiring a necessary base substance for a new technological age, while the sellers are content to take losses so as to enable the new regime. At the same time, the balance is weighed against the economic collapse of certain key world industries as others come to the fore. In short, the scientific Day of the Ark is close upon us and it seems we are to give with one hand in order to receive with the other.

The Golden Fleece

Our fascination with gold is the same fascination which persists with regard to the Ark, and the reason why the latter became a relic of sacred quest. We have always known that the Ark was important – not because it contained the Ten Commandments (which it did not), but because it was the key to a secret for which gold was the ultimate catalyst. This secret was symbolized in Greek legend by the enigmatic Golden Fleece sought by Jason and the Argonauts – an epic tale which predated the final compilation of the Old Testament.[9] In his *New System of an Analysis of Ancient Mythology*, the noted 18th-century English mythologist Jacob Bryant drew attention to the nominal similarity between the definition Ark and Jason's ship *Argo*. The ship was said to have been called after her builder, Argus, whose name was the word used in Greece to denote a Watcher or Guardian. In the course of their exploits, the Argonauts were taken by Zeus to the Isle of Electris. This was the island from where amber was obtained in the Valtiki Sea, and the Hellenic word for amber was *electron*. It was known that when amber was rubbed with a soft cloth, it would attract pieces of paper and particles to it by way of an unseen charge. The term used to describe this frictional force was *electrikus*, from which derived the modern word "electricity."

In 1598, a text entitled *Aureum Vellus* (Golden Fleece) was published in Germany by the philosopher Salomon Trismosian.[10] He cited that, contrary to the romantic notion of the woolly ram's skin of perceived mythology, the historical Fleece was actually a skin in the sense of a vellum. Indeed, the etymology does confirm this, with the English word "fleece" stemming from the Middle High German *vlûs*, which related simply to a sheep's skin. The *Golden Fleece*, stated Trismosian, was a parchment which contained the secrets of gold and the Philosophers' Stone from "the kings and sages of the Egyptians, Arabs, Chaldeans, and Assyrians." In this same regard, many other adepts were convinced that the secrets of hermetic alchemy were contained within the textual body of the Jason legend. A century or so ago, the French philosopher Fulcanelli wrote: "The fable of the *Golden Fleece* is a cryptic story of the whole hermetic work, which is to produce the Philosophers' Stone,"[11] and in more recent times the Swiss analytical psychiatrist Carl Gustav Jung made a similar association in his book *Psychology and Alchemy*.[12]

Much earlier, in the 2nd century, Charax of Pergamos wrote of the sublime art of writing on parchment with gold[13] – an ancient science called *chrysographia*. This is apparent in the Greek mythology of Nephele (the wife of King Athamas, *c.* 1200 BC), who gave her children, Phrixos and Helle, the *Golden Scroll of Testimony*, written on sheepskin with gold. There is a general consensus in alchemical texts that the *Golden Scroll* and the *Golden Fleece* were one and the same, but the 18th-century hermeticist Naxagoras went even further, suggesting that they were each also synonymous with the Emerald Tablet of Hermes.[14]

Alongside all this, Moses was considered to have been a primary guardian (an *argus*) of the hermetic wisdom, which came out of Egypt. He was recorded as a student of Hermes in the *Turba Philosophorum* (Assembly of the Philosophers) – a 12th-century Latin work translated from early Hebrew and Arabic sources. The transmutation of gold was even called the Mosaico-hermetic Art. Such references[15] date back to a 3rd-century treatise entitled *The Domestic Chemistry of Moses*, progressing to the famous 10th-century Arabic *Kitāb al-fihrist* (Index Book) of Ibn al-Nadim. Subsequently, there followed the 12th-century *Mirqraot G'dolot* Bible commentaries of the Spanish Jew Abraham Ibn Esra, and the *Alchymica* of the 17th-century German philosopher Johann Kunckel of the Académie Royale.

Whether from Jewish, Muslim, Christian, or other sources, Moses was revered by all as a primary exponent of the hermetic philosophy. In respect of his firing the golden calf to transform it to a powder, the same point is consistently made in old texts (*see* "The Ultimate Goal," pages 13–14) – that heating gold produces molten gold, while continued burning simply turns it black and unrenderable. The common interpretation of Exodus 32:20 is therefore misleading until one understands the physics of monatomic (single-atom) gold powder, achievable by the arc-light fire of the *electrikus* (electricity). According to Qabalistic doctrine, the whole mystery of the cherubim rests upon an understanding of alchemical principles as described in the hermetic text of Job 28:5–6. This brings all that we have discussed (the fire, bread, stone, sapphire, and gold) together in one equation: "As for the earth, out of it cometh bread; and under it is turned up as it were fire. The stones of it are the place of sapphires; and it hath dust of gold."[16]

The Emerald Tablet

So far we have encountered the ancient Sumerian *Table of Destiny*, the Testimony *Sappir* of Moses, and the parchments of the *Golden Fleece* and the *Golden Scroll*, each of which was said to hold the sacred secrets of ages past. Whether the *Table of Destiny* and the *Sappir* were in any way textual is not known, but it is most unlikely. They were simply said to "contain" great wisdom. The *Golden Fleece* was, however, said to be an alchemical manuscript.

Within the Old Testament we have yet another old wisdom text in the book of Proverbs. This constitutes a series of wise sayings attributed to King Solomon, and they might well have been used by him – but they were in the first instance Egyptian. They were, in fact, translated almost verbatim into Hebrew from the writings of an Egyptian sage called Amenemope,[17] and they are now held in the British Museum. Verse after verse of the book of Proverbs can be attributed to this Egyptian original. Additionally, it has now been ascertained that the writings of Amenemope were themselves extracted from a far older work called *The Wisdom of Ptah-hotep*,[18] which emerged more than 2,000 years before the time of King Solomon (*see* Appendix IV for an Amenomope comparison).

The annals of ancient Freemasonry contain a document from around 1450, which lays down some of the old Charges of the Craft, currently held at the British Museum.[19] It was published by Richard Spencer of London in 1861 and, in allusion to its then editor, is now known as the *Matthew Cooke Manuscript*. Within the original 15th-century text is an Old English version of a story dating back to biblical times. It tells of how the sciences which formed the bedrock of Freemasonry began with the sons and daughter of Lamech, namely Jabal, Jubal, Tubal-cain, and Naamâh, as detailed in Genesis 4:19–22. Lamech was fourth in succession from Enoch, the son of Cain (Genesis 4:17–18). Relating to such matters as geometry and metallurgy, the manuscript explains that "there were two manner of stones of such virtue that the one would never burn, and that stone is called *marbyll*, and the other stone that would not drown in water, and that stone is called *latres*. And so they devised to write all the sciences they had found in these two stones."

In part of the text the stones are referred to as "pylers," and this has generally been assumed to relate to "pillars," as was also given in the 19th-century English translation from the 1st-century work of Josephus, who had related a version of the same story.[20] The translation from Josephus has, however, been criticized by scholars because of its many inaccuracies, among which are the renderings of "brick" and "stone" for the Hebrew words equivalent to *marbyll* and *latres*. Similarly, the word "pillar" was wholly misleading and led to the illusion of two great columns, which appeared to have no geographical location. Given that Lamech and his sons lived before the biblical Flood, the stones became legendarily known as the Antediluvian Pillars.

The mistake here is that there are two very distinct words used in old Hebrew, each of which has been translated to "pillar" in the English Old Testament. They are *'ammud* and *mazzebah*.[21] The first denotes a pillar as might be a column in architecture or a column of smoke, but the second has a rather different connotation. It might refer to a stela or altar stone, but was equally applied to the stone that Jacob used for a pillow and set up for a *mazzebah* at Beth-el (Genesis 28:18). As *mazzebahs*, therefore, the antediluvian stones of the *Cooke Manuscript* were correctly designated before the translatory error as "stones" of *marbyll* and *latres*. The former might perhaps have been marble or some crystalline rock, while the other was corrupted in some writings to *laterus* and then reckoned to be laterite, a red iron-based clay used for bricks and road surfaces. The fact is that the nature of *latres* is as obscure as that of *sappir*, although early masonic tradition presumes it to have been a type of metal.[22]

It is said that after the Flood, the stones' content was tran-scribed onto an emerald tablet by Hermes Trismegistus (Hermes the Thrice Great). This was the name given by the Greek Neoplatonists to the Egyptian scribal god Thoth, revered as the founder of alchemy and geometry. Following the teachings of Plato (*c.* 429–347 BC), the Neoplatonists[23] claimed that the human intellect was not related to the mater-ial world, and that individual spirituality would increase in relation to one's contempt for earthly values. The relevance of Hermes was that his special knowledge was held to represent the Lost Wisdom of Lamech as preserved in the antediluvian stones. Tradition has it that, in time, the Emerald Tablet of Hermes was inherited by the Greek philosopher Pythagoras (*c.* 570–500 BC).

Although Thoth was worshipped as a deity in his own right in Egypt, he was rather more a scribe and messenger to the higher ranking gods.[24] The Greeks therefore associated him with their own messenger god Hermes (known to the Romans as Mercury), who bore the caduceus and serpent device of Askle-pios. Because of this cross-culture referencing, there are some significant differences in the portrayal of this multi-named char-acter, but in all cases he was associated with wisdom, alchemy, and intellectual pursuits. A Gnostic document, found at Cheno-boskion in Egypt and known as the *Treatise of Hermes Trismegis-tus*, states: "It is thus by degrees that the adepts will enter into the way of immortality, and will attain to a conception of the Ogdoad, which in turn reveals the Ennead."[25] The Ogdoad (eightfold) corresponds to the heaven of the stars, outside the individual heavens of the planets, and the Ennead (ninefold) refers to the great outer heaven of the universe. The separate heaven of Earth itself was called the Hebdomad (sevenfold). The Egyptian cult-center of Thoth was at Khemenu (now el-Eshmunein). This was the town of the Ogdoad, personified by eight gods (four male and female pairs). They were Nun and Nunet, Heh and Hehet, Kek and Keket, and Amun and Amunet.

Thoth was reckoned to have written 42 books containing all the wisdom of the world, many of which were dossiers of great magic, while as Hermes Trismegistus he was credited with much the same. His revered Emerald Tablet contained the most ancient of all alchemical formulae, which were of great significance to the early mystery schools. Its text related both to the alchemy of metals and the divine alchemy of human regeneration, along with matters of science, astronomy, and numerology. Known to Rosicrucian adepts as the *Tabula Smaragdina Hermetis*, the Emerald Tablet was recorded as "the most ancient monument of the Chaldeans concerning the Philosophers' Stone." This is very much the same as was stated by Salomon Trismosian in respect of the Golden Fleece.

It is because of Hermes Trismegistus that alchemy is referred to as the "hermetic" art, and it is from the hermetic fusion of glass in early Egypt that we derive the present-day term "hermetically sealed" glass.[26] The term "alchemy" comes from the Arabic *al-khame* (the blackness) and is defined as the science which overcomes the blackness, or that which enlightens through intuitive perception. Alchemy also had an association with the mysterious Khem of Mendes, often portrayed as a goat and identified with a certain angelic Azazel of Capricorn. The book of Enoch (written in the 2nd century BC, but excluded from the Old Testament) defines Azazel as a Watcher – or in old Greek, an *Argus*, as applied to Jason's ship, *Argo*. It is said in Enoch that Azazel made known to men "all the metals, and the art of working them."[27]

Extant translations of the Emerald Tablet date from the 700s, beginning with that of the Islamic philosopher Jabir Ibn Haiyan, who also wrote of the alchemical School of Pythagoras (the *Ta'ifat Fthaghurus*). Apollonius of Tyana[28] (also known as Balinus), from the Temple of Asklepios in Aegae, apparently discovered the Pythagorean relic in the 1st century, from which time many notable philosophers have studied and made use of the text. Prominent among these was Sir Isaac

The crucified serpent of Nicolas Flamel.

Newton, president of London's scientific Royal Society from 1703.

Lost for ever, though, is the famous *Book of Thoth* (a designation applied, however, to the Tarot), which explained the secrets of regeneration and longevity. Along with other hermetic texts and over half a million irreplaceable documents of history, science, and philosophy, it was destroyed by a fevered Christian mob in AD 391. Led by the Roman-appointed Bishop Theophilus, they marched upon the Serapeum, where the collection was held in the great Library of Alexandria, and razed it to the ground in order to clear the field for the doctrines of new Church-approved literature. In this regard, Rome was said to have crucified the serpent of wisdom, just as Jesus (a purveyor of that wisdom) had been crucified by the same establishment. There are various allegorical representations of this act, perhaps the best known of which is in the 14th-century *Livre des figures hyéroglyphiques* of the hermetic philosopher Nicolas Flamel.

PART II

Electrikus

Judgment of the Archon

Clouds and darkness are round about him;
Righteousness and judgment are the habitation of his throne.
A fire goeth before him,
And burneth up his enemies round about.
His lightnings enlightened the world:
The earth saw, and trembled.
The hills melted like wax at the presence of the Lord ...
Psalm 97:2–5

From the 4th-century time of St. Augustine of Hippo, many interpretations have been published in respect of this biblical Psalm of the judgmental Archon. It has certainly provided suitable invective for the preachers of fiery damnation and the vengeful God of wrath. The message is, nevertheless, Ark-related and is reminiscent of the Israelite scene at Mount Horeb: "And all the people saw the thunderings, and the lightnings, and the noise of the trumpet, and the mountain smoking: and when the people saw, they removed, and stood afar off. And they said unto Moses, Speak thou with us, and we will hear: but let not God speak with us, lest we die" (Exodus 20:18–19).

As pointed out in 1977 by the author Jerry L. Ziegler, when studying the phenomenal nature of *YHWH*: "A text without a context is simply a pretext."[1] It is therefore necessary to find contexts for Bible passages like these, since they are quite divorced from the Church notion of God as a caring heavenly Father. In fact, statements such as, "Let not God speak with us, lest we die" are far more in keeping with the modern scientific view of God as a powerful energy force, rather than a divine character.

At various stages of the Old Testament (from the moment of his direct association with Mount Horeb and the Ark) God is portrayed as sending out arrows of lightning.[2] He was said to exist between the cherubim and was at his most fiercely judgmental when the penetrative lightning stone of the *Urim-Schamir* was present. In mystic and masonic lore, God has been called the Archon, the Architect, and the Archetype, and he dwelled in a House of Judgment called the Archeion. The Ark-light above the mercy seat was dignified as being God's "presence" and was immediately responsible for the transmutation of gold into the sacred "bread of the presence" (*mfkzt*). This leads to an intriguing hypothesis relating to the Ark of the Covenant, which might perhaps resolve the mystery of the cherubim.

Without any explanation in Exodus, the *Urim* and *Thummim* appeared at Mount Horeb as if Moses had previously been familiar with them. We know from the Bible that Moses was an Egyptian (Exodus 2:19), and from Manetho's *Aegyptiaca* (*c.* 300 BC) that he had been trained as a temple priest at Heliopolis. Moreover, Phinheas the Levite (son of Eleazar),[3] in whom the "everlasting priesthood" was confirmed (Numbers 25:11–13), bore the same name as Panahesy, the Egyptian Governor of Sinai who happened to have been the Chief Servitor of Aten at Akhenaten's temple of Amarna.[4] Although the Sinai mountain is called Mount Horeb (Cherub Mountain) in the Bible, it subsequently became known as *Serâbît el Khâdim* – the full translation of which is "Prominence of the Servitor."

Across the river from Amarna lies the modern city of Mal-lawi (Malleui) which means, quite literally, City of the

Levites, and the High Priest of Akhenaten's Amarna Temple was Meryre.[5] His name was equivalent to the Hebrew Merari: one of the sons of Levi (Genesis 46:11), and it is evident that Moses' pharaonic association with the Israelites was established in Egypt long before he led them into Sinai. Moses was defined in hermetic tradition as having been a master alchemist and, according to Exodus, he did indeed perform a most remarkable transmutation of gold into the mysterious powder of projection by the use of fire. But this was no ordinary fire – it was the fire of the Ark-light: the "presence" of God, which crashed and sparked, sending out spears and bolts of deadly lightning. The point of interest is that this lightning, along with the *Sappir* and all else of relevance, was associated with Mount Horeb before Bezaleel was said to have built the Ark of the Covenant – not as a *result* of his building it.

When the Israelites first arrived at the mountain, the Lord was said to have descended in the fire of a furnace, and the mount quaked greatly (Exodus 19:18). Even before that, Moses had seen the mysterious burning bush and been advised to remove his shoes (Exodus 3:1–5). If the golden Ark was directly associated with these phenomena, as appears to be the case, it becomes apparent that the Ark was already in situ at the mountain temple prior to the Israelite arrival. Indeed, as we shall discover, the Ark was necessary for producing the *mfkzt* powder of gold, and the workshop for this purpose had been operative at Mount Horeb from the reign of pharaoh Sneferu, more than 1,300 years before the time of Moses.

The recognizable context that we are seeking for all this divine lightning and arcane fiery activity is undoubtedly electricity – the power of the *electrikus*. The parallel hypothesis is that Bezaleel did not build the Ark after all. Maybe he built the Tabernacle's altars and other accoutrements, but the Ark (whose story was written up by scribes many centuries after the event) could well have been at Horeb all along. If so, then the nature of the cherubim can be reconsidered in a wholly new light.

Arks of the design and style depicted in Exodus were historically Egyptian, not Israelite or Hebrew – a good example being the Anubis Ark discovered in 1922 by Howard Carter at the tomb entrance of Tutankhamun. The cherubim on the golden shrine of Akhenaten's son Tutankhamun are not dissimilar to those in the popular imagery of the Ark of the Covenant – neither are those on his sarcophagus, nor on that of his immediate successor, Pharaoh Aye. Although denied to Israelite art (by virtue of the law against graven images of life forms), such winged figures were indeed common in the ancient world of Asia and the Middle East. It is therefore quite feasible that a pre-Mosaic Egyptian Ark would have been topped with angelic cherubs, just as the Tutankhamun Ark was guarded by Anubis. In this regard, our initial Sinai guide, Sir W.M. Flinders Petrie, came to much the same conclusion, stating: "In the holiest of all things, the Ark of Yahweh of the Hebrews, there were cherubs, one on each end of the mercy seat with wings covering the mercy seat. This agrees with the description of the Egyptian ark of the gods with figures of the goddess Ma'at with wings covering the ark."[6]

Ma'at, the goddess of truth and law, was said to be the daughter of Ra and, in keeping with the Ark "presence," she too was concerned with judgment – though rather less violently. Her weighing of "truth in the balance" was conducted with a feather,[7] and truth was identified with gold, the most noble of metals. When the souls of the early pharaohs passed into the Afterlife, they were tested by the funerary god Anubis against the judicial feather of Ma'at.

St. Elmo's Fire

"And the sight of the glory of the Lord was like devouring fire on the top of the mount in the eyes of the children of Israel" (Exodus 24:17).

To place the mountain in its own individual context, it is fair to say that the initially visible, and clearly awesome, fire on the thunderous peak was not necessarily due to the Ark as such. The Sinai plateau is a traditionally stormy region, where the sky abounds with electricity – giving rise to the phenomenon known as St. Elmo's Fire. This is a type of continuous electric spark called a "glow discharge." It occurs when high-voltage electricity affects a gas, and is seen when the air and ground below a storm become electrically charged. The voltage tears the air molecules apart and the gas takes on a fiery glow, requiring about 30,000 volts per sq cm. Sharp grounded points such as masts and aerials can, however, trigger it at lower levels down to 1,000 volts.

In essence, St. Elmo's Fire is illuminated plasma. Plasmas can carry electric currents, generate magnetism, and are the most common form of universal matter.[8] Gas (including atmospheric gas: air) is composed of molecules. These are composed of atoms, which are in turn composed of electrons and clusters of proton particles. When high-voltage electricity is applied to the gas it causes the electrons and protons to be pulled away from each other, transforming the gas into a glowing mixture of separate proton clusters and electrons. The precise color of the resultant plasma fire depends on the type of gas involved, but it is generally a blue-violet in the Earth's atmosphere.

Unlike ball lightning, which can float around, St. Elmo's Fire associates itself with the objects to which it is attracted, and it will spit, spark, and crackle like fire, although it is heatless and non-consuming. These objects can be anything from a high-peaked mountain to a low-level shrub, as in the account of Moses and the burning bush: "And he looked, and, behold, the bush burned without fire, and the bush was not consumed" (Exodus 3:2). Pointed objects, such as ships' masts and church steeples, are especially susceptible to the phenomenon. Many sailors have been as astonished as Moses to discover that a mast which they undoubtedly saw ablaze remained untouched and intact after the event. It was from this that the mysterious fire derived its name because St. Elmo (c. 300 AD, who preached during storms)[9] was the patron saint of sailors.

Compared to the atmosphere, the earth is a good conductor, having the ability to discharge electricity with a flourish at its mountaintops. It is therefore not surprising that the gods of old were so often associated with mountains. Indeed, the Bible cites a good deal of early worship in "high places."[10] It is also not surprising that in such an electrically charged environment Moses was advised to remove his shoes. If a person's body is not grounded directly to the earth it will acquire a charge according to the potential of the atmosphere at its head. Dry leather soles would act as a resistance and inhibit the flow of charge from the body. This would not in itself be a problem, but if the person then touched something that was electrically grounded, a shock would result.[11] A similar static charge can sometimes be experienced in a minor way when touching metal filing cabinets and the like.

Ancient Batteries

Electricity in its natural form was plainly well-known to the ancients, whatever they might have called it. In fact, *YHWH* (breathalyzed without the subsequently added vowels) might be as explanatory as any other audible description, and it was said that the priests could only utter the unspeakable name "under their breath." According to the Judaeo-Egyptian papyrus entitled *Zeus Thunderer, King Adonai, Lord Iaooue*, the non-vocalized breath pronunciation of *YHWH* was "iauooe"[12] – rather like a whispered "he-ewe." What is more relevant, however, is that they somehow learned how to capture the power and glory of *yhwh*, enhance it, and use it to astonishing effect.

One way or another, electricity was always perceived as the manifestation of a god associated with mountains, whether that god be Zeus, Yahweh, or some other. In his scholarly work, *The Shining Ones*, linguist and geologist Christian O'Brien relates the derivation and derivatives of the ancient word *El*, which defined a god or lofty one (as in El Elyon and El Shaddai), but which in all its variant forms denoted a bright or shining being.[13] The terms electricity, electron, and electrikus all stem, therefore, from an original base concerning the "bright substance of God."[14]

In 1938, the German archaeologist Wilhelm Koenig made the first thorough examination of a curious clay jar (one of a number), lodged in the National Museum of Iraq, where it is still on display. Pale yellow in color, about 15 cms high and 7 cms wide at its top-end, the bulbous pot has been dated at around 2,240 years old and attributed to the Parthians. They ruled much of the Middle East at that time, when Ptolemy III was the pharaoh in Egypt. The jar's top opening housed a 9-cm high copper cylinder, held in position by an asphalt plug, while running down through the center of the cylinder was an iron rod, which projected just a little above the lead-covered stopper. The iron rod stopped short of the bottom end of the copper tube, which was sealed with a crimped copper disc overlaid with asphalt.

It became evident that the jar was nothing less than a battery, requiring only an acidic liquid such as vinegar to make it active. Confirmation of the artifact as an electric cell was obtained and it became known as the Baghdad Battery. Then, following World War II, Willard M. Gray of the General Electric Laboratory in Pittsfield, Massachusetts, constructed an exact replica of the device. With the addition of citric acid, two volts of electricity were obtained – a feat not achieved by this method (or so it had been thought) until the early 19th century. Consequently, as confirmed in the April 1957 issue of *Science Digest*,[15] the latter-day Count

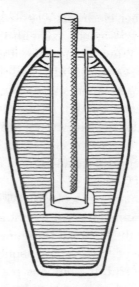

The Baghdad Battery.

Alassandro Volta had not invented the "voltic-pile" battery in 1800; he had reinvented it.[16]

Also discovered by Dr. Koenig in the Iraq Museum were copper utensils from ancient Sumer, which had been electroplated with silver. He surmised that the plating was indicative of such batteries in practical use, although these plated artifacts were many centuries older than the battery he had examined. In all, there were five such battery jars at the Museum, and the point was made that a considerably increased voltage would be obtained by connecting the tops of their protruding rods together. Subsequently, the German scientist Dr. Arne Eggebrecht repeated the replication process, doing precisely that, and performed successful electroplating with gold.

Gold of the Gods

Time now to return to Hathor (the patroness of Serâbît el Khâdim) and to her other temple, with its intriguing under-

ground crypt, at Dendera, a little north of Luxor. This is one of
the oldest sacred locations in Egypt and has been claimed by
many as the burial ground of Osiris.[17] It is here that we find
hieroglyphic inscriptions which tie Hathor even more firmly
to the kingly House of Gold. Translated in the 1980s by the
Egyptologist Sylvie Cauville for the Institut Français d'Arche-
ologie Orientale, the legend reads: "Ra opened his eyes inside
the lotus as it emerged from the primordial chaos and his eyes
began to weep, and droplets fell to the ground. They were
transformed into a beautiful woman who was named Gold of
the Gods,[18] Hathor the Great, Mistress of Dendera." Hathor
appears on the earliest historical record ever to be found in
Egypt: the famous green-slate *Narmer Palette* (from beyond
3000 BC),[19] and she is the only goddess ever to be shown full
face.

The first temple at Dendera had been built during the Old
Kingdom reign of the Great Pyramid pharaoh Khufu. He was
the son of Sneferu, which dates Dendera (originally Tentirys)
to the same period as the Serâbît temple and the early days of
mfkzt production, around 4,500 years ago. The above-ground
temple presently on the Dendera site is a later construction
from the 1st-century BC era of the Ptolemies. Associated with
both Hathor and Queen Cleopatra VII, one of the building's
key features was its impressively designed ceiling map of the
sky. Known as the Dendera Zodiac, only a plaster copy now
remains – the original being on display in the Louvre
Museum, Paris. The great mystery of Dendera lies, however,
deep within its old underground crypt, close to the Gold
House. Here, the walls of the southern crypt are adorned with
large pictorial carvings that have long baffled Egyptologists
because of their extraordinary portrayals. The images are of
priests holding long balloon-like objects with serpents inside,
while other characters perform supportive roles (*see* Plate 14).
The ostensibly lightweight or weightless tubes are connected
by lotus-stem cables to a box upon which sits Heh, the god of

infinite space, and their extraordinary size is either symbolic of their great importance or indicative of their actuality.

In his 1961 book *Forvunen Teknik*, the Swedish engineer Henry Kjellson noted that the hieroglyph concerning the serpents translated to *seref*, relating to a "glow" or a "flame," and he speculated that perhaps it was an electrically centered tableau. Subsequently, the Scottish scientist Ivan T. Sanderson and other investigative technicians came to similar conclusions,[20] and the bulbous devices were likened to electron tubes as in cathode ray technology.[21] (It was back in 1838 that Michael Faraday first described the characteristics of the colorful "glow" which occurs when a high voltage is applied to electrodes in a partially evacuated glass tube.)[22]

The Stockholm engineer Ivan Tröeng also confirmed in his *Kulturer Före Istiden* that he felt the Dendera petroglyphs

Mysterious relief at the Hathor temple in Dendera.

represented electrical apparatus with high-tension insulators in the nature of *djed* pillars. The word *djed* relates to "support" or "durability," and such pillars appear extensively, along with the *ankh*, in Egyptian artwork – often worn as amulets (talismanic charms). Looking somewhat like a spark plug or an insulated electrode, the *djed* pillar was said in mythology to symbolize the backbone of Osiris, who was himself depicted as a *djed* in the British Museum's *Papyrus of Hunefer* from around 1370 BC. As can be seen in museums, *djed* amulets are generally quite small, maybe just a couple of centimeters in length – but they are still called "pillars" or "columns." With reference to our earlier mention of the Antediluvian Pillars (*see* "The Emerald Tablet," page 92), it can be seen that the word "pillar" related to shape or a supportive function, not to size.

Once the Dendera crypt had been emptied of sand in the late 19th century, the carved depictions were eventually brought to public notice by the photographs of the French Egyptologist Emile Chassinat. In 1934 he produced four volumes of his work, entitled *Le Temple de Dendera*, for the French Institute of Oriental Archaeology.[23] It was subsequent to these publications that Sylvie Cauville began her book series of the Dendera hieroglyphic translations for the same Institute.[24]

When I first saw the Dendera representations, my mind was immediately cast back to the 1960s, at which time I was working with Scientific Department technologists of London's National Gallery in the field of fine art conservation. In particular, I was studying the research of Dr. Carl Dame Clarke who, from his base at the School of Medicine, University of Maryland, had introduced the use of Röntgen rays (x-rays) to the examination of paintings and pigment analysis. This was a significant aid to the science of art preservation, which was then undergoing a major transition in Britain. Helmut Rhuemann, who had been chief restorer at the Berlin State Galleries from 1929, had come to London to work alongside Sir Kenneth

Clarke, Director of the National Gallery, and it was Rhuemann who established the Gallery's Scientific Department, along with the Technology Department at the Courtauld Institute.

What struck me with the Dendera petroglyphs was that the priestly, cable-connected ampoules looked very much like Dr. Röntgen's original 19th-century x-ray tubes, and I recalled his 1896 discovery that "when x-radiation passes through the air, the air becomes an electrical conductor." If it is indeed the case, as so many have speculated, that the Dendera crypt displays tableaux of an electrical nature, then the ampoules certainly resemble the original Crookes tubes[25] as used by Röntgen at the Physical Institute of the University of Würzburg.

In the course of a continuing Dendera debate, scientists argue in favor of an ancient cathode tube heritage, and some researchers have proposed a form of light bulb. Meanwhile, mythologists prefer the idea of an embryonic serpent cult, theologians perceive a pagan birthing ritual, and esotericists have suggested Dendera as portraying an underground Creation epic. But what of the Egyptologists? What do the front-line classical archaeologists have to say on the subject? The answer is: nothing very much. Upon direct enquiry, a representative of one of Britain's foremost museums stated, "There is hardly anything out of the ordinary in these scenes, but their precise significance is difficult to summarize." Not out of the ordinary! They are unique, which is precisely why he found them difficult to summarize. A more honest answer should have been, "We haven't a clue."

What is known without doubt is that the petroglyphs are in some way connected with the goddess Hathor – and we know from the inscriptions in that very crypt that Hathor, the Mistress of Dendera and of Serâbît el Khâdim, was called the "Gold of the Gods." Ultimately, this leads to a fascinating scenario concerning the mysterious shapes, and when I asked a nuclear physicist what he thought they might be, his answer was immediate and intuitively relevant. We shall return to these depictions later in our story as the evidence unfolds.

Flame of the Ark-light

Looking once more at the arkite etymology, we have seen that in old France the Latin *arca* (box or chest) became *arch*, and then *arc*, as is the proper English form of ark today; also that a medieval association was made with an arch as in "architecture," "arcade," and "architrave." The curved shape of an arch was that of a bow (Latin: *arcus*), from which derived "archery," while in electrical terms an arc is a luminous discharge between two electrodes.

There is, therefore, a direct linguistic and historical relationship between arcs and arches, both of which definitions derive from the original Greek *ark* and the Latin *arca*. Consequently, Ark-light and arc-light are synonymous, and it was in 1822 that the British chemist Sir Humphrey Davy placed two carbon poles a short distance apart, connected them to an electricity supply and produced a brilliant arc of light – just like that described between the biblical cherubim. Subsequently, he appointed the young bookbinder Michael Faraday to be his laboratory assistant. Faraday's own study of arc-light led him into the field of gaseous tubes, while also ascertaining that a change in a magnetic field was necessary to create a current.

It was not long before arc-lamps became a regular feature of public buildings, exhibition halls, railway yards, and the like. By 1910 it was announced that some 20,000 arcs had been installed in British cities. And so it was that, three and a quarter millennia after the time of Moses, sparking light-giving devices were once again being called "arcs."

During the pioneering years of this public service development in the late 19th century, there was no national grid system to produce a constant flow of electricity. Batteries and generators had to be used on a limited scale, and capacitors

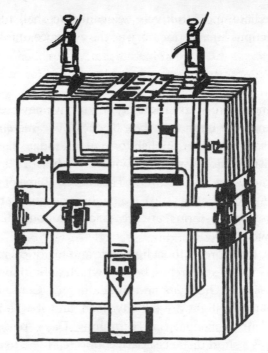

19th-century Ark capacitor.

(condensers) evolved for the purposes of storing and distributing the charge. The capacitor on which the 19th-century models were based had been invented over 100 years earlier by Pieter van Musschenbroek, professor of physics at Leiden University in Holland. His 1745 device was a glass jar, partially filled with water with a brass wire protruding through its cork stopper. Static electricity was produced by friction and stored, via the wire, in the jar. The important part of the exercise arose when a student received a prodigious shock from the apparatus. A circle of volunteers then joined hands from the jar and back again, each receiving the shock as the current passed through them. This proved that electricity was transferable from one body to another when one had a surfeit of electricity and the other had spare capacity. The principle was subsequently improved by coating the jar's outer surface with metal foil, so that the glass became an insulator between it and the conductive water. A further coating of foil inside the jar then dispensed with the need for water altogether.

Early industrial capacitors of the latter 1800s did not look too dissimilar to some of today's high voltage models. Their principle was called "dielectric" and their construction was very straightforward. They consisted of parallel-plate layers of a conductive metal, separated by a non-conductive material: an insulator called a "dielectric medium." Each of the conductive plates (effectively the positive and negative) was connected to a corresponding electrode.[26] The operation was, and still is, much like that of a gas tank, and the amount of electricity a capacitor will hold (its capacitance) depends on the pressure (voltage) applied to it.

Turning back to the Old Testament, it seems that this description of an electrical capacitor is precisely the same as the description of the Ark of the Covenant. Exodus 37:1–2 explains: "And Bezaleel made the ark of shittim wood ... and he overlaid it with pure gold within and without." Here, then, are the necessary components: two plate-layers of gold (an excellent electrical conductor), sandwiching a non-conductive dielectric insulator of acacia wood. Exodus 37:7 continues: "And he made two cherubims of gold," placing one at each end of the mercy seat (the box top). These were the uppermost outer electrodes, needing only for each to be connected to its respective golden plate-layer. Even at low electrical potentials, such a device would become charged over a period of time, with a discharge facility arcing from the cherubim that would be instantaneous.

As we saw earlier, the Semitic root word for the Ark was *āron*, which specifically applied to the act of "gathering" (becoming charged). Given a suitable abundance of atmospheric electricity, a capacitor the size of the Ark could charge to many thousands of volts, and its resultant arcing power would be substantial – certainly enough to kill, as was the case with Uzzah and the sons of Aaron. More importantly, though, direct current arcing is precisely the process used in today's scientific laboratories to produce monatomic high-spin gold – once called *mfkzt* or *shem-an-na*: the mystical white powder of the highward fire-stone.

The Orbit of Light

Masters of the Fire-stone

When discussing the *Urim* and *Thummim* earlier (*see* "Ring of the Testimony," page 41) we touched on the subject of iridium crystal. Before progressing to the nature of the highward fire-stone, it is necessary to look a little more circumspectly at iridium and other platinum group metals (PGMs), since they are central to understanding *mfkzt*. Along with platinum, the other five PGMs are iridium, palladium, rhodium, osmium, and ruthenium. Because of the ultimate strengths of the metals, they are now used in surgical, optical, and dental instruments, crucibles and thermocouples, machine bearings, electrical switch contacts, and all manner of precision devices down to the tipping of needles and pen nibs.

It is generally cited in encyclopedias and reference books that PGMs came to our attention as late as the 19th century, and perhaps the best known is palladium. Used extensively by jewelers, palladium is often alloyed with gold to produce the metal popularly known as "white gold." It is said that palladium was first discovered in Brazil, California, and the Urals in 1803, and was named after the asteroid Pallas in that year. Iridium, osmium, and rhodium are also given the same date of recognition, with ruthenium following in 1843. However, it is now plain from discoveries relating to the distant BC years that the ancients were fully aware of the individual properties of these platinum group metals. Iridium crystal (although transmuted from a platinum group metal) glows with transparent color like any precious gemstone. The name "iridium" was applied in 1803 by virtue of this very iridescence (from the Latin *iris*: rainbow). Brought to earth by meteorites, iridium is an extraterrestrial metal, which can form its own rare glass-like rock, which the ancients called *sappir*. This was the *Schethiyâ*, "stone of heaven," said to have been present beneath the Jerusalem Temple, as identified in the old tenets of Royal Arch Freemasonry. Seemingly, it was also present at Mount Horeb, as detailed in Exodus 24:10, "and there was under his feet as it were a paved work of sapphire stone, and as it were the body of heaven in his clearness."

In 1968, a joint Cornell and Harvard University expedition unearthed the gold refinery of the legendary King Croesus, who reigned in Lydia (Western Turkey) in the middle 6th century BC. Subsequently, the expedition's assistant director, Prof. Andrew Ramage, collaborated with Paul Craddock, head of the metals section at the British Museum, to document a full and recently published report of the find at Sardis, entitled *King Croesus' Gold*.[1] The revelations have proved so astonishing that they would have been ridiculed if hypothetically proposed, and would doubtless have been sidelined if they had emanated from a non-academic source. As it is, the weight of scholastic authority is such that the disclosures cannot be ignored. Contrary to all textbooks and scientific understanding hitherto, the Sardis refinery has provided incontrovertible proof that PGMs were known and understood in far off times.

Although classified as a "group," the individual platinum metals have different qualities – not least in that platinum, palladium, and rhodium are soluble in molten gold, whereas iridium, osmium, and ruthenium are not. Hence, the modern manufacture of white gold is not a complex process, but iridium (with its high specific gravity) will naturally sink to the bottom of molten gold. Since trace elements of these metals often exist as silvery inclusions in gold deposits, it is now common practice to extract them in order to maintain the purity of gold, and it is essential to extract those elements with a high specific gravity, otherwise they will corrupt any manufacturing process. This extraction is carried out by a procedure called "electrolysis" – the decomposition of a substance by the application of an electric current.[2]

Electrolysis requires an electrolyte (an ionized solution or molten metallic salt) to complete an electric circuit between two electrodes (the cathode and anode). When these electrodes are connected to a source of direct electrical current, the cathode becomes negatively charged, while the anode becomes positively charged. When electroplating, the plating metal is generally the anode, and the object to be plated is the cathode. As we have seen, (see "Ancient Batteries," page 104) multiples of the Baghdad Battery were capable of electroplating on a limited scale, but at the Sardis refinery something far more sophisticated emerged. Here was not only a facility for large-scale electroplating, but also evidence of the highly skilled ability to separate platinum metal elements and impurities from gold. In discussing the ancient records, Craddock stated, "Given the background of the great difficulties encountered in their removal from gold in the 19th century, it could seem little short of incredible to suggest that the ancients knew how to remove the inclusions."[3]

More remarkable is the fact that there was no reason for King Croesus or anyone of his era to regard naturally unearthed gold as being in any way impure or corrupt just because it had some copper, silver, or a PGM within it.[4] How could the Lydians possibly have known? Why would they care?

Our modern perception of "pure gold" as a precisely defined element is a relatively new one, as is the applied Law of Constant Composition. It has therefore been concluded that no one from the past could possibly have known about the composition of completely pure elemental substances. After all, the *Periodic Table of Elements* was not formulated until the Russian chemist Dmitri Mendeleyev published the first arrangement of 63 elements, based on atomic mass, in his 1869 *Principles of Chemistry*. The fact is, nevertheless, that the ancients were indeed aware of elemental impurities, and even the Old Testament has seven nouns applicable to gold: *zahav, paz, ketem, harus, s'gor, ophir*, and *baser*. For instance, *zahav tahor* refers to "pure gold"[5] as specified for the lid of the Ark of the Covenant.

Apart from the use of electrolysis, corruptive elements can be removed from gold by a process called "cupellation," as was used by some coin manufacturers to extract inherent base metals from gold. The impure metal was melted with lead and subjected to a *c*. 1100° C blast of air to oxidize the lead along with the base metals, leaving the gold separate. If silver had to be removed from gold, then a method called "parting" was used, which involved acidic salts such as sodium chloride, saltpeter, elemental sulfur, and antimony sulfide. However, this was all the stuff of medieval alchemists and, as the Sardis authors pointed out, even advanced 19th-century cupellation had no effect whatever on platinum metal elements. They were also immune to acid dissolution as used in parting. It took the scientific introduction of electrolysis in recent times to remove platinum group elements from gold satisfactorily – and yet the Lydians were doing it 2,500 years ago!

There are numerous texts from even more ancient Mesopotamia and Egypt, which refer to the assaying and refining of gold, but they are records of weights, measures, and quantities, rather than descriptions of technology. The only specific mention in this regard is that it was done with fire, but until now this has been conveniently disregarded as a mistaken notion. The invention of gold leaf was impossible before methods were perfected to free gold of impurities so that it could be beaten to a micron of thinness.[6] However, fine gold leaf has now been discovered in Mesopotamia from the 3rd millennium BC. Even at that early stage, the skill existed to remove silver, copper, and PGMs from alluvial gold.[7] Also, gold chisels from that same era (discovered in the Sumerian royal grave at Ur, by Sir C. Leonard Woolley and the joint 1923 team from the British Museum and the University of Pennsylvania) are now established as being plated with gold over a less pure alloy.

It is clear from all this that PGMs were not discovered in the 19th century, but were rediscovered and newly named. Moreover, it has now been ascertained that classical writers, such as Plato and Pliny, wrote about platinum metal elements in gold, calling them *adamas*.[8] Prior to the discovery of the Croesus refinery, these references had not been understood, because it never occurred to anyone that the ancient scholars could possibly have been referring to a supposed discovery of our modern era.

In ancient Sumer, PGMs (*adamas*) were classified as *an-na* (fire-stone). Because of the bright silvery color described in old records, the mysteriously designated shining metal was long presumed to have been tin by misguided metallurgical adepts of the Middle Ages, while others who knew something of cupellation and parting strove earnestly with salts, sulfurs, and mystical solutions, endeavoring to extrapolate gold from lead. This leaves us in no doubt that, although PGMs were a part of ancient technology, they were (just like electricity) lost to us for many centuries until archaeological and geological research caught up with them again.

Iridium is a very rare element on Earth, but geologists have discovered its existence in quantities up to 30 times the norm in crust layers where meteorites containing the substance have landed in the distant past.[9] The Sumerians and ancient Egyptians clearly knew about the properties of gold and of how to alloy it with other noble metals. The Master Craftsmen were adepts too in the workings of PGMs, which, just like gold, could be taken to the exotic "highward" state of the *shem-an-na* (highward fire-stone) or *mfkzt*. This means that they not only knew and worked with these metals, but that they also pioneered the science of atoms and nuclei – for the "highward" state of the white powder (gold or PGM) is only achieved through the high-spin metallurgical experience.

Although the current names of the platinum group metals are relatively new to us, the metals themselves are far from new. However, given the extraterrestrial nature of iridium in particular, it is intriguing to discover that we have this very metal within our own bodies. Recent tests have shown that, by dry-matter weight, over 5% of brain tissue is composed of iridium and rhodium in the high-spin state.[10]

The Plane of Shar-On

So, what precisely is the "highward" condition that converts gold and other noble metals into the impalpable white *mfkzt* powder of the Paradise Stone? And what exactly was its advantage when ingested by the ancient kings of the House of Gold in Mesopotamia, Egypt, and, later, Judaea?

In modern scientific terms, "highward" is identified as "high spin" – that is to say an element in a high-spin state. A normal atom has around it a screening potential – a positive screening produced by the nucleus. The majority of electrons going round the nucleus are within this screening potential, except for the very outer electrons. The nucleus goes to the highward or high-spin state when the positive screening potential expands to bring all the electrons under the control of the nucleus.

These electrons normally travel around the nucleus in pairs: a forward-spinning electron and a reverse-spinning electron. But when these come under the influence of a high-spin nucleus, all the electrons begin spinning in the same direction.

When perfectly correlated, the electrons turn to pure white light and it becomes impossible for the individual atoms in the high-spin substance to hold together. On that account, they cannot retain the metallic state, and the substance falls apart to become a white monatomic powder.[11]

In simple terms, the white powder is created by striking the metal sample, under strictly controlled conditions, for a pre-determined time, with a designated high heat from a DC electric arc: a single-directional current between two electrodes. But the truly unusual thing about the powder is that, through continuous sequences of heating and cooling, its weight will rise and fall to hundreds of percent above its optimum weight, down to less than absolutely nothing. Moreover, its optimum weight is actually 56% of the metal weight from which it was transmuted. So, where does the other 44% go? It becomes nothing but pure white light, and translates into a dimension beyond the physical plane – the dimension of the Orbit of Light, which the ancients called the *Plane of Shar-On*, or the *Field of Mfkzt*. At the zero-weight stage, not only does the substance become invisible and weigh less than nothing, but the pan in which it sits also registers less than its starting weight. This conforms precisely with the Alexandrian text (*see* "Sacred Manna," page 24), which states that, when placed in the scales, the Paradise Stone can outweigh its quantity of gold, but when it is converted to dust, even a feather will tip the scales against it.

An experiment conducted in the USA in the late 1970s demonstrated the effect of the mystical white light in open-air conditions, without the controls of vacuums and inert gases necessary for contained results. In this test the monatomic substance completely disappeared in an enormous blaze of light equivalent to thousands of flash bulbs. It was, in effect, an explosion, but there was absolutely no blast, and an unsupported pencil (that was stood on its flat end within the explosion) was left standing upright afterwards.[12] This was entirely reminiscent of the burning bush which Moses saw at Mount Horeb, which was seemingly ablaze, but was not consumed by the fire (Exodus 3:4).

In the May 1995 issue of *Scientific American*, the effect of the platinum group metal ruthenium was discussed in relation to human DNA. It was pointed out that when single ruthenium atoms are placed at each end of a short strand of DNA, it becomes 10,000 times more conductive. It becomes, in effect, a superconductor. For some time, chemists had suspected that the double helix might create a highly conductive path along the axis of the molecule, and here was confirmation of the fact.[13] Similarly, the *Platinum Metals Review*[14] has featured regular articles concerning the use of platinum, iridium, and ruthenium in the treatment of cancers, which are caused through the abnormal and uncontrolled division of body cells.[15] When a DNA state is altered, as in the case of a cancer, the application of a platinum compound will resonate with the deformed cell, causing the DNA to relax and become corrected. Such treatment involves no surgery; it does not destroy surrounding tissue with radiation, nor kill the immune system, as does chemotherapy.

The medical profession entered the high-spin arena when the biomedical research organization Bristol-Myers Squib[16] announced that ruthenium atoms interact with DNA, correcting the malformation in cancer cells. (Monatomic gold and PGMs are in effect "stealth atoms," and it has now been ascertained that body cells communicate with each other by way of stealth atoms through a system of light waves.) What the new science determined was that monatomic ruthenium resonates with the DNA, dismantles the short-length helix, and rebuilds it again correctly – just as one might demolish and resurrect a dilapidated building.

It is known that both iridium and rhodium have anti-ageing properties, while ruthenium and platinum compounds interact with the DNA and the cellular body. It is also known that gold and the platinum metals, in their monatomic (single atom) high-spin state, can activate the endocrinal glandular system in a way that heightens awareness and aptitude to extraordinary levels. In this regard, it is considered that the high-spin powder of gold has a distinct effect upon the pineal gland, increasing melatonin production. Likewise, the monatomic powder of iridium has a similar effect on the serotonin production of the pituitary gland, and would appear to reactivate the body's "junk DNA," along with the underused parts of the brain.

Only in recent times have medical scientists identified the hormonal secretion of the pineal gland. It was isolated in 1968, and became known as melatonin, which means "nightworker" (from the Greek *melos*: black, and *tosos*: labor) because people with a high melatonin output react strongly to sunlight which affects their mental capability. By virtue of this, they are night operatives, and melatonin is called the "hormone of darkness," being produced only at night or in the dark.[17] (Blind people produce above average quantities of melatonin, which heightens their senses other than sight.) Exposure to an excess of natural light makes the pineal gland smaller and lessens spiritual awareness, whereas darkness and high pineal activity enhance the keen intuitive knowledge of the subtle mind, while reducing the stress factor.

Melatonin is manufactured by the pineal gland through an activated chemical messenger called serotonin. This transmits nerve impulses across chromosome pairs at a moment (known as *meiosis*) when the cell nuclei divide and the chromosomes halve, to be combined with other half-sets upon fertilization.[18] Melatonin also enhances and boosts the body's immune system, and those with high pineal secretion are less likely to develop cancerous diseases. High melatonin production heightens energy, stamina, and physical tolerance levels, and it is directly related to sleep patterns, keeping the body temperately regulated with properties that operate through the cardiovascular system. It is the body's most potent and effective antioxidant, and it has positive mental and physical anti-ageing properties.[19]

It is of particular significance that, irrespective of all today's costly and extensive research in these areas, the secrets of the highward fire-stones were known to our ancestors many thousands of years ago. They knew that there were superconductors inherent in the human body; they were the elements of individual consciousness which they called the "light body" (the *Ka*.)[20] They knew that both the physical body and the light body had to be fed to increase hormonal production,[21] and the ultimate food for the latter was called *shem-an-na*. This was manufactured by the priestly Master Craftsmen of the temples (the guardians of the House of Gold) for the express purpose of deifying the kings.

Realm of the Genies

Shaped like a pine cone and about the size of a grain of corn, the pineal gland is centrally situated within the brain, although outside the ventricles and not forming a part of the brain matter as such. It was thought by the French philosopher and optical scientist René Descartes (1596–1650) to be the "seat of the soul"[22] – the point at which the mind and body are conjoined. The ancient Greeks considered likewise and, in the 4th century BC, Herophilus described the pineal gland as an organ which regulated the flow of thought.

Greek mystics carried symbolic wands topped with pine cones, and in the reliefs of old Mesopotamia, priestly figures are often seen holding pine cones to identify supreme intellect.[23] Generally (and especially in Assyrian reliefs), their cones are strategically pointed towards the heads of the kings (*see* Plate 15). Sometimes portrayed with eagle, griffin, or fish headdresses, these wise men were called the Apkallu sages (an Akkadian term from the Sumerian *ab-gal*, meaning "great director"),[24] and their transcendent abilities were conveyed by depicting them with four wings.[25]

In addition to the pine cones (*pinus brutia*, representing the pineal body),[26] the Apkallu also carried small situlas (bucket-like receptacles called *banduddû*), and, when not attending the kings, they were customarily depicted nurturing the Plant of Birth (the *Kiskanu* tree). This sacred plant represented the immortality of the kingship with which they were entrusted. In Babylonia, an Apkallu guardian was classified as an *Alad*,[27] while in the Arabic world he was a *djinni* (or *jinni*, meaning "genius"), from which derived the familiar French word *genie*. These protective words, *alad* and *djinn* (plural of *djinni*) form the root of the name Aladdin in the *Arabian Nights* stories.

Many of the best Apkallu reliefs (now displayed in museums around the world) were discovered in the middle 1800s at the Nimrud palace of King Ashurnasirpal II, who reigned in Assyria 883–859 BC,[28] and at the Khorsabad palace of Sargon the Great (720–705 BC). In accordance with traditional practice, the Apkallu (*Ab-gal*) of this era were akin to the earlier Great Ones of the Egyptian temples, who were responsible for maintaining the light-bodies of the pharaohs.

Archaeologists and museum authorities continue to be undecided about what these Genies carried in their situla receptacles. The most common theory is that it was perhaps pollen gathered from the Plant of Birth and figuratively conveyed, by way of the cones, to the kings as a fertility rite. However, there is no record that the Apkallu were in any way concerned with fertility; their duty was to minister to the kings as the ultimate guardians of sovereignty. Moreover, the Plant of Birth was a purely symbolic tree (like the Tree of Life) from which, in accordance with the *Sumerian King List* (*c.* 2000 BC),[29] the kings were said to have been fed. Its representation was directly concerned with the Mesopotamian *Gra-al*: the "nectar of supreme excellence" called the Gold of the Gods which was a designation of the goddess Hathor in Egypt.[30] By virtue of this, and given that the kings were fed with the high-ward fire-stone of the *shem-an-na*, it seems beyond doubt that the substance carried by the Genies was not pollen, but the *mfkzt* powder of gold.

In the early 15th-century writings of the French alchemist Nicolas Flamel, both the "plant" and the "powder of gold" were brought together, along with the customary reference to serpents, in explaining the route to the Philosophers' Stone (*see* "The Ultimate Goal," page 13). From 22 November, 1416, and as esoterically obscure as all such alchemical texts, comes confirmation from the most famed hermeticist of them all, that the Philosophers' Stone was the enigmatic powder of gold. An extract from Nicolas Flamel's last testament of that date reads: "For in that this *argent vive*, being joined with the sun and moon, was first turned with them into a plant ... and afterwards by corruption into serpents which ... being perfectly dried and digested made a fine powder of gold, which is the Stone."

Unlike so many alchemical adepts of the Middle Ages who failed in their enterprise, Flamel's story was remarkably different. Born of humble parents, he began his working life as a clerk scrivener (a document copyist) and, in the course of this came upon an extraordinary old copper-bound work by a Jewish philosopher called Abraham. Having purchased it for two florins, he studied the book for over 20 years before embarking on its practicalities, whereupon his resultant success transformed his poor existence into one of considerable prosperity. During the latter part of his life, he founded a number of hospitals and chapels in Paris and Boulogne, where there emerged many wonderful tales of his extreme benevolence.

With gold being the traditional emblem of kingship, from early times pine resin was directly identified with pineal secretion (melatonin). It was often used, along with boswellia sap, to make frankincense (the incense of priesthood). Hence, gold and frankincense were the traditional substances of the priest-kings of the Grail bloodline, together with myrrh (a gum resin used as a medical sedative), which was symbolic of death. In the ancient world, higher knowledge was identified as *daäth* (whence: death), and the terms "tomb" and "womb" were considered interchangeable and mutually supportive as routes to the higher knowledge.[31] The New Testament describes how the three substances, gold, frankincense, and myrrh, were presented to Jesus by the ascetic Magi (Matthew 2:11), thereby positively identifying him as a dynastic priest-king of the House of Gold.

The pineal gland is impregnated by eternal ideas, and gives us the possibility of formulating our own conceptions. It is an organ of thought by means of which we acquire inner perception and can thereby change eternal ideas into earthly conceptions. Yogi masters associate the pineal gland with the *Ajna Chakra* (Sanskrit: *ajna*: command; *chakra*: wheel). Chakras are energy centers corresponding to each of the glands of the endocrine system and yogis believe that the pineal gland is a receiver and sender of subtle vibrations which carry thoughts and psychic phenomena. (Endocrine glands, named from the Greek verb "to arouse," are ductless glands which secrete directly into the bloodstream.) The pineal gland is also known as the Eye of Wisdom, the chakra of the mind, of heightened self-awareness, and inner vision,[32] representing the ability to see things clearly with intuitive knowledge. The onset of puberty is directly controlled by the pineal gland and melatonin secretion is at its highest during childhood and the teenage years. It appears that above-average melatonin production in childhood, although heightening the extent of young intellect, can also be an inhibitor of early sexual development,[33] since the two aspects are in physical conflict during the growing years.

The Pineal Eye (the Third Eye) is a metaphoric eye, but it is found as a physical, seeing entity between the brain and skull cavity of many lizards. Hinduism claims that everyone has a

Third Eye – an all-seeing channel for sacred powers, located centrally behind the forehead. In fact, the Third Eye is an anatomical reality like the pineal gland. Yogic teaching suggests that the Pineal Eye is significant in the process of becoming aware, for this is the ultimate source of obtaining light out of darkness.[34] A spiritual person will automatically perceive with the Third Eye, the subtle eye of insight, rather than be duped by mundane eyes which identify only physical presences. Such presences are defined by their place within arbitrary time, but to the pineal graduate there is no time to calculate, for he/she lives in a dimension where time and space are of little consequence.

We are all surrounded and bombarded by thought-fields, and the thoughts we claim as our own are like a continuous universal broadcast. Some thoughts are cosmic in origin, while others are like broadcasts from local stations.[35] The pituitary gland is the primary radio receiver, channeling all wavebands and frequencies. It transmits selected frequencies (through secretions) directly to the pineal gland, which then amplifies certain broadcasts for transmission throughout the body.[36] The pineal gland has total control over what it will and will not transmit through its regulated manufacture and release of the hormone melatonin. High melatonin production thereby increases the facility for receiving and transmitting high-frequency cosmic and local broadcasts, and leads to a greater state of cosmic awareness – a state of "knowing." In this regard, it is interesting to note that the Pineal Eye has been found to contain very fine granular particles, rather like the crystals in a wireless receiving set.[37]

We have seen how the spiraling serpent of wisdom was represented in the insignia of the American, Australian, and British Medical Associations (*see* "The Curious Spiral," page 32). However, other worldwide medical relief institutions use two coiled serpents, spiraling around the winged caduceus of the messenger-god Mercury (Hermes). In these instances, the

Double-serpent caduceus of Hermes.

central staff and serpents represent the spinal cord and the
sensory nervous system, while the two uppermost wings
signify the brain's lateral ventricular structures. Between these
wings, above the spinal column, is shown the small central
node of the pineal gland.[38] The combination of the central
pineal and its lateral wings are referred to in some yogic
circles as the Swan, and this is emblematic of the fully enlightened being. It is the utmost realm of Grail consciousness
achieved by the medieval Knights of the Swan, epitomized by
such chivalric figures as Perceval and Lohengrin.[39]

In the hermetic lore of the ancient Egyptian mystery
schools, this process of achieving enlightened consciousness
was of express importance, with spiritual regeneration taking
place by rising degrees through the 33 vertebrae of the spinal

column[40] until reaching the pituitary gland which invokes the pineal body. The science of this regeneration is one of the lost keys of wisdom, and it is the reason why true ancient Freemasonry was founded upon 33 degrees.[41]

Beyond Zero

Not only is the powder of the highward fire-stone capable of raising human consciousness, it is also a gravity-defiant superconductor. One of the great researchers into gravity from the 1960s was the Russian physicist Andrei Sakharov, and the mathematics for his theory (based on gravity as a zero-point) were published in the *Physical Review* by Hal Puthoff of the Institute for Advanced Studies.[42] Puthoff has since made the point that, because gravity determines space-time, then monatomic white powder is capable of bending space-time.[43] It is "exotic matter," he explained, with a gravitational attraction of less than zero. In addition to the substance being contrived to weigh less than nothing and to disappear into an unknown dimension, the pan in which it is placed can also be caused to weigh less than nothing. So, under the right circumstances, the powder is capable of transposing its own weightlessness to its host, which might be a pan, or might very well be an enormous block of stone.

Perhaps there is a clue here as to how the Egyptians built the pyramids and erected other great monuments.[44] Were the massive stone blocks weighing many tons apiece raised to great heights, with such accuracy, by hundreds of thousands of slaves using nothing but ropes and ramps over an undefined period of time, as is the common speculation? As unsuccessful latter-day attempts to replicate that process have proven, they clearly were not. To construct an inclined plane to the top of the Great Pyramid at a gradient of 1:10 would have required a ramp 4,800 feet (*c.* 1,460 m) in length, with a volume three times greater than that of the pyramid itself.[45] In reality, the building process might have been far more straightforward, and a good deal now points to the possibility that such constructions were aided by the technology of the superconductive fire-stone. This would certainly account for the large volume of its manufacture at the Mount Serâbît temple of Hathor. Indeed, the very word "pyramid" derives from the Greek word *pyr*, which means "fire" (whence *pyre* and *pyro*), denoting that the pyramids were, one way or another, "fire-begotten."[46]

The three pyramids of Giza are assigned as the pharaonic tombs of Khufu, Khafre, and Menkaure, yet for all the investigation of their known internal and subterranean chambers and passages, no bodily remains have been found in these monuments. Nor have the bodies of these Old Kingdom pharaohs been found anywhere else. In the secret repository of the King's Chamber, within the Great Pyramid, age-old tradition relates that the builders had placed "instruments of iron, and arms which rust not, and glass which might be bended and yet not broken, and strange spells"[47] but what did the first explorers of the 9th-century Caliph Al-Ma'mun find, having tunneled their way into the sealed chamber? Then, as today, the only furniture was a lidless, hollowed granite coffer,[48] containing not a body, but a layer of a mysterious powdery substance. This was superficially determined to be grains of feldspar and mica,[49] which are both minerals of the aluminum silicate group.

During the course of the recent white powder research, aluminum and silica were two of the constituent elements revealed by conventional analysis of a granular sample known to be a 100% platinum group compound. Standard laboratory testing is carried out by striking a sample with a DC arc for 15 seconds at a sun-surface temperature. However, a continuation of the burn time, way beyond the normal testing procedure revealed the noble metals of which the substance truly consisted. It is because of the limitations placed on the conventional testing sequence that 5% by dry weight of animal brain tissue is said to be carbon, whereas more rigorous analysis reveals it as the platinum group metals iridium and rhodium in the high-spin state. In view of this, the once-sealed King's Chamber appears to have been contrived as a superconductor, capable of transporting the pharaoh into another dimension of space-time through his polar magnetic aura. It was here that the pharaoh's rite of passage to the Afterlife was administered in accordance with the *Book of the Dead* (*see* "Sacred Manna," pages 24–5) – a passage facilitated by the repeated question, "What is it?" (*Manna?*).

King Solomon's Secret

Royal Generation

Returning now to the Mosaic era and continuing the story of the Ark, we should first look at the ambiguous biblical chronology. Among the more repetitive features of the Old Testament are its frequent narrative references to time spans of "forty years." Not the least of these is the period which the Israelites are said to have spent in the Sinai wilderness after their sojourn at Mount Horeb and before they eventually entered Canaan.[1] This 40-year period of desert wandering is important enough to be mentioned numerous times in the books of Numbers and Deuteronomy, with later confirmations in Psalms and the books of the Prophets.

A key aspect of those years is that the Israelites seemed to spend a good deal of their time "murmuring!"[2] They murmured against Moses, they murmured against Aaron, they murmured against their new Lord, and against all and sundry. Clearly they were not at all impressed with the Moses tour; they complained about the environment, the food, the lack of water, the snakes, and about having to confront the hostile native inhabitants. Finally, the Lord became so fed up with their incessant murmuring that he delivered them into the hands of the Philistines for yet another 40 years![3]

In understanding the relevance of all this, it is important to recognize two salient facts. First, that when the five books of the Pentateuch[4] were written, the Hebrew language did not distinguish between past tenses as we do today. There was only one past tense and it referred, with equal significance, to events that "happened," "have happened," and "had happened." Linguistically, there was no difference between what took place 1,000 years before and what occurred yesterday. Moreover, the words for "day" and "year" were used with unbridled flexibility, which made eventual translation into languages with more concrete ideas of time very difficult.[5]

Having said this, it is clear from the Dead Sea Scrolls that there was a particular significance to the term "forty years" since it was the definition of a period of royal generation. Today's generation standard (the average period in which offspring take the place of their parents) is reckoned at 30 years or so, but the dynastic standard in Bible times (between a father's maturity and his heir's maturity) was determined at 40 years.[6]

The Bible's first mention of kingship in the line from Abraham's wife Sarah is given in Genesis 17:19. In reference to her son Isaac, it is related that the Lord said, "I will establish my covenant with him for an everlasting covenant, and with his seed after him."[7] The male generational precedent for the royal line is then cemented with: "And Isaac was forty years old when he took Rebecca to wife ... and Rebecca his wife conceived."[8] In respect of their son Esau it is then stated: "And Esau was forty years old when he took to wife Judith."[9]

Esau's twin brother Jacob (the second born) is later cited as the progenitor of the Israelites, having changed his name to Israel at Bethel before moving into Egypt, where the strain evolved.[10] However, this was many centuries before the family achieved its kingly station in Jerusalem, and the important link in the chain was not Jacob but Esau, whose line descended to Queen Tiye, the junior wife of pharaoh Amenhotep III, father of Akhenaten the Moses (*see* Chart: The Egyptian Connection, pages 331–2).[11] It was from the daughter of Akhenaten's second wife Mery-khiba (also styled Mery-amon/Miriam), who was born to his father and the Mesopotamian princess Gilukhipa, that the royal line came out of Egypt with the Exodus and descended to the Davidic Royal House of Judah.

Hence it is that, once we see this royal line from Isaac and Esau finally established on the throne of Jerusalem, the "forty-year" standard is brought right back into literary play. 1 Kings 2:11 states: "And the days that David reigned over Israel were forty years." Subsequently, with regard to his son King Solomon, 1 Kings 11:42 states: "And the time that Solomon reigned in Jerusalem over all Israel was forty years." Moving on to Solomon's descendant King Joash, 2 Kings 12:1 continues: "And forty years reigned he in Jerusalem." The true periods of their reigns did not appear to have concerned the Old Testament scribes. What they knew, from the prevalent customs of their own era, was that 40 years was the accepted generational standard between one dynast's maturity and the next, and they ascribed this term to the kingly reigns of particular importance.

Precisely the same was done by the New Testament Gospel writer of Matthew. In detailing the male-line descent from King David down to Jesus (between Solomon and Joseph – spanning about 1,000 years), he listed 25 generations of 40 years each.[12] However, the Gospel compiler of Luke preferred reality to the rule, and gave a more complete list of 40 generations at 25 years each, in accordance with a more logical record.[13]

What this all means is that, when it is said that the Israelites were in the Sinai wilderness for 40 years, the reference is actually to the fact that they were there until the next son was born in the royal line. The parents in question were Khiba-tasherit (the daughter of Moses and Miriam) and her husband Rama of the family of Judah (*see* "Beloved of Khiba," page 61; *see* also Chart: Out of Egypt, pages 333–5).

Conquest of the Ark

It was determined that the line could only take up its kingly role when established in Jerusalem at the site of Mount Moriah, where Abraham had offered his son Isaac as a sacrifice to the El Shaddai many centuries before.[14] The Lord had made his pact with the generations of Isaac, and, in respect of his mother, Sarah, it had also been decreed that "She shall be a mother of nations; kings of people shall be of her."[15] At Sinai, the strains from Isaac's sons, Esau and Jacob-Israel, had come together in the tribal line of Judah. The Mosaic mission was, therefore, to reach Mount Moriah, where the Royal House of Judah would be enthroned.

There were, of course, the indigenous tribes to encounter en route: Canaanites, Amalekites, Edomites, and the like – so this was clearly not a journey of friendly migration. It was, by all standards, an invasion, and the ultimate ambition was conquest. This is made apparent at the outset in Numbers 31:8–10, which tells of their campaign against the Midianites: "And they slew the kings of Midian beside the rest of them that were slain ... And the children of Israel took all the women of Midian captives, and their little ones, and took the spoil of all their cattle, and all their flocks, and all their goods. And they burnt all their cities wherein they dwelt, and all their goodly castles, with fire." Subsequently, there were to be more fearsome adversaries than the Midianites but what the Israelites had, which the others did not, was the most powerful of all known weapons, the Ark of the Covenant.

As they traveled, the Ark was sent on before them,[16] with Moses crying. "Let thine enemies be scattered, and let them that hate thee flee before thee." Their experience was not without some self-inflicted injury, however, and on one occasion an accident caused the Ark to blaze its fire in their own midst, killing some of the Israelites.[17] Soon afterwards, the importance of the Ark in battle becomes clear when, having left it at a base camp, a company of Israelites was routed by Amalekite warriors.[18]

The plan was to move north-eastwards out of Sinai, with an incursion into the Canaanite land to the west of the Dead Sea and the River Jordan (modern Israel). But there were five great fortresses guarding the southern route to Moriah, in view of which Moses decided to swing up east of the Dead Sea, so as to come back across the Jordan and enter Canaan from the north. This meant crossing the frontiers of the Edomites, Amorites, Moabites, and Ammonites, which they appear to have done without too many problems. Soon the Israelites were the masters of Transjordan and made their way northwards to retrace across the river above the Dead Sea at Jericho.[19]

In the course of this, while surveying Canaan across the water from Mount Nebo, Moses died[20] and was succeeded as leader of the tribes by his chief minister's son Joshua. It was he who led the final thrust into Canaan, commencing with one of the best-known incidents in Old Testament history: the siege of Jericho. With the Ark at the head of his army,[21] Joshua advised all but its Levite bearers to stay well behind by about 1,000 yards/meters.[22] Then, with a biblical repeat of the parting of the Red Sea story (to establish Joshua's scriptural position as a worthy leader), the Ark was said to have parted the River Jordan to make possible their crossing (Joshua 3:13–4:24). In real terms, the river is quite narrow at that point and has always been very fordable in places. Even when in full spate from its upper reaches, debris will cause it to dam, and chronicles of the past six centuries record the Jericho stretch as being dry for up to 24 hours at a time.[23]

When across the water, an armed contingent (along with seven priests blowing ramshorn trumpets) preceded the Ark

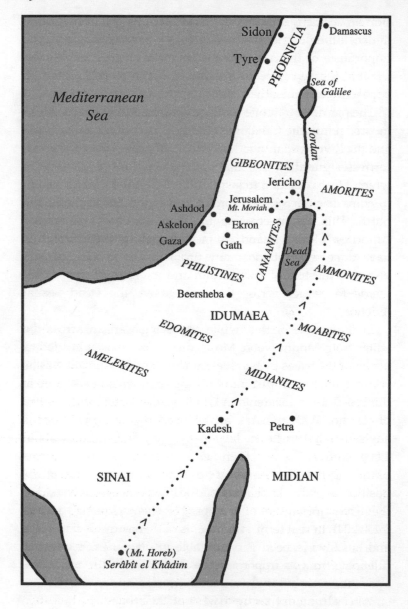

Journey of the Ark.

bearers to compass the city of Jericho once a day for six days. On the seventh day, they made seven circuits, whereupon a final blast of the trumpets and a shout from the Israelites brought the city wall tumbling down (Joshua 6:12–20). With apparent ease, they then took Jericho by storm, killing every man, woman, and child except for the family of the harlot Rahab, who had aided their advance scouting party.[24] The Israelites were then firmly on the soil of Canaan, which they regarded as their "promised land."

Archaeologically, the destruction of the Jericho fortress has been dated between 1400 and 1250 BC,[25] which coincides with our Egyptian exodus date of around 1330 BC (*see* "The Burning Bush," page 46). A rather more accurate guide was established in 1997 when cereals from the ground layer at Jericho immediately before its fall were carbon-dated to about 1315 BC.[26] This means that Joshua's Israelite army of 40,000 men arrived at that time or soon afterwards.

Plainly, no amount of shouting or trumpet blowing could actually bring down a stout city wall such as that at Jericho. Excavations in the 1900s revealed that there were two parallel constructions of about 27 feet high (*c.* 8 m), with the main inner wall being 12 feet thick (*c.* 4 m).[27] By virtue of the extent of damage to the massive mud-brick fortification, it has been suggested that an earthquake was responsible, but that would have affected the Israelites outside as well as the residents within. Far more likely, the Ark would have caused the destruction, but if so that would mean its power was considerably greater than that of a conventional capacitor.[28] To accomplish such devastation, it would need to have been capable of enormous violence and, as we shall see when evaluating the science of its construction in association with the *mfkzt* firestone, it certainly may have had that potential.

With a foothold secured west of the Jordan, Joshua then formed an alliance with locally suppressed Gibeonites and set his sights towards the Canaanite settlement at Ai, near Bethel.

The Kingdoms of Judah and Israel.

Like Jericho, Ai was strongly fortified,[29] but this battle was won by contriving a feint retreat after an initial assault. This drew the military guard of Ai out after them into a strategically laid ambush (Joshua 8:15–20) while, at the same time, other Israelites swept down from the hills to set the city ablaze. Subsequently, further key settlements were taken and in the course of this, the Israelites annexed traditional Canaanite places of worship such as Hebron, Shechem, and Beersheba, just as the later Christians did with the old druidic sites in Europe.[30]

The Song of Deborah

Although not yet ready to establish a new kingdom, the Israelites did have a need for some overall management as their disparate tribes began to operate independently of one another. They settled on the concept of appointed Judges (militarily empowered magistrates), who would see them through about 250 years until the monarchy was constituted. During this period, however, it is apparent that they were in no way united in matters of religion. At Shechem, they had been gathered by Joshua to give their allegiance to Jehovah,[31] but after their leader's death they also began to worship Canaanite deities such as Baal and Ashtoreth.[32]

Not only were the Israelites of that era polytheistic, just as their forebears had been in Egypt, but they were also pretty wayward and violent in their social conduct. The rape of the maidens at Shiloh provides a good example,[33] as does the sacrifice of Jepthah's daughter as a thanksgiving for their victory over the Ammonites in Gilead.[34] As stated in Judges 17:6: "Every man did what was right in his own eyes" – but this was hardly the route towards building a cohesive, confederate society!

The major Judges of the colonizing years were Othniel, Ehud, Deborah, Gideon, Jepthah, Samson, and Samuel. The prophetess Deborah (the first female leader since Miriam, and a veritable Joan of Arc figure) was prominent among these and, together with her chief commander Barak, she instigated the most major assault since the days of Joshua. This led to the defeat of the formidable Canaanite charioteers of King Sisera at Har Megiddo (Armageddon),[35] thereby gaining the Valley of Jezreel for the Israelites, as well as their previously occupied high ground in the Galilean hills. Archeological discoveries determine that the event took place in about 1125 BC,[36] and its story was preserved in the evocative *Song of Deborah*, which she is said to have sung to the assembled throng after the battle (Judges 5).[37]

Israel's next major triumph came under the leadership of Gideon, when they were challenged by hordes of Midianites, mounted on camels.[38] This must have come as some surprise, for tame camels were very new to the ancient culture, receiving no mention in Egyptian, Syrian, or Mesopotamian record prior to that date.[39] (Such references as those when Rebecca watered her father's camels in Genesis 24:10 are mistranslations, which should in fact denote donkeys.)[40] In the face of these unwelcome marauders, Gideon resorted once more to the use of trumpets – this time 300 of them, blown in unison at night, while pitchers were broken and lamps were fired around the sleeping enemy's encampment.[41] In essence, Gideon fought his surprise war against the camels rather than against the men, and the animals fled in terror, with their riders running after them.

The story of Samson (that redoubtable giant of a Judge) is well-known, but the important aspect of his legend is that it is our first introduction to the most intimidating of all Israel's enemies: the Philistines. Heavily armed, they had arrived by sea, like plundering Vikings, in about 1300 BC, with a trail of death and destruction behind them in Crete, Cyprus, Asia Minor, and Phoenicia. They had completely obliterated the Hittite empire, and the Egyptians called them the *Pelestia*, which in Hebrew was *Peleshti*.[42] In all their years of wreaking havoc through the Mediterranean, only pharaoh Rameses III ever defeated them on both land and sea.[43] Claiming a stretch of coast in southern Canaan, these maritime warriors established the five city kingdoms of Askelon, Ashdod, Ekron, Gaza, and Gath, which together became known as Palestine. At the same time, the Israelite invaders held the north of Canaan, and they each had their sights set towards the occupation of the whole.[44]

Notwithstanding the continued struggle which persists between the Israelites and Palestinians over the same land today, the fact is that, in that era, they were both unwelcome invaders of Canaan. The Israelites had evolved through some four centuries in Egypt, prior to which their patriarch Abraham and his forebears were from Ur of the Chaldees in Mesopotamia (modern Iraq).[45] Meanwhile, the Hebrews (from *eber*, meaning "other side") were the people from *eber hannahor*: the "other side of the river" (the Euphrates), as explained in Joshua 24:3.[46] These were the trading descendants of Abraham's sixth generational ancestor Eber (Heber), and the Egyptians called them *Apiru* or *Habiru*.[47] As described in Genesis 11:28–32, the "other side of the river" was the land of Haran in the kingdom of Mari in Mesopotamia.

The newly dubbed Palestinians (Philistines) hailed from Caphtor[48] (called Kafto in the Ramesside inscriptions),[49] a coastal region of southern Anatolia (modern Turkey), whose capital was Tarsus. This was the land of the Luwians,[50] who had arrived in about 2000 BC, bringing an Akkadian language and script from Mesopotamia. The chances are that, in more distant times, the Israelites and Philistines had related Mesopotamian origins.

Famed for wielding the jawbone of an ass for his weapon,[51] and for killing a lion with his bare hands,[52] Samson's great strength was said to emanate from his long hair. On learning this secret, his treacherous wife Delilah cut his hair while he slept and betrayed his whereabouts to the Philistines, who seized and blinded him. Undaunted, however, Samson miraculously regained his strength and pulled down the support pillars of his captors' temple, killing himself and everyone within.

Having moved through these tales of Israelite folk heroes (doubtless with reference to popular legends of their time), the Bible scribes then get back on track with the last and greatest of the Judges, Samuel. At the same time, these tales remind us that the Ark of the Covenant is still very relevant to the story (Judges 20:27). It is then brought back to the forefront of operations once the accounts of those individual champions of tradition are said and done.

Royal David's City

In practical terms, the Philistines were far better equipped than the Israelites, having up-to-date military technology and weaponry from their experience in more advanced lands. They also introduced iron and iron-smelting into Canaan, having learned the techniques from the Hittites, so their hardware and armor were far more efficient.[53] What they did not have, however, was the Ark of the Covenant and, despite all their potentially winning might, they knew they would have to capture it if they were to defeat their Israelite adversaries.

Samuel's story is linked from the outset with an old Canaanite sanctuary at Shiloh, where the Ark was ritually housed when not carried into battle. The problem was that, with the Philistines operating from their five key centers, the Israelite troops were necessarily split into separate units so they might protect their borders, and the Ark could not be everywhere at once. As a result, the tribal factions became autonomous and disunited, in the course of which the Philistines managed to outwit the unit concerned and seize the Ark.[54] They took it to their citadel at Ashdod, but the residents were smitten by its emissions and fell victim to the terrible consequences. And so the Ark was taken to Gath, and then to Ekron, but the results were the same and there was "deadly destruction" in the cities. Those who were not killed by its rays suffered dreadful afflictions, so the Philistines decided that it should be returned to the Levites at Bethshemesh.[55]

Since Samuel was a priestly seer rather than a warrior, reprisals against the Philistines were taken up by the largest and bravest of the Israelites, a Benjamite named Saul, who was installed as king in the field, contrary to Samuel's advice. Setting up his court at Gibeah, Saul managed to unite the tribal factions against the enemy for a while, but he was no diplomat and soon alienated his own priests, scores of whom he put to the sword for not showing full allegiance to his position.[56] Whereas Saul felt he was the chosen king, to be succeeded by his son Jonathan, the majority viewed his status as being purely military and temporary. As far as they were concerned, the true king-elect was David of the House of Judah, who also happened to be Saul's son-in-law (married to his daughter Michal). What made Saul's position all the more uncomfortable was that his son Jonathan was a close friend of David, who was greatly admired for his battlefield slaying of the Philistines' giant champion Goliath of Gath.[57]

Knowing that Saul was intent on taking David's life, Jonathan warned his friend, who duly took his army into the hills of En-gedi to await the king's assault. Saul eventually came with 3,000 men but, in separating him from his troops, David forgave the man and set him free. Shortly afterwards Samuel died and, wanting then to know his own fate, Saul consulted the wise witch of Endor. She, however, conjured the ghostly shade of Samuel to advise him that he and his sons would soon fall in battle against the Philistines. And so it was that, when Jonathan was slain on the field of Mount Gilboa, Saul, who had rejected the Ark of the Lord, knew that his hour of humiliation had come. Not wishing to be killed by the enemy, he elected instead to fall on his own sword, and the Royal House of David was eventually proclaimed.[58]

With the Ark back in action, David defeated the Philistines in a series of battles, moving ever southwards towards Mount Moriah with a mustered force of 30,000 men. The Ark was transported throughout on a specially made cart, and it was when it swayed during this journey that Uzzah the carter inadvertently touched it and was killed on the spot.[59] David was concerned that only the Levites, with their special clothing and training, could handle the sacred relic, when he (even as their king) could not. He donned a priestly *ephod* and danced before the Ark, but knew that despite everything he could never touch it for fear of his life. At length, he and the Israelites reached Mount Moriah, and Zadok the high priest led the Ark into the old Jebusite city, where the Davidic court was established and the king enthroned. As a result of David's leadership, Philistine domination was at an end in southern Canaan, where the land was renamed Judah and its capital was called Yuru-salem: City of peace.

Having subjugated the regions of Edom, Ammon, and Moab, along with bordering Aramaean centers such as Damascus and the Canaanite conclaves of Megiddo and Beth-shean, David became more of an emperor than a king. He established trading relations with the Phoenicians of Hamath, Tyre, and Sidon, and constructed his court on the traditional Egyptian model of his ancestors. It was administered by appointed officials, with a military commander, a chancellor, a chronicler,[60] two chief priests (Zadok and Abiathar), and a vizier, just as retained by the pharaohs. He also had his own harem in the style of other Eastern monarchies.

David's reign was not without its turmoils, though, and at one point his own eldest son Absalom led a revolt against his father, only to be killed in the process – resulting in the famous lament "O Absalom, my son."[61] A struggle for succession then erupted, with the Judah faction supporting David's next eldest son, Adonijah, and the Jerusalem faction backing the younger Solomon (a son of David and Bathsheba the Hittite). When David eventually died, Solomon's supporters were by far the more powerful, having in their number Zadok the priest, Nathan the prophet, and Benaiah, captain of the palace guard. They had Adonijah executed,[62] his supporters exiled, and Solomon became the new King in Jerusalem.

The Fire-stone Project

Finally, in about 968 BC, after a lengthy history of battles and journeying from those far-off days at Mount Horeb, the Ark found its long-sought place of residence in King Solomon's Jerusalem. Although generally portrayed by his familiar nominal style (meaning "peaceable"), Solomon's given legitimate name was actually Jedidiah.[63] His father's true name is uncertain, since the titular style of David has predominated (although never recorded as a personal name before that time). Mesopotamian texts from the palace of Mari refer, however, to the *Dâvìdum* as might be the "Caesar" (Emperor), and the title has stuck with him as a name to the present day.[64] In reality, Solomon and his successors were all Davids (*Dâvìdums*).

Quite suddenly, with the installation of Solomon, the old kingly traditions of the early line are seen to have re-emerged – not least of which was the resurrected gold culture: "Now the weight of gold that came to Solomon in one year was six-hundred threescore and six talents."[65] "And all King Solomon's drinking vessels were of gold … It was nothing accounted of in the days of Solomon[66] … And King Solomon made two hundred targets of beaten gold; six hundred shekels of gold went to one target[67] … And he made three hundred shields of beaten gold; three pounds of gold went to one shield[68] … Moreover the king made a great throne of ivory, and overlaid it with the best gold."[69] The list of golden artifacts is seemingly endless – and all this was additional to the extensive use of gold in the construction and furnishings of his famous Temple.

Unlike his warlord of a father, Solomon was reputed as a prince of peace. He did not embark on any expansionist campaigns, although building defensive garrisons for his chariots and cavalry, notably at Hazor, Megiddo, and Gezer. He also built store centers and appointed 12 regional governors for his administrative districts. Given that the Israelites had no maritime experience, Solomon forged good relations with the Phoenician merchants, and King Hiram of Tyre helped him build a fleet of ships to operate in the Red Sea. The fleet was based at Ezion-geber, which enabled Solomon to enter the lucrative horse trade, as a result of which he had 40,000 stalls of horses for his chariots and 12,000 horsemen.[70] Even his Jerusalem city stable was extensive and, when excavated by the Knights Templars around 2,000 years later, it was reported that it was "a stable of such marvelous capacity and extent that it could hold more than 2,000 horses."[71]

Noted for his wisdom and philosophical writings, the high point of Solomon's fame was the Temple which he built near David's palace to house the Ark of the Covenant. For this construction, King Hiram of Tyre came again to his aid, supplying designers, craftsmen, and materials. The director of operations was another Hiram, also from Tyre, a skilled artificer in metalwork.[72] According to masonic lore, this Hiram was surnamed Abif, although he is not named as such in the Bible.[73] Far from being a wholly Jahvist place of worship, the Temple was modeled on aspects of Middle Eastern tradition. At its entrance (and in line with Phoenician temple custom) were two free-standing pillars: *Jachin* (denoting "establishment") and *Boaz* (meaning "in strength:" the name of the great-grandfather of David). Masonic ritual tells that these bronze pillars were hollow constructions which contained the constitutional Rolls of the Craft. The Temple walls and ceiling were lined with Lebanon cedar, and decorated with cherubim, palms, pomegranates, and lilies. The doors and floor were made of olive and pine – and all of this, from floor to ceiling, was overlaid with gold.[74] Central to the overall theme was the designated Holy of Holies: the *Sanctum Sanctorum*, which housed the Ark of the Covenant, guarded by two giant cherubim[75] (additional to those on the Ark itself). But there was another dominant feature, which has caused considerable bewilderment because its function was never explained.

1 Kings 7:23–26 tells of a massive container, which Hiram made for the Temple court. However, the description strays a little from the context of the original Greek text, so it is necessary to concentrate on the Septuagint book of 3 Kings for a more authentic account. It relates that this was a circular bronze receptacle of some 15 feet (c. 3.8 m) in diameter and 7.5 feet (c. 1.9 m) in height, with its metal being a palm-span (about 3 inches/7.5 cm) thick. Its rim was fashioned like an open lotus flower, and it stood upon the statues of 12 great bronze oxen. In all, it held "three-thousand measures" of its accompanying wagons, and there were 10 of these. They were also made of bronze, open-topped, richly decorated with lions and cherubs, and set upon 27-inch (c. 68.5 cm) chariot wheels. Additionally, it is related that Hiram made the cauldrons and the shovels.

The questions which naturally arise are: What on earth would such an enormous tank be doing in a temple? What would have been stored in it? And why the wagons and shovels? Another question which follows just as naturally is: notwithstanding all the gold used for the Temple project itself, what could Solomon possibly have been doing with a supply of such vast quantities each year?

It has been suggested that the great vessel was a laver for priests to wash themselves in, but with its top at around 12 feet (over 3.5 m) from the ground, including the oxen supports, this is hardly likely. In fact, unless the priests were all over 7-feet tall, they would have needed to swim, rather than wash! Apart from that, the Temple's lavers are separately mentioned in 1 Kings 7:38. The Hebrew scholar and Dead Sea Scrolls translator, Yigael Yadin, has made the point that the Hebrew consonants sometimes translated to "laver" from old texts (the *Temple Scroll* for example) comprise the same consonantal sequence that could equally translate to "platform," "pillar," or other constructions.[76]

So, what could possibly have been kept in the brazen container? To answer this, we can return to where our story began, at the Sinai mountain temple of Serâbît el Khâdim, with Sir W.M. Flinders Petrie. When he wrote his report about the discovery of the mysterious white powder in the temple's chambers, he stated (thinking at first, before his tests, that it was a fine ash) that there was an estimated 50 tons of the substance stored there. Everything points to the fact that, with the Ark firmly installed and operative, King Solomon had finally resurrected the Sinai manufacturing plant in Jerusalem, and was trading *mfkzt* fire-stone with the Egyptians, Phoenicians, and others for his shipping fleet, military protection, horses, chariots, and other expensive services rendered during the course of his reign – not to mention all the building supplies for his Temple and palace. Septuagint 3 Kings 5:7 and 10:11 confirm the deal, stating that King Hiram of Tyre supplied the raw gold from the mines of Ophir, near Sheba,[77] while his requirement in return for this and all his favors was that Solomon should "give bread[78] to my household."

Into the Darkness

Kebra Nagast

We have seen (*see* "Conflict of Deuteronomy," pages 63–4) how the 14th-century Christians of the Ethiopian Orthodox Church figuratively hijacked the Ark as a relic of the Abyssinian emperors in the *Kebra Nagast* (Glory of Kings). The book suggests that a secret son called Bayna-lekhem (Menyelek) was born to King Solomon and the Queen of Sheba – a son who stealthily removed the Ark from the Temple of Jerusalem, then carried it through Arabia and across the Red Sea to Ethiopia. It is difficult to imagine how anyone could "stealthily remove" something weighing around a ton and a half without being noticed, but it is worth looking at this legend in greater detail to see how it stands up against the Bible's own account of the Ark. If there were any foundation to the Ethiopian text, the Ark should not appear in the Hebrew scriptures after the time of King Solomon. The fact is, however, that it is recorded in the Old Testament as being in Jerusalem through many generations of Solomon's successors. So, why would an anonymous Ethiopian scribe go to such lengths to concoct an immediately disprovable story?

Back in AD 330, Emperor Constantine the Great had split his Roman Empire formally in two, with the West governed from Rome and the East from Byzantium (in north-western Turkey), which he renamed Constantinople. But not long afterwards the Western Empire collapsed – demolished by the Visigoths and Vandals. The last Roman Emperor, Romulus Augustulus, was deposed by the German chieftain Odoacer, who became King of Italy in AD 476. In the absence of an Emperor, the prevailing High Bishop, Leo I gained the title of *Pontifex Maximus* (Chief pontiff or bridge-builder), later known as the Pope (*Papa*: Father). In the East, the story was different and the Byzantine Empire was destined to flourish for another thousand years.[1]

From the 5th century, the Church of Rome continued in the West, while the Byzantine Church emerged from its centers at Constantinople, Alexandria, Antioch, and Jerusalem. Each of the Churches sought supremacy over the other, and a main point of contention was an argument as to whether Jesus was the Son of God or whether he was God incarnate. Along with this, the nature of the Holy Spirit (or Holy Ghost) became a matter of heated discussion, and the whole affair became known as the Trinity Debate. This erupted into a fever in 867, when Patriarch Photius of Constantinople excommunicated Pope Nicholas I of Rome because he fronted an inferior Faith!

The Catholics of Western Christendom then decided to ratify what was called the *Filioque Article*. This had been introduced at the Council of Toledo in 598, and it declared that the Holy Spirit proceeded "from the Father and from the Son" (Latin: *filioque*). The Eastern Orthodox bishops claimed otherwise, stating that the Spirit proceeded "from the Father through the Son" (Greek: *dia tou huiou*). It was a somewhat intangible and extraordinary point of theological dispute, but it was good enough to split formal Christianity down the middle. In reality, it was simply a trivial excuse to perpetuate the dispute over whether the Church should be politically managed from Rome or Constantinople. The result was the formation of two quite distinct Churches from the same original, and the unresolved dialogue drove a wedge firmly between the factions.[2]

In the course of this, the Eastern believers had begun to contrive a separate religious heritage for what they considered to be the true Faith. To further this, they looked specifically at the Old Testament scriptures, rather than at the 1st-century teachings of Peter and Paul as used by the Catholics. Their objective was to prove that orthodox Christianity had evolved more directly from the precepts of Mosaic Law and had a truly ancient tradition. The problem was that everyone knew the Old Testament constituted the religious framework of Judaism, which was distinct from Christianity. It was therefore determined to cement the notion that, irrespective of Jesus' personal involvement as a "member" of the movement, Christians had actually existed before there were Hebrews! A solution to this end was found in rewriting the Old Testament stories to give them a fresh Byzantine message for Christians in countries such as Egypt, Syria, and Ethiopia.

Among the newly contrived fables was an Ethiopic work called *The Book of Adam and Eve*, subtitled *The Conflict of Adam and Eve with Satan*, which was produced sometime in or after the 6th century.[3] This lengthy book features Satan as a central character, and goes so far as to say that the cross of Jesus was erected on the very spot where Adam was buried! A similar work, entitled *The Book of the Cave of Treasures* (*M'ārath gaze*), is a 6th-century Syriac compendium of earthly history from the Creation of the world to the Crucifixion.[4] Once again, Satan appears as the constant protagonist of evil. In one instance, Adam and Eve are seen to be dwelling in a cave when Satan comes 14 times to tempt them, but each time an angel of God puts the demon to flight. The book even maintains that orthodox Christianity was in place before the time of Adam and Eve! Another volume along similar lines is *The Book of the Bee*[5] – a Syriac text from about 1222, compiled by Bishop Shelêmôn of Basra, Iraq. Its title is explained by virtue of the fact that it "gathered the heavenly dew from the blossoms of the two Testaments, and the flowers of the holy books," thereby applying Christian doctrine to the traditional Jewish scriptures which it strategically reinterpreted.

If these books can be said to have anything in their favor it is that their Old Testament genealogies are very much in accordance with the far more ancient Jewish works such as the *Book of Jubilees*. Apart from that, they are no more than fictional fables, designed to undermine historical record, and they are contrary to all original Sumerian, Canaanite, and Hebrew archives. It was into this tradition that the *Kebra Nagast* was born. Its sole purpose was to bestow a Judaic heritage on the Kings of Ethiopia by portraying them as descendants of King Solomon and inheritors of the Ark of the Covenant. The book gives no details of the generations from Solomon, but simply applies the heritage of Judah to a certain Emperor Yekuno Amlak, who began the so-called Solomonid dynasty in Ethiopia from 1268.[6]

Word of the *Kebra Nagast* filtered into European consciousness in 1533, when the Portuguese envoy Francisco Alvares returned from a visit to Ethiopia. Just prior to that, the Spanish chemist Enrique Cornelio Agrippa had translated the Ethiopic work in his 1528 *Historia de las cosas de Etiopía*. Another translation was made in the early 1600s by the Jesuit priest Manuel Almeida, who had been a missionary in Ethiopia. But it was not until the close of the 18th century, when the Scottish explorer James Bruce of Kinnaird released his *Travels in Search of the Sources of the Nile*, that the fabulous content of the *Kebra Nagast* became more widely known in the West.

The Ethiopian Ark is currently said to be held under the auspices of the Church of St. Mary of Zion in Axum (Aksum), supposedly kept in a crude 1960s building called the *Enda Tsallat* (Chapel of the Tablet) – although no one ever gets to see it. In fact, its only known description comes from the 13th-century writing of an Armenian known as Abu Salih – but the item he described bore little resemblance to the biblical Ark of the Covenant. Salih wrote that it stood about knee-height, with golden crosses and precious stones on its lid, and was generally kept upon the altar.[7] This relic (whatever it might have been) is similar in shape and size to the supposed Ark which is carried in procession today, but always under veiling drapes which prohibit any sight of it. Called a *manbara tabot*, it is actually a casket which contains a venerated altar slab known as a *tabot*. The reality is that, although the Axum chest might be of some particular cultural significance in the region, there are *manbara tabotat* (plural of *tabot*) in churches across the breadth of Ethiopia. The *tabotat* which they contain are rectangular altar slabs, made of wood or stone. Clearly, the prized *manbara tabot* of Axum is of considerable sacred interest and, by linguistic definition, it is indeed an ark – but it is not the biblical Ark of the Covenant, nor anything remotely like it.

The Queen of Sheba

Having skipped the Sheba legend in our chronological discussion of King Solomon, this is a more appropriate stage to consider the illustrious and mysterious Queen of the South. The *Kebra Nagast* labels her as Makeda of Ethiopia, but she is not personally named in the Bible, nor identified in any authentic or historically recognized document. Notwithstanding this, and contrary to numerous literary claims that the land of Sheba (sometimes Sāba) is difficult to identify, it is actually specified in the Assyrian inscriptions of King Tiglathpileser III (*c.* 745–727 BC) and of Sargon II (*c.* 720–705 BC). Making it perfectly clear that Sheba was the land of the Sabaeans (the *Sāba'aa*), the latter inscription (from around 707 BC) associates a prevailing Queen Samsé of Aribû with It'amara, King of Sheba. His realm was to the far south of Palestine and Jordan in the Arabian Peninsula which now includes Yemen. Bordering the eastern flank of the Red Sea above the Gulf of Aden, the Semitic rendition of the name Sāba was Sheba.[8]

The Queen of Sheba makes her brief biblical appearance before Solomon in 1 Kings 10:1–13 (repeated in 2 Chronicles 9:1–12), which states somewhat ambiguously that "she came to prove Solomon with hard questions." The account relates that she arrived with a great caravan, bringing spices, gold, and precious stones for the King of Judah, whose unparalleled wisdom was renowned far and wide. Apart from these things, there is little more to the story. The Queen was satisfied with Solomon's wise answers and very impressed by his royal court. Then, after a mutual exchange of abundant gifts, she departed. Most probably, however, her visit was to do with negotiations concerning the sacred fire-stone for her household, and 1 Kings 10:10 specifies that she had brought Solomon 120 talents (about 5.5 tons) of gold.[9]

In linguistic terms, the word *sheba* defined an "oath"[10] and it was not uncommon in usage. Hence, the Queen of Sheba has also been called "Queen of the Oath," and Solomon's mother Bathsheba was the "Daughter of an Oath." In its variant forms the name crops up a number of times in the Old Testament, including Seba, son of Cush,[11] Sheba, son of Joktan,[12] and Sheba, son of Bichri,[13] along with the place name Beer-sheba.[14]

The Queen of Sheba's introduction into the story of King Solomon is a literary non-event, spanning just a dozen short verses and with no apparent outcome. It does, however, set a scene for the portrayal of Solomon's own prestige, and maybe that was the reason for its inclusion in the narrative. How better to demonstrate the wisdom and wealth of the mighty King than to have the Queen of an historically great trading nation confide, "Thy wisdom and prosperity exceedeth the fame which I heard." (I Kings 10:7.)

The land of Sheba was certainly noted for its spices and gold, just as portrayed, but as for the Queen, there is no mention of her age, her looks, nor anything about her. And yet there is a compelling romance in the mystique of the woman with the wealth-laden camel train that has led artists and writers to develop a mythology of her over the centuries. The Queen of Sheba was a perfect candidate for the strategically delusive, but nonetheless adventurous, *Kebra Nagast*. There was so little said about her in the Bible that the Queen's enigma was ripe for an embellishment that would somehow complete her portrait in a way that would satisfy an understandable intrigue.

Guardians of Destiny

Turning now to the biblical Ark, we see that, in complete contrast to the *Kebra Nagast*, the Old Testament docs indeed confirm that the Ark was in Jerusalem long after Solomon's era (*c.* 968 BC). King Hezekiah of Judah (12th lineal descendant of Solomon) was said to have prayed before the Ark (2 Kings 19:15). In the subsequent reigns of Kings Manasseh and Amon, the Ark was removed to a Levite sanctuary while there was a degree of disturbance and sectarian conflict at the Temple. Later, when recounting the reign of Hezekiah's great-grandson, King Josiah of Judah, 2 Chronicles 35:3 relates how Josiah decided that the Ark should be returned to its proper abode. He "said unto the Levites that taught all Israel, which were holy unto the Lord, Put the holy ark in the house which Solomon the son of David king of Israel did build; it shall not be a burden upon your shoulders." This was over 360 years after Solomon built the Temple and shortly before the first invasion of Jerusalem by Nebuchadnezzar of Babylon in around 597 BC.

With this instruction carried out, it would seem logical that when Nebuchadnezzar's troops descended upon the Temple, they would have carried away the Ark with their loot, but it appears they did not. Inventories of some key items of plunder are given in 2 Kings 25:13–17 and Jeremiah 52:17–23, but the Ark does not feature. It does feature, however, in numerous Hebrew texts confirming that prior to the invasion it was secreted by the prophet Jeremiah. Not surprisingly, therefore, a related prophecy is found in the Old Testament book of Jeremiah, which states: "The ark of the covenant of the Lord: neither shall it come to mind: neither shall they remember it; neither shall they visit it." (Jeremiah 3:16).

In the Old Testament Apocrypha, a complementary entry is also found in 2 Maccabees 2:5, while 2 Esdras 10:22 laments that the Levites were taken into captivity, continuing: "Our candlestick is put out, the ark of our covenant is spoiled, our holy things are defiled." Various commentaries in the Hebrew Talmud recall that Jeremiah secreted the Ark below ground near the Temple's Holy of Holies,[15] and the tradition was so strong that it survived the centuries even after the 10th-century Masoretic Hebrew Bible was written.

What is clear in all this is that from the time of King Solomon's reign, the Ark was not used, and the Temple's gold culture came to an abrupt end as disputes prevailed over kingship between the northern territory of Israel and the southern land of Judah. Although Solomon's son, Rehoboam, naturally succeeded in Jerusalem as King of Judaea, a revolt over labor levies in the north led to the installation of the Ephraimite Jeroboam as an independent ruler of Israel in *c.* 928 BC. This coincided with a dynastic change in Egypt, when a Libyan chief named Sheshonq married an Egyptian heiress and became the new pharaoh. Being unfamiliar with the true Egyptian culture, this ex-commander of the Meshwesh (a Libyan police force) decided to re-cement Egypt's dominion over Palestine in accordance with the *Israel Stela* (*see* "Right of Succession," page 54). Sheshonq (called Shishak in the Bible) therefore launched an assault against Rehoboam and surrounded Jerusalem.[16] He removed a number of easily portable valuables from the Temple, to prove his supremacy over the King of Judah, and then immediately turned his sights northwards against the kingdom of Jeroboam, who duly fled across the Jordan.[17] A composite record of the campaign was later inscribed on the walls of the temple of Amun at Thebes.

The Ark of the Covenant was not listed in Sheshonq's table of plunder, but Bible references to it after the event relate it as being more ceremonial than functional. With the nation now divided, the main thrust of the ensuing narrative centers on the continuing struggle between the Kings of Judah and Israel. One way or another, the Bible and other Jewish records are consistent in stating that the Ark was eventually hidden in the reign of Josiah so as not to be seized by the Babylonians.[18] The retrospectively written 2 Chronicles 6:1 explains that the Lord would indeed dwell in the thick darkness. Then, at the very end of the Bible, Revelation 11:19 (written in the 1st century AD) confirms that the Ark, with its thunders and lightnings, was still resident in the Temple of Heaven. In his *Miohnch Torah* of 1180, the Spanish philosopher Moses Maimondes told that Solomon had constructed a special hiding place for the Ark deep beyond winding tunnels – the same crypt which had been used by his son Rehoboam when Shishak of Egypt invaded. Later, in 1648, Rabbi Naftali Hertz explained, in his *Emeq ha Melek* (Valley of the King), how the holy relic had been safely stowed before the Temple was destroyed.

At the center of all accounts concerning the Ark's protective stowage is Jeremiah, and it is to his personal history that we must turn for the rest of the story. Although generally portrayed in Church teachings as a prophet, Jeremiah was a man of particular influence. As identified in Jeremiah 1:1, he was the son of Hilkiah, a priest of Anath who became the High Priest of Jerusalem and discovered the *Book of the Law* secreted in the Temple (2 Kings 22:8 and 2 Chronicles 34:15). Moreover, Jeremiah was the captain of Hilkiah's Temple Guard. Prior to Nebuchadnezzar's invasion, Hilkiah instructed Jeremiah to have his men secrete the most sacred Temple treasures in the vaults beneath – including the Ark of the Covenant. This was duly done, with the Guard forming an elite Order of the Temple so as to retain the record of the hoard.

And so it was that, when Nebuchadnezzar ravaged the Temple, specific items such as the Ark and the anointing stone of the Kings of Judah were not on the list of plunder. The venerated Stone of the Covenant was the pillow on which Jacob was said to have laid his head to see the ladder reaching up to Heaven at Beth-el (Genesis 28:18–22). El Shaddai had promised Jacob on that occasion that his seed would generate a line of future kings – the line which, in due course, became the dynasty of David and Solomon.

With the treasures secure from Nebuchadnezzar, Josiah then came against another enemy, and was killed in battle against pharaoh Nekau of Egypt at the Palestinian battlefield of Meggido.[19] His son Jehoahaz was installed as his successor, but Nekau dethroned him in favor of his younger brother Eliakim, who became King Jehoiakim.[20] With Jerusalem's taxes being paid to the pharaoh, the city was in a weak condition, and it was then that Nebuchadnezzar launched the first of his anticipated assaults from Babylon, maneuvering pharaoh Nekau firmly out of the picture. King Jehoiakim then died, to be succeeded by his son Jechoniah, but Nebuchadnezzar struck again with a far more vigorous invasion. The Temple was raided and Jechoniah was taken hostage with some 10,000 Israelites to begin the 70-year Babylonian Captivity (2 Kings 24:10–20).

With Jerusalem in chaos, Jechoniah's uncle Mattaniah succeeded as the resident King Zedekiah of Judah. But 11 years later, Nebuchadnezzar returned, whereupon Zedekiah was taken to Babylon and blinded.[21] On that occasion the Temple was totally destroyed by the Babylonian captain Nebuzar-adan, who took its famous pillars, Boaz and Jachin, along with Solomon's container tank and other architectural features. The sons of Zedekiah were murdered, but his daughter Tamar (Tea) was rescued by Jeremiah, who removed her (via Egypt and Spain) to safety in Ireland. In the interim, Jeremiah had retrieved the sacred Stone of the Covenant before

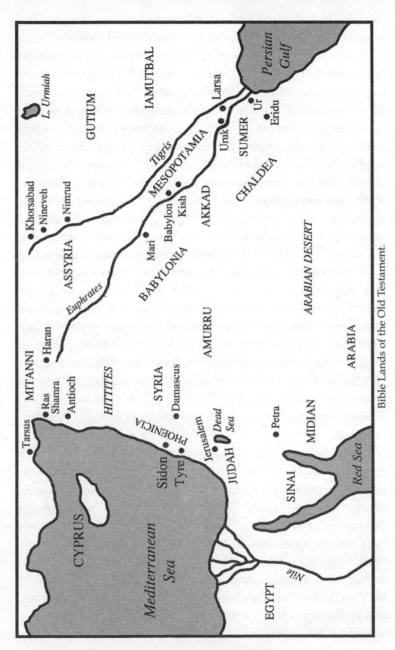

Bible Lands of the Old Testament.

the Temple was demolished, and he carried this also to Ireland where it became known as *Lia Fáil*: the Stone of Destiny.[22]

In all, it would seem that around 50,000 captives were transported to Babylon in the deportations of Nebuchadnezzar. According to Jeremiah 29:5–7, they lived freely in their own homes, ran their own farms and businesses, generally conducting their lives as normal. Their princes and governors might have been badly treated, but the people as a whole appeared to fare rather well, and they are not portrayed anywhere as having been slaves or bonded servants. So, why were they taken? The Bible tells that it was God's retribution against them because their ex-king Manasseh had erected altars to the Canaanite god Baal.[23] It did not matter that Manasseh's grandson, King Josiah, had destroyed these altars with the people's blessing.[24] In any event, Jehovah decided to take his revenge, saying, "I will wipe Jerusalem as a man wipeth a dish … and deliver them into the hand of their enemies … They have provoked me to anger since the day their fathers came forth out of Egypt."[25] It is then explained that: "At the commandment of the Lord came this upon Judah, to remove them out of his sight for the sins of Manasseh, according to all that he did."[26]

This explanation might be sufficient to satisfy scriptural requirement, but in practical terms it makes little sense. Nebuchadnezzar was not a servant of Jehovah and would certainly not have masterminded such an incursion to appease the god of a foreign nation. His reason for taking so many hostages must, therefore, have been substantially different from the scenario as portrayed. He could easily have overthrown Jerusalem and taken control in Judaea (as the Romans did in later times) without the inconvenience of taking such a vast number of captives. In the longer term, they might well have contributed to the Babylonian economy, but in the short term it would have been an expensive and unnecessary exercise.

What had happened was that, between 612 and 609 BC, the mighty Assyrian state of King Ashur-banipal collapsed in ruins at the hands of the neighboring Babylonians and Medes, who became the new masters of Mesopotamia. The primary palace of Nineveh had been looted and razed to the ground, and what followed was a colossal building program, with Babylon becoming the largest and most beautiful city in the Middle East.[27] In a relatively short space of time, Babylon became the world center of a great literary and architectural renaissance. Its unsurpassed library collection was the perfect environment for the Israelite scribes who scoured the archive for details of their own ancestral history, resulting in the early narrative of the Old Testament. Not least among Babylon's stunning features were the famous Hanging Gardens (one of the Seven Wonders of the World) and the exquisitely glazed Ishtar Gate – one of eight monumental entrances to the new city. The immediate requirement was for a substantial workforce of many thousands – either to serve directly in the extensive building project, or to supplement the businesses and trades of those Babylonians who were seconded to it. To satisfy this, Nebuchadnezzar did not have to look very far, and he elected to obtain the necessary manpower from nearby Judaea.

Some decades later, when Cyrus II of Persia occupied Babylon in 538 BC, he permitted the descendant Israelite exiles to return to Judaea. Of those who elected to leave what had effectively become their new homeland, the first wave traveled to Jerusalem with Jechoniah's descendant, Prince Zerubbabel, in about 536 BC. Around 20 years later a new Temple was completed on the old site, but there were to be no more reigning kings of the House of Judah. Their overlords were Darius I and his successors of the Persian Empire. What the Israelites did have, though, from the libraries of Babylonia, were the prototypes for a patriarchal history that was to form the structural base for the books of their emergent Old

Testament. Also, unbeknown to them, the arcane treasures of Jeremiah's Jerusalem cache were still buried beneath the foundation rubble of the second Temple. The book of 2 Chronicles 5:9, compiled between 300 and 250 BC, long after the second Temple was built,[28] states in respect of the Ark, "There it is unto this day."

This sacred and valuable hoard might have been lost forever were it not for the records of Hilkiah's Temple Guard, which had been removed to the West with Jeremiah. French Templar chronicles of the Middle Ages confirm that the catalogued treasure (secreted by Jeremiah and guarded by the descendant brethren of the Jerusalem Order) became the specific responsibility of the Templar Grand Knights of St. Andrew, formally instituted by the Crusader King Baudouin II of Jerusalem in 1118. They were called the Guardian Princes of the Royal Secret: the inheritors of an Order established by Hilkiah the High Priest over 1,700 years before.[29] It was the allotted task of these knights to excavate the Temple site and bring out the treasures while the Western princes held Jerusalem for a while in the early crusading era. As we shall see, they did precisely that, with the result that they became the most influential and powerful organization the world has ever known.

After the Captivity

With the repatriated Israelites under Persian control and their own reigning dynasty at an end, they were also subject to the official Aramaic imperial language. The high priest of the new Temple became the head of a culture that was then wholly centered on religion, and their newly defined Law of God became the recognized law of the land (Ezra 7:23–26). With the Persian government prevailing for two centuries, it is at this point that the Old Testament tails off, and there is a period of more than 350 years before the New Testament begins.

The intervening era began with the rise to power of Alexander the Great of Macedonia, who defeated the Persian Emperor Darius III in 333 BC. Destroying the city of Tyre in Phoenicia, he then moved into Egypt and built his citadel of Alexandria. With full control of the hitherto Persian Empire, Alexander then pressed on through Babylonia, moving ever eastward, until he finally conquered the Punjab. At his early death in 323 BC, his generals took control. Ptolemy Soter became Governor of Egypt, Seleucus ruled Babylonia, while Antigonus governed Macedonia and Greece. By the turn of the century, Palestine was also enveloped within the Alexandrian domain.

At that stage a new force gathered momentum in Europe: the Republic of Rome. In 264 BC the Romans ousted the Carthaginian rulers of Sicily – also capturing Corsica and Sardinia. The great Carthaginian general Hannibal then retaliated by seizing Saguntum (in modern Spain) and advanced with his troops across the Alps, but he was checked by the Romans at Zama. Meanwhile Antiochus III (a descendant of the Macedonian general Seleucus) became King of Syria. By 198 BC he had rid himself of Egyptian influences to become master of Palestine. His son, Antiochus IV Epiphanes, then occupied Jerusalem – an action that promptly gave rise to a Jewish revolt under the Hasmonaean priest Judas Maccabaeus. He was killed in battle, but the Maccabees achieved Israelite independence in 142 BC.[30]

In the continuing struggle, the Roman armies destroyed Carthage and formed the new province of Roman North Africa. Further campaigns brought Macedon, Greece, and Asia Minor under Roman control. But disputes raged in Rome because the Carthaginian (or Punic) wars had ruined the Italian farmers while simultaneously enriching the aristocracy, who built large estates utilizing slave labor. The Democrat leader Tiberius Gracchus put forward proposals for agrarian reform in 133 BC, but he was murdered by the Senatorial Party.

His brother took up the farmers' cause and he too was murdered, with the Democrat leadership passing to the military commander Gaius Marius.

By 107 BC Gaius Marius was Consul of Rome. But the Senate found its own champion in Lucius Cornelius Sulla, who eventually deposed Marius and became Dictator in 82 BC. A horrifying reign of terror ensued until the Democrat statesman and general Gaius Julius Caesar gained popularity and was duly elected to primary office in 63 BC.

In that same year, Roman legions marched into the Holy Land, which was already in a state of sectarian turmoil. The Pharisees, who observed the strict ancient Jewish laws, had risen in protest against the more liberal Greek culture. In so doing, they also opposed the priestly caste of Sadducees, and the unsettled environment rendered the region ripe for invasion. Seeing their opportunity, the Romans, under Gnaeus Pompeius Magnus (Pompey the Great), subjugated Judaea and seized Jerusalem, having annexed Syria and the rest of Palestine.

Meanwhile, the Roman hierarchy was undergoing its own upheavals. Julius Caesar, Pompey, and Crassus formed the first ruling Triumvirate in Rome, but their joint administration suffered when Caesar was sent to Gaul and Crassus went to supervise matters in Jerusalem. In their absence, Pompey changed political camps, deserting the Democrats for the Republican aristocrats, whereupon Caesar returned and civil war ensued. Caesar was victorious at Pharsalus, in Greece, and eventually gained full control of the Imperial provinces when Pompey fled to Egypt.

Until that time, Queen Cleopatra VII had been ruling Egypt jointly with her brother, Ptolemy XIII. But then Caesar visited Alexandria and conspired with Cleopatra, who had her brother assassinated and began to rule in her own right. Caesar went on to campaign in Asia Minor and North Africa, but, on his return to Rome in 44 BC, he was murdered by

Republicans. His nephew Gaius Octavius (Octavian) formed a second Triumvirate with General Mark Antony and the statesman Marcus Lepidus. Octavian and Mark Antony defeated the foremost of Caesar's assassins, Brutus and Cassius, at Philippi in Macedonia, but Antony then deserted his wife Octavia (Octavian's sister) to join Cleopatra. At this, Octavian declared war on Egypt, and was victorious at the Battle of Actium, following which Antony and Cleopatra committed suicide.

Palestine, at that juncture, was composed of three distinct provinces: Galilee in the north, Judaea (Judah) in the south, and Samaria between. Julius Caesar had installed Antipater the Idumaean as Procurator of Judaea, with his son Herod as the Governor of Galilee, but Antipater was killed shortly afterwards and Herod was summoned to Rome for appointment as King of Judaea.

This was the harsh environment into which Jesus was born: a climate of oppression controlled by a puppet monarchy and a highly organized military occupational force. The Jews were desperate for a Messiah (an Anointed One, from the Hebrew verb *maisach*: "to anoint") – a forceful liberator to secure their freedom from the Roman overlords.

PART III

A Parallel Dimension

The Hudson Files

Before continuing our chronological sequence of events through the Gospel era and beyond, this is a suitable point at which to consider the fire-stone phenomenon in greater detail. In doing so, we can establish its technological relevance today, and better understand its awesome functions when related to the Ark and the *electrikus* of ancient times.

In old Mesopotamia the exotic white powder of gold and platinum group metals was called *shem-an-na*. In ancient Egypt it was *mfkzt*. Either way it was "highward fire-stone." Today it is recognized as a high-spin, single-atom substance for which the scientifically coined term is ORME (Orbitally Rearranged Monatomic Element). Let us now look at recent and current events in this regard, beginning with the extraordinary story of how *mfkzt* was rediscovered and subsequently developed within the last two decades. It is a story of ingenuity, tenacity, expenditure, and achievement – but a story with a dark twist of governmental intervention.

It all began in 1976 in a place that could not be more aptly named for the Philosophers' Stone discovery. The place was Phoenix, Arizona, where David Hudson was a wealthy, third-generation cotton farmer. His father had been Commissioner of Agriculture for the State, and he was farming around 70,000 acres in the Yuma Valley. David had a 15,000 square-foot home, 40 employees, a $4 million credit line with the bank, and described himself as "Mr. Material Man." Little was he to know that his routine, profit-based existence was soon to be consumed by an arduous alchemical quest that would over-turn every conservative instinct to launch one of the most enterprising pioneers of our age.[1]

A natural difficulty with farming in Arizona is that the soil suffers from a high sodium content, which causes the surface to be crunchy, black, and impenetrable by water. To combat this, David was using tanker-truck loads of highly concen-trated sulfuric acid, injecting some 30 tons per acre into the ground. With irrigation trucks following behind, the acid and water frothed and foamed, breaking down the alkaline crust to a manageable consistency, which (with added calcium carbonate to buffer the acid and preserve the trace nutrients) formed a two-year program towards making the soil suitable for crops.

In the course of analyzing soil constituents that were not dissolved by the acid, one particular material had a most unusual quality. When heat-dried in the Arizona sun (about 115° centigrade at 5% humidity) after precipitation, it would flare into a great blaze of white light and totally disappear. Dried more slowly out of sunlight, the substance was then tested (as in fire assaying) by mixing it in a crucible with lead. The premise is that, when molten, those metals which are lighter than lead float out, while those with a heavier specific gravity do not. In this particular test, the mysterious substance proved to be a dense, weighty metal, which settled (as would gold or silver) to the bottom of the lead. The odd thing was that metals such as gold and silver are soft and can be beaten to the thinnest leaf – but this material was different and when struck with a hammer it shattered like glass! When analyzed at a commercial laboratory, it was said to be iron, silica, and aluminum. But this was clearly not the case; it would not dissolve in sulfuric acid, nitric acid, or hydrochloric acid, whereas iron, silica, and aluminum would have been annihilated by such procedures.

The next step was to hire a Ph.D. at Cornell University, who was an expert in precious elements. He explained that Cornell had a machine which could analyze down to 3–5 parts per billion. So the mysterious substance (known to be a precious element) was subjected to the prized technology and once again the result revealed that it was iron, silica, and aluminum! It transpired that there were some small impurities affecting the analysis, so these were fully removed, still leaving 98% of the original sample, which was tested again. The result was staggering. The glowing white bead was there for all to see, but the equipment registered it as "pure nothing!"

An expert spectroscopist was then brought into the picture. Trained in West Germany at the Institute for Spectroscopy, he had been the senior technician for a company in Los Angeles which manufactured spectroscopic equipment. He designed the spectroscopes, blueprinted them, constructed them, tested them, and used them. He surely had to be the man for the job.

Arc Emission Spectroscopy involves placing a sample in a carbon electrode cup and another electrode is brought down above it to strike an arc. As the current flows, the elements in the sample ionize, giving off their individually specific light frequencies, which are then read to determine the analysis. After about 15 seconds at 5,500° centigrade, the carbon electrode burns away, so laboratories have to limit their tests to this burn time. The problem is that the analysis identifies elements in order of their boiling temperatures – taking the lowest reading first. Limited arcing exposure therefore gives a limited result.

By virtue of the burn-time limitation, the spectroscopist was unable to help with his standard equipment. Plainly, 15 seconds was not sufficient to bring the material to its boiling temperature, not even at sun-surface heat. A sample was then sent to England's Harwell Laboratories of AEA Technology in Oxfordshire for neutron activation analysis – but even they could not obtain a suitable reading.[2] However, the Soviet Academy of Sciences had the answer.[3] For satisfactory results, they explained, a spectroscopic arcing burn-time of 300 seconds was necessary (20 times longer than was possible anywhere in the West). To achieve this, the process is sheathed in an inert gas, such as helium or argon; this excludes oxygen from the carbon electrode and prevents it from burning away. There was nothing for it but to obtain the details and build the necessary equipment to Russian specifications. Then, using an original raw sample, the tests were done again.

As expected, during the first 15 seconds it read: iron, silica, and aluminum, with small traces of calcium, sodium, and a little titanium. With these items now boiled away, all readings stopped and, just as had happened at Cornell, the main 98% sample registered as absolutely nothing; 20 seconds went by, 25, 30, 35, 40 – and all the way to 70 seconds: still nothing. Then, suddenly, the substance became real again, registering as palladium; after another 20 seconds, it recorded platinum – and after that (as each of the successive boiling temperatures was reached) came ruthenium, rhodium, iridium, and osmium at 220 seconds.[4] It transpired that the tiny white bead was composed entirely of platinum group elements which, by standard Western testing, had previously registered as nothing.

With Siegfried, the German spectroscopist, still in charge, the tests (with numerous analytical variations) were continued and repeated over the course of two and a half years, and there was no doubt that around 98% of the hitherto unidentifiable product consisted of noble metals in a state not normally recognizable. The richest known platinum group deposits in the world are half a mile underground at the Bushveld Igneous Complex in South Africa,[5] where a narrow seam contains one-third of an ounce per ton of platinum metals. It was discovered that (in a not obviously metallic form) the Phoenix farm soil contained 7,500 times this amount, at an astonishing 2,400 ounces per ton!

Up to this stage, the research had remained a quiet and relatively private affair – but it was clear that the eyes and ears of officialdom would soon be pointed in its direction. In the world market, platinum group metals were selling for unusually high prices, with rhodium (the majority constituent of the farm deposit) selling at about $3,000 per ounce. Clearly, something very important was emerging from Arizona, and not even David Hudson had any idea where eventually it would lead.

Defying Gravity

A new participant then came onto the scene – a Ph.D. in metal separation systems from the US Department of Energy's metalurgical school at Iowa State University. He was a consultant for Motorola and Sperry, and had worked with rare earths and the majority of elements on the Periodic Table. After collecting his own ground samples and working on the project for three years, he finally announced that the substance was indeed registering the precious metal elements in a form completely unknown to science. He further confirmed the same ounces-per-ton as revealed by the earlier Russian spectroscopic analysis.

From 1983 until 1989, the research continued, with a Ph.D. chemist, three master chemists and two technicians working full time. With assistance from the Soviet Academy of Sciences, and with the US Bureau of Standards Weights and Measures information as a starting base, they learned how to make qualitative and quantitative separations of each of the enigmatic elements. They bought pure precious metals (gold, rhodium, osmium, iridium, and ruthenium) from Johnson

Matthey, studied cluster chemistry and, with the most sophisticated computer-controlled equipment from Dow Chemical,
ascertained how to break all the elemental bonding.

David Hudson then learned that scientists at General Electric were researching a new fuel-cell technology using
rhodium and iridium. So he made contact with them and went
to meet their senior catalytic chemist and the team in Massachusetts. They confirmed that they too had experienced the
white-light explosions and that they were having problems
with a material derived from rhodium tri-chloride, which
simply would not react to analysis. They asked for comparison samples from the Phoenix research, and established that
they did not have to manufacture their fuel-cell requirement
from purchased rhodium and iridium after all; they could
obtain it in a ready monatomic form. A tentative deal was
agreed between the parties, with the GE men subsequently
establishing a separate company to manufacture the cells in
Waltham, MA. Meanwhile, David Hudson was advised to
patent his discoveries – so in 1987 and 1988 he filed US and
worldwide patents (22 in all) for the newly designated
Orbitally Rearranged Monatomic Elements (ORMEs).[6]

To comply with patent requirement, further research tests
were necessary to provide specific data relating to weights
and measures. A machine for thermo-gravimetric analysis was
acquired to facilitate absolute atmospheric control of the
samples, while continually weighing them during the process.
The substance was heated at $1.2°$ C per minute, and cooled at
$2°$ C per minute. They found that when the material was
oxidized, it rose to 102% of its starting weight, and when
hydrogen-reduced it weighed 103%. But the great surprise
came when the substance changed from its original dullness to
the familiar whiteness of its bright bead and subsequent
powder. At that moment the sample's weight fell dramatically
to 56% of its starting weight. Where on earth, they wondered,
did the other 44% go? Further heating at $1160°$ C in a vacuum

then transformed the precious substance into a wonderfully clear glass, at which point the material weight returned to its original 100%. It was seemingly impossible, but it happened time and time again!

Totally bewildered, the scientists continued their investigations. When repeatedly heated and cooled under inert gasses, the cooling processes took the sample to an amazing 400% of its starting weight. But when heated again it weighed less than nothing – way below zero. When removed from its pan, the pan actually weighed more than it did with the material in it, and it was perceived that the white sample had the ability to transfer its weightlessness to its supporting host. Even the pan was levitating!

The manufacturers of the equipment were consulted, and their checks confirmed that the machinery was fully efficient with every substance they tested. The sole exception to any rule was the white Phoenix powder. It always fell to 56% of its original weight, and would then rise to 300–400% on cooling – or to way below zero when reheated. On consulting technicians at the Varian Corporation in California,[7] they confided that, if the weight loss were to occur on cooling, they figured the white powder was superconducting but, they said, "Inasmuch as you are heating the material, we don't know what you've got, or what's going on here." However, they were plainly unaware that high-temperature superconductors had been discovered in 1986 at the IBM Research Laboratory in Zurich.[8] Prior to this it was thought that they were only stable at extremely low temperatures achieved with the use of liquid helium.

With a voltmeter and live electrodes touched to the ends of a white powder sample, its electrical conductivity was checked, only to reveal that there was no conductivity whatever; it might just as well have been a heap of talcum. A superconductor works quite differently to a conductor in that it does not allow any voltage potential or any magnetic field to exist within itself; it is a perfect insulator when superconduct-

ing, but it is remarkably sensitive to magnetic fields of infinitely minute proportions and will respond to incalculably
small magnetic forces (amounting to just about nothing).

Superconductors

It seems that flowing within a superconductor there is a
single-frequency light, which flows (like liquid light) at the
slower-than-light speed of sound. It has a null magnetic field,
which repels North and South magnetic poles alike, but has
the capability to absorb high magnetic energy to produce even
more light. In fact, the Earth's magnetic field can give sufficient energy to a superconductor for it to levitate – and that
was precisely what happened to the ostensibly missing 44%
weight; the material was beginning to levitate, and therefore
was not registering properly on the scales. When the weight
registered as zero or less, the superconducting material was in
a full state of levitation. Also, the sample was a light-produc-
ing light reflector, which is what made it a brilliant white.
When the light flows within a superconductor it produces
around it a field which excludes all external magnetic fields.
Named after the German physicist Walter Meissner, who
published the discovery in 1933, it is called the Meissner Field,
and it is this which excludes all external magnetic fields from
the sample. Magnets, by virtue of being repelled, will actually
levitate above a superconductor.

A superconductor does not conduct by way of standard
conductivity, but by way of the frequency of its inherent light.
When external electrons are tuned to that same frequency, it
will conduct them. When two superconductors are linked by
their Meissner Fields, over any distance, the two can act as one
in a process called "quantum coherence." Electricity (in
contrast) has to flow through physical contacts. Even light
itself can be transmitted between superconductors. The interesting thing about light is that, like most perceived reality, it

does not exist within any particular realm of space. Light can be seen to fill a space – but more and more (in fact, limitless) light can be added to that same space, making it brighter and brighter. By this same means, any amount of energy can be stored in a superconductor, and transferred over any distance on a quantum wave which knows no boundaries of space or time. As stated by David Hudson in one of his related lectures: "You literally start the superconductor flowing by applying a magnetic field. It responds to this by flowing light inside and building a bigger Meissner Field around it. You can put your magnet down and walk away. Come back a hundred years later and it is still flowing exactly as when you left. It will never slow down. There is absolutely no resistance; it is perpetual motion and will run for ever."

Just as the ex-General Electric scientists had deduced, a monatomic (single atomized) superconductor could enable the perfect environmentally friendly fuel-cell, and Hudson struck his deal to supply their newly established independent company, Giner Inc.,[9] with the ready material. It is not difficult to imagine that trouble would ensue once this news became more widely known. Superconducting fuel-cells might be the perfect alternative to pollution from combustion engines on the ground, on sea, and in the air. It is something that we would all welcome, and has to be the solution for the future. But, in the short term, what would become of the mighty oil industry which underpins the world economy? It would, of course, collapse, and there are too many powerful vested interests to allow that to happen in a hurry. In 1989, at a high point of excitement and enthusiasm, David Hudson made plans to build an extensive plant for the ORMEs enterprise. But at the same time, moves were afoot in the corridors of industrial power to thwart his interests, along with the environmental and health interests of us all.

It was at that stage that a mysterious sponsor made contact. Posing as an enterprising benefactor who wished to support the project financially, he detailed certain aspects of the research that no one outside the immediate team (each of whom had signed a confidentiality agreement) could possibly have known. No one that was, except the US Department of Defense. When filing his patents, Hudson had been obliged to supply information to the Department because they said his technology concerning superconductivity was "of strategic importance to this country." Hudson employed a private detective, who discovered the man to be a military official operating out of Langley Air Force Base, Virginia. Further investigation revealed that he was employed to invest government money from a designated Swiss bank account so that the Department of Defense could become a strategically secret partner in select ventures. Needless to say, Hudson declined the offer, but was then advised that he would never be allowed to complete his enterprise in matters of superconductivity!

Stealth Atoms and Space-time

To this point, with the assistance of a Canadian placement company, the $2.5 million necessary to begin the Arizona plant was scheduled for provision by the Legal & General Assurance Group. The matter had not been in doubt, and their precious metals consultant had spent 10 days evaluating the reports in Phoenix and at General Electric. But suddenly the picture changed. L & G now required far more research information, including that which was protected by the team's confidentiality agreements. At the same time, David was informed from government sources that the neutron diffraction studies (required to prove the superconductivity of his samples) would be tactically delayed for up to three years! From that moment it was clear that his patents would be affected, and that he would have to continue funding the project himself, particularly since otherwise he could not be sure whether incoming investors were government operatives seeking to access confidential research information. Additionally, it became obvious that the way to protect the time frame of his patents was to publish openly certain information and to give a series of recorded lectures.

Earlier we touched briefly on the involvement of Hal Puthoff, Director of the Institute for Advanced Studies in Austin, Texas[10] (see "Beyond Zero," page 130). We can now widen the story, since it was after this stage of development that he met with David Hudson. In his studies of zero-point energy and gravity as a zero-point fluctuation force,[11] Puthoff had determined that when matter begins to react in two dimensions (as Hudson's samples were doing), it should theoretically lose around four-ninths of its gravitational weight. That is about 44%, precisely as discovered in the white powder experiments. Hudson was therefore able to confirm Puthoff's theory in practice, explaining that when entering a superconductive state the monatomic powder registers only 56% of its previous weight; also that when heated it can achieve a gravitational attraction of less than zero – at which point the weighing pan also weighs less than it did when empty. Since gravity determines space-time, Puthoff concluded that the powder was "exotic matter" and was capable of bending space-time. However, he continued, the mfkzt powder would then be resonating in a different dimension, under which circumstance it should become totally invisible. Again, Hudson confirmed that this was precisely the case; the sample certainly did vanish from sight when its weight disappeared.

What was being said here was not simply that the substance could be moved out of perceptual vision, but that it was literally transported into an alternative parallel plane – a fifth dimension of space-time. The proof of this was ascertained by attempting to disturb and scoop the substance with spatulas while it was invisible, so that it would be positioned differently when it returned to a visible state. But this did not happen and the substance returned to precisely the same position and shape that it was last seen. Nothing was moved or disturbed in the invisible interim, simply because it was not there. In short, it was not invisible: it had actually altered its physical state and had transposed into another dimension. Puthoff explained that it was like the difference between a conventional Stealth aircraft, which cannot be detected by radar, as against one which can literally disappear into another dimension. This, then, is the superconductive dimension of the Orbit of Light – the *Plane of Shar-On*, or, as the Egyptian tomb records called it, the *Field of Mfkzt*.

In the early 1990s, seemingly from out of nowhere, articles concerning "stealth atoms" and superconductivity began to appear with great regularity in the Science press.[12] The Niels Bohr Institute, University of Copenhagen,[13] the USA Department of Energy's Argonne National Laboratories, Chicago,[14] and their Oak Ridge National Laboratory in Tennessee[15] all confirmed that the elements which had been filed in the Hudson patents existed in the monatomic high-spin state. The scientific terminology to describe the phenomenon is Asymmetrical Deformed High-spin Nuclei. They are superconductors because high-spin atoms can pass energy from one to the next with no net loss of energy.

Manipulation of space-time also became a subject of special interest, leading to an astonishing May 1994 announcement in the journal *Classical and Quantum Gravity*. Written by the Mexican mathematical scientist Miguel Alcubierre, it stated: "It is now known that it is possible to modify space-time in a way that allows a spaceship to travel at an arbitrarily large speed by a purely local expansion of the space-time behind the spaceship and an opposite contraction in front of it – a motion faster than the speed of light, reminiscent of the warp drive of science fiction."[16]

This was followed a few months later by a related article in the *American Scientist*. In this study, Michael Szpir showed how Alcubierre's concept did not violate Einstein's theory that no object can travel faster than light. He explained that, when in warp mode, the craft would not actually be traveling at all. The theoretical acceleration would be enormous, but the true rate of acceleration would be zero.[17] Here was a form of speed-of-light travel that required minimum time and minimum fuel. Only the necessary chunk of space-time would ostensibly have moved from in front of the craft to be relocated behind it by means of contraction and expansion respectively. But what was the necessary device to make this possible? The Alcubierre article explained that: "exotic matter will be needed to generate a distortion of space-time." Britain's BBC News science editor, Dr. David Whitehouse, subsequently reported that "the idea relies on the concept that, to physicists, space is not empty ... Space has a shape that can be distorted by matter ... The starship would rest in a warp bubble between the two space-time distortions."

So, what is the "exotic matter" to which Alcubierre referred? It is matter which has a gravitational attraction of less than zero. Szpir described it as "matter with the curious property of having a negative energy density, unlike normal matter (the stuff that makes up people, the planets and the stars), which has a positive energy." The necessary exotic device is an operative superconductor, and Hal Puthoff had already explained that, in this regard, the Phoenix *mfkzt* was "exotic matter" with the ability to bend space-time. No wonder the eyes of governmental officialdom were set towards David Hudson and his arrangement to supply the fuel-cell scientists. If they were not able to gain a controlling interest through investment, they were determined by one route or another to curtail or topple his private enterprise.

In addition to Hudson's patents concerning PGMs in general, were his patents concerning the amazing phenomenon of high-spin gold. Since the standard US spectroscopy tests were not sufficient to determine the metal from its monatomic state, Argonne National Laboratories had been asked to prove the procedure by making the white powder from a starting base of pure yellow-gold metal. (A signed affidavit was required by the Patent Office.) For this purpose, the head of ceramics and superconductivity at Argonne passed David to a metallurgical chemist who, in accordance with the Hudson specification, produced the high-spin snow-white powder from pure gold. When analyzing the resultant material, however, his equipment registered it as iron, silica, and aluminum, just as he had been warned it would! When signing the required affidavit, the chemist made specific mention of the fact that (despite any further tests that might be conducted), he positively guaranteed the material to be 100% gold since it was transposed from pure gold in his own laboratory.

Subsequent to this, Hudson was then asked to reverse the process fully by turning the powder back into a piece of metal-lic gold. It was like asking someone to remake an apple from a pan of apple sauce – seemingly impossible! Early trials led to some disastrous results, with expensive electrodes burning away in less than a second. Even worse, short wavelength gamma radiation was produced, which fragmented the labora-tory equipment. By late 1995, the difficulties had been over-come and the figurative apple had indeed been rebuilt from the apple sauce. From this, there was no doubt that it was possible (just as in ancient metallurgical lore) to manufacture gold from a seemingly non-gold base product. From a commencing sample which registered as iron, silica, and aluminum, emerged an ingot which analyzed as pure gold. After centuries of trial, error, frustration, and failure, the Philosophers' Stone of ancient times had at last been rediscovered.

Judgment Day

From the onset of his research to 1995, David Hudson's personal expenditure for the ORMEs investigations had amounted to some $8.7 million, and now the processing plant had to be built. ORMES L.L.C. was established as the company to develop the project, with regular *Newsletter* updates on progress issued by the affiliated Science of the Spirit Foundation to a subscribing membership.[18]

With a suitable site acquired, and the necessary constructional permissions duly obtained, the building and fitting work began. In the interim, with the $2.5 million building requirement raised from Science of the Spirit Foundation membership subscriptions,[19] all was progressing well at the plant. Interest in the products had widened and, in November 1996, it was announced that ORMES L.L.C. interests would be expanding into metal catalysts, metalo-ceramics, and the supply of precious metals for commercial application.[20]

The first major problem arose when they were ready to finalize the plant's electric power installation. The County inspector announced that, although formal approval for electrical supply had been granted, there was a "zoning" problem which would take many months to resolve. Again it was apparently a matter of classification, and a notice was received, stating: "No one is doing anything similar to what this plant will be doing, and it will not fit into any of the Government categories."[21] Undaunted, and not willing to be pressured into calling his products "drugs," "fuels," or whatever, Hudson decided to wait out the months before grid connection by using an independently installed generator. Unfortunately, the inevitable accident occurred soon afterwards in June 1998 when 4,500 gallons of nitric acid leaked into a secondary containment facility. When the emergency services team arrived, they sprayed foam onto the acid instead of simply diluting it with water, as a result of which a red gas cloud lit up the sky. The moment of reckoning had arrived – and so did the men from the Department of Environmental Quality (DEQ). Hot on their heels were others from the Occupational Safety and Health

Administration (OSHA) and the Environmental Protection Agency (EPA).

Despite the fact that the spillage was internal, contained, and no toxic residue was determined by the subsequent DEQ tests, the EPA demanded that all chemical equipment was to be disassembled and removed immediately from the plant. Over and above this, a punitive six-figure fine was imposed. David Hudson, who had been through a period of ill health in the previous year, was then hospitalized for major bypass surgery after a heart attack. In the course of this, and irrespective of his building regulation approvals, planning permissions were granted for a number of residential homes in close proximity to the ORMEs plant. Ten years before, when encountering early difficulties with the Department of Defense, Hudson had been advised that he would never be allowed to complete his enterprise in matters of superconductivity (see "Superconductors," page 178), and this was clearly the moment of final judgment. There was now no way that the site could become operative and, although legalities were thrashed to and fro over many months, David was finally obliged to write, in November 2000, that he had been "regulated out of existence."

It was the tragic end of a great pioneering era – but the science remains. The problem is that it is now being pursued by those with far less socially motivated interests. It is now destined to become a science for the big league players at government departmental and corporate levels. Consequently, the stakes are high and the precious metals markets have moved on to a new platform of strategic operation. As oil begins its downward slide to become the fuel of yesteryear, the future masters of the globe will be those who control the gold and PGM supplies. These are the materials of future industry in a world of superconductor technology – an anti-gravity realm of levitation, teleportation, parallel dimensions, and space-time manipulation. But, let it not be forgot in the annals of time, that it all began with one man's enthusiastic tenacity and a family farm in Phoenix, Arizona. (*See* Appendix V: "Towards the Vanishing Point", for additional information concerning ORMEs and cancer research.)

The Quantum Protocol

Transition Elements

As we progress towards completing our journey with the Ark of the Covenant, we shall be looking not just at matters of electronic arcing and ORMEs transmutation, but at such things as superconductors and parallel dimensions.

Despite the fact that the Old Testament does not specifically mention that the *manna* powder was placed in the Ark, the tradition has prevailed by virtue of the New Testament reference in Hebrews 9:4. This tells of "the ark of the covenant overlaid round about with gold, wherein was the golden pot that had the manna." What becomes apparent from this (given the superconductive attributes of the ORME powder) is that the Ark would itself have been a powerfully generative superconductor. Consequently, there is no reason to doubt any of the biblical statements concerning the Ark's ability to levitate and emit violently destructive forces, whether as straightforward light beams or as harmful rays.

Central to the Periodic Table is a group of elements known as the Transition elements. They include silver and the light platinum group: palladium, rhodium, and ruthenium, along with gold and the heavy platinum group: platinum, iridium, and osmium. Also included are the non-precious elements, copper, cobalt, and nickel. It is the Transition Elements which are capable of transmuting to the monatomic state of the high-ward fire-stone.

The monatomic state occurs when the time-forward and time-reverse electrons correlate around the nucleus of a substance so that its individual atoms cannot bind together as a solid (*see* "The Plane of Shar-On," page 120). Instead, it becomes a powder of single atoms.

Within the body of an atom, electrons travel around the nucleus inside and outside a screening potential. In essence, they are maintained within inner and outer shells. Elements with fewer electrons in the outer shells than in their inner shells tend to be electropositive, while those with fewer in the inner shells tend to be electronegative. What makes the Transition elements different from the norm is that they have a unique uncertainty in their electron status. Under specific conditions the electrons in the outer orbitals can interface with those in the inner orbitals.

In the majority of elements, atoms cluster together in groups of two or more, but the atoms of Transition elements are not able to bind chemically since they are too far apart.[1] This encourages the monatomic state in which the atoms interact in two dimensions. Only when the repulsive force is overcome can the atoms aggregate to become metal.

In their monatomic condition the atoms of the Transition elements lose their chemical reactivity, changing the configuration and shape of their nuclei. Nuclei are not round; they normally have a shape ratio of 1.3:1. However, the nucleus of a monatomic atom elongates from this to a 2:1 ratio (twice as long as it is wide), or beyond this to a cigar shape which is called "superdeformed." This superdeformation is directly related to the "spin state," when moving from low-spin to high-spin. Back in the 1960s it was discovered by magnetic field researchers that high-spin atoms were capable of passing energy from one to another with no net energy loss. This is "superconductivity." All that is needed to set the energy flow in motion is the application of an external magnetic field.

David Pines, study professor of physics at the University of Illinois Center for Advanced Study has stated that "Superconductivity is perhaps the most remarkable physical property in the universe." Similarly, nuclear physicist Dr. Daniel Sewell Ward explains that "Superconductivity is infinitely more than a physics phenomenon of the first order. It may be one of the fundamental linking mechanisms in an unlimited and connected universe."

Levitation and Teleportation

Within the world of superconductors there are two main types. A perfect superconductor with a single vibrational phase that repels all magnetic invasion is called Type-1. These include monatomic gold and platinum group elements. Type-2 superconductors (metallic compounds including copper, lead, niobium, and niobium-titanium) have a mixed state behavior, which affords some external magnetic penetration.

Type-1 superconductors function perfectly because their forward and reverse spin electrons pair up as mirror images without destroying each other. They become single frequency photons – no longer particles, but light-bearing waves. These waves are the key to the quantum protocol because, in essence, the photons represent the Quanta – quantities of energy proportional to the frequency of the radiation they represent (from the Latin *quantus*: "how much"). These mirrored photons, which flow on the quantal wave of a superconductor are called Cooper Pairs[2] and they create a Meissner Field – a unique magnetic field with no North or South polarity. When activated, this resists all other magnetic fields, so that the superconductor becomes diamagnetic – a state in which it repels, and is repelled by, strong magnetic fields. This offers immediate levitational possibilities.[3]

In discussing mirror electrons in a state whereby they will destroy each other, Professor Stephen Hawking refers to the duplicate electron as an "antielectron" which can annihilate. To demonstrate the annihilation, he states "If you meet with your antiself, do not shake hands; you would both vanish in a great flash of light!"[4] This, of course, is precisely what David Hudson and the General Electric team discovered in their research tests. However, neither Hawking, Hudson, nor anyone else has described such electron particle annihilation in a form that demolishes, leaving residue – simply that a vanishing act is performed, whereby the substance concerned disappears. As pointed out by Hal Puthoff, this is not a state of invisibility, but of transportation into another dimension of space-time (*see* "Stealth Atoms and Space-time," pages 180–1).

A good working example of magnetic levitation is provided by the Maglev train, one of which was commercially operated in Birmingham, England as an experimental shuttle in the 1990s. Such trains literally float by way of strong superconductive magnetism, thereby eliminating friction between the vehicles and their tracks. The prototype was tested in 1990 in Japan, followed by the nationally funded Yamanashi Maglev Test Line, which opened on 3 April 1997. Two years later[5] the MLX01 vehicle attained a fully levitated speed of 343 miles per hour. The United States Government has now earmarked nearly a billion dollars for Maglev improvement, and Germany's commercial Maglev train service is scheduled for 2006.

Once magnetically triggered, the Meissner Field of a Type-1 superconductor will continue to function ad infinitum. Also, when two Meissner Fields touch, the quantal wave between them is similarly perpetual. A superconductive trigger can be minuscule in potential (a twinkling star for example), and ultimately a continuous energy can be obtained from the vacuum of the universal zero-point.

In short, a superconductor is a substance that can transport electron energy with no resistance and no dissipation of that energy. Without any physical contact, superconductors will conduct energy (such as light and electricity) over any distance for any length of time. They could also be the key to the distance teleportation of physical matter – even the teleportation of life forms. The following is extracted from a USA Department of Energy statement, via their Newton Bulletin Board System Division at Argonne National Laboratory: "The technique is to prepare a pair of coupled quantum systems." Explaining that one of these would be placed somewhere far away, it continues: "It is then possible to make a measurement of the local system, transmit the result of the local measurement and reconstitute a new quantum on the other side … People can (by this means) in principle be transported by sending enough classical information."[6]

NASA and Argonne Laboratory scientists confirm that it will also be possible to duplicate matter instead of transporting it, since the bizarre rules of light and matter are determined on atomic scales. In this realm, the NASA Office of Biological and Physical Research confirms that "Matter can be in two places at once. Objects can be particles and waves at the same time." In quantum mechanics nothing is certain, only probable or improbable. The improbable feat of "stopping" light has now been accomplished by two teams – one led by Ron Walsworth, a physicist at the Harvard-Smithsonian Center for Astrophysics, and the other by Lene Hau of Harvard University's Department of Physics. Not only can light be stopped in its tracks, stored, and released again at will, but its immense speed (the speed of light) can currently be controlled down below the speed of a bicycle. The possibilities are mind-boggling and even textual information (encoded in atoms) could be conveyed on a light wave.[7]

Quantum entanglement allows two particles to behave as one, no matter how far apart they are. Sougato Bose of Oxford University and Dipanker Home of the Bose Institute, Calcutta, have demonstrated a single mechanism that could be used to entangle atoms or molecules that are light-years apart. Anton

Zielinger, a quantum physicist at the University of Vienna, has shown that this is possible with large molecules.[8] Clouds of trillions of atoms have been linked through quantum entanglement by Eugene Polzik's team at the University of Aarhus in Denmark.[9] This, say NASA scientists, is the stuff of *Star Trek*'s teleportation of matter by way of a light beam, whereby a body's molecular pattern is atomically rearranged and sent to another destination.

Sacred Science

It is important to establish a base-line acceptance of the principles we have discussed since they are outside the scope of generally imparted public information. Only by conceding to the cutting-edge science of superconductors and their phenomenal attributes can we achieve an understanding of what finally happened to the Ark of the Covenant.

Eminent modern scientists have not only confirmed the existence of parallel dimensions, teleportation, and the like, but have also expressed their particular concern that the public are kept in the dark about such matters. To demonstrate the dilemma that faces us in this regard, the following extracts are given from a lecture presentation by nuclear physicist Daniel Sewell Ward, Ph.D. to the International Association of New Science Forum in Fort Collins, Colorado, October 1999:

A plethora of evidence suggests that a profoundly important and basic science capable of explaining a vast array of otherwise anomalous observations exists ... Of particular importance are the subjects of sacred science (including mathematics, physics, and health/longevity) and the degree to which such subjects have been withheld from seekers and investigators.

A widely acknowledged truism is that "knowledge is power." Significantly, secret knowledge or teachings held by a limited elite constitute the potential for even greater power. It is apparently for this reason that the world history of the last several thousand years has had embedded in its scope the underlying theme of the struggle for control and power based on esoteric knowledge, understandings and wisdom.

From the mystery schools of ancient Egypt and Greece, to the Jerusalem treasures uncovered by the Knights Templars ... to the modern day guarded secrets of the Trilateral Commission and various other secretive organizations, the greatest heritage of the human race has been carefully and studiously withheld from the mainstream of society. Understandings and techniques which afforded the potential for enormous enlightenment and evolution of the individual have been historically held for the exclusive use of those in power ... The fact that there have been many forces (particularly religions) which have made every effort to attack truth as a means of preserving their own view of the universe is perhaps the primary case in point. Curiously, the quest for the outright destruction (as in the case of the burning of the Library of Alexandria) or the placing of severe limitations on the dissemination of knowledge is also based on control and power issues. Within the confines of this world-class power struggle, much esoteric wisdom and knowledge has been kept from public view both as a means of protecting the underlying truths as well as using them (or eliminating them) in order to profit thereby.

Suddenly (in historical terms) Pandora's box has been overturned and individuals outside the elite groups ... have begun to glimpse, study, and understand the heretofore secrets of esoteric knowledge. And with the dissemination of such understanding into the mainstream, the control of one human over another is being lessened ... For the individual seeker of truth and enlightenment, suddenly the history of conspiracy to deny the existence of such wisdom becomes less important than the understandings of how one applies these fundamental teachings.

Clearly, much of what is known today derives from the normally open process of learning and discovery down through the ages. Historically, we have the dissemination of knowledge via apprenticeship, where the holder of the knowledge (the master) shares his understanding with someone (the apprentice) who has earned the rights to such knowledge through the demonstration of his or her worthiness … Schools have also existed to disseminate wisdom and knowledge, with such schools ranging in size from carefully limited mystery schools, to schools for the greater elite, to public education …

The Sumerian civilization constitutes the earliest record of human endeavor which is amply supported by physical evidence in the form of writings and artifacts. Particularly striking is the apparent fact that civilization blossomed in the Tigris–Euphrates valley with all manner of new and heretofore absent innovations and aspects of civilization. Suddenly there was writing, animal husbandry, irrigation for farming, temples for worship, and so forth …

It seems clear, for example, that Moses, as a Prince of Egypt, was amply instructed in the ancient mysteries, and shared a portion of his education with the Israelites in the form of the Ark of the Covenant. The Templars came into existence during the Crusades at the turn of the last millennium, and it was they who apparently discovered a wealth of information contained in the environs of Jerusalem …

The good news is that such information has become increasingly available … This has been due in large part to the discovery and decipherment of ancient writings. These writings include such things as the Egyptian *Book of the Dead,* the *Dead Sea Scrolls* and the *Nag Hammadi Codices.* In addition, much of the more esoteric wisdom in the form of *ha Qabala,* the Tarot and other books have been handed down through the ages and outside the confines of secret societies. There is additional evidence that much of the information is being purposefully disseminated, as if a decision has been made to bring a much larger segment of the population into the fold of understanding ... Truth has a way of inevitably rising to the surface ...

A key question is whether or not the proliferation of our under-standing of sacred geometry and mathematics is the result of accidental discovery or intentional dissemination of informa-tion. On the one hand, geometry and numbers are imminently discoverable, due in part to the simplicity of the logical process employed. All one really need do is ask the right question, and the mathematics fairly rushes to show itself ... But is there more of which we are unaware? Is the current trend in state-of-the-art physics into zero-point energies and multiple dimensions beyond our four-dimensional space-time continuum a foray into heretofore secret knowledge, or merely the advance of knowl-edge into the reality of the universe?

In the final analysis, there do appear to be many questions begging for answers, and that eager and enthusiastic attempts will be rewarded ... In this view, it's no longer a question of whether or not someone is worthy of knowing the secrets, but rather an encouragement to go out and discover the wonders of the universe for one's self. In effect, there's still room at the top of the learning curve for anyone interested in pursuing the matter.

Return to Dendera

In the light of this insightful perspective, it occurred to me that I should seek Dr. Daniel's opinion concerning the mysterious Hathor-related petroglyphs at Dendera. These are the strange bulbous objects adorning temple walls, which we considered earlier (*see* "Gold of the Gods," pages 106–11). Here was a qualified physicist in the vanguard of modern science, who also has an aptitude for ancient history. He pointed out that

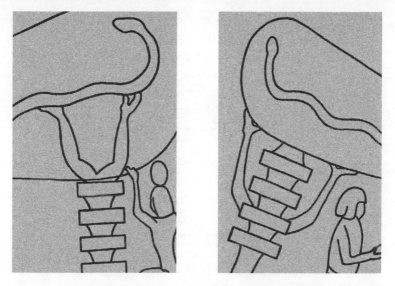

Djed arms at Dendera. Inside and outside the fields.

there were certain important differences between the individual temple reliefs. For example, whereas some of the images show arms seemingly supporting the ampoules from beneath, there are also versions where the *djed* pillar arms extend into the confines of the bubbles where the serpents are suspended. This suggests that the bubbles/tubes/ampoules are not physical objects at all, but representative of a significant area or aura within – rather like the speech bubbles in cartoons, where the spoken words are the relevant factor, not the bubble outlines.

The *djed* arms closer to the serpents are more muscular than the arms of other *djeds* or characters which touch only the perimeters. Where the *djed* hands extend within, the serpents have five or six waves, but when limited to the outer confines, the serpents have fewer waves. This might suggest a defined process of invigoration taking place within the confines.

Another feature of these portrayals is the presence of the falcon of Horus in some of the reliefs. The Horus effect is an important factor of the *mfkzt* (white powder) scenario, and the "golden tear" from the eye of Horus was directly associated with its godly attributes. In the *Papyrus of Ani Pyramid Text*, the pharaoh in search of enlightenment in the *Field of Mfkzt* (*see* "Field of the Blessed," pages 8–10), states: "I am purified of all imperfections. What is it? [*Manna?*] I ascend like the golden hawk of Horus. What is it? I come by the immortals without dying. What is it? I come before my father's throne. What is it?"

According to the related inscriptions at Dendera, the priestly character in charge of the ritual is identified as being Ka, a type of physical soul – the same as the pharaonic "light body," called the *Ka*, that was fed with the regenerative *mfkzt* of enlightenment. Moreover, the tubular shapes all extend, like encapsulated ether from the stems and sepals of lotus plants, while the inscriptions identify the serpents as Harsomtus, the divine child of Horus and Hathor. Lotus flower shapes were also predominant among the vessels discovered at the Horeb temple in Sinai, and the rim of King Solomon's great bronze container was also fashioned like an open lotus flower (*see* "The Fire-stone Project," pages 147–50). From the oldest of recorded Sumerian times, the lotus (lily) was representative of the "divine essence:" the nectar of supreme excellence called (just as was Hathor) the Gold of the Gods.[10]

All of this discussion took place after my initial question. What my physicist colleague actually said, before getting into any such detail, was that the bulbous extrusions looked very much like representations of "flux tubes" – that is to say, superconductive Meissner Fields. When two Meissner Fields touch (*see* "Levitation and Teleportation," page 190), they produce a perpetual quantal wave, and in every instance of the Dendera reliefs, the pairs of fields (with their inherent serpent waves) are just about touching. It could therefore be the case that the portrayals demonstrate the preparatory set-up for Hathor's flux-tube gateway to the hyper-dimensional *Field of Mfkzt*.

Rite of Passage

When endeavoring to comprehend some of the mind-blowing science encountered in pursuing this book's quest, I was advised by an astrophysicist not to try and understand it. "You don't even have to believe it," he said, "because it is not about belief. You simply have to recognize that, beyond the bounds of any conventional belief or understanding, it is quite simply here. It is science and it exists." To cite Professor Stephen Hawking: "Only a few people can keep up with the rapidly advancing frontier of knowledge, and they have to devote their whole time to it and specialize in a small area. The rest of the population has little idea of the advances that are being made or the excitement they are generating."[11]

With these thoughts in mind, it occurred to me that if these phenomena are here now, then they must always have existed. The only difference is that, as with all things that suddenly resolve into the light of day, we have simply rediscovered some of the modes of operation and have dubbed them with new scientific names. If there is superconductivity now, then there was superconductivity in medieval times. Moreover, there was superconductivity in the days of Moses and back in the days beyond – but instead of Argonne National Laboratories, Cornell University, and the Institute of Advanced Studies there were the Temples of Karnak, Horeb, and Dendera. As naturally occurring phenomena, there were also magnetic waves and Meissner Fields in those days. The people of the era perhaps knew nothing about the mechanics of these in the way that our modern scientists comprehend them, but operationally they certainly knew enough of their existence to describe the *Field of Mfkzt* and its rite of passage.

It came to mind so often in the early stages of this work that my studies in the fantastic world of quantum physics kept presenting revelations that seemed to require enormous leaps of faith. However, I soon discovered that only by taking those leaps could the next stages and their own resultant leaps be encountered. This appears to be precisely what the world of quantum theory is all about. It is why (despite all its positive and proven discoveries) it is still classified as "theory," because there is always another hurdle beyond and so the ultimate problem is never solved. It did not take long to recognize that even the perceived leaps of faith were just illusions. There were actually no leaps to be made, and it had nothing whatever to do with faith. The quantum comfort zone is encountered the moment one removes the blinkers of conditioned restraint. From that moment everything flows naturally on a quantum wave so that the instinctive response to each new revelation is intuitive acceptance. As the physicist said, "It is science, and it is here" – and as was attributed to the wisdom of King Solomon in the Bible's Old Testament:

> The thing that hath been, it is that which shall be.
> And that which is done is that which shall be done.
> And there is no new thing under the sun.
> *Ecclesiastes 1:9*

13

Fire in the Desert

Enigma of the Grail

We have seen how the Philosophers' Stone was featured in the Holy Grail legends of the Middle Ages (*see* "Sacred Manna," pages 24–8), and of how it was linked to the alchemical mythology of the Phoenix which rises from the ashes of enlightenment. Matters such as these have long puzzled those who attempt to view the Grail tradition as a Christian prerogative, since the Phoenix and Philosophers' Stone are often perceived as matters of the occult. There is in fact a strange enigma here because, even though the Grail is generally considered to be a Christian relic, the Church actually proclaimed Grail lore an unofficial heresy at the Council of Trento (Northern Italy) in 1547. It was at this same Council that the choice of books for the approved New Testament was finally ratified from an original selection made long before at the Council of Carthage in AD 397.

When we looked at the *Gra-al* legacy of old Mesopotamia (*see* "Realm of the Genies," page 124), it was apparent that the Chalice and Bread symbolism was part of Semitic culture in the days of Abraham and Melchizedek (as featured in Genesis 14:18) from around 1960 BC. The greatest anomaly is that the Church should set its official sights against the Grail while usurping the most pertinent symbol of the heritage as its own.

The sacrament of the Eucharist (or Holy Communion) is blatant in its use of the chalice of wine, representing the Messianic blood, along with wafers of bread representing the body. Apologists for this custom cling to the notion that it stems from the Last Supper incident when Jesus offered the wine and bread to his Apostles,[1] without considering that he was himself performing an age-old rite.

As evidenced in the *Community Rule*, one of the Dead Sea Scrolls, the Last Supper corresponds to the Messianic Banquet held at Qumrân. The primary hosts of the banquet were the High Priest and the Messiah of Israel[2] – that is to say, the prevailing Messiah (Anointed One), not necessarily Jesus in particular. According to the scroll, the Nazarene community was represented by appointed officers who formed the Council of Delegate Apostles. Written about 50 years before the birth of Jesus, the *Community Rule* lays down the correct order of precedence for the seating at the banquet and details the ritual to be observed at the meal, concluding: "And when they gather for the community table ... and mix the wine for drinking, let no man stretch forth his hand on the first of the bread or the wine before the priest, for it is he who will bless the first fruits of the bread and wine ... And afterwards, the Messiah of Israel shall stretch out his hands upon the bread, and afterwards all the congregation of the community will give blessings, each according to his rank."[3]

Another aspect of the Grail legends which has baffled many is that they contain numerous venerative references to prominent characters of Jewish history. Also, there is a consistency of Jewish names and others of Jewish extraction – names such as Josephes, Lot, Elinant, Galahad, Bron, Urien, Hebron, Pelles, Joseus, Jonas, and Ban.

Specifically regarded as the most Christian of knights is the champion Galahad, who was identified in early texts as Gilead. The original Gilead, however, was a Hebrew son of Michael, the great-great-grandson of Nahor, brother of

Abraham (1 Chronicles 5:14). Gilead means "a heap of testimony," and the mountain called Gilead was the Mount of Witness (Genesis 31:21–25). Galeed was also the name given to Jacob's cairn, the heap of the witness in Genesis 31:46–48.

Prominent in the Grail stories, which emanated from a French Templar environment in the 12th century, is Joseph of Arimathea, but there is another who was held in the highest esteem from more ancient times. He was the Hasmonaean priest Judas Maccabaeus, who died in 161 BC. From the Franco-Flemish *High History of the Holy Grail* (compiled in around 1220) comes this conversation between Sir Gawain and Joseus of the Grail family:

> "Sir Knight," said he to Messire Gawain, "I pray you bide ... and conquer this shield, or otherwise I shall conquer you ... for it belonged to the best knight of his faith that was ever ... and the wisest."
>
> "Who then was he?" said Messire Gawain.
>
> "Judas Machabee was he."
>
> "You say true," saith Messire Gawain, "and what is your name?"
>
> "Sir, my name is Joseus, and I am of the lineage of Joseph of Abarimacie."

Why Judas Maccabaeus? He does not feature in the authorized Bible. There is, however, an historical void between the Old and New Testaments, and it is within this period that we find the history of Judas and the Hasmonaean Maccabees (*see* "After the Captivity," page 164). Fortunately, their story is detailed at length in the 1st-century writings of Flavius Josephus (who was himself of Hasmonaean birth) and also in the apocryphal *Books of Maccabees*, which were added to the original Septuagint Bible before the final canon was established without them. Apparently, the reason they were not selected was because they were solely concerned with the affairs of man, and not with the affairs of God!

It is by virtue of this missing aspect of the authorized canon that the Gospel stories of Jesus emerge in a Roman environment which is quite divorced from the Old Testament scriptures. Hence, the Gospel perspective is veiled to the extent that Jesus has been presented in a confusingly unique role instead of being seen as part of a continuous sequence of historical events. It also facilitated the dismissal from mainstream record of a second Royal House of Judah which, in the lead-up to the Herodian era, held equal rank with the House of David to which Jesus belonged. Also veiled within this hidden period was the continuing story of the traditional gold culture and the establishment of Qumrân by the Dead Sea.

The House of Hasmon

Judas, known as the "Hammerer" (*Maqqaba*) was a son of the priest Mattathias of Modin, near Jerusalem, and his shield (as alluded to in the Grail story) was a legend in its own time. Inscribed on it was the rhetorical question, "Who is like you among the gods?" As a result of Judas' nickname, his successors became known as Maccabees, and were dubbed with the surname Maccabaeus. In broader terms, they were known as Hasmonaeans, after their ancestor Hasmon (Asmonaeus), the great-grandfather of Mattathias.

In the footsteps of his father, Judas took up arms against the Seleucid kings of Syria, who had overrun Jerusalem. They were the successors of Alexander the Great's Macedonian general Seleucus, and consequently they imposed Greek tradition and religion on the people of Judaea. The main Seleucid antagonist of the era was King Antiochus IV, who had become allied with brothers of the Aaronite High Priest of Jerusalem. They usurped their family's legacy to side with the invader, while introducing Greek gods and worship to the Temple. The

Torah scrolls were burned with pig fat, circumcision was banned, and the Greek language was made compulsory on pain of death.

With the wayward Jerusalem priests supporting the insurrection against their own Jewish culture, Mattathias of Modin initially took up the challenge with a guerrilla force that was later inherited by his son Judas. Over a number of years, Judas defeated several Syrian armies in great battles, with many thousands of men on each side. In the course of all this, Jerusalem was wrecked, but on 25th Kisev (November) 165 BC Judas finally ousted the towering image of Zeus and rededicated the Temple to the Jewish faith. The city's Menorah was lit to begin an eight-day festival of celebration, and the annual feast of Hanukkah[4] was born.

That was not the end of the Hasmonaean Revolt, for there were still Syrians to defeat in the hills and surrounding country. However, this was the incident which led to a new princely reign in Jerusalem under Judas's brother Jonathan. To expedite this the Hasmonaeans gained the military backing of Rome (the new rising power in the Mediterranean world), thereby achieving complete Judaean independence from c. 142 BC. However, just a few decades later, the Romans themselves became the new overlords of Judaea.

Victorious as the Maccabees had been against Antiochus of Syria and his successor Demetrius I, a good deal of social damage had been done because the arduous campaign had involved fighting on the Sabbath. A core of ultra-strict Jewish devotees known as the *Hasidim* (Pious Ones) strongly objected to this and, when the triumphant House of Hasmon took control, setting up their own dynasty in Jerusalem, the *Hasidim* not only voiced their opposition but marched en masse out of the city. Subsequently, they established their own community in the nearby wilderness of Qumrân, a few miles east of Jerusalem, on the Dead Sea. According to the *Copper Scroll*, old Qumrân was called Sekhakha.

The *Books of Maccabees* relate how Hyrcanus, the nephew of Judas, became both King and High Priest in Jerusalem – succeeded by his sons Aristobulus and Alexander, then by Alexander's sons Hyrcanus II and Aristobulus II, followed by Aristobulus II's son Antigonus. At last, after many centuries since the Babylonian Captivity, there was a reigning dynasty again in Judaea, but the House of Hasmon came to an abrupt end when their princess Mariamme married Herod, an Idumaean Arab commander. The adventurous story of this marriage and the surrounding Roman–Egyptian intrigue of Antony and Cleopatra is told at length by Flavius Josephus in his *Wars of the Jews* and *Antiquities of the Jews*,[5] but the net result was that when Antigonus died in 37 BC the sole Hasmonaean heiress was his niece (Herod's wife) Mariamme. With Roman assent, Herod became the new resident king in Jerusalem.

The period of formal occupation at Qumrân seems to have commenced in about 130 BC, with the Essene therapeutics consolidating the settlement in around 100 BC.[6] The Essenes were a philosophical healing community, with a culture more Greco-Egyptian than Israelite. Jewish chronicles describe a violent Judaean earthquake around 70 years later in 31 BC,[7] which caused an evacuation of the settlement. This is confirmed at Qumrân by a break between two distinct periods of habitation.[8] In the *Wars of the Jews*, Josephus explains that the Essenes were practiced in the art of healing and received their medicinal knowledge of roots and stones from the ancients.[9] Indeed, the term Essene might refer to this expertise, for the Aramaic word *asayya* meant physician and corresponded to the Greek word *essenoi*.

The second residential period began during the reign of Herod the Great. Apart from the evidence of the Dead Sea Scrolls (unearthed from 1947), a collection of coins has also been amassed from the Qumrân settlement.[10] They relate to a time span from the Hasmonaean ruler John Hyrcanus (135–104 BC) to the Jewish Revolt of AD 66–70 against the Romans. Many relics of the era have since been discovered and, during the 1950s, more than a thousand graves were unearthed at Qumrân. A vast monastery complex from the second habitation was also revealed, with meeting rooms, plaster benches, huge water cisterns, and a maze of water conduits. In the Scribes' room there were ink wells and the remains of the tables on which the Scrolls had been laid out – some more than 17 feet (c. 5 m) in length.[11] It was confirmed by archaeologists and scholars that the original settlement had been damaged in the earthquake and rebuilt by the Essenes in the later Herodian era. The white-robed Essenes were one of three main philosophical Jewish sects (the other two being the Pharisees and the Sadducees). They were allied to the mystics and healers of the Egyptian Therapeutate, as were the Nazarene family of Jesus, who were resident at Qumrân. In principle, the Essenes were the old aristocrats, who longed for a return to the great days of Israel and the Royal House of David.[12]

Keepers of the Covenant

During the reign of Herod the Great (37–4 BC) vast sums of money were expended in Jerusalem, but this was in the wake of a massive disaster which beset the kingdom in 25 BC. In that year the rains failed and there was no harvest in Palestine or Syria.[13] There was neither seed nor corn, and all the goats and sheep had died. Josephus commented that, to feed the people in the face of this adversity, Herod stripped all the gold and silver from his palace, sending it to Petronius, the prefect of Egypt, for supplies from the pharaonic granaries. This, along with clothing and other needs, was distributed freely throughout the realm in exceptional quantity.[14] After two long years, the crisis was over, but the Jerusalem coffers were completely bare. Herod (at his kingly best) had saved the nation from utter catastrophe, but he and his court had become completely broke in the process.

Within a very short time, however, Herod was conducting his economy on an amazingly lavish scale. His donations and bequests were enormous – far in excess of the calculable tax revenues. On top of that he extended and rebuilt the Temple of Jerusalem so that, within a new complex of over 35 acres, it was bigger than the Acropolis in Athens and was the most magnificently appointed construction of the era. Thousands of masons worked on the colossal project over many years – but where did all the money come from? Moreover, in line with the question regarding the pyramids and other gigantic monuments of Egypt (*see* "Beyond Zero," pages 130–2), how did they move and raise the millions of massive stones, so many of which weighed over 50 tons apiece? Indeed, in the wall structure that remains today, there are still corner-stones weighing over 80 tons each at more than 100 feet (over 30 m) above the foundations.[15]

History has it that, from his bankrupt starting base, Herod accumulated the new wealth of Jerusalem from export trading, especially with his mother Kufra's[16] wondrous rock-cut city of Petra in South Jordan below the Dead Sea. Petra, with its valuable spice and marble trades was an extremely wealthy center, governed then by the Nabataean Arab ruler, King Aboud. Petra's engineers were noted far and wide as experts in hydraulic systems, and this unique expertise was another of the city's famed exports. In fact, Petra's economy was essentially export based, and they required very little from outside. What they did import were expensive luxuries such as silks from China, ivory from Africa, and rare gems and woods from India.[17] So, what was King Herod selling to Petra's governors to reap such incredibly high rewards from an ostensibly poor Judaean base that seemingly had little to offer? The answer is that he appears to have been replicating what King Solomon had done long before – selling the most prized and valuable of all known products: highward fire-stone.

As mentioned, the Essenes of Qumrân were attached to the Egyptian Therapeutate – the White Brotherhood of the Karnak temple craftsmen. They referred to themselves in the Dead Sea Scrolls as the New Covenant (*Berith Hadashad*),[18] while the Arabs called them *Nazrie ha-Brit* (Keepers of the Covenant),[19] from which stems the designation "Nazarene." (Contrary to common opinion, the Nazarene sect of Jesus had nothing whatever to do with Nazareth. They were the Dead Sea guardians of the arcane secrets of the Covenant in the traditions of Moses and Solomon.)

In the various excavations at Qumrân since the 1950s, the most striking characteristic of the impressive monastery buildings is the number and size of the water cisterns, and the extraordinary complexity of the conduits and channels.[20] An aqueduct on the western side ran from the Judaean hills to carry the fresh water supply, but other water courses led directly from the salt-laden Dead Sea. Not the least of these was the 314-foot (95 m) Mazin channel, a little below Qumrân. This water, with its high mineral content, was quite unsuitable for drinking or washing. But then, as now, it contained a remarkably high quantity of ORME gold – natural *mfkzt*. Recent experiments reveal that Dead Sea precipitate contains 70% gold in the monatomic state, along with 30% magnesium.[21] Further application of the dried precipitate with hydrochloric acid will dissolve the magnesium, leaving pure white *shem-an-na* powder. Unlike Solomon, who manufactured the Philosophers' Stone from conventionally mined gold, the Essene method was rather more like David Hudson's in that the monatomic material was refined and perfected from a readily available source. To suit Herod's purposes, it would have been easy enough to conduct this operation in secret within the confines of a desert monastery some miles from Jerusalem.

Josephus relates that, in matters of business, the Essenes would only trade for money with those outside their own community, but would freely give and receive from each other as a matter of common exchange, rather than buying and selling.[22] Therefore, any goods or income derived from the Herodian establishment for services rendered were for the benefit of all at Qumrân, but the on-sale revenues derived by the King from the Nabataeans and others were clearly far in excess of anything passed on as consideration to the Essenes.

It seems that, despite the biblical black mark against Herod for his supposed slaying of the infants when Jesus was born, history records him as a competent and well-regarded king. He even converted to a form of Judaism in order to aid his acceptance by the people, although he had a string of 10 wives and upheld other customs of his Arab upbringing. Notwithstanding this, there was a governmental problem in that Herod's authority was subject to the superior rule of the Roman Procurator of Judaea, who was based in Caesarea. The Roman regime was harsh in the extreme and more than 3,000 summary crucifixions were carried out to coerce the population into submission. Unfair taxes were levied, torture was commonplace, and the Jewish suicide rate rose alarmingly. There was not much that Herod could do about this and the people never blamed him personally – but his son, King Herod II Antipas, was of a different nature. He was very much a part of the Roman machine, and just as cruel – notorious in the Gospels as the Herod who beheaded John the Baptist.

It was during the early reign of Herod-Antipas that all trading liaison with the Essenes ceased. Subsequently, it was from their base at Qumrân that the vehemently aggressive Zealot movement against the Roman overlords emerged under the warlord Judas the Galilean. Born of Hasmonaean stock from John Hyrcanus, Judas took the same guerrilla route as his ancestral namesake Judas Maccabaeus. Eventually, the Zealots fronted a fierce campaign against the incoming Governor of Jerusalem, Pontius Pilate, and this led to a full scale Jewish revolt against the Romans in AD 66.

Quite how and when the discovery of ORMEs in the Dead Sea precipitate was first made is impossible to know. It might even have been a revelation from times long before in the Genesis era. We know from recent laboratory experiments that this superconductive substance can produce lethal gamma rays and it is highly dangerous if mishandled. It is possible, therefore, that the Dead Sea centers of Sodom and Gomorrah fell victim to a fire-stone radiation catastrophe when they were destroyed by fire and brimstone nearly two millennia before Qumrân was settled in the region.[23]

From the time of Abraham and the Righteous King, Melchizedek, the fire-stone "bread" of the Covenant was always associated with "righteousness." Through the era of the Davidic House its provision was supervised by the Zadok priests (*tsedeq/zaddik*: righteous), a dynastic style which was retained within the Essene community structure.[24] The Old Testament book of Ezekiel establishes that the sanctuary of the Covenant would remain with the sons of Zadok.[25] In the *Damascus Document* of the Dead Sea Scrolls, the prevailing Zadok was revered as the Teacher of Righteousness. His primary adversary is given as one called the Wicked Priest, and in this regard the Sodom and Gomorrah imagery is seen as a weighing of the balance between the righteous and the wicked (as described in Genesis 18: 23–33). Hence, the "bread of the presence" was deemed to be the Covenant food of the "righteous," which the "wicked" sought to devour.

None of the Scrolls is more full of allegory and allusion than the *Habakkuk Pesher*, which uses Essene scribal codes and metaphor throughout. In telling how the Zadokite's *mfkzt* craftsmanship was appropriated by the officiating priest of the Herodian establishment, it treats the Righteous Teacher as representing the bread itself, stating that he was confronted by the Wicked Priest in order to swallow him. One thing of which we may be sure, however, is that the Ark of the Covenant was not available or in use during the Hasmonaean or Qumrân eras. Its only Dead Sea Scrolls mention is in the *Damascus Document* (from around 100 BC), which explains that it had been hidden long before.

14

The Desposyni

Paradox of the Nativity

Arriving now at the time of the New Testament Gospels, we
have reached the subject era of *Bloodline of the Holy Grail*. Since
that book comprehensively deals with the life, ministry, and
marriage of Jesus, we shall not dwell on these matters again
here. This is a good opportunity, however, to expand on a few
aspects which have prompted specific enquiry over the years.
In doing so, we can move rather conveniently, via the legacy
of Jesus, into the medieval period leading to the Jerusalem
retrieval of the Ark of the Covenant.

A question which has been raised many times is: how does
the mortal figure of Jesus (the son of Mary and Joseph) reconcile with his Christian depiction as the son of God? To answer
this, the best place to look is in the New Testament itself. At
the same time, we can clarify some of the other scriptural
discrepancies concerning Jesus' birth and ancestry.

There is a significant difference between what Christians
are taught about the Nativity, as against what the Bible actually states. For example, it is commonly reckoned that Jesus
was born in a stable – and yet there is not one single reference
to a stable in any authorized Gospel. Certainly, there is no
mention of an ox, an ass, nor any of the dutiful creatures
which are classically portrayed at the scene. Surprisingly, only

two of the four Gospels (Matthew and Luke) discuss the birth of Jesus, while Mark and John completely ignore the event.

The Gospel of Matthew opens the New Testament with the statement: "The book of the generation of Jesus Christ, the son of David, the son of Abraham." A detailed lineal descent then follows in Matthew 1:2–16, culminating with the summary that it represents 42 male-line generations from the time of Abraham. Subsequent to this, the Gospel tells of the Nativity in Bethlehem, plainly stating in Matthew 2:11 that Jesus was born in a "house."

The Gospel of Luke begins with the arrival of John the Baptist and, on reaching the time of Jesus' birth, gives yet another generational list, commencing in reverse with Jesus' father, Joseph, and going all the way back (beyond Abraham) to Adam, who is called "the son of God" (Luke 3:38). In comparing the parallel sequences of the four Gospels, this is chronologically the first New Testament mention of the term "son of God," and it relates not to Jesus but to his far distant ancestor.

The word "stable," so commonly used in connection with the birthplace of Jesus, is specifically an English definition of a place for rearing and keeping horses – hence, horses of a particular stable. It does not, and never has, related to any other breed of animal, neither is it synonymous with a farm-yard outhouse, as depicted in the Christmas card sense of the Bethlehem Nativity. The notion of an outhouse as a birthplace for Jesus arose from the single statement in Luke that he was "laid in a manger" – but a manger is not a building, it is an animal feeding box. Luke 2:7 relates that this was done because there was "no room for them in the inn." The concept of an animal shed as an alternative to the inn was thus conjectured purely on the basis of this one comment, while ignoring the fact that Matthew specifies the location as a "house."

The historical fact is that there were no inns in the region, and the word "inn" was a corrupt translation. As confirmed in

Smith's Bible Dictionary,[1] "Inns, in the modern sense, were unknown in the ancient Middle East, where it was common to invite travelers into one's home, and was regarded as a pious duty to do so." Notwithstanding this, the rest of the Luke verse concerning the "inn" was also poorly translated. The original Greek text actually states that there was "no *topos* in the *kataluma*" – that is to say, there was "no place in the room."[2] In practice, it was quite common for mangers to be used as substitute cradles in emergency or for sake of convenience (cradles, mangers, and coffins were all made at the same workshops). A better translation of the Luke verse which has caused the confusion would be: "The baby Jesus was laid in a feeding-box because there was no cradle provided in the room."

In relating Jesus' lineage, Matthew and Luke do not agree on the genealogy from King David. Matthew gives the kingly line from David's son Solomon, whereas Luke details a descent from another of David's sons, Nathan. However (after 22 subsequent generations in Matthew and 20 in Luke), both lists eventually coincide with Zerubbabel. At this point, they agree that he was the heir of Salathiel (Shealtiel) after the Babylonian Captivity in accordance with the Old Testament books of Ezra 3:2 and Haggai 1:1.[3] In discussing the ostensibly variant Solomon and Nathan genealogies, Eusebius, 4th-century Bishop of Caesarea, referred to a 100-year-old letter written by the historian Julius Africanus. This, he said, clarified that a natural father was not necessarily the father in terms of the law. It was, he stated, all a matter of guardianship and upbringing, but that "the memory of both was preserved – of the real and nominal fathers."[4]

This apologetic explanation does not make much sense because genealogy is about natural parenthood (even if illegitimate). It is only concerned with matters of law when the inheritance of specific titles are involved. A more honest reason for the discrepancy would be that important females of the bloodline were not included in the lists. The book of 1 Chronicles 3:10–17 confirms the patrilinear descent of Zerubbabel from King Solomon (as given in Matthew), whereas Zerubbabel's mother was descended from Nathan, who is cited in Luke (*see* Chart: The Royal House of Judah, pages 338–43).

Having converged on Zerubbabel, the lists in Matthew and Luke then diverge again. Matthew traces Jesus' descent from a son named Abiud, while Luke takes a course from a son called Rhesa. This discrepancy occurs for precisely the same reason as before. Both of Jesus' parents were descended from Zerubbabel, but Mary's line descended from Abiud, while Joseph's lineage stemmed from Rhesa. (*see* Chart: The Family of Jesus, pages 375–9).

Jesus' paternal grandfather is called Jacob according to Matthew 1:16 but, in Luke 3:23, he is said to be Heli. Again, both versions are correct. Joseph's father, Heli, held the traditional distinction of "Jacob" in his patriarchal capacity within the Nazarene community.[5]

The genealogical list in Matthew, from David to Jacob-Heli (spanning about 1,000 years), contains 25 generations at 40 years each, so as to comply with the royal generation standard (*see* "Royal Generation," page 133.) Luke, on the other hand, gives 40 generations at a more comprehensible 25 years each. Hence, Luke places Jesus in the 20th generation from Zerubbabel (*c.* 536 BC), whereas Matthew places him in the 11th generation.

In relating the story of the Nativity, Matthew and Luke disagree as to the dating of the event. Matthew 2:3 states that it was while Herod reigned in Judaea. Then, in detailing the King's son as Archaelus (Matthew 2:22), the particular Herod in question is determined historically as Herod I, the Great, who died in the year we now classify as 4 BC. Luke 2:1–2 gives an alternative time frame, claiming that Jesus was born in the year of the Judaean census of Emperor Augustus, when Cyrenius was Governor of Syria. One has to look no further than the 1st-century *Antiquities of the Jews* by Flavius Josephus to establish that there was indeed a census in Judaea conducted by the Roman senator Cyrenius (Quirinius) at the behest of Caesar Augustus.[6] This took place in the last regnal year of Herod's son Archaelus, who was deposed in AD 6.[7]

The overall biblical picture is as follows: Neither Mark nor John make any reference to the Nativity or to the genealogical descent of Jesus, while both Matthew and Luke give male-line ancestries down to Jesus' father Joseph. Matthew states that Jesus was born in a house, while Luke gives no specific location, and these two Gospels disagree on the date of the event by at least 10 years!

This dating anomaly is explained by the fact that, according to Essene tradition, there were two relevant births to consider – a boy's physical birth and his community birth. A son was, in effect, "reborn" at the age of 12 when, dressed in a simple robe, he would undergo a ritual re-enactment of birth. He would thus symbolically be born again and installed as an initiate into his community position.[8] The later Merovingian royalty of Gaul (France) followed a similar practice in that kings' sons were granted an hereditary right to dynastic kingship by initiation on their twelfth birthday. The Essene custom of community birth is clearly evidenced in the Gospel of Luke 2:1–12, although it was completely misunderstood in the 17th-century translation. Consequently, Jesus' own ritualistic initiation was chronologically confused with his physical birth.

Just as in the Gospel of Matthew, Luke sets the Nativity (the actual birth of Jesus) during the latter reign of Herod the Great, who died in 4 BC. But Luke then states that Cyrenius was the Governor of Syria at the time, and that the Emperor Caesar Augustus had implemented a national census. In reality, Cyrenius was never Governor of Syria while Herod was alive. He was appointed to the office in AD 6 when, according to Josephus, there was a head count in Judaea conducted by Cyrenius on behalf of Caesar Augustus. This is the only recorded census for the region; there was none in Herod I's time. The census was held 12 years after Jesus' actual birth – precisely in the year of his customary community birth.

This error in translation was in turn responsible for the chronological confusion that surrounds the story of how Jesus was delayed at the Temple when in Jerusalem with his parents (Luke 2:41–50). The event is reported as occurring when Jesus was 12 years old, but it should relate to his designated "twelfth year." That is not 12 years after his birth into the world, but 12 years after his birth into the community. At the Passover of that year, Jesus would have been 24. He would then have been raised from initiate to full community manhood, but instead of accompanying his parents to the related celebrations, he stayed behind to discuss his Father's business. That is to say his spiritual father (the Father of the Community), who at that time was the priest Eleazer Annas.[9]

The calculation which follows is straightforward. Jesus was aged 12 in AD 6 at the time of the Judaean census. This places his actual birth in the notional year of 7 BC, which was indeed during the latter reign of Herod the Great. The year of Jesus' birth is often given as being 5 BC (for example, in the *Oxford Concordance Bible*). The first published sequence of biblical dates appeared in AD 526, as calculated by the monk Dionysius Exiguus. By his reckoning, Jesus was born in the Roman year 754 AUC (*Anno Urbis Conditae*, meaning "Years after the founding of the City [of Rome]"). This was equivalent to the restyled date of AD 1, which makes sense of the *Anno Domini* (Year of Our Lord) classification. It was subsequently decided that, since Jesus was born in the reign of King Herod, then he must have been born before Herod's death in 750 AUC, which had been designated as 4 BC. Hence, the birth year of Jesus was amended in the records to 5 BC, thereby making a complete nonsense of the already cemented BC and AD classifications.

That apart, a better guide to the Nativity date is to use the first-hand time frame of Flavius Josephus, by way of which 7 BC emerges as being rather more precise.

By virtue of this, the recent worldwide Millennium festivities might well have celebrated 2,000 years of an arbitrarily introduced Roman calendar, but they were seven years too late to have any relevance to the birth of Jesus.

Son of God – Son of Man

Despite the fact that the Gospel of John does not detail the Nativity, John 7:42 does make an important retrospective announcement regarding the ancestry of Jesus: "Hath not the scripture said, that Christ cometh of the seed of David, and out of the town of Bethlehem, where David was." In addition, St. Paul's Epistle to the Romans 1:3-4 refers to "Jesus Christ our Lord, which was made of the seed of David according to the flesh; and declared to be the Son of God." Again, in Mark 10:47 and Matthew 22:42 Jesus is called the "son of David." In Acts 2:30, Peter (referring to King David) calls Jesus the "fruit of his loins, according to the flesh." These entries, along with the male-line genealogical lists in Matthew and Luke, make it abundantly clear that Jesus was of straightforward human descent from King David. Over and above that, St. Paul wrote that Jesus was "declared" to be the son of God; while in the Annunciation sequence of Luke 1:35, it is similarly stated that Jesus would be "called" the son of God.

The fact of Jesus' Davidic paternal descent is made even more apparent in Hebrews 7:14, which relates to his appointment in the high priestly Order of Melchizedek. From the time of Moses and Aaron, only the tribe of Levi had any automatic right to Israelite priesthood. The tribe of Judah, which included David and his dynasty down to Joseph, held the privilege of kingship, but not of priesthood. In writing his epistle to the Hebrews, St. Paul clarified the matter of Jesus' new priestly status with the following: "It is evident that our Lord sprang out of Judah, of which tribe Moses spake nothing concerning priesthood." (Hebrews 7:14.) Just before this, in Hebrews 7:12, the point is made that, to accommodate this divergence from custom, there was "made of necessity a change also of the law." Nothing is mentioned here about Jesus being able to be whatever he wanted because he was the son of God – only that the law had to be amended because of his birth into the Davidic line of Judah.

When confronted by others to the effect that he was the son of God, Jesus generally avoided the issue. In Matthew 26:63–64, when asked by the High Priest whether he was in truth the son of God, Jesus replied, "Thou hast said" – implying that the priest had said it, not he. In Luke 22:70, Jesus answered in virtually identical terms: "Then said they all, Art thou then the Son of God? And he said unto them, Ye say that I am." On other occasions, Jesus responded to the effect that he was the son of man (as in Matthew 26:63–64).

The perception of Jesus as the physical son of God emanates from things said about him by others in the text. For example, John 20:31 states, "But these things are written, that ye might believe that Jesus is the Christ, the Son of God." Similarly in Acts 9:20 when Paul is said to have preached that Christ was the son of God. There are 45 such entries in the New Testament, which state that Jesus was "declared to be," "preached as," "believed to be," "was called" the son of God. Alternatively, there are 90 mentions of his being the "son of man," the majority of which references were made by Jesus himself.

As we have learned, Adam was the first of the line to be called the "son of God." More important to the overall picture is that the Bible cites certain deserving people as being the "children of God," commencing in the New Testament with Jesus' own words in Matthew 5:9: "Blessed are the peacemakers, for they shall be called the children of God." Once again, just as in the case of Jesus, the operative word is "called."

1 *Israelites with the Ark of the Covenant at the Wall of Jericho*
by Jacques J. Tissot (1836–1902)

2 *The Golden Calf worshipped by the Israelites in Sinai*
by Jacques J. Tissot (1836–1902)

3 Ruins of the Hathor mountain temple at Serâbît el Khâdim

4 Mount Horeb cave entrance in the temple at Serâbît el Khâdim

5 *Ezekiel's Vision* — Cherubim and the Celestial Throne
by Sir Peter Robson, 2001

6 *Rise of the Phoenix*
by Sir Peter Robson, 2001

7 *Tuthmosis III in battle at Armageddon*
by H.M. Herget, 1940

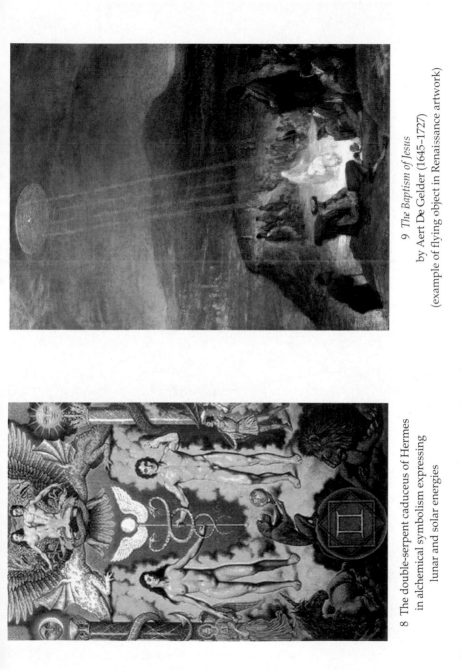

8 The double-serpent caduceus of Hermes
in alchemical symbolism expressing
lunar and solar energies

9 *The Baptism of Jesus*
by Aert De Gelder (1645–1727)
(example of flying object in Renaissance artwork)

10 *The Plague of Ashdod* — Philistines and the Ark of the Covenant
by Nicolas Poussin, 1630

11 Winged cherub on the golden shrine
of Tutankhamun

12 The Egyptian Ark of Tutankhamun
with Anubis guarding the royal shrine

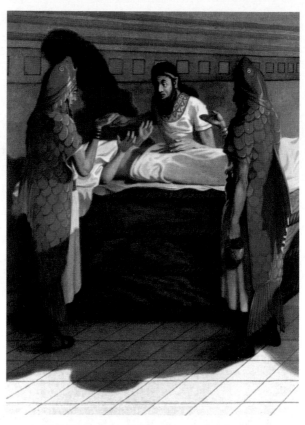

13 *Mesopotamian fish-garbed Apkallu physicians*
by H.M. Herget, 1940

14 Mysterious relief at the Temple of Hathor, Dendera

16 Chartres labyrinth design from a 2nd-century Greek document as copied by Vilars Dehoncort

15 Assyrian Apkallu – Pine-cone Genie and the King, from the Nimrud Palace of Ashurnasirpal II, c. 870 BC

17 *King Solomon and the Brazen Vessel*
by Jacques J. Tissot (1836–1902)

18 Vaulted cistern of *Bahr El Khabeer* beneath the Temple of Jerusalem
by William Simpson, 1870

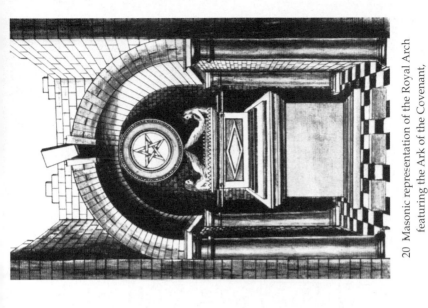

19 The Royal Society, by John Evelyn, 1667. Bust of Charles II, with Viscount Brouncker, Sir Francis Bacon, and the Angel of Fame from the Rosicrucian *Fama Fraternitatis*

20 Masonic representation of the Royal Arch featuring the Ark of the Covenant, by Laurence Dermott, 1783

21 *Destiny of the House of Gold*, by Sir Peter Robson, 2002

22 The labyrinth at Chartres Cathedral

23 *La Dompna del Aquae*
Mary Magdalene arrives in Provence, by Andrew Jones, 2001

24 *The Execution of Jacques de Molay*
Paris, 18th March 1314

25 *Knights Templars at the Paris Chapter House, 22nd April 1147*
by François-Marius Granet, 1844, Château de Versailles

All things considered, the term "son of God," as applicable to Jesus, was a figurative and symbolic description, whereas his physical lineage from King David is given on numerous occasions as being the human reality of his position. The most important thing here is that it was the kingly line of David which was especially considered to be God's offspring, not Jesus as a lone individual. This premise is laid down in 2 Samuel 7:13–14, where God is recorded as announcing in respect of King David: "He shall build an house for my name, and I will stablish the throne of his kingdom for ever. I will be his father, and he shall be my son."

Virgin and the Carpenter

This is a good time to recap (*see* "Giver of Life," page 17) in respect of Jesus' father, Joseph, being misidentified in translation as a carpenter. The original Greek texts refers to him by the style of *ho tekton*, derived from the Aramaic term *naggar*. This should not have been translated as "carpenter," but as "craftsman."[10] As pointed out by the Semitic scholar Dr. Geza Vermes, the descriptive word would more likely define a scholar or master. It certainly did not identify Joseph as a woodworker. More precisely, it defined him as a learned man with great skills in his occupation. In practice, after the Old Testament styles of Tubal-cain, Bezaleel, and Hiram of Phoenicia, Joseph could well have been a master artificer in metals at the Qumrân fire-stone refinery.

A similar error was made in respect of Jesus' mother, Mary, who is given in the modern Gospels as being a virgin. However, the Semitic word translated to become "virgin" was *almah*, which actually meant no more than a "young woman."[11] The comparative word denoting physical virginity was *bethulah*. In Latin, the word *virgo* meant, quite simply, "unmarried" and, to imply the modern connotation of "virgin," the Latin noun would need to be qualified by the adjective *intacta* (as in: *virgo intacta*), denoting absence of sexual experience.[12]

The physical virginity attributed to Mary becomes even less credible in relation to the dogmatic Catholic assertion that she was a "virgin forever," as established at the Council of Trullo in 692. It is no secret that Mary had other offspring, as confirmed in each of the Gospels: "Is this not the carpenter's son? Is not his mother called Mary and his brethren, James, and Joses, and Simon, and Judas?" (Matthew 13:55). In both Luke 2:7 and Matthew 1:25, Jesus is cited as Mary's "firstborn son." Furthermore, the quotation from Matthew describes Jesus as "the carpenter's son" (that is, the son of Joseph) and Luke 2:27 clearly refers to Joseph and Mary as Jesus' "parents." Matthew 13:56 and Mark 6:3 also indicate that Jesus had sisters. They are named in the *Panarion* and *Ancoratus* of Epiphanius as being Mary, Salome, and Anna (Joanna).[13] Sisters of Jesus are also mentioned in the *Protevangelion* of James,[14] in the Gospel of Philip,[15] and in the Church's *Apostolic Constitutions*. In the New Testament Gospels, they appear at the cross and the tomb of Jesus, along with Mary Magdalene. Mary and Salome appear, for example, in Mark 15:47, while Joanna and Mary appear in Luke 24:10. In these and other such Gospel listings (six in all), Mary Magdalene is always the first named in order of rank as the "first lady": the Messianic queen.[16]

Jesus' sister Mary (known as Mary of James[17] or, more popularly, Mary Jacob) accompanied Mary Magdalene to Gaul in AD 44,[18] as detailed in *The Acts of Magdalene* and the ancient MS *History of England* in the Vatican Archives. St. Mary Jacob[19] was a Nazarene priestess, who became better known in Europe as Mary the Gypsy. In England her cult was widespread in medieval times, and she is portrayed as a mermaid alongside Mary Magdalene in a window at the Church of St. Marie in Paris.

Burning the Evidence

In addition to recounting the Bethany marriage of Jesus and Mary Magdalene, *Bloodline of the Holy Grail* details the subsequent births of their children and the family's Grail-related history thereafter. A related sequence worth amplifying here is the official persecution which beset the generations of Messianic family heirs. This has been a subject of particular reader interest because it is not conveyed in the established teachings of Imperial Roman history.

Following the 1st-century Judaean Revolt and the sacking of Jerusalem by General Titus in AD 70, the Roman overlords were reputed to have destroyed all records concerning the Davidic legacy of Jesus' family. The destruction was far from complete, however, and relevant documents were retained by the Messianic heirs, who brought the heritage from the Holy Land to Western Europe.

Writing in about AD 200, the chronicler Julius Africanus of Edessa[20] recalled how waves of refugees had fled Jerusalem and Judaea to perpetuate their tradition in the northern reaches of Mesopotamia, Syria, and southern Turkey. Known as the "Father of Christian chronography," Africanus made his reputation by translating into Latin a series of Aramaic works by the 1st-century disciple Abdias, the Nazarene representative in Babylon. The *Books of Abdias* amounted to 10 volumes of first-hand Apostolic history. However, like so many important eyewitness accounts of the era, their content was rejected outright at the Council of Carthage in AD 397 for inclusion in the Christian canon.[21]

In his *Ecclesiastical History*, Eusebius of Caesarea confirmed from the writings of Africanus that the Messianic heirs were called the *Desposyni* – ancient Greek for "Heirs of [or belonging to] the Lord [or the Master]."[22] This was a hallowed style reserved exclusively for those in the same family descent as Jesus.[23] The word is not to be found used in any other context, and Africanus even went to the trouble of explaining it in his account. The term *Desposyni* was apparently confined to Jesus' immediate relatives and heirs, as one might these days determine the hub of a dynastic royal family.

The annals explain that, in the time of King Herod-Antipas, documents of genealogical record relating to the family of Jesus were burned at the King's instruction.[24] Later, when the legions destroyed Jerusalem, the Roman governors had all Messianic records burned so as to prevent future access to the details of the family pedigree. For all that, Africanus confirmed that "a few careful people had private records of their own ... and took a pride in preserving the memory of their aristocratic origin." These included the *Desposyni* of the Savior's family.

The 2nd-century Palestinian historian Hegesippus reported in his *Hypomnenata* (Memoirs) that Emperor Vespasian (AD 69–79) went so far as to order that no member of the Messianic house should be left alive and that "all descendants of King David should be ferreted out."[25]

Eusebius confirmed that, notwithstanding this persecution, the *Desposyni* leaders became the heads of their sects by way of a strict dynastic progression. But, wherever possible, they were pursued to the death – hunted down like outlaws[26] and put to the sword by Imperial command. Hegesippus also wrote that after Vespasian, during the reign of the Emperor Domitian (AD 81–96), the execution of all *Desposyni* was ordered by Imperial decree. Among those seized were Zoker and James, sons of Jesus' brother Jude.[27] The same is also reported by Hegesippus during the subsequent reign of Emperor Trajan (*c*. AD 110), when the *Desposynos* Simeon was crucified for belonging to the Lord's family!

Fr. Malachi Martin (a Jesuit professor, who lately served in Rome with Cardinal Augustine Bea and Pope John XXIII) relates that in AD 318 a *Desposyni* delegation journeyed to Rome, where, at the newly commissioned Lateran Palace, they were given audience by Bishop Silvester. Through their chief spokesman Joses, the delegates argued that the Church should rightfully be centered in Jerusalem, not in Rome. They claimed that the Bishop of Jerusalem should be a true hereditary *Desposynos* of the Savior's family, while the bishops of other major centers – such as Alexandria, Antioch, and Ephesus – should also be related. Not surprisingly, their demands were in vain, for Silvester was hardly in a position to countermand the decrees of Emperor Constantine. The men were duly advised that the teachings of Jesus had been superseded by a doctrine more amenable to Imperial requirement, and that the power of salvation rested no longer in Jesus, but in the Emperor himself![28]

Voyage of the Magdalene

In establishing the new Roman Church in a hybrid form that was distinctly different from earlier Christianity, the bishops of Emperor Constantine introduced specific rules of operation. One of these was the 4th-century rule of celibacy, which became a canon law in 1138, and which persists even today. This was in direct contradiction of St. Paul's statement in 1 Timothy 3:2–5 that a bishop should have a wife and children, for a man with his own household is better qualified to take care of the Church. Even though the bishops elected to uphold the teachings of Paul in general terms, they chose to disregard this explicit directive so that Jesus' own marital status could be ignored.

At the same time, when collating the New Testament from AD 367, numerous Gospel texts were not selected because they upheld the status of women in Church and community society. Consequently, out of dozens in the original selection, only four Gospels (Matthew, Mark, Luke, and John) were afforded recognition by the new Church. The titles of around 50 of the original Gospels are known, and texts are extant for

20 of them. Among the better known of these are the Gospels of Philip, Thomas, and Mary Magdalene, discovered at Nag Hammadi, Egypt, in 1945.[29]

Most prominent in the ranks of Jesus' female companions was Mary Magdalene. Early Christian texts describe her as "the woman who knew the all of Jesus." She was the one whom "Christ loved more than all the disciples;" she was the apostle "endowed with knowledge, vision, and insight far exceeding Peter" and she was the beloved bride who anointed Jesus at the Sacred Marriage (the *Hieros Gamos*) at Bethany.[30] Born of high-ranking Hasmonaean stock, Mary was the designated *Magdal-eder* – the Watchtower of the flock – and she was always associated with wisdom (*sophia*), symbolized by the sun, moon, and a halo of stars. The female gnosis of the goddess Sophia was deemed to be represented on Earth by the Magdalene, who fled to French exile in Provence, bearing the child of Jesus. In The Revelation 12:1–17, St. John tells of Mary and her son, describing her persecution, flight, and the continued hounding of "the remnant of her seed," who were among the *Desposyni*.

By virtue of Mary Magdalene's heirs, who opposed the male-dominated Apostolic Succession of the papal Church of Rome, women were barred from Catholic ordination. Women, other than Jesus' mother, were relegated to a position of insignificance, and even Mother Mary (although revered) was denied any ecclesiastical status, while at the same time being designated a virgin. By this strategy, the heirs of Jesus were eclipsed and the bishops were enabled to reinforce their claim to holy authority by means of a contrived heritage from St. Peter.

The Life of Mary Magdalene by Raban Maar (776–856), Archbishop of Mayence (Mainz) and Abbé of Fuld, incorporates many traditions about Mary dating back to early times. A copy of the Maar manuscript was unearthed at Oxford University in the early 1400s and the work had been cited in the *Chronica Majora* of Matthew Paris, in around 1190. It is also listed in the

Scriptorum Ecclesiasticorum Historia literaria Basilae at Oxford. *Saint Mary Magdalene* by the Dominican friar Père Lacordaire (published after the French Revolution) is a particularly informative work, as is *La Légende de Sainte Marie Madeleine* by Jacobus de Voragine, Archbishop of Genoa (b. 1228). Both de Voragine and Maar state that Mary's mother Eucharia was related to the Hasmonaean royal house of Israel.

Another important work by Jacobus de Voragine is the famous *Legenda Aurea* (Golden Legend), one of the earliest books printed at Westminster, London, by William Caxton in 1483. Previously published in French and Latin, Caxton was persuaded by William, Earl of Arundel, to produce an English version from the European manuscripts. It is a collection of ecclesiastical chronicles detailing the lives of selected saintly figures. Highly venerated, the work was given public readings on a regular basis in medieval monasteries and churches. One particular narrative from the *Legenda* tells of Mary Magdalene's voyage to Gaul, along with Lazarus, St. Maxim, Mary Jacob, and others, landing near Marseilles. The most active Magdalene cult was eventually based at Rennes-le-Château in the Languedoc region. Elsewhere in France there were many shrines set up to Ste. Marie de Madeleine. These included her burial place at St. Maximus, where her sepulcher and alabaster tomb were guarded by Cassianite monks.

In December 2001, the gnostic oratorio, *The Marriage at Cana* (which relates the story of Mary Magdalene's life), had its world premier performance at London's Royal Opera House, Covent Garden. Based upon *Bloodline of the Holy Grail*, I was privileged to write the libretto, with the music composed by Jaz Coleman, composer in residence for the Prague Symphony Orchestra. At this Opera House event, a specially commissioned new painting by Andrew Jones was unveiled, depicting the expectant Mary Magdalene's historic arrival on the shore of Provence. Entitled *La Dompna del Aquae* (The Great Lady of the Waters), this exquisite work is featured in Plate 23.

A Noble Artificer

If Jesus had been tried and punished for his supposed crime against the Judaean state, why would his relatives and heirs of subsequent generations be pursued and persecuted throughout the Empire?

In certain circles, the family was extremely influential and posed a significant threat to the Imperial structure – but there was rather more to it than that. Jesus' brother James had been the Nazarene Bishop of Jerusalem, and being the second son, had held the community distinction of "Joseph," with Jesus being the recognized "David." All senior dynasts of the line were individually classified as the Dâvìdum of the House of Bread (*Beth-le-hem*) (*see* "The Fire-stone Project," page 147). James inherited the "Joseph" distinction, becoming the Divine Highness (the equivalent of today's crown prince: Royal Highness). As such, he was, in Nazarene community terms, the Joseph *ha Rama-Theo*, becoming better known in phonetic transliteration as Joseph [of] Arimathea.

Outside the Bible, he was reputed as an artificer in metals – a *ho tekton*: a "master craftsman" just like his father, and like Bezaleel, Hiram, and others of the fire-stone tradition. He was recorded as a *noblis decurion* (noble decurio) and, while the Magdalene centers were being established in the South of France, Joseph/James was granted a wealth of tax-free land at Glastonbury in England. A decurio was an overseer of mining estates,[31] and his land grant was made by King Arviragus, the brother of Caractacus, Pendragon of the Isle (*Pen Draco Insularis*). Their dynasty was called the House of Camu-lôt (meaning "curved light" – later romantically corrupted to Camelot).

Joseph's daughter, Anna, married into the Camu-lôt dynasty, whose curved light emblem was a rainbow, and from them a great line of Celtic kings descended. Meanwhile, in Gaul, the priestly House of Jesus and Mary Magdalene became known as the Fisher Kings – ultimately to found the French monarchy. It was from this combined scenario that the most romantic of all traditions evolved, for it was said that Mary and Joseph had brought with them the greatest of all treasures: the Holy Grail.

The Grail was many things (both physical and spiritual) but, in one guise or another, it always represented the Blood Royal: the Messianic *Sangréal* of Judah. It is for this very reason that the concept of the Holy Grail has remained beyond the grasp of understanding – because the root of its bloodline significance has not been common knowledge since it was suppressed by the Church in early medieval times. This period is generally referred to as the Dark Ages – an era about which little is historically known, especially in the Celtic realms. This does not mean that no one was writing history, but that the majority of genuine records from that period were confiscated and destroyed, to be supplanted by the religiously biased compositions of monks with predetermined vested interests. Their given duty was to support and promote newly contrived Church dogma, irrespective of the truth. Fortunately, many pre-Church chronicles from the 1st to the 4th centuries have survived, while some brave churchmen of later times preferred to maintain the traditional romance of earlier records in defiance of the official doctrine.

The term Grail derived from the *Gra-al* of old Mesopotamia, called the "nectar of supreme excellence" and Gold of the Gods (*see* "Realm of the Genies," page 124). The light bodies (the *Ka*) of the ancient Sumerian kings had been fed with the *Gra-al*, which was superseded in Egypt, Babylonia, and Assyria by the highward fire-stone, the *shem-an-na*, the *mfkzt*: the white powder of gold.[32]

This, then, was the great threat posed to Imperial Rome and to the later Roman Church by the *Desposyni*. Notwithstanding all the military might of the Emperors, and the subsequent authority of the Popes, they still did not hold the great secret of Camu-lôt – and their ultimate quest was the same as it had always been: to obtain the Ark of the Covenant. In the meantime, Jeremiah's old Order of the Jerusalem Temple Guard had progressed through the Irish and Scots kings in descent from Tamar (the daughter of King Zedekiah), whom he had carried to safety in Ireland (*see* "Guardians of Destiny," page 157). Eventually, with his Merovingian cousins reigning in France, High King Arthur mac Aedàn of Dalriada (the Western Highlands) constituted the *Sangréal* Order of the Round Table as the figurative guardians of the sacred relic in AD 574.

By 751, Pope Zachary had ousted the Merovingian Fisher Kings, to install his own chosen dynasty in France. But this was to little avail, and by 807, King Eochaid IV of Scots (6th-generational descendant of Arthur's brother) had struck a binding treaty with the new Emperor Charlemagne of the Franks. By that time, the Jerusalem anointing stone of Beth-el (the *Stone of Destiny*) had long been in Scotland, along with Jeremiah's arcane record of the Temple vault (most probably held by the Irish–Scots mission of St. Columba). This might have been the perfect moment to retrieve the Ark, for the Roman Empire had collapsed and the *Desposynic* Franco–Scots alliance was strong. Jerusalem was, however, then under Muslim control (as it had been for some time) and a wonderful mosque had been built on the old Temple site. It was now quite inaccessible.

PART IV

Hermetic Renaissance

Knights of the Temple

Following the Roman destruction of Jerusalem and the Temple by General Titus in AD 70, the inhabitants scattered, leaving the city a desolate ruin for over six decades. In AD 132 Emperor Hadrian began a rebuilding scheme, with a temple dedicated to Jupiter planned for the old Temple Mount. This prompted an unsuccessful Jewish revolt under the guerrilla leader Shimon Bar-Kockba, at the end of which the surviving Jews were banished or sold into slavery. Henceforth, Jewish study and worship were proclaimed capital offences and Jerusalem was renamed *Aelia Capitolina* by the Romans.[1]

After the 5th-century collapse of Imperial Rome, Jerusalem came under full control of the Byzantine authorities. It was later conquered by Persians, and then by the forces of the lately established Islam under Caliph Omar ibn Al-Khattab in 638. He constructed a mosque (later called the El-Aqsa Mosque) on the old Temple site, and soon afterwards the Dome of the Rock shrine (now the foremost Jerusalem land-mark) was built nearby on the Mount Moriah Rock of David.[2] Subsequent earthquakes caused damage to both buildings, necessitating restorations and improvements. In the course of all this, Christians were permitted to continue using their churches, in particular the 4th-century Church of the Holy

Sepulchre. Jews were also readmitted and allowed to build synagogues. They had lost their Temple Mount and Moriah Rock to the Muslim foundations, but lived in reasonable harmony with their neighbors. They might have been humiliated by Islam, but the Muslims did not persecute and slaughter them as the Imperial Romans and Byzantine Christians had done.

A major change occurred when Seljuk Turks invaded Jerusalem in 1077, while simultaneously posing a severe threat to the Byzantine Emperor Alexius I. These tribes from Turkestan had swept into Asia Minor and adopted the Islamic faith, but their Sultan,[3] Malik Shah, challenged the Muslim supremacy of the Caliphs (the successors of Mohammed). This caused great consternation for Muslims of the Caliphate, also for the Jews and Christians alike – as a result of which, the princes of Western Europe decided to take Jerusalem under their own control.

Their military Crusade was initiated in 1095 when Pope Urban II raised a formidable army, led by the best knights in Europe. They were coordinated by Adhemar, Bishop of Le Puy, and in the vanguard was Robert, Duc de Normandie, together with Stephen, Comte de Blois, and Hugh, Comte de Vermandois. The Flemish contingent was led by Robert, Comte de Flandres, and included Eustace, Comte de Boulogne, with his brothers Godefroi de Bouillon and Baudouin. The South of France was represented by Raymond de St. Gilles, Comte de Toulouse.

Godefroi de Bouillon was the Duke of Lower Lorraine. He had succeeded to the title through his famous mother, St. Ida, from whom he gained the castle and lands of Bouillon – estates which he mortgaged to the Bishop of Liège in order to fund his Holy Land campaign. By the time that the First Crusade was under way, Godefroi had become its overall commander and, on its eventual success against the Seljuks in 1099, he was proclaimed King of Jerusalem. In the event, he preferred not to use the dignity of King, assuming instead the alternative distinction Defender of the Sacred Sepulchre.

Of the eight Crusades, which persisted until 1291 in Egypt, Syria, and Palestine, only Godefroi's First Crusade was to any avail, but even that was marred by the excesses of irresponsible troops who used their victory as an excuse for wholesale slaughter of Muslims in the streets of Jerusalem. Not only was Jerusalem important to the Jews and Christians, but it had become the third Holy City of Islam, after Mecca and Medina. As such, the city sits at the heart of continuing disputes today.[4]

The Second Crusade to Edessa, led by Louis VII of France and the German Emperor Conrad III, failed miserably. Then, around 100 years after Godefroi's initial success, Jerusalem fell to the mighty Saladin of Egypt in 1187. This prompted the Third Crusade under Philip Augustus of France and Richard the Lionheart of England, but they did not manage to win back the Holy City. The Fourth and Fifth Crusades centered on Constantinople and Damietta. Jerusalem was reclaimed briefly from the Saracens after Emperor Frederick II's Sixth Crusade, but was finally conceded to Saladin's successor in 1244. Louis IX then led the Seventh and Eighth Crusades, but fell short of reversing the situation. By 1291, Palestine and Syria were firmly under Muslim control, and the Crusades were over.

During this crusading era, a number of knightly Orders emerged, including the Order of Sion, founded by Godefroi de Bouillon in 1099.[5] Others were the Knights Protectors of the Sacred Sepulchre and the Knights Templars. Soon after his Jerusalem triumph, Godefroi de Bouillon died in 1100, to be succeeded as King by his younger brother Baudouin of Boulogne. After 18 years, Baudouin was followed in 1118 by his cousin, Baudouin II du Bourg. According to the orthodox accounts, the Knights Templars were founded in that year as the Poor Knights of Christ and of the Temple of Solomon. They were said to have been established by a group of nine

Frenchmen, who took vows of poverty, chastity, and obedience, and swore to protect the Holy Land. The Frankish historian, Guillaume de Tyre, wrote at the height of the Crusades (c. 1180) that the function of the Templars was to safeguard the highways for pilgrims. But, given the enormity of such an obligation, it is inconceivable that nine poor men succeeded without enlisting new recruits until they returned to Europe in 1127. In truth, there was a good deal more to the Order than conveyed in Guillaume's account.

The Knights were actually in existence for some years before they were said to have been founded by Hugues de Payens, a cousin and vassal of the Comte de Champagne. Their function was certainly not highway patrol, and the King's chronicler, Fulk de Chartres, did not portray them in that light at all. They were Godefroi's front-line diplomats in a Muslim environment and, in 1114, the Bishop of Chartres had called them the *Milice du Christi* (Soldiers of Christ). In 1118, the specially commissioned Templar Grand Knights of St. Andrew (the Guardian Princes of the Royal Secret) were installed at Baudouin II's palace, which was located at the El-Aqsa Mosque on the site of the old Temple of Jerusalem. When Baudouin moved his quarters to the domed citadel on the Rock of David (which was then a Christian shrine called *Templum Domini*),[6] the Mosque was left entirely to the Knights. Their ambition was to excavate the site and to retrieve the treasure that had been stowed by Jeremiah and Hilkiah's Temple Guard over 1,700 years before. Deep beneath the mosque was the original vault complex, which had remained sealed and untouched since Bible times, and it was known by St. Bernard to contain the wealth of Old Testament Jerusalem, including the Ark of the Covenant.

Hugues de Payens was appointed commander of the project, with the Flemish knight Godefroi Saint Omer as his second-in-charge. Another recruit was André de Montbard, a kinsman of the Count of Burgundy. In 1120 Fulk, Comte d'Anjou (father of Geoffrey Plantagenet, the progenitor of England's Plantagenet kings) also joined the Order, followed in 1124 by de Payen's liege lord, Hugues, Comte de Champagne. The Templars' patron and protector was the Cistercian Abbot, St. Bernard de Clairvaux,[7] who was related to the Comte de Champagne. Indeed, it was on land donated by the Count that Bernard built the Cistercian monastery of Clairvaux in 1115. Contrary to popular belief, the Knights were far from poor, and there is certainly no record of these illustrious noblemen policing the bedouin-infested highways for the benefit of pilgrims. The task of ministering to wayfarers was actually performed by the separate Knights Hospitallers of St. John of Jerusalem. As distinct from the Templar Cross (red on white), the Hospitallers used a different color scheme (silver on black) in the same octagonal design, and their pilgrims' hospital in Jerusalem had been founded before the Crusades in about 1050.[8]

Council of the Ark

By 1127, the Templars' search was over. They had retrieved not only the Ark, but an untold wealth of gold bullion and hidden treasure, much of which had been safely stowed below ground long after Hilkiah's time, prior to the Roman invasion in the 1st century BC. In *The Histories* [of Imperial Rome], Senator Cornelius Tacitus had recalled the surprise of Pompey the Great, stating that when he entered the Temple in 63 BC "the sanctuary was empty and the Holy of Holies untenanted."[9]

In the light of the Templars' overwhelming success, Hugues de Payens received a summons from St. Bernard to attend a forthcoming Council at Troyes. It was to be chaired by the papal ambassador, the Cardinal Legate of France. Hugues and a company of Knights duly left the Holy Land with their auspicious find and St. Bernard announced that the Jerusalem mission had been fulfilled. Fearing that the Vatican authorities would be intent on sequestrating what they had found, he wrote: "The work has been accomplished with our help, and the Knights have been sent on a journey through France and Burgundy, under the protection of the Count of Champagne, where all precautions can be taken against all interference by public or ecclesiastical authority."[10]

The Champagne Court at Troyes was well prepared for the cryptic translation work to follow and, in readiness, had sponsored an influential school of Judaic studies. The Grand Council was held in 1128, at which time international status as a Sovereign Order was conferred upon the Templars, while their Jerusalem headquarters became the governing office of the capital city. Under St. Bernard, the Knights were duly established as a Cistercian Order and Hugues de Payens was formally installed as Grand Master. St. Bernard subsequently preached the Second Crusade at Vézelay to King Louis VII and a congregation of 100,000, and his Constitutional Oath of the Knights Templars required the "Obedience of Bethany: the Castle of Mary and Martha."[11] In due accord, the great Basilica of St. Mary Magdalene was then constructed at Vézelay.

Following the Council of Troyes, the Templars' rise to prominence was remarkably swift as they became engaged in high-level politics and diplomacy in Europe and the Middle East. Just 11 years later, in 1139, Pope Innocent II (another Cistercian) granted the Knights international independence from obligation to any authority save himself. Irrespective of kings, cardinals, or governments, the Order's only superior was the Pope, and they were granted vast territories and substantial property across the map from Britain to Palestine. *The Anglo-Saxon Chronicle* states that when Hugues de Payens visited England's Henry I, "the King received him with much honour, and gave him rich presents." The Spanish King, Alfonso of Aragon, passed a third of his kingdom to the Order and the whole of Christendom was at their feet.

Notre Dame

When news spread of the Templars' incredible find, the Knights became revered by all and, notwithstanding their Jerusalem wealth, large donations were received from far and wide. No price was too high to secure affiliation and, within a decade of their return, they were the most influential body the world has ever known. Nevertheless, despite the prodigious holdings of the Order, the individual Knights were bound to a vow of relinquishment. Whatever his station in life, every Templar was obliged to sign over title to his possessions – yet the sons of nobility still flocked to join the Order. Being so well funded, the Templars established the first international banking network, becoming financiers for the Levant and for practically every throne in Europe.

Just as the Order grew to high estate, so too did the Cistercians' fortune rise in parallel and, within 25 years of the Council of Troyes, they could boast more than 300 abbeys. But that was not the end of it, for the people of France then witnessed the most astounding result of the Templars' newfound technology. City skylines began to change with immeasurable drama as their great Notre Dame cathedrals, with majestic Gothic arches, rose from the earth. The architecture was phenomenal – impossible, some said, and still baffling to architects today. The pointed ogives reached incredible heights, spanning hitherto insurmountable space, with flying buttresses and thinly ribbed vaulting. Everything pulled upwards and, despite the thousands of tons of richly decorated stone, the overall impression was one of magical weightlessness. Using Hiramic geometry and levitational techniques from long distant times, the masons constructed the finest holy monuments ever to grace the Christian world.

The cathedrals were mainly the work of the Children of Solomon – a guild of specialist masons instructed from the newly acquired arcane knowledge of St. Bernard's Cistercian

Order. As explained by the 19th-century French hermeticist Fulcanelli, the design was called Gothic (*Art Gothique* or *Argot*) from the *langue argotique*: the guardian language of the Golden Fleece which applied to transmutation alchemy.[12] St. Bernard had translated the secret geometry of King Solomon's masons who, under their own master, Hiram (a Phoenician craftsman from Tyre), were qualified by degrees of knowledge and proficiency. By virtue of this, Hiram was destined to become a key symbolic figure in later Freemasonry as Hiram Abif, which is said to mean Excellent Father.[13]

Built above earth locations where the telluric forces were heightened by deep underground caverns or wells, the cathedrals were all commenced at much the same time, although some took more than a century to complete. Notre Dame de Paris was begun in 1163, Chartres in 1194, Reims in 1211, and Amiens in 1221. Others of the same era were at Bayeux, Abbeville, Rouen, Laon, Evreux, and Etampes. In accordance with the hermetic principle "As above, so below," the combined ground plan of the Notre Dame cathedrals replicates the Virgo constellation.[14]

Notable among the authorities on the history of Chartres is Louis Charpentier, whose research and writings have done much to increase the understanding of Gothic architecture. He tells that at Chartres the telluric earth currents are at their highest and the site was recognized for its divine atmosphere, even in druidic times. So venerated is the location of Chartres that it is the only cathedral not to have a single king, bishop, cardinal, canon, or anyone interred in the soil of its mound. It was an original pagan site, dedicated to the Mother Goddess – a site to which pilgrims traveled long before the time of Jesus. Its altar was strategically erected above the *Grotte des Druides*, which housed a sacred dolmen[15] that was said to mark the Womb of the Earth.

One of the greatest mysteries of Gothic architecture is the stained glass used in the cathedral windows. This particular type of glass first appeared in the early 12th century, but disappeared just as suddenly 100 years later. Nothing like it had ever been seen before, and nothing like it has been seen since. Not only is the luminosity of Gothic glass greater than that of other schools, but its qualities of light enhancement are far more effective. Even in twilight, this glass retains its brilliance way beyond that of any other. True Gothic glass also has the unique power to transform harmful ultra-violet rays into beneficial light, but the secret of its manufacture was never revealed, although it was said to have been a product of hermetic alchemy. Those employed to perfect the glass were Persian philosophical mathematicians from the school of Omar Khayyām. They claimed that their method incorporated the *Spiritus Mundi*: the cosmic breath of the universe. This is now known to have been the white light of the Philosophers' Stone, for their glass was made from high-spin metals. (Many of the windows seen at Notre Dame cathedrals today are not of true Gothic glass; they are replacements and donations from other churches following the extensive damage of World War II.) Akin to the crystal pavement of Moses in Exodus 24:10, a New Testament reference in this regard is to be found in the book of The Revelation 21:18, 21, which states in connection with the cosmic Jerusalem: "And the city was pure gold, like unto clear glass ... And the street of the city was pure gold, as it were transparent glass."

As mentioned earlier (*see* "The Plane of Shar-On," pages 120–4), the optimum weight of the *mfkzt* powder (the Philosophers' Stone) is 56% of the metal weight from which it was transmuted, with the other 44% becoming pure white light. When the white powder of a highward metal (gold or a PGM) is subjected to a specific heat, it transforms immediately to glass and the metal concerned will determine the individual color and qualities of the glass. Not only is wonderfully clear glass produced by this method, but the missing 44% light (the *Spiritus Mundi*) can be made to reappear within the glass, which then returns to its optimum 100% metallic weight. This demonstrates that the 44% never actually disappears: it simply moves into a state of weightlessness beyond the mortal plane: the dimension known to the ancients as the Plane of Shar-On (the Realm of the Orbit of Light).

In 1989, Antoine Faivre, professor of the *Ecole Pratique des Hautes Études*[16] at the Sorbonne University, Paris, spoke of the *Spiritus Mundi* at the Netherlands Alchemy Conference in Gronigen. He cited the German hermeticist Hermann Fictuld who, in his 1749 publication, *Aureum Vellus*, described the *Spiritus Mundi* as being the natural environment of "astral gold," as represented in the legend of the Golden Fleece.[17]

In addition to the Jerusalem treasure, the Templars also found a wealth of ancient Hebrew and Aramaic manuscripts, providing first-hand accounts that had not been edited or tampered with by any ecclesiastical authority. Their documentary discoveries were substantial, including numerous books from Persia and the East. There were ancient Essene works predating Jesus Christ, and volumes from Arabian and Greek philosophers – all of which were destined to be condemned by the Church. There were also volumes concerning numerology, geometry, architecture, and music, along with manuscripts pertaining to metals and alloys. In all, the Templars returned to Europe with the combined knowledge of thousands of years of study, all written down for posterity.

In the light of this, along with the fact that the Knights subsequently refused to bear the upright Latin Cross (which they perceived as an instrument of torture), it was widely accepted that they possessed an insight which eclipsed conventional Christianity – an insight which permitted them the certainty that the Church had misinterpreted both the Virgin Birth and the Resurrection of Jesus. They were nevertheless highly regarded as holy men, and were firmly attached to the Cistercian Popes of the era. In times to follow, however, the once revered knowledge of the Templars led to their persecution by the Popes of other Orders, and by the savage Dominican friars of the Inquisition.

The Vatican authorities were fully aware that the Templars had returned from Jerusalem with more than documents and bullion. They knew that among the Temple hoard was a particularly great and sacred treasure. At that stage they had no way of knowing what it might be, but their intelligence revealed that it was so astonishing as to be far beyond any material wealth.

Inquisition

Back in the 8th century, King Pepin the Short of the Carolingian Franks had agreed to set up a Jewish kingdom within the territory of Burgundy – a kingdom that would have at its head a recognized descendant of the Royal House of David.[18] This was in return for help from the Jews of Narbonne in driving out the Islamic Moors from the city. Consequently, the Jewish kingdom of Septimania (the Midi) was established in 768, from Nimes to the Spanish frontier, with Narbonne as its capital. Pepin's son and successor, Emperor Charlemagne the Great from 800, was pleased to confirm Septimanian independence under the Potentates of Judah. The decision was also upheld by the Caliph of Baghdad and, reluctantly, by Pope Stephen in Rome. All acknowledged Prince Guilhelm of the House of Judah to be a true bloodline successor of King David, and in 791 he instituted his famous Judaic Academy of St. Guilhelm at Gellone.

More than 300 years later, the Davidic succession was still extant in the Spanish Midi to the south of Burgundy, although the notional kingdom had ceased to function as a totally independent state. In 1144 the English monk, Theobald of Cambridge, confirmed (when initiating a charge of ritual murder against the Jews of Norwich): "The chief men and rabbis of the Jews who dwell in Spain assemble together at

Narbonne, where the Royal Seed resides, and where they are held in the highest esteem." In 1166, the chronicler, Benjamin of Tudela, reported that there were still significant estates held by the prevailing Davidic heirs: "Narbonne is an ancient city of the Torah.[19] Therein are sages, magnates, and princes, at the head of whom is Kalonymos, son of the great Prince Todros of blessed memory, a descendant of the House of David, as stated in his family tree. He holds hereditaments and other landed properties from the rulers of the country, and no one may dispossess him."

St. Bernard and his Cistercians made good use of the re-established Judaic Academy at Gellone when compiling their translations from the old Jerusalem manuscripts after the Council of Troyes. However, this gave cause for great concern among the Catholic bishops, who could not discover any part of what was going on. They knew that Gellone had long been a Mary Magdalene cultural seat, and that the Templars swore their Oath to Bethany and the Magdalene. Moreover, the Notre Dame cathedrals were originally dedicated to her as "Our Lady." Also, south of Gellone near Narbonne was Rennes-le-Château, where the church had been consecrated to Mary Magdalene in 1059. This region (west-north-west of Marseilles, on the Golfe du Lion) was then known as Languedoc – a name derived from the people's own unique language: the *langue d'oc*.

The bishops were convinced that, whatever the nature of the Templars' secret treasure, it resided somewhere in Languedoc to the south of France, and so, in 1209, Pope Innocent III decided to send in his troops. A papal army of some 30,000 soldiers descended upon the region under the command of Simon de Montfort. They were deceitfully adorned with the red cross of the Holy Land Crusaders, but their purpose was immeasurably different. They had been sent to exterminate the ascetic Cathari sect (the Pure Ones), whom the Pope and King Philippe II of France were convinced guarded the mysterious treasure and were in league with the Knights Templars against the Church of Rome.

The slaughter continued for 35 years, claiming tens of thousands of lives and culminating in a hideous massacre at the seminary of Montségur, where more than 200 hostages were set upon stakes and burned alive in 1244.[20] In religious terms, the doctrine of the Cathars was essentially Gnostic; they were notably spiritual people, who believed that the spirit was pure but that physical matter was defiled.[21]

The Languedoc region was substantially that which had formed the 8th-century Jewish kingdom of Septimania and, like the Templars, the Cathars were expressly tolerant of the Jewish and Muslim cultures. They also upheld an equality of the sexes[22] but, for all that, they were condemned and violently suppressed by the Catholic Inquisition (formally instituted in 1233) and were charged with all manners of blasphemy and sexual deviance. Contrary to the charges, the witnesses brought to give evidence spoke only of the Cathars' church of love and of their unyielding devotion to the ministry of Jesus. They believed in God and the Holy Spirit, recited The Lord's Prayer and ran an exemplary society with its own welfare system of charity schools and hospitals.

In practical terms, the Cathars were simply non-conformists, preaching without license and having no requirement for appointed priests or the richly adorned churches of their Catholic neighbors. St. Bernard had said that "No sermons are more Christian than theirs and their morals are pure" – yet still the papal armies came, in the outward guise of a holy mission, to eradicate their community from the landscape.

The edict of annihilation applied not only to the mystical Cathars themselves, but to all who supported them – which included most of the people of Languedoc. At that time, although geographically a part of France, the region was a semi-autonomous state. Politically, it was more associated with the northern Spanish frontier, having the Count of

Toulouse as its overlord. Classical languages were taught, along with literature, philosophy, and mathematics. The area was generally quite wealthy and commercially stable, but all this was to change in 1209 when the papal troops arrived in the foothills of the Pyrenees. In allusion to the Languedoc center at Albi, the savage campaign was called the Albigensian Crusade[23] – at least that is what we are told. However, the name has a far more important implication. "Albi" was, in fact, a variant of the old Provençal word *ylbi* (a female elf) and the Cathars referred to the Messianic succession of Mary Magdalene (the *Sangréal*: Holy Grail) as the *Albi-gens*: the Elven bloodline.

Of all the religious cults that flourished in medieval times, Catharism was the least menacing, and the fact that the Cathars were associated with a particular ancient knowledge was no revelation; Guilhelm de Toulouse de Gellone had established his Judaic Academy in the region more than four centuries earlier. However, this very fact (along with the notion that the Cathars held an unsurpassed treasure more historically meaningful than the root of Christianity) led Rome to only one conclusion: the Ark of the Covenant, the Testimony of Judah, and the Jerusalem manuscripts must be hidden in Languedoc. This, it was felt, was enough to blow the lid off the fundamental concept of the Roman Church, and there was only one solution for a desperate and fanatical regime. Consequently, the instruction was given to the papal army: "Kill them all!"

16

The Hidden Scroll

Scourge of the Templars

The Albigensian Crusade in Languedoc ended in 1244, but it was to be another 62 years before King Philippe IV of France and Pope Clement V were in a position to harass the Knights Templars in their bid for the arcane treasure. By 1306 the Jerusalem Order was so powerful that Philippe IV viewed them with the utmost trepidation. Philippe owed a great deal of money to the Knights and was practically bankrupt. He also feared their political and esoteric might, which he knew to be far greater than his own.

Until that time the Templars had operated without direct papal interference, but King Philippe managed to change this. Following a Vatican edict forbidding him to tax the clergy, the French king arranged for the capture and murder of Pope Boniface VIII. His successor, Benedict XI, also met his end in mysterious circumstances, to be replaced in 1305 by Philippe's own candidate, Bertrand de Got, Archbishop of Bordeaux, who duly became Pope Clement V. With this new French Pope under his control, Philippe drew up his list of accusations against the Knights Templars. The easiest charge to lay was that of heresy, for it was well-known that the Knights did not hold with the established doctrines of the Virgin Birth and Crucifixion. It was also known that their diplomatic and business affairs involved them with Jews, Gnostics, and Muslims. With contrived papal support, King Philippe then persecuted the Templars in France and endeavored to eliminate the Order in other countries. (The word "heresy" is defined as a belief or practice contrary to the orthodox doctrine, but it actually derives from the Greek *hairesis*, meaning "choice." Thus, a charge of heresy was a denial of the right of choice.)

On Friday 13th October 1307, Philippe's henchmen struck with a vengeance and Templars were seized throughout France. Captured Knights were imprisoned, interrogated, tortured, and burned. Paid witnesses were called to give evidence against the Order and some truly bizarre statements were obtained. The Templars were accused of a variety of practices deemed unsavory, including necromancy, homosexuality, abortion, blasphemy, and the black arts. Once they had given their evidence, under whatever circumstances of bribery or duress, the witnesses then disappeared without trace. But, despite all this, the King did not achieve his primary objective, for the Templar treasure remained way beyond his grasp. His minions had scoured the length and breadth of Champagne and Languedoc but, all the while, a majority of the hoard was hidden away in the Treasury vaults of the Order's Chapter House in Paris.

In 14th-century France and Flanders, most aristocratic families had sons within the Church – if not as bishops, then as abbots of allied Orders. The Chaplain of the Manor of La Buzadière was one of these noblemen and, shortly before the papal edict against the Templars, there were seven Templar guests at the Lord of the Manor's castle.[1] At this gathering, the Knights were alerted to the impending Inquisition and duly raced to Paris, where they informed their hierarchy of King Philippe's plan. Then, with an auxiliary contingent, they traveled to St. Malo, spreading the word abroad. The seven Knights were Gaston de la Pièrre Phoebus, Guidon de Montanor, Gentilis de Foligno, Henri de Montfort, Louis de Grimoard, Pièrre Yorick de Rivault, and Cesare Minvielle.

At that time, the Grand Master of the Order was Jacques de Molay. Knowing that Pope Clement V was a pawn of King Philippe, Molay arranged for the Paris hoard to be removed in a fleet of 18 galleys from La Rochelle on the Charente coast.[2] Most of these ships sailed to Scotland,[3] and some to Portugal, but Philippe was unaware of this and arranged for the Templars to be pursued throughout Europe. With most of the portable treasure safely dispatched, Molay and some key officers remained in France to continue their work – a primary aspect of which was to get word to those Knights who were not aware of the impending onslaught. Couriers sped far and wide with their message of warning, but in many cases they were too late and their colleagues had already been seized.

Knights were arrested in England, but north of the Border in Scotland the papal Bulls were ineffective. This was because King Robert the Bruce and the whole Scottish nation had previously been excommunicated for taking up arms against the Catholic King Edward II of England.[4] Edward was initially reluctant to turn against the Knights but, as King Philippe's son-in-law, he was in a difficult position and was obliged to comply with the rule of the Inquisition. Many Templars were arrested in England, while their lands and preceptories were confiscated and subsequently passed to the Knights Hospitallers of St. John.

In Scotland, however, the story was very different since an alliance with the Templars had been struck long before in 1128. Hugues de Payens had first met King David I of Scots soon after the Council of Troyes, at which time St. Bernard de Clairvaux had integrated Scotland's Celtic Church within his wealthy Cistercian Order. King David had granted Hugues and his Knights the lands of Ballantradoch by the Firth of Forth (now the village of Temple), and they established their primary seat on the South Esk. Indeed, both David and his sister were married into Godefroi de Boullion's Flemish House of Boulogne, and by way of these marriages there were direct family ties between King David, Hugues de Payens, and the Crusader Kings of Jerusalem.

It is important to recognize that there was no Franco–Scots language barrier since France and Scotland had been formally linked for trading and military purposes for many hundreds of years by way of the *Auld Alliance*.[5] This treaty, formally styled "The League Offensive and Defensive," had been struck between Emperor Charlemagne of the Franks and King Eochaid IV of Scots in 807. It was by virtue of this that the Scots Guard (the *Garde Ecossais*) became the official household bodyguard of the French Royal House of Valois in the days after Philippe IV's Capetian dynasty. In this respect, the Scots Guard was prominent in Joan of Arc's cavalry at the famous Siege of Orléans against the English in 1429.

Following the Templar Fleet's voyage from Brittany, 50 or so French Knights settled in Scotland's Mull of Kintyre. Later, on 24th June 1313 (realizing that their Grand Master, Jacques de Molay, could soon be executed in Europe), they applied the provisions of the Order's revised Constitution of 1307 and appointed a Knight named Pièrre d'Aumont as their Scottish Grand Master. On the nearby island of Islay, and at Kilmartin on the mainland, there are numerous Templar graves still to be found, and some of their distinctive tombstone slabs depict the occupants as Knight Officers of the original Templar Fleet.

Under the auspices of King Robert the Bruce and his excommunicated clergy, the Order was restructured into a Church, with a hierarchy quite independent of Rome. The Templar Church had abbots, priests, and even bishops – but no cardinals, and certainly no Pope. In preparation for a war against the English, they began to train the Scottish troops in the hit-and-run warfare tactics established in the Crusades. Templar gold was then used for an arms supply to be manufactured in Ireland. (From 1314, Robert's brother, Edward Bruce, was King of Ireland until his death in 1318.)

If ever England's House of Plantagenet had designs on the Scottish realm, these designs were dramatically heightened by the arrival of the Templars, and the eventual result was the 1314 Battle of Bannockburn. This battle was fought only three months after the Templar Grand Master, Jacques de Molay, was burned at the stake[6] in France for refusing to reveal the Order's secrets to the Inquisitors of King Philippe IV.

Subsequent to Bannockburn, the Knights became part of the Scottish Government as the appointed royal bodyguard, and were established as official Guardians of the Kings of Scots. The Order was then promoted and encouraged by the succeeding Stewart kings. Considerable tracts of land were passed to the Order (especially around the Lothians and Aberdeen) and the Knights also took possession of properties in the Western regions of Ayr, Lorne, and Argyll.

The year 1317 saw a change in the administration of the Templars. Many had died at Bannockburn and, with their ranks depleted, it was thought advisable to invite Scottish knights into the Order. The King of Scots was installed as the hereditary Sovereign Grand Master and, from that time, whoever held the ultimate office of chancellery was known as the Prince (or Count) St. Germain. Bruce took this original titular style and constituted a new Order for the purpose, calling it the Order of the Elder Brethren of the Rosy Cross. Several of the Rosy Cross Knights then sailed to France for a meeting with Pope John XXII at Avignon.

Despite the Templars' abandonment of any papal affiliation, this new Order was not apparent as a Templar institution, and since the Pope held the international reins of Chivalric Orders, a meeting was necessary for registration. Gaston de la Pièrre Phoebus was the senior representative for the mission, and Pope John agreed to issue a Charter so long as his own nephew, Jacques de Via, became the operative Grand Master. However, de Via died on 6th May 1317, and the position immediately became vacant, whereupon the Knights elected Guidon de Montanor (who was then in Scotland), and they duly returned with the necessary Charter of Incorporation, which they presented to King Robert.[7]

In the event, the papal edict of Scots excommunication did not last indefinitely, and it was lifted in 1323 when Pope John XXII recognized Robert the Bruce as the true King of Scots. By virtue of this recognition, many historians have presumed that the Knights Templars must have been disbanded in Scotland, but this was not the case – it was simply that Bruce had contrived the secret Order to become even more secret. In constituting his Order of the Rosy Cross for Templars who had been valiant at Bannockburn, Bruce had provided a very successful cover.

It was during these Templar-influenced times that the Scottish national banking system evolved from the Order's financial experience in Europe and the Middle East. Scotland's soil held significant gold reserves and the Knights were quick to put these resources to use. This underground wealth was one of the reasons why the Plantagenet English were so keen to gain dominion in Scotland.[8] At a Paris banquet, hosted by King James V of Scots (1513–42) and his wife, Madeleine de France, more than 300 French guests were each presented with a goblet filled to the brim with Scottish gold. The Crown of Scotland (with its magnificent gems, and pearls from the River Tay) is made from Scottish gold and even today, as reported recently in the British national press, there are two gold mines currently being worked in Perthshire.[9]

The Third Degree

Along with the Children of Solomon, other masonic brotherhoods of medieval France were the Children of Father Soubise, and the Children of Master Jacques.[10] When the 14th-century Inquisition against the Templars was in full swing, these guilds were equally at risk. Being practitioners of the hermetic Craft, they held privileged information concerning the workings of sacred geometry according to their attained degrees. There were three such degrees: Apprentice Companion, Attained Companion, and Master Companion – just as there are now three degrees in the mainstream of modern speculative Freemasonry. This is why, following the Inquisition of the Templars, a severe interrogation to extract vital or secret information under duress is often called the Third Degree.

Although modern Freemasonry is said to derive from the medieval guilds of Europe, it had far more distant origins in the days of the ancient Master Craftsmen. Carvings on the Egyptian obelisk in Central Park, New York, have been identified as masonic symbols from the time of pharaoh Tuthmosis III (c. 1468–1436 BC).[11] He was the great-great-grandfather of Moses and the founder of an influential society of scholars and philosophers, whose purpose was to preserve the sacred mysteries. In later times, the Samaritan Magi were members of the Order, being attached to the ascetic Egyptian Therapeutate at Qumrân in Judaea. It was from Egyptian custom that Akhenaten the Moses continued the concept of temple ritual when he created the Tabernacle in Sinai, subsequent to which the tradition was taken into Canaan. Prior to that, the Canaanites and early Hebrews had used simple outside stone altars as places of reverence and sacrifice, such as those erected by Noah and Abraham (Genesis 8:20 and 22:9).

A second Egyptian obelisk from the Temple of the Sun – known as Cleopatra's Needle (relating to Queen Cleopatra VII, although it predated her by more than 1,000 years) – stands on the Thames Embankment in London. It is 68 feet, 6 inches (20.88 m) high[12] and weighs 186 tons. These two granite obelisks were originally entrance pillars to the Egyptian Temple at Heliopolis, but were moved to Alexandria in 12 BC, then to London and New York in 1878 and 1881 respectively. In 1926, Eugene Canseliet, a student of the French alchemist Fulcanelli, collated his master's notes for a work published as *Les mysteres des cathedrales*. In this he specifically inscribed a citation to the Heliopolis Brotherhood (*Le Fraternite d'Heliopolis*).

In line with the Egyptian practice of placing freestanding pillars at temple entrances, the Phoenician architect Hiram had introduced the same theme at the porch of King Solomon's Temple in Jerusalem. The pillars, with their rounded capitals, were akin to the designs of Tyre goddess worship, and were also similar to the fertility symbols dedicated to Astarte in Canaan. The Jerusalem brazen pillars were called *Jachin* and *Boaz* (1 Kings 7:21 and 2 Chronicles 3:17), and are reckoned by Freemasons to have been built hollow in order to serve as repositories for the Constitutional Rolls of Masonry. Moreover, although the Temple was considered by the Old Testament scribes to have been dedicated to Jehovah and designed primarily to house the Ark of the Covenant, its construction was not limited to the masculine principle of God. It was constructed largely in keeping with traditional custom and incorporated both the male and female geometric energies.

Masonic lore relates that the Temple was completed in seven years, at the end of which time Hiram was murdered and placed in a shallow grave. His death is said to have come about through his refusal to impart the Master Masons' secrets to the lesser initiated workers. Today, the symbolized slaying of Hiram Abif features significantly in the Third Degree ceremony of Freemasonry, when the candidate is struck down and raised again from the darkness of his grave by the use of a peculiar grip (called the Lion's Paw) and a particular bodily attitude. Modern Freemasonry is speculative rather than operative, but even in Hiram's day the society of Dionysian Artificers to which he belonged had its own lodges, symbols, and passwords. One symbol was the ascia (the mason's trowel), an emblem used by the later Pythagoreans and Essenes. It is also found in the catacombs of Rome, where portrayals of masonic initiation were painted in the tombs of the persecuted Innocenti.

The Flame of Innocence

While compiling this chapter, I received a call from Adriano Forgione, editor of the Italian magazine *Hera* in Rome. "Have you heard about the recent archival discovery at the Vatican?" he asked excitedly. I had to admit that I had not, but before long a related six-page article and photographs appeared in *Hera*.[13] This led to a lengthy feature article in Britain's foremost daily newspaper, *The Times*, entitled: "Vatican File Shows Pope Pardoned Massacred Knights."[14]

With today's Pope currently seeking Muslim forgiveness for the Crusades, *The Times* correspondent in Rome suggested that perhaps he should also apologize for the 14th-century Inquisition of the Knights Templars. Despite everything previously known about the liaison between Pope Clement V and King Philippe IV of France to bring down the Order and execute its Grand Master, Jacques de Molay, it now transpires that Pope Clement had actually exonerated the Knights before Philippe let loose his henchmen for their wholesale massacre!

This announcement was recently made by Dr. Barbara Frale, a researcher at the Vatican School of Paleontology who, on 13th September 2001, discovered a hitherto unknown scroll, signed by Clement V, hidden away in the Vatican's Secret Archive. Now dubbed the *Chinon Parchment*, the document tells of a 1308 interrogation of de Molay and the Chapter House Templars by papal ambassadors at Chinon Castle in the Loire. Subsequent to his inquiry into the validity of King Philippe's charges against the Knights, Pope Clement's scroll states in conclusion, "We hereby decree that they are absolved by the Church, that they are restored to communion and that they may receive the holy sacraments."

In addition to this, it appears that Clement had severely criticized King Philippe, writing: "While we were absent you turned your mind to the Knights Templars and their property. You have even gone so far as to incarcerate them, and what pains us most is that you have not released them. On the contrary, we have heard that you have done more, inflicting in addition to their imprisonment further suffering." This protest was formalized in the Bull *Subit Assidue* of 5th July 1308, in which Clement accused the French Inquisitor, William of Paris, of failing to advise the papal authority of the arrests.

Unfortunately for the Templars, the Pope's words were completely disregarded by the King of France. Clement, with his new papal See at Avignon, was not in a position to enforce the terms of his decree, and his cardinals in Rome were similarly powerless against the despotic French monarch. Consequently, some while later, at the Council of Vienne in 1312, Pope Clement tried another strategy by formally terminating the Templars' chivalric status in an attempt to have de Molay and the other prisoners handed over to the papal curia for a more comfortable house arrest. By this means, he figured that an official trial could be conducted under his jurisdiction, and that the Knights would be reprieved in due course. But it was to no avail, and the debate became so protracted that, during the course of it, Clement V drew near to his death. At this, King Philippe did not waste another moment. With no active Pope to consider, he had de Molay and his companions removed to an island on the River Seine. Then, without trial, they were burnt at the stake on 18th March 1314. Clement died a month later at Roquemaure, on 20th April, and shortly after that King Philippe also died. Subsequently, there was no Pope elected for two years until John XXII took office in 1316.

Interestingly, the recent discovery of the *Chinon Parchment* has made it clear that the document had not been a secret to the Vatican officials, even though they thought it was lost. Notwithstanding Pope Clement's endeavor towards justice, the content of his scroll was known, but had been kept secret for the past 900 years. When questioned after the find by the Catholic daily paper *L'Awenire*, a Vatican spokesman said that, as far as they knew, it had been lost in the early 19th century at the time of Napoleon.

Although there is no doubting the authenticity or content of the scroll, there is still an element of manipulative untruth which emanates from its ostensibly forgiving ink. In fact, for many reasons, it signifies collusion of a "good cop–bad cop" style between Clement and Philippe. For all its length and fine wording, the only people to whom it was published at the time (apart from King Philippe and his Inquisitors) were de Molay and his fellow Knights in prison. It is reasonable to conjecture that perhaps Clement and the cardinals might not have been able to force King Philippe into compliance with the decree, but there were other monarchs who would clearly have been more obedient. The Kings of Portugal and Spain, for example, would undoubtedly have welcomed such a papal absolution for the Knights, while King Edward II of England would have been most relieved to have a legitimate reason to stand firm against his dictatorial French father-in-law. Outside France, however, there is no record of any monarch knowing anything about the *Chinon Parchment* at the time.

It rather looks as if Clement and Philippe were playing both ends against the middle. While Philippe was hounding and torturing the Templars in the hope of submission, Pope Clement was playing his part by trying to gain the Knights' confidence, as if siding with them. It is no secret that, in the final event, they were both after precisely the same thing. They desperately wanted to know the whereabouts of the Templar treasure and to gain particular access to that one formidable item which had made the Knights so feared and revered since their 1127 return from Jerusalem: the Ark of the Covenant.

Rise of the Phoenix

Beneath the Temple Mount

That the Ark had been hidden at the time of King Josiah (*c.* 597 BC), is not in doubt (*see* "Guardians of Destiny," pages 157–8). Not only does the Old Testament confirm many times that it was housed in the Jerusalem Temple for 15 generations after King Solomon's era (*c.* 375 years) before being secreted, but it is also mentioned outside the Bible. Written in around 100 BC, the *Damascus Document* of the Qumrân Dead Sea Scrolls confirms that the Ark had been hidden.[1]

Similarly, there is no doubt that the Ark was held in the Jerusalem Holy of Holies prior to being concealed from Nebuchadnezzar of Babylon. Its Temple location has been physically established, in complete accord with the Bible, by its still visible setting in the floor of the *Sanctum Sanctorum* – an inset depression of 53 inches x 31 inches facing the entrance.[2] As stated by King Solomon in 1 Kings 8:21: "And I have set there a place for the Ark."

Interestingly, this rectangular floor setting further establishes that the Ark was placed with its short side forward to the approach, not lengthwise as is often imagined. The Holy of Holies was only 20 cubits square and, as given in the Talmud,[3] the Ark's carrying shafts were 10 cubits in length, so they would have needed the entrance space in order to be withdrawn once the Ark was lowered into position.[4]

Also not in doubt are the histories of the constructional stages of the First and Second Temples on the original square platform of Solomon's design, and on the adjusted platform of Zerubbabel's replacement building, as supervised by the prophet Nehemiah. The subsequent platform extension made by the Seleucid Kings of Syria[5] (to house a fortress in 186 BC) has been positively indentified, together with the further Hasmonaean extension of 141 BC and the later extension by King Herod the Great (37–4 BC).

The whole complex is now known as the *Haram el Sharif* (Noble Sanctuary) and, from the days of Solomon to the time of Herod, the foundation increased dramatically in size, making it the largest man-made building platform in the classical world.[6] Herod's final construction occupied a space of some 144,000 square meters, compared with 30,000 for the Acropolis in Athens.[7] It had an outer wall that was 16 feet thick (nearly 4.9 m) and many of its stones weighed as much as 80 tons. In his awestruck, first-hand description of the edifice, Flavius Josephus used such words as "incredible," "immense," and "amazing."[8] The Roman senator Tacitus recorded in *The Histories* that water was supplied to the enclosure by an ever-flowing spring, with additional tanks for collecting rainwater.[9] Additionally, the *Middoth* tractate of the *Mishnah* (the earliest rabbinic codification of the Law, from about AD 200) relates that there was a great wheel, which drew water from the underground Golah Cistern.[10]

In the 1860s, the British explorer Sir Charles Warren conducted extensive excavations beneath the Temple Mount for the Palestine Exploration Fund,[11] and the related photograph collection (currently held by the Fund) is very revealing. To begin, his team dug a number of vertical shafts down to the bedrock, and then opened lateral tunnels between them to identify the walls of the original square foundation and its subsequent extensions. Having achieved that, they went even deeper

Subterranean chamber beneath the Temple of Jerusalem.

into the limestone rock itself, where they discovered an astonishing subterranean labyrinth of winding corridors and
passages. Branching off these were large storage facilities and a
virtual fairyland of cleverly engineered caves and water
cisterns.[12] Fortunately, as well as the monochrome photographs,
some of this was captured in color by the Victorian artist
William Simpson, famed for his paintings of the Crimean War
just a few years earlier. (He had been sent to Jerusalem to record
the Warren expedition for the *London Illustrated News*.)

It was during the course of these Palestine Exploration
Fund excavations that the original square foundation of King
Solomon's original Temple was found. Its lower retaining
walls were still intact, and their masonry techniques were
quite distinct from those of the Second Temple and later buildings. That this exploratory dig took place when it did was
truly fortuitous because it has never been repeated, apart from
a mapping survey by British military engineers shortly after-

wards in 1894. The whole underground area has since become inaccessible by virtue of Muslim political and religious sensibilities.[13] One reward from the 1894 project was the discovery of a Templar cross, a broken Templar sword, and other related items in the tunneling.[14]

The Royal Arch

Although it has been confirmed by many that the origin of Freemasonry dates back to very early times in Egypt and Babylonia, it is noticeable that the tenets of the modern Craft are firmly cemented with King Solomon's Temple in Jerusalem. This is characterized by ritual and by certain ceremonial questions and answers – for example, *Question*: "Where was the first lodge?" *Answer*: "In the porch of Solomon's Temple." And *Question*: "In what part of the Temple was the lodge kept?" *Answer*: "In Solomon's porch at the west end of the Temple, where the two pillars were set up."[15]

Central to the theme of Third Degree Freemasonry (*see* "The Third Degree," pages 252–5), is Solomon's chief mason Hiram Abif. According to the ritual, he was slain by the three lesser masons, Jubela, Jubelo, and Jubelum, for not revealing the secrets of the Master Craftsmen. Individual rituals vary slightly but, in essence, one man struck him with a 24-inch gauge (alternatively a plumb rule), another with a square (or level), and the other with a stone maul. They buried him over the brow of Mount Moriah and placed a sprig of acacia on the shallow grave. When Hiram's body was discovered, Solomon instructed some Fellowcraft (Second Degree) Masons to disinter him, but he could not be raised by clutching his hand with either the Entered Apprentice grip or the Fellowcraft grip (the first two masonic handshakes). Only by taking a firm hold of his wrist and using advantageous bodily leverage (called the "five points of fellowship") could he be raised. He was then buried with dignity and a suitable epitaph near the *Sanctum Sanctorum*.

What is especially interesting about this sequence is that those Fellowcrafts concerned were said to have been instructed by Solomon to don aprons (*ephods*), as had the Levite guardians of the Ark. Also, they were to wear gloves and to divest themselves of all metal objects which they might carry on their persons or in their pockets. The same is repeated today when masonic initiates are relieved of all coins and metal objects. These days, the gesture is reckoned to be symbolic of vulnerability, but this would not have been a necessary requirement for Solomon's diggers – so perhaps something rather more scientific motivated the original tradition.

Royal Arch Masonry, which emerged in the 1700s from an arcane heritage, is generally worked as an addition to the Third Degree. It is commonly held that modern "speculative" Freemasonry evolved from past "operative" masonry but, whether or not this is the case, Royal Arch Masonry appears to have a very different root, despite the fact that it has been tagged on to the Hiramic ritual.[16] The Royal Arch tenets and symbols have a positive alchemical aspect which are more akin to Rosicrucian metaphysical philosophy. One of its key differences is that, instead of being concerned with raising a dead Master from an ignominious grave, it has a distinct crypt legend as its theme. It is partially rooted in Old Testament lore, but also has a parallel flavor from Templar Europe in much later times. Royal Arch masonry also has elements of a Scottish tradition concerning knights of the crusading era who discovered a secret vault in Jerusalem. Additionally, the ritual is concerned with the importance of a particular "keystone," which is graphically depicted as being divorced from its Arch (*see* Plate 20 image by Laurence Dermott, 18th-century Secretary of the Royal Arch).

Initially, England's Grand Lodge hierarchs were wholly opposed to the integration of Royal Arch Masonry within the designated structure. But supporters of the more ancient aspect pressed their claim to authenticity and this led to a dispute between the so-called Ancients and Moderns. Eventually, however, the latter agreed to accept Royal Arch ritual as an extension of their Third (Master Masons) Degree, but only on the understanding that certain amendments were made.

Freemasonry did not emerge in England until the mid-17th century, but in Scotland the Lodge of Aberdeen was recorded in 1541. Indeed, according to the Rite of Strict Observance, speculative Masons from operative French guilds were in Aberdeen as early as 1361. Also, the lodge at Stirling was reputed to have had a masonic chapter as early as 1590 – at which time various high degrees were being worked, including Rose Croix, Knight Templar, and Royal Arch.

At that time the Scottish Templars were under the leadership of David Seton (a kinsman of Lord George Seton and his sister Mary Seton – one of the legendary "Four Maries" who accompanied Mary Stuart to France in 1548, and returned with her as Mary, Queen of Scots, in 1561). Seton reconstituted the Stuart Order under a new identity as the Knights Templars of St. Anthony,[17] and in 1590 land grants were made to the Order by King James VI, requiring that they should found operative hospitals. A further grant, awarded in 1593, was specifically for a monastery and hospital at Leith.[18] The latter was founded in 1614 to become King James's Hospital, and duly bore the royal coat of arms.

The first inductions into English Freemasonry are recorded from 1641, when rituals were formalized during the reign of King Charles I Stuart. Nevertheless, it was his father, King James VI of Scots (James I of England), who had previously established the fraternal concept on an informal basis south of the Border.

Noted as the first Freemason in England was the Scottish statesman Sir Robert Moray, who was the London Attaché for Cardinal Richelieu of France and was of enormous influence in Court and Government circles.[19] Subsequently installed was the hermetic scholar Elias Ashmole (founder of Oxford

University's Ashmolean Museum) and William, Viscount Brouncker, president of London's Gresham College at the time of King Charles II. Mutual interests in hermetic alchemy and sacred science brought these men together in 1660 to form the Royal Society of London, along with other Rosy Cross adepts such as Robert Boyle, William Petty, and Christopher Wren. Royally chartered by their patron King Charles II in 1662, their motto was established as *Nullis in verba*, which roughly translates to "Take no one's word for it" – a motto which had previously been used by the Rosicrucian philosopher Sir Francis Bacon. Indeed, the Society's inaugural picture, published in 1667, depicts a bust of King Charles, along with Viscount Brouncker and Sir Francis Bacon, who had died many years before. Also featured in the engraving is the Angel of Fame from the *Fama Fraternitatis* of the 1614 *Rosicrucian Manifestos*.

A New Philosophy

The Royal Society's interest in alchemy and gold was notably encouraged by the Cambridge Platonist, Henry More, and his pupil Anne, Viscountess Conway of Ragley Hall, who nurtured a group of intellectuals called the Hartlib Circle, to which Robert Boyle and the physician William Petty belonged. They recognized that medieval alchemy, in the way it was generally portrayed (the manufacture of gold from base metal), was a delusion conveyed to the outside world by propagandists and failed adepts. Alchemy, they knew, was a combination of practical and spiritual arts, which had its root in ancient metallurgy, while also applying to the enlightened state of being (the golden state) which could be achieved by the mundane person (symbolized by lead).

At the hub of it all was Gresham College itself, established in 1597 (where the NatWest Tower now stands in Cheapside, London) as a memorial to Sir Thomas Gresham who had conceived and funded the project. Thomas Gresham, the

Tudor royal agent in Antwerp, was a Provincial Master of the Rosicrucian Order and brother-in-law to the Rosicrucian heraldist Sir John Thynne of Longleat. The latter's treatise, *Homo Animal Sociale*, is a lengthy discourse on matters concerning Egyptian hieroglyphics and Druid writings, compiled long before the days of archaeological discovery.

During the 11-year Commonwealth and Cromwellian Protectorate from 1649 (which followed the Civil War between the Royalists and Parliamentarians), alchemical texts from Tudor times had been hard to come by. If not confiscated by the parliamentary Roundheads, they were hidden away to elude discovery. But with the 1660 Restoration of Charles II Stuart, a new enlightenment of initiates began. This enlightenment made it quite clear that the Philosophers' Stone (despite all the puritanical rhetoric) had nothing whatever to do with making gold, for it was itself made of gold, and was indeed the magical "powder of gold," just as Nicolas Flamel and Eirenaeus Philalethes had written (*see* "The Ultimate Goal," page 14 and "Realm of the Genies," page 124).

The new philosophy of these scientific pioneers, with their extraordinary insight, was indeed like the Phoenix rising from the ashes, and their era of amazing discovery was unique in Western history. What especially intrigued the fraternity was that the Philosophers' Stone was traditionally associated with the defiance of gravity, and this compelling subject was a primary focus of their study, leading to the famous gravity discoveries by Robert Hooke and Isaac Newton. Additionally, they knew that the Stone was directly related to higher degrees of consciousness and perception, while being represented by the legendary Phoenix which rises from destruction in a blaze of rebirth and new light (*see* "Sacred Manna," pages 24–8).

Robert Boyle was a great mystery to his friends outside the Society. His father, the Earl of Cork, was the richest man in Britain, yet few men worked so hard and long without the need for personal gain. Being such a high-profile figure, Robert suffered considerably from clerical harassment and was regarded as highly suspicious by the Church because of his determined research into matters of the occult. The bishops were well aware that he had his own specially equipped alchemical workshop, and they watched him very closely. However, Boyle refused to take Holy Orders (as scientists were supposed to do in those times), and he wrote at length concerning magic and the Philosophers' Stone. Ostensibly a scrupulous man, it is clear that Boyle confronted a real dilemma in his work. He stated that so much traditional alchemical writing was too obscure to be of any real value, but nevertheless studied all he could in order to pursue his research.

Whether Boyle actually succeeded in making the Philosophers' Stone is unclear and seemingly unlikely, but there is no doubt that he saw it in operation after a Viennese friar had found a quantity of the mysterious powder secreted in a small casket within a pillar at his monastery. In his related report to the Royal Society, Boyle made particular mention of the powder's ability to manipulate specific gravity – something which has now been proven in today's laboratory research. What he never imagined, of course, was that over three centuries later it would be discovered to manipulate space-time, thereby becoming a substance of primary interest to an international space industry.

The Vienna account is reminiscent of a similar box of alchemical powder which the Elizabethan magus John Dee had once obtained from the Dissolution remnants of Glastonbury Abbey. More importantly, Boyle managed to discover an Eastern source of the Philosophers' Stone in its natural state, without having to go to the trouble of manufacturing it. This, once again, is something which recent discovery has proved to be possible.

In his subsequent Royal Society *Philosophical Transactions* article, Boyle noted that his objective was not to make gold,

but to "produce good medicines for general use." He nevertheless conceded, with amazing foresight, that it was dangerous research since the Stone, if misused, could "disorder the
affairs of mankind, favor tyranny, and bring a general confusion, turning the world topsy-turvy."

By virtue of a later program to sanitize the early Royal
Society's occult image in the Hanoverian era, Robert Boyle's
alchemical pursuits were strategically lost to academia until
modern times. He is now best remembered for Boyle's Law
concerning the volume of gases, along with his research into
the elasticity of air, but few have recognized that his tireless
work and findings were fuelled by an overwhelming desire to
understand the nature of the great alchemical secret.

Another Royal Society Fellow with an enormous talent was
Sir Isaac Newton, who was also an ardent alchemist. He
embarked on a translation of the *Emerald Tablet* and the *Corpus
Hermeticum* of Hermes Trismegistus, and was especially interested in the *prisca sapienta* (a unified theory of the law of the
Universe), which he referred to as the Frame of Nature. This
thought process was directly allied with the underlying
maxim of Hermes: "As above, so below." It denotes that the
harmony of earthly proportion is representative of its universal equivalent – in other words, that earthly proportion is the
mundane image of cosmological structure. From the smallest
cell to the widest expanse of the galaxies, a repetitive geometric law prevails, and this was understood from the very earliest of recorded times.

Newton's religious leaning was distinctly Arian, a form of
Christianity which denied the divinity of Jesus and rejected
any concept of the Holy Trinity. Albeit he was a deeply spiritual man, and an authority on early religion, he constantly
maintained that the New Testament had been strategically
distorted by the Church before its publication. One of his foremost studies concerned the structure of the ancient kingdoms,
and he claimed the pre-eminence of the Judaic heritage as an

archive of divine knowledge and numerology.[20] In fact, Newton was so immersed in the hermetic lore of ancient times that, in a 1942 wartime lecture to the Royal Society, the renowned economist and political commentator John Maynard Keynes referred to him as "the last of the Sumerians."

Secrets Denied

These, then, were some of the great men who were involved in the front-line workings of original Rosicrucian metaphysical science. They were truly Freemasons of the old school. Through studying the secrets of the ancient archons and applying the arcane principles of hermetic philosophy, they and their colleagues numbered among the greatest scientists of all time. However, following the 1688 deposition of the Royal House of Stuart by the Whig aristocrats of London's Westminster Parliament, Scottish Freemasonry and Templar-based Rosicrucian philosophy moved into European exile with them. By the early 1700s, Newton and others were obliged to adopt a more clinical image as their old culture moved from Britain's shores to be overshadowed by an austere new regime. In this regard, the subsequently reigning House of Hanover (an incoming German dynasty from 1714) introduced its own masonic lodges and the Grand Lodge of England was constituted in 1717 (subsequently, as it became more widely affiliated, to become United Grand Lodge). The problem was that their new form of Freemasonry (which became known as the *York Rite*) was centered upon very restricted information and, since its founders were not themselves initiates of the higher degrees, they justified their position by claiming that the true secrets of the Craft had been lost to a bygone era.

To further strengthen its weak position on this front, the Hanoverian Government of King George III went so far as to introduce a Secret Society Act in 1799. This proscribed the working of any masonic degrees higher than those of York, and specifically forbade teachings and ritual that were Templar based. This was the final nail in the coffin of old style Freemasonry in Britain. Even Scotland's ancient Kilwinning Lodge, which dated back to the days before Robert the Bruce (possibly even to the 12th century), was compelled to toe the line under threat of losing its Charter.[21] Henceforth, substitute secrets of a rather pointless and ritualistic nature were introduced – "until such time," it was said, "that the old secrets are rediscovered." Resultantly, for nearly three centuries, Freemasons of this new school have gleaned nothing of any real consequence. It is of little wonder that they are so intent to preserve a facade of knowing important secrets which they cannot reveal – for the biggest secret of all is that they are never taught what the true secrets are!

It may come as a surprise to many that Solomon's Temple did not always hold the pre-eminent position in Freemasonry that it has enjoyed since the 18th century. In an early document of the generally styled Old Charges – The *Regius Manuscript* from about 1399 – it is declared that the First Excellent Grand Master was not Solomon but Nimrod, the mighty hunter of Babylon, who features in Genesis 10:8–10. In this context, he is misidentified with the building of the Tower of Babel, which was actually constructed by King Ur Baba long after Nimrod's time in around 2000 BC. Notwithstanding the chronological discrepancy, the *Regius MS* relates that Nimrod taught all the masonic signs and tokens to distinguish his builders and their Craft from the rest of mankind.[22]

Despite the British restrictions, the old scientific movement prevailed in parts of Europe, and notable in this Rosicrucian arena until his death in 1784 was the influential Marquis de Montferrat, the prevailing Comte de St. Germain.[23] As mentioned earlier (*see* "Scourge of the Templars," page 247), the titular style of St. Germain was held by the Masters of the Elder Brethren of the Rosy Cross from its introduction by Robert the Bruce in 1317.

The Art of Hermes

Although the ritual of Royal Arch Freemasonry is ostensibly devised around a vault discovery, it seems likely that in older times its origin was arkite and hermetically based. Indeed, the pre-England *Constitutions* of 1723 specify no less than 23 times that it is about the cultivation of a "Royal Art" – each time written in capitals or italics.[24] Also from the 1723 ritual comes the *Question*: "Whence comes the pattern of an arch?" – to which is given the correct ceremonial *Answer*: "From a rainbow."[25] This is interestingly reminiscent of the "curved light" emblem of the alchemical House of Camu-lôt (*see* "A Noble Artificer," page 228).

There is no doubt that many of the engravings in Robert Fludd's Rosicrucian journal, *Clavis Philosophiæ et Alchymiæ Fluddianæ*, published in the 1630s, are prototypes of later masonic devices. Some Tracing Boards[26] of the 18th-century lodges are similarly constructed. Also, a popularly used lodge Deacon's jewel of the era carried a depiction of Hermes himself.[27] So, what happened to these Rosicrucian and hermetic aspects of early Freemasonry? How were the real secrets of Elizabethan and Stuart times forgotten, to be replaced by strange rituals, which are beyond even the modern participants' ultimate comprehension? Plainly, an alchemical remnant persisted in the Georgian 1700s, especially while the younger colleagues of those such as Isaac Newton and Christopher Wren were still alive, but by the 1800s all trace of anything scientifically worthwhile had gone.

The final change of emphasis occurred in 1809, when a heated dispute arose between King George III's sons, Edward and Augustus (younger brothers of George Augustus, who became King George IV). Prince Edward, the Duke of Kent,[28] was a Freemason of the new *York Rite* of the House of Hanover, but his brother Prince Augustus Frederick, Duke of Sussex, was a *Scottish Rite* Knight Templar and (despite his father's position) was allied to the exiled House of Stuart.[29]

Edward endeavored to sway his brother's allegiance, but failed and compromised by creating a pseudo-Templar branch within the English masonic structure. This fell under his own Kent protectorate and persists today, although it is quite divorced from legitimate Templarism.

An engraver called Alexander Deuchar then approached Edward of Kent for a Charter to establish an anti-Stuart Templar authority in Scotland. The Duke agreed, and in 1811 the new foundation became known as the Scottish Conclave, with Deuchar as its Grand Master and Edward as the Royal Grand Patron.

From 1826, the Grand Master of the original Templars in Scotland was Robert Martin of the Irish Grand Encampment. He denounced Deuchar's establishment on 28 December 1827, proclaiming that neither the Duke of Kent nor Deuchar had the right to pretend that they were Knights of the Temple. The Duke was, however, the King's son and there was little that Martin could do to counter his mock establishment. Consequently, the original Scots and Irish Encampments became allied to the Stuart Templars and their *Scottish Rite* in France – especially to the *Chapitre Primordian de Rose Croix*, which had been constituted in Arras by Bonnie Prince Charlie and the Comte de St. Germain in 1747. The Duke of Kent had no way of infiltrating this activity outside Britain, and so he concocted a series of spurious additional degrees and introduced what is still referred to as *Scottish Rite* in Britain and North America today. So, what happened to the lost secrets of the original scientific fraternities? Nothing. They still exist – but they are certainly lost to masonic institutions which fall under the jurisdiction of the Kent Protectorate.

The Lord of Light

The black-and-white checkered pavement of the masonic lodges is sometimes held to be related to the floor of

Solomon's Temple, but this is not a biblical representation and no such thing is mentioned in the Old Testament or in any other related text. In fact, 1 Kings 6:15 and 30 specifically state that the Temple floor was made of fir planks covered with gold. By virtue of this, the lodge pavement design is often a subject of discussion in masonic circles, with a number of viewpoints having been put forward over the years. Whatever else might be its origin, it does reflect the black-and-white checkered war-banner of the Knights Templars. Called the *Beaucéant* (alternatively, *Baussant*), the banner depicted – just as is said of the masonic pavement – the changing relationship between constraint and freedom, between ignorance and enlightenment, between Darkness and Light.[30]

One of the symbolic words in Royal Arch ritual, said to have been discovered in a First Temple vault when the foundation was being prepared for Zerubbabel's Second Temple, is *Jah-Bul-On*. This is reckoned to be a combination of Hebrew, Mesopotamian, and Egyptian words, meaning "I am the Lord, Father of All" (or words to that effect, depending on the particular ritual used). It is sometimes lengthened to "I am and shall be; Lord in Heaven; Father of All"[31] – or even unfathomably extended to "I am that I am, the Alpha and Omega, the Beginning and the End, the First and the Last, who was and is, and is to come, the Almighty."[32]

Whatever the case, *Jah-Bul-On* is a triune god principle, conjoined from different cultures and relating to the three aspects of the Grand Architect of Masonry: *Jahweh* – stated simply as *Jah* in Psalm 68:4 (Hebrew),[33] *Bul* (alternatively *Baal* or *Bel*: Canaanite) and *On* (Egyptian), which translate to "I am/the Lord/On." However, the last word, *On* (as cited in Genesis 41:45) defines the Egyptian sun-god and was an alternative name for Heliopolis, the Egyptian temple-city of Annu and Ra, called the House of the Sun.[34] As such, the term *On* was specifically related to "light." A more accurate translation of *Jah-Bul-On* would therefore be: "I am the Lord of Light."

With Light predominating as a requirement, in its greater and lesser forms, throughout all masonic ritual, there are indeed some key pointers to old secrets within the Royal Arch ceremony. This arrived in 18th-century England from Ireland and Scotland as a remnant of a more philosophical branch of Freemasonry, which had otherwise been exiled. Since speculative Masonry of the original Scottish style evolved directly from a Templar legacy in the Gaelic realms, it is clearly the case that its importance was a Templar importance and its secrets were Templar secrets. Undoubtedly, the Jerusalem Temple was of great significance to the early Knights Templars, but not because it was Solomon's project, or because Hiram Abif was murdered there. It was important because of what they unearthed at the Jerusalem site and brought back to the West in 1127.

The story of Hiram Abif, as related in Freemasonry, is not mentioned in the Bible or in any other chronicle because it is an allegory in itself, not a history. Consequently, in the same way as the checkered pavement debate, it has provoked an amount of discussion, and a number of books by those seeking to find an origin for the legend. In its broader context, however, it is the story of an important disinterment from an ignoble darkness, followed by an auspicious relocation in the realm of light. This concept is clarified from the very outset of initiation with the ritual question: "What is the predominant wish of your heart?" – to which the given correct answer is "Light."

The Hiramic legend (with its ritualistic unearthing and relocation of the Master) could be no less than an allegorical account of the disinterment and relocation of the Ark of the Covenant, which appears not only in Royal Arch imagery, but (even though not directly featured in the Degree rituals) proudly surmounts the United Grand Lodge coat of arms at its crest. Additionally, current Royal Arch ritual explains that towards the end of the 18th century there was a dispute over

United Grand Lodge of England Coat of Arms surmounted by the
Ark of the Covenant.

an aspect of the Jewel of the Chapter, as a result of which part
of the ritual was reinterpreted. Prior to that, a combination of
descriptive wording in the lodge explanation of the jewel
reads: "*Nil nisi clavis deest … Templum Hierosolyma … clavis ad
thesaurum … theca ubi res pretiosa deponitur,*" which translates
to: "Nothing is wanted but the key … the Temple of Jerusalem
… the key to the treasure … a place where a precious thing is
concealed."

The Resting Place

Rosary of the Philosophers

In determining the site and method of the Templars' inspired relocation of the Ark, there are certain key elements to take into account. Of primary importance is the involvement of "light." Next is the requirement for a "keystone" (or copestone) to be in position. Additionally, the Royal Arch account of the Jerusalem Temple's underground vault (where the masons found the secret *Jah-Bul-On* inscription and a mysterious scroll) makes particular reference to an engraved "plate of gold," said to have been discovered on a marble pedestal.

Rather than referring to Hiram Abif's "first lodge" at Solomon's Temple (as given in the Third Degree), the Royal Arch ritual refers to an earlier event. In this instance, it is related that the First or Holy Lodge was held "at the foot of Mount Horeb in the wilderness of Sinai," where Moses, Aholiab (son of Aaron), and Bezaleel presided. It is then stated that the Second Lodge was held at the Jerusalem Temple – not in the porch, but "in the bosom of the holy Mount Moriah," with King Solomon, Hiram of Tyre, and Hiram Abif presiding.

What then was engraved on the golden plate? According to masonic teaching, there were (apart from the ineffable name of God) two integrated geometric shapes: an equilateral triangle within a circle. Graphically, these are depicted in Royal Arch

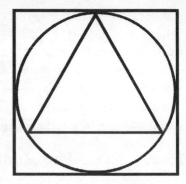

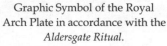

Graphic Symbol of the Royal
Arch Plate in accordance with the
Aldersgate Ritual.

Graphic Symbol of the
Philosophers' Stone as in the
Rosarium Philosophorum.

documents as a pair of concentric shapes in the surround of a
square – essentially three shapes in all: a circle, a square, and a
triangle.

What does the overall graphic symbolize? The ritual relates
that the secret is "more precious than rubies, and all the things
thou canst desire are not to be compared with her ... She is a
tree of life to them that lay hold upon her ..." (This statement
comes from the Old Testament book of Proverbs 3:15–18.)

Let us now look at the hermetic work known as the *Rosarium Philosophorum* (The Rosary of the Philosophers), published
in 1550 within the alchemical volume *De Alchemia opuscula
complura veterum philosophorum.*[1] In respect of the Philosophers' Stone, it states that its emblem is drawn by means of a
round circle, a quadrangle [a square], and a triangle. The
graphic symbol of the Philosophers' Stone, as determined by
the *Rosarium Philosophorum*, is therefore much the same as the
Royal Arch graphic, which is in turn related to the golden
plate discovered in the Jerusalem Temple vault.

A further point of considerable interest now arises from the
18th-century Royal Arch depiction by Laurence Dermott (*see*
Plate 20). He was Secretary of the Ancient Grand Lodge in
England from 1751 (traditionally spelt "Antient"), prior to the

Ancients and Moderns combining to form the United Grand Lodge of England in 1813. In this regard, Dermott was the primary protagonist for the acceptance of Royal Arch within the modern masonic structure. His picture identifies the Jerusalem vaulted chamber by way of an updated architectural arch with its keystone removed. Beneath, on a checkered pavement, is the marble pedestal. But where is the golden plate that was supposedly discovered upon it? In its place, we have no less than the Ark of the Covenant itself, which forms the centerpiece of the portrayal.

This image should now be compared with the philosophical Royal Society engraving from over a century before (Plate 19). Again, we have an arched chamber, the same checkered floor, and a central pedestal. The difference is that King Charles II takes the place of the Ark in the form of a stone bust. As the descendant Grand Master of the Household Orders from old Scotland, King Charles (a designated Knight Templar from birth)[2] was the royal patron of the Society's Rosicrucian interest in the Philosophers' Stone. In the 1667 depiction, Viscount Brouncker's pointing finger leaves us in no doubt of Charles's importance in the portrayal. His aunt, Princess Elizabeth (the daughter of King James I), had married Frederick V, Elector Palatine, in 1613. Their son (Charles I's cousin) Rupert, Prince Palatine of the Rhine, was a Rosicrucian Master of Heidelberg. Moreover, the Rev. John Wilkins (author of the controversially hermetic book, *Mathematicall Magick*, and Warden of Wadham College at Oxford University) was not only chaplain to Prince Rupert, but was also the initial founder and primary instigator of the one-time Baconian *Invisible College* which ultimately became the scientific Royal Society of natural philosophers.[3]

As mentioned earlier (*see* "Scourge of the Templars," page 247), Edward Bruce (brother of Robert the Bruce of Scots) was King of Ireland subsequent to the Templars' 1307 exile from Europe. Arms were provided from the Templar Grand Priory of Ireland for Chevalier Hugues de Crecy, who commanded the Templar contingent at Bannockburn in 1314, and the emergent Irish lodges were called "encampments." In the 1700s, Laurence Dermott was attached to the Irish Grand Encampment before introducing the Royal Arch working to England. The Chapter's heritage was, in no uncertain terms, Templar based and it seems likely that the current ritual is a legacy from the 12th-century Templar excavations in Jerusalem. Although Royal Arch ritual and imagery relate emblematically to a vault discovery of the Ark and the Philosophers' Stone by masons at the time of Zerubabbel's Second Temple (*c.* 536–520 BC), it was most likely based on the Knights Templars' discovery of the very same in the early 1100s.

While the Ark was a prerequisite for manufacturing the sacred Stone of the white powder gold (the *mfkzt* or *shem-anna*) in Mosaic and Solomonid times, it was also a storage receptacle for the substance, which caused it to be superconductive, hence its levitative and related powers. The Ark and the Philosophers' Stone, although not synonymous, are inextricably linked and, while the Royal Arch graphic is emblematic of the Stone (in accordance with the *Rosarium Philosophorum*), Dermott's own original portrayal is far more explicit in depicting the Ark itself.

Yielding the Ark

As a further confirmation that the Ark was indeed buried at King Josiah's instruction before Nebuchadnezzar's onslaught in 597 BC, we can now turn to Talmudic writings (*see* "Guardians of Destiny," pages 157–8). In the Hebrew *Mishnah* (Yoma 52b), it is specifically stated: "Before the destruction of the first Holy Temple, King Josiah ordered the Ark to be hidden to prevent its capture." In continuation, it is said that the *Shemen ha Mishchah* was also secreted with the Ark, as a result of which the high priests could not afterwards be anointed. The word *mishchah* refers to "anointing" (whence, *Messiah*: Anointed One), and the *Shemen ha Mishchah* is traditionally reckoned to have been the "anointing oil" of the Messiahs. Linguistically, that is precisely what the term does now mean, but etymologically *shemen ha* bears a striking resemblance to the Mesopotamian term *shem-an-na*: the highward fire-stone of the white powder gold – the Philosophers' Stone of Messianic inheritance.

In consideration of the ancient Apkallu genies (*see* "Realm of the Genies," page 124), we saw how a key function of these priestly sages of Mesopotamia was to sanctify the kings. Their symbolic instrument of sanctification was a pine cone, called a *mullilû*, meaning "purifier,"[4] and their purification substance was the *shem-an-na* powder, which they carried in their situlas. This magical "powder of projection" was directly related in Assyrian reliefs to the Tree of Life (the Plant of Birth) and it is said in masonic ritual concerning the Temple secret: "She is a tree of life to them that lay hold upon her." The purification connection is further substantiated by the *Temple Scroll* of the Dead Sea Scrolls when dealing with the subject of King Solomon's great brazen storage container (*see* "The Fire-stone Project," pages 147–9). It was housed, relates the *Temple Scroll*, in the Purification Chamber.[5] It is likely that although *Shemen ha Mishchah* customarily has been associated with anointing oil, and has long meant precisely that in the Hebrew language, it was originally a reference to the purification *shem-an-na* of the Philosophers' Stone, which was stowed within the Ark when it was hidden by Josiah and Jeremiah.

In order to set the revelatory scene concerning the present whereabouts of the sacred Ark, it is worth establishing and confirming certain tenets of the Templar tradition as they exist today. To this end, a verbatim extract can be given from a ceremonial address by a Knight Grand Commander of the Chivalric Order of the Temple of Jerusalem to a Masonic Templar Chapter of the Grand Lodge of Scotland in 1990. This took place at the 12th-century Cistercian chapel of Newbattle Abbey in the Lothians. The Lodge was specially convened to celebrate the 20th August feast day of the Templars' original patron and protector St. Bernard de Clairvaux, and the relevant text is as follows:

> In 1127 Hugues de Payens received word that he must come back to his native France to take part in the proceedings of the Council of Troyes, headed by none less than the Cardinal Legate of France: Pope Honorius II's personal representative. However, the power behind the cardinal, whose word was law and total obedience, was the abbot Bernard de Clairvaux of the Cistercian Order. Hugues de Payens was related to Bernard and to the Count of Champagne, but he did not come back to his cousins empty handed – far from it. Trunks of ancient books were given to St. Bernard, together with the prize of all, the Ark of the Covenant.

St. Bernard's own record of the 1127 Templars' return from Jerusalem (*see* "Council of the Ark," page 237) was unequivocal in confirming that the Knights and their cargo had been placed "under the protection of the Count of Champagne, where all precautions can be taken against all interference by public or ecclesiastical authority." Right from the outset, Bernard knew that significant Church interest would be prompted by their discovery, to the extent that the valuable consignment was placed under military guard for its journey through France and Burgundy. This fanatical Church interest in the sacred treasure continued for centuries at the expense of countless lives. It led to the Albigensian Crusade, the Templar persecutions, and to the Catholic Inquisition in general.

In our earlier study of the Templars prior to their persecution and exile (*see* "Notre Dame," pages 239–43), we witnessed the greatest architectural fruit of their labors as being the awesome Gothic cathedrals of France. It is in this connection that we discover the last historical reference to the Ark of the Covenant in the public domain. At Chartres, the most sacred of all the cathedrals, the Ark is depicted undergoing transportation in a small stone relief. This carving, on a northern portal column of the Gate of the Initiates, is accompanied by an inscription in an arcane form of Latin. Areas of encrustation and erosion, along with some small French Revolution damage, have made translation difficult over the years, but recent laser cleaning has helped considerably. To the best of anyone's decipherment, it reads: "*Hic Amittitur Archa Federis*,"[6] and this translates to: "Here is let go the Ark of the Covenant," "Here is sent the Ark of the Covenant," or "Here is yielded the Ark of the Covenant."[7] Whichever way the sentence is translated, it at no time refers to the Ark being lost or hidden by the Templars – simply that it was "let go," "sent," or "yielded" from "here" – from Chartres.

The Final Performance

One of the most curious and frequently discussed features of Chartres Cathedral is its labyrinth. It is curious because, although labyrinths are both ancient and multicultural, they have never at any time been associated with Christianity. This caused the Catholic clergy to destroy French labyrinths at Auxerre in 1690, Sens in 1768, Reims in 1778 and Arras in 1795. Jean-Baptiste Souchet, a canon of Chartres who died in 1654, wrote that he considered the Cathedral's labyrinth to be "a senseless game, a waste of time."[8] However, unlike his counterparts, he never dared to attempt desecration at Chartres, and it remains today the largest, best preserved and traditionally the most sacred of all labyrinths from medieval times.

Set as a paving inlay within the nave, the Chartres design precisely replicates a labyrinth from a 2nd-century Greek alchemical manuscript. During the 1220s this was copied into the *Album de croquis* (sketchbook) of the Cistercian advisory clerk Vilars Dehoncort from Picardy (*see* Plate 16), and it had become a Chartres masonic reality by the time the first stage of the Cathedral was completed in 1260. Dehoncort's unique sketches, on parchment sheets in a pigskin wallet, were held in the late Middle Ages at the Paris monastery of St. Germain, and were passed to the Bibliothèque Nationale in 1795.[9] Accompanying architectural and window designs, the portfolio includes many sketches of animals, along with masonry and carpentry techniques, plus extraordinary hydraulic and clockwork mechanisms, which have led Dehoncort to be hailed as the Gothic Leonardo. (Subsequent to a modernization of his name in the 19th century, he is now generally referred to as Villard de Honnecourt.)[10]

The meandering path of the Chartres labyrinth has a length of over 860 feet (*c.* 261.5 m).[11] It was specifically referred to as the "Journey to Jerusalem"[12] and was called the "Labyrinth of Solomon," representing in particular the brazen vessel of his Temple. Indeed, the *Dictionnaire des Symboles* makes the point that its purpose was to provide a magical function,[13] which *The Encyclopedia of Religion* clarifies as being the *decensus ad inferos* – a descent into darkness and a return into the light.[14]

A record of the Chartres labyrinth at Lucca Cathedral in Italy (where the design is miniaturized on a pillar) states: "This is the labyrinth built by the Cretan, Daedalus. No one has ever found the way out except Theseus, thanks to Ariadne's thread"[15] (*see* legend in Appendix VI, pages 400–3). The anomaly here is that it is perfectly easy to find the return route at Chartres, since there are no diversions or dead ends, and the ways in and out are the same. The mystery lies in the fact that the labyrinth is alchemically devised for the sole purpose of the *decensus ad inferos*. Hence, when properly operative, it is the route to an enveloping field of light – the same as the ancient *Field of Mfkzt* (*see* "Field of the Blessed," pages 8–9). The distance between the center of the labyrinth and the West door is practically the same as that between the West

The Chartres labyrinth.

door and the West Rose window above it. The base of the triangle is the distance from the center of the labyrinth to the center of the window. The window depicts the *Last Judgment*, and if the West facade were folded down onto the nave floor, the labyrinth and the West Rose would correspond.

Returning for a moment to the lodge ritual of Freemasonry, there is a scripted ceremonial conversation which takes place between the Worshipful Master and his Wardens concerning the West and the Lost Secrets. The Master asks – *Question*: "How do you hope to find them?" *Answer*: "By the center." *Question*: "What is a center?" *Answer*: "That point within a circle from which every part of its circumference is equidistant."[16] In this regard, it is pertinent to note that the symbol of a "point within a circle," so familiar to Freemasons, is identical to the hieroglyph for Light displayed in the Shrine of the Kings at the Hathor temple of Serâbît el Khâdim, where our journey began (*see* "The Great One," page 10).

Relating this to the Royal Arch discovery of the Temple vault items which represented certain masonic secrets, and if the Chartres labyrinth constitutes the route to the Light according to Rosicrucian tradition, then we should rightly expect to find a golden plate at its center. However, there is no such plate on the floor of the nave.

Notwithstanding this, what we do find in the bare, and ostensibly unfinished, center of the labyrinth are a number of metal studs, shaved down to floor level. In this regard we can consult the 17th-century writings of Sire Charles Challine, Seigneur de Messalain, who died in 1678. His journal records that a bright golden plate did indeed occupy the labyrinth's central rose. Further investigation reveals that in 1792, when the Cathedral's iron bells were melted down for cannon during the Napoleonic Wars, the heavy plate was also removed at that time.[17] It transpires that it was over 4 feet 6 inches in diameter (approaching 140 cms) and was actually of shining copper. The writings of Challine and others relate that, in accordance with the Italian reference at Lucca, its engraved scene depicted Theseus and the Minotaur, along with Ariadne and her ball of thread from the Cretan legend.

Since copper, a soft metal, would have been of little use for the making of cannon or armor, the Chartres plate was possibly removed for some distinctly different purpose at that time. It could simply have been stolen by revolutionaries, or perhaps its removal was more a matter of safe keeping – maybe even by the Templars themselves. If this were the case, then there is a chance that it still exists, although I can find no record of its stowage. In *The Hiram Key*, Christopher Knight and Robert

Lomas present a well-founded suggestion that the Royal Arch scroll from the Jerusalem Temple was secreted by the Templars at Rosslyn Chapel, near Edinburgh.[18] In their book, *Rosslyn*, Tim Wallace-Murphy and Marilyn Hopkins also conclude that the Jerusalem scrolls unearthed by the Templars are most likely at the Chapel.[19] If they are correct – and there is every reason to support their research in this regard – then Rosslyn might also be a likely residence for the Chartres plate, which was steeped in a replication of the same Royal Arch tradition.

Copper (*see* "Levitation and Teleportation," page 190), is a powerful Type-2 superconductor, which will superconduct in the presence of large magnetic fields and currents. In doing this (as explained in the *Chemical and Engineering News*),[20] the copper will expel the magnetic field to the point of its lower critical level, thereby creating a "flux tube" between it and the ultimate magnetic source. The magnetic field in the flux tube is generated by supercurrents that circulate around the tube and restore the Type-2-expelled field by the current around its periphery. Thus the flux tube becomes a vortex. In a way, such vortices are (according to ancient interpretation) not unlike that from the thunderstone of Jacob, which constituted the stairway to heaven at Bethel, wherein the angels ascended and descended.[21] Similarly, there is the story of the whirlwind which conveyed Elijah to heaven.[22]

To facilitate this flux tube process, a magnetic generator or Type-1 superconductor would be required to focus its energy onto the copper plate which, being a magnetic expellent, would be milked of the non-penetrative energy by the vortex tube. Nuclear physicist Daniel Sewell Ward, Ph.D. explains that the magnetic generator would be rather like an Admiral directing operations from his flagship far offshore, while his destroyer (the copper plate) takes care of the business at hand. The distance between them is entirely irrelevant since super-conductors, once in resonance, will operate over any expanse of space and time.

Our labyrinthine journey, therefore, is to the center and to the shining plate of final judgment. However, if the alchemy of Solomon's vessel is to be activated, a super-charged magnetic force is required from above – in essence, we need the Royal Arch "keystone" of the vortex. Is there such an item at Chartres? Actually, no – a fire in 1836 completely engulfed and destroyed the wood-framed roof of the Cathedral, which was subsequently rebuilt. But what of times before that?

One of the original Founding Fellows of London's Royal Society in 1662 was the metrologist and mineralogist Dr. Martin Lister. A close associate of Elias Ashmole and the Rosicrucian circle, Lister was also a renowned naturalist and a Fellow of the Royal College of Physicians. Lister visited France in 1698, ostensibly to meet with colleagues of the Académie Français and to compare notes on scientific achievement. He was especially intrigued when learning of a new metal pen in those days of quills, and wrote also in his memoir about Chartres. "There used to be in the heights of the Cathedral," he explained, "a substantial lodestone of strong magnetic virtue."[23]

Such high-power lodestones are generally of meteoric origin, like the thunderstones of legend. They are rich in magnetic iron and are often further enriched with iridium: a powerful Type-1 superconductor. Often these thunderstone meteorites are as small as tennis balls, but sometimes they are quite huge. In the 18th century, a 1,600-pound lodestone (c. 726 kgs) was discovered in Russia, and in 476 BC a thunderstone "as large as a chariot" fell to earth in Thrace.[24]

The craftsmen of ancient Egypt certainly knew about the properties of these stones, referring to them as *res mehit ba*, meaning "north-south iron."[25] But they also knew about the supreme qualities of another very precious material, which they called *tchām*. The precise nature of this substance is now unknown, but it is apparent from inscriptions that it was specifically used for the crowns of obelisks and pyramidions – the apex tips of pyramid capstones.[26] David Hudson's research into the nature of *tchām* led him to the conclusion that it was a bright gold-based or platinum-based ORME glass and, in view of its association with the *Field of Mfkzt*, it was undoubtedly superconductive. When writing about the mysterious *tchām* in 1924, E.A. Wallis Budge, Curator of Egyptian Antiquities at the British Museum, stated that it was plainly of considerable value, and yet none has ever been found. Interestingly, his investigations revealed that *tchām* and the pyramidions probably disappeared at the time of pharaoh Akhenaten.[27]

And so, in medieval Templar times, the perfect stage set for creating a conical flux tube vortex, with a base area of around 4.5 feet across, was in place at Chartres Cathedral. Above was the Type-1 superconducting thunderstone, and below was the Type-2 superconducting plate. All that was needed to start the frequency flow and excite the energy of this magical environment was voltage. Enter stage, the capacitorial arcing device – the Ark of the Covenant, beneath the keystone, in readiness for the final performance.

The Portal

In placing the Ark within the arena to activate the vortex, an extension to the scene then arises for, as we have seen, the Ark of gold containing the *mfkzt* fire-stone was itself a superconductor with its own Meissner Field. Under such a circumstance the result can be awesome.

Not only would the Ark levitate, it would begin to defy all known parameters of gravity and space-time, for superconductivity is not about particles and matter; it is about Light and it exists in a world of its own. To quote David Hudson once again: "In superconductivity, all atoms in a material act like a single atom, where time is timeless. They are coherent, resonating in unison with the zero-point energy" (precisely as has been confirmed by Dr. Hal Puthoff of the Institute of Advanced Studies).

In the quantum domain of Superstring Theory, there is an assumption that there are ten dimensions of space-time – one of time, three of space as we know it, and six spatial dimensions which have collapsed into a different scale of perception (rather like digital compression in a computer). In a recent BBC radio broadcast, Britain's Astronomer Royal, Sir Martin Rees, spoke of parallel dimensional research not as a newly theoretical enterprise, but as being an "arcane" science. "Space is the underlying nature of reality," he explained, "but everything we think of as material, and therefore, composed of particles, is actually made from vibrations." Hence, it is not difficult to understand that if the vibrational frequency is changed, then the nature of reality also changes. There is no boundary around reality – only our notional perception of it is constrained by being based on the experience of our own space-time. We know, for example, that two material objects cannot occupy the same space, but that immaterial things like light, smell, and sound appear to do just that. What quantum analysis seeks to question, therefore, is our perspective of material reality.

Continuing with Sir Martin Rees' explanation: "Superstring Theory is based on the concept of space on a tiny scale. It is not just up and down, left and right, back and forward, but crumpled up in a series of harmonics and motions." Just as the string of an instrument is tuned by tension, the musical note produced is altered by a change in that tension. Particles are similarly affected by tension (by their mode of excitation). We are used to seeing our reality at a particular level of tension, but when the tension changes and the particles take a different form, they are in a vibrational state that is different to our own personal tuning. Hence, we do not see them as a composed object any more. That does not mean they are not there, but that they have moved into another realm of existence.[28] Just as Hal Puthoff explained with the white powder experiments (*see* "Stealth Atoms and Space-time," pages 180–4), such an object would have become weightless in our gravity, and will have moved beyond the visual perception of our familiar space-time.

Based on all the available historical evidence, a number of scholars and writers, such as Louis Charpentier, have put forward their belief that the Ark of the Covenant has its final resting place at Chartres Cathedral.[29] Others, such as Trevor Ravenscroft and Tim Wallace-Murphy, have been far more explicit in stating this as a certainty.[30] In all this, however, it is so easy for us to be duped by our own familiar concept of vibrational reality. This leads us to ask such questions as: Is it buried in a crypt, or perhaps lodged within a wall? What we need to do is to view the picture through the allegory of the Rosicrucian archive and to apply our modern scientific knowledge of superconductors and hyper-dimensional states. Templar-instigated Royal Arch symbolism is forthright in announcing where the Ark is lodged, and how the lost secrets may be found.

With another quotation from Dr. Daniel Ward, the following is explained from his viewpoint as a practicing physicist:

At the level of Superstrings, matter winks in and out of existence – that is in and out of our three-dimensional universe. But there is an event horizon (where whatever goes in can no longer send light messages out because the light is itself gravitationally bound), such that the light from an object becomes effectively invisible – or simply not in three dimensions. At the same time, in the phenomenon of Sonoluminescence [the emission of short-wavelength light from an excitement of low-density sound], the extreme accelerations result in a flash of light, perhaps looking like Star Trek's *Enterprise* going into warp drive. The idea is that a superconducting object implodes, either into the collapsed other six dimensions, or through a portal into fully expanded dimensions.

This then is the Realm of the Orbit of Light: the *Plane of Shar-On*, the *Field of Mfkzt* that was known (even if not scientifically understood) by the Master Craftsmen of ancient times. Progressing the Chartres tableau through to its logical flux-tube conclusion, therefore, the Ark of the Covenant is doubt-less precisely where it has been since before 1307. In the resultant scientific scenario it resides majestically within the aura of the labyrinth at Chartres Cathedral, having moved through the superconducting vortex portal of another parallel dimension of space-time.

Hic Amittitur Archa Federis: "Here is yielded the Ark of the Covenant."

Notes and References

Chapter 1: House of Gold

1 Exodus 3:1, 17:6.
2 In its original form, the Old Testament was written in a Hebrew style consisting only of consonants. In parallel with this, a Greek translation emerged in about 270 BC for the benefit of the growing number of Greek-speaking Hellenist Jews. This became known as the Septuagint (from the Latin *septuaginta*: 70) because 72 scholars were employed in the translation. Some centuries later, a Latin version of the Bible, known as the Vulgate (because of its vulgar or common use) was produced around AD 385 by St. Jerome for use in the Christian Church (including the New Testament). Then a revised Hebrew Old Testament (on which today's Jewish Bible is based) was introduced by Masoretic scholars in around AD 900. It was, however, the older and more reliable Septuagint that was used for translating the King James Authorized English-language edition, issued in 1611.
3 *See* Chapter 5, under "Chariots and Cherubim."
4 Petrie, Sir W.M. Flinders, *Researches in Sinai*, John Murray, London, 1906, p. 72.
5 *Ibid.*, p. 85.
6 Gardner, Laurence, *Genesis of the Grail Kings*, Bantam Press, London, 1999, ch. 19.
7 Ashmolean Museum, Oxford; British Museum, London; Cairo Museum; Chadwick Museum, Bolton; Haskell Museum at Oriental Institute, Chicago; Manchester University Museum;

Museum of Art and History, Brussels; National Museum of Ireland, Dublin; National Museums of Scotland, Edinburgh; University College, London.

8 Rohl, David M., *A Test of Time*, Century, London, 1995, ch. 4, p. 113.

9 Cerny, Jaroslav (ed.), *The Inscriptions of Sinai*, Egypt Exploration Society, London, 1955.

10 The Lotus Eaters (or *Lotophagi*, pronounced "ltofji") were a fabulous people who occupied the north coast of Africa and apparently lived on lotus flowers. These flowers were said to produce forgetfulness and happy indolence. In Homer's *Odyssey*, when Odysseus landed among them, some of his men ate the food. They forgot their friends and home and had to be dragged back to the ships. *The Lotus Eaters* by Alfred, Lord Tennyson, has become a classic of English poetry.

11 Petrie, Sir W.M. Flinders, *Researches in Sinai*, p. 85.

12 Kitchen, Kenneth Anderson, *Ramesside Inscriptions*, B.H. Blackwell, Oxford, 1975, p. 1.

13 An ornamental oval-shaped inscription denoting a royal name.

14 Cerny, Jaroslav (ed.), *The Inscriptions of Sinai*, vol. 2, p. 7.

15 The Rosetta Stone (now in the British Museum) was found near Alexandria in 1799 by Lieutenant Bouchard of the Napoleonic expedition into Egypt. The black basalt stone from about 196 BC carries the same textual content in three different scripts: Egyptian hieroglyphs, Egyptian demotic (everyday cursive writing) and scribal Greek. Through comparative analysis of these scripts (with the Greek language being readily familiar), the hieroglyphic code was revealed; it was then cross-referenced with pharaonic cartouches of the Egyptian kings.

16 Cerny, Jaroslav (ed.), *The Inscriptions of Sinai*, vol. 2, p. 9.

17 *Ibid.*, vol. 2, pp. 45–6.

18 Petrie, Sir W.M.F., *Researches in Sinai*, p. 101.

19 Cerny, Jaroslav (ed.), *The Inscriptions of Sinai*, vol. 2, p. 119.

20 *Ibid.*, vol. 2, p. 205.

21 British Museum, *Hieroglyphic Texts from Egyptian Stelae*, British Museum, London, 1911, Stela 569.

22 Exodus 20:23. Similarly, Exodus 20:4 gives an earlier dictate against the making of graven images.

23 Philalethes, Eirenaeus, *Introitus apertus ad occulusum regis palatium: Open entrance to the closed palace of the King – Secrets Revealed*, Musaeum Hermeticum, Amsterdam, 1667.

24 Philalethes, Eirenaeus, *Tres tractatus de metallorum transmutatione – Brief Guide to the Celestial Ruby*, Musaeum Hermeticum, Amsterdam, 1668.

25 *Pharaoh* = Great House.

26 De Lubicz, R.A. Schwaller, *Sacred Science*, Inner Traditions, Rochester, VT, 1982, ch. 8, p. 182–3.

Chapter 2: The Paradise Stone

1 Osman, Ahmed, *Moses, Pharaoh of Egypt*, Grafton/Collins, London, 1990, p. 172.

2 Sitchin, Zecharia, *The 12th Planet*, Avon Books, New York, 1978, ch. 12, p. 337.

3 Wilson, A.N. *Jesus*, Sinclair Stevenson, London, 1992, ch. 4, p. 83.

4 Carlyon, Richard, *A Guide to the Gods*, Heinemann/Quixote, London, 1981, p. 276.

5 "Fountain of Youth: Telomerase," in *Science*, vol. 279, 23 January 1998, p. 472, published by the American Association for the Advancement of Science.

6 Bodnar, Andrea G., Quellette, Michel, Frolkis, Maria, Holt, Shawn E., Chiu, Choy-Pik, Morton, Gregg B., Harley, Calvin B., Shay, Jerry W., Lichtsteiner, Serge, and Wright, Woodring E., "Extension of Life Span by Introduction of Telomerase into Normal Human Cells," in *Science*, vol. 279, 16 January 1998, pp. 349–52.

7 An excellent work in this regard is Brenner, Sydney (ed.), *Telomeres and Telomerase*, Ciba Foundation and John Wiley, New York, NY, 1997. For specific details concerning telomerase and reproductive cells, *see* p. 133 by Calvin B. Harley of the Geron Corporation.

8 *Ibid.*, p. 188 for Robert Newbold on gene isolation.

9 Diploid status relates to two chromosome sets per cell.

10 Bodnar, Andrea G., and others in *Science*, vol. 279, 16 January 1998, pp. 349–52.

11 Armstrong, Karen, *A History of God*, Ballantine, New York, NY, 1994, ch. 1, pp. 14, 20–21.

12 *See* Chapter 1, note 2.

13 Hastings, James, *Dictionary of the Bible*, T. & T. Clark, Edinburgh, 1909, under "God."

14 Charpentier, Louis, *The Mysteries of Chartres Cathedral*, Research Into Lost Knowledge Organization, and Thorsons, Wellingborough, 1972, ch. 18, p. 147.

15 Vermes, Geza, *The Complete Dead Sea Scrolls in English*, Penguin, London, 1998, p. 85.

16 Hastings, James, *Dictionary of the Bible*.

17 Further references also in Leviticus 24:5, Numbers 4:7, 1 Samuel 21:6, 1 Kings 2:4, 2 Chronicles 2:4, Matthew 12:4, Mark 2:26, Luke 6:4, Hebrews 9:2.

18 Hastings, James, *Dictionary of the Bible*, under "Shewbread." Also Mills, Watson E. (ed.), *Lutterworth Dictionary of the Bible*, Lutterworth Press, Cambridge, 1994. The books of 1 Samuel and 1 Kings are the same book in the Septuagint, as are 2 Samuel and 2 Kings. Whereas the King James Bible has only two books of Kings, the Septuagint has four.

19 Velikovsky, Immanuel, *Ages in Chaos*, Sidgwick & Jackson, London, 1952, ch. 4, p. 160.

20 Relating to *man-hu*, pronounced "manna."

21 Josephus, Flavius, *The Antiquities of the Jews* in *The Works of Flavius Josephus*, (trans. William Whiston), Milner & Sowerby, London, 1870, III, 1:6.

22 Before modern science discovered the phenomenon of white-powder gold in 1979, the manna which fell to the ground like snow, and which was eaten by the Israelites in Sinai was suggested to be a resinous secretion from the tamarisk plant. Crystalline grains of tamarisk resin were recorded in 1483 by Breitenbach, Dean of Mainz, who confirmed that they blew around like small beads at daybreak. The German botanist G. Ehrenburg explained in 1823 that tamarisk trees exuded the white crystals when attacked by a particular type of plant louse native to Sinai. *See* Keller, Werner, *The Bible as History*, (trans. William Neil), Hodder & Stoughton, London, 1956, pp. 129–31. Had this actually been the case, however, the Israelites would have known precisely what it was, and would not have asked the question: *manna?*

23 Complete texts from about 1425 BC based on earlier texts from the 3rd millennium BC. *See* Budge, Sir Ernest A. Wallis (trans.), *The Book of the Dead*, University Books, New York, 1960, p. ix, and 3.

24 Weigall, Arthur, *The Life and Times of Akhenaten*, Thornton Butterworth, London, 1910, p. 17.

25 Hall, Manly P., *The Secret Teachings of All Ages*, Philosophical Research Society, Los Angeles, CA, 1989, p. LXXIX.

26 *See* Chapter 1, note 24.

27 Loomis, Roger Sherman, *The Grail: From Celtic Myth to Christian Symbolism*, University of Wales Press, Cardiff, 1963, p. 210.

28 Lewis, H. Spencer, *The Mystical Life of Jesus*, Ancient and Mystical Order Rosae Crucis, San Jose, CA, 1982, pp. 191–2.

29 A sister language to the Vedic Sanskrit of India.

30 Loomis, Roger Sherman, *The Grail: From Celtic Myth to Christian Symbolism*, pp. 212–13.

Chapter 3: Light and Perfection

1 Hall, Manly P., *The Secret Teachings of All Ages*, p. XCVIII.

2 Genesis 11·28, 15·7.

3 Suarès, Carlo, *The Cipher of Genesis*, Samuel Weiser, Maine, 1992, pp. 19–21, 154.

4 Gardner, Laurence, *Genesis of the Grail Kings*, ch. 7, p. 62 ff.

5 Black, J., and Green, A., *Gods, Demons and Symbols of Ancient Mesopotamia*, British Museum Press, London, 1992, p. 173. Also *see* Hastings, James, *Dictionary of the Bible*, under "Urim and Thummim."

6 Graves, R., and Patai, R., *Hebrew Myths: Genesis*, p. 53. In the esoteric Jewish tradition, the Table of Destiny was also called the *Book of Raziel* (one of the seven archangels of the book of 1 Enoch 20:4).

7 Hastings, James, *Dictionary of the Bible*, under "Jewels and Precious Stones" – items: sapphire and jacinth.

8 Browne, Lewis (ed.), *The Wisdom of Israel*, Michael Joseph, London, 1948, p. 13.

9 Scholem, Gershom G., *Major Trends in Jewish Mysticism*, Thames & Hudson, London, 1955, p. 163.

10 Patai, Raphael, *The Hebrew Goddess*, Wayne State University Press, Detroit, MI, 1967, p. 114.

11 Scholem, Gershom G., *Major Trends in Jewish Mysticism*, p. 156.

12 The Talmud is essentially a commentary on the *Mishnah*, compiled originally in Hebrew and Aramaic. It derives from two independently important streams of Jewish tradition: the

Babylonian and the Palestinian. The *Mishnah* (Repetition) is an
early codification of Jewish law, based upon ancient compilations
and edited in Palestine by the Ethnarch (Governor) Judah I in the
early 3rd century AD. It consists of traditional law (*Halakah*) on a
wide range of subjects, derived partly from old custom and
partly from biblical law (*Tannaim*) as interpreted by the rabbis
(teachers).

13 Jones, Bernard E., *Freemasons' Book of the Royal Arch*, George G.
Harrap, London, 1957, ch. 11, p. 137. *See* also *Encyclopaedia Judaica
Decennial*, Keter Publishing, London, 1997, under "Even
Shetiyyah."

14 Hall, Manly P., *The Secret Teachings of All Ages*, p. fac. LXXVII.
Also, Horne, Alex, *King Solomon's Temple in the Masonic Tradition*,
Aquarian Press, London, 1971, ch. 9, p. 165.

15 Day, David, *Tolkien's Ring*, HarperCollins, London, 1994, ch. 12,
pp. 129–30.

16 Smith, Dr. William, *Smith's Bible Dictionary* (1868 revised),
Hendrickson, Peabody, MA, 1998.

17 Josephus, Flavius, *The Antiquities of the Jews*, Bk. III, ch. VII:5.

18 Hastings, James, *Dictionary of the Bible*, under "Dress" – item:
apron.

19 From the First Epistle of John – 1 John 1:5.

20 Carlyon, Richard, *A Guide to the Gods*, p. 312.

21 From around 200 BC.

22 The biblical term used to denote the serpent was *nahash* – from
the consonantal stem *NHSH*, which meant "to decipher" or "to
find out." *See* Sitchin, Zecharia, *The 12th Planet*, ch. 13, p. 371.

23 Josephus, Flavius, *The Wars of the Jews*, (trans. William Whiston),
Milner & Sowerby, London, 1870, II, ch. 8:6.

24 December 1958 edition.

25 *Nature*, 6 August 1960, vol. 187, no. 4736, pp. 493–4.

26 Maiman's story and the subsequent 30 years of wrangling over
patents, with Nobel Prizes going to Townes and Schawlow, is
told in Maiman, Theodore, *The Laser Odyssey*, Laser Press, Blaine,
WA, 2000. Also in Taylor, Nick, *Laser*, Simon & Schuster, New
York, NY, 2000.

27 The first *Enûma elish* tablets to be discovered were unearthed in
the 1848–76 excavations of Sir Austen Henry Layard, from the
library of King Ashur-banipal at Nineveh. They were

subsequently published by George Smith of the British Museum in 1876 under the title *The Chaldean Account of Genesis*. Other tablets and fragments containing versions of the same epic were found at Ashur, Kish, and Uruk, and it was ascertained from colophons (publishers' imprints) that an even older text existed in a more ancient language. This conveyed the same story of how a certain deity had created the heavens and the Earth, and everything on Earth, including humankind. For the complete text, *see* Heidel, Alexander, *The Babylonian Genesis*, University of Chicago Press, Chicago, IL, 1942.

28 Hastings, James, *Dictionary of the Bible*, under "Covenant, Book of the."

29 In Exodus 16:33–34, long before the Ark is ever discussed, Moses advised Aaron to take a pot of manna and "lay it up before the Lord," whereupon Aaron is said to have "laid it up before the Testimony." Then in Numbers 17:8–10 Aaron's rod was said to have budded in the tabernacle, and was brought "before the testimony to be kept for a token against the rebels."

30 Hastings, James, *Dictionary of the Bible*, under "Ornaments 4."

31 *See* Gardner, Laurence, *Realm of the Ring Lords*, HarperCollins, London, 2003, ch. 5, pp. 53–5.

32 Following Joseph Smith's 1827 account of the *Book of Mormon*, the concept of the singular *Urim-Thummim* was pursued in William Muss-Arnolt, "The Urim and Thummim – Suggestion as to their Original Nature and Significance," in *American Journal of Semitic Literature*, XVI, Chicago, 1900, p. 218, seq.

Chapter 4: Out of Egypt

1 Church, Rev. Leslie F. (ed.), *Matthew Henry's Commentary on the Whole Bible*, Marshall Pickering, London, 1960, Genesis XIV: 13–16/I.

2 *See* Chapter 1, note 2.

3 Kramer, S.N., *Sumerian Mythology*, Harper Bros., New York, 1961, pp. 44, 59.

4 O'Brien, Christian and Barbara Joy, *The Genius of the Few*, Dianthus, Cirencester, 1999, ch. 2, p. 27.

5 Osman, Ahmed, *Moses, Pharaoh of Egypt*, ch. 17, pp. 172–3.

6 Josephus, Flavius, *Against Apion*, (trans. William Whiston), Milner & Sowerby, London, 1870. I:26–7.

7 *Ibid.*, I:31.

8 Josephus, Flavius., *The Antiquities of the Jews*, II, 10.

9 Breasted, James H., *The Dawn of Consciousness*, Charles Scribner's Sons, New York, NY, 1934, p. 350. Also Osman, Ahmed, *Moses, Pharaoh of Egypt*, ch. 6, p. 66.

10 Freud, Sigmund, *Moses and Monotheism*, pp. 12–13.

11 The Josephus version is that the Egyptian word for water was *mo*, while those that were saved from the water were called *uses*. From this combination of words, he says, derived the name *Mo-use*. Josephus, Flavius, *Antiquities of the Jews*, II, 9:6.

12 Osman, Ahmed., *Moses, Pharaoh of Egypt*, ch. 6, p. 66.

13 For detailed accounts of all, with notes and source references, *see* Gardner, Laurence, *Genesis of the Grail Kings*, especially chs. 7–10.

14 Roux, Georges, *Ancient Iraq*, George Allen & Unwin, London, 1964, p. 128.

15 Porter, J.R., *The Illustrated Guide to the Bible*, Duncan Baird, London, 1995, p. 72.

16 Osman, Ahmed., *Moses, Pharaoh of Egypt*, ch. 1, p. 15.

17 At that time Sitamun was very young, which has led some Egyptologists to reckon she was perhaps a daughter of Amenhotep, but she was his junior sister – *see* Osman, Ahmed, *Stranger in the Valley of Kings*, Souvenir Press, London, 1987, pp. 14, 66. A cartouche of Sitamun at the Metropolitan Museum, New York, describes her as "The Great King's daughter," which is to say the daughter of Tuthmosis IV, not of Amenhotep III – *see* Gardiner, Alan, *Egyptian Grammar*, Griffith Institute, Ashmolean Museum, Oxford, 1957, Excursion A, p. 74.

18 Osman, Ahmed, *Moses, Pharaoh of Egypt*, ch. 6, p. 61.

19 The first son born to Tiye was called Tuthmosis and he certainly did die prematurely (a whip bearing his name was found in the tomb of Tutankhamun). *See* Clayton, Peter A., *Chronicle of the Pharaohs*, Thames & Hudson, London, 1994, p. 120.

20 Also called Zarukha. The fortified frontier settlement of Zaru was built on the site of the Hyksos city of Avaris. In later times it was reconstructed to become known as Pi-Rameses in the reign of Rameses II, who had been the mayor of Zaru. Pi-Rameses is often said to have been a grain storehouse center, but this description has now been overturned. It was thought to be such because an inscription relating to a public official was translated to define

him as an "overseer of granaries." It now transpires that the correct translation is "overseer of foreign lands." *See* also Osman, Ahmed, *Stranger in the Valley of Kings*, pp. 111–12; and Peet, T. Eric, *Egypt and the Old Testament*, Liverpool University Press, Liverpool, 1922, p. 84.

21 Nefertiti's mother is often said to be unknown, although it is recognized that she was raised by Tey, the wife of Yuya and Tuya's son Aye. *See* Clayton, Peter A., *Chronicle of the Pharaohs*, p. 121. Nefertiti was, however, the daughter of Amenhotep III and Sitamun, and it was by way of marriage to Nefertiti that Amenhotep IV (Akhenaten) secured his right to the throne. *See* Osman, Ahmed, *Moses, Pharaoh of Egypt*, p. 62.

22 It was the mitochondrial DNA of the matrilinear succession that was important to the dynasties. Although mitochondria is inherited from mothers by both sons and daughters, it is only passed on by the daughters, since this DNA resides within the female egg cells. *See* Jones, Steve, *In the Blood: God, Genes and Destiny*, HarperCollins, London, 1996, ch. 2, p. 93.

23 Gardiner, Alan, *Egyptian Grammar*, Excursion A, p. 75; and Clayton, Peter A., *Chronicle of the Pharaohs*, p. 78. Amenhotep IV was also called Amenemhet IV and Amenemes IV.

24 The Israelite concept of a god without an image was already established in Egypt before Akhenaten came to the throne. What he uniquely did was to install Aten as the sole god of Egypt. It was the world's first example of religious intolerance at a State level – a strict monotheism foisted upon the people. It was this somewhat discordant concept of the One God in Egypt that originally inspired the 1930s research of Sigmund Freud, leading him to associate Moses with the reign of Pharaoh Akhenaten.

25 Osman, Ahmed, *Moses, Pharaoh of Egypt*, ch. 17. p. 167.

26 Rohl, David M., *A Test of Time*, p. 197.

27 *Ibid.*, p. 199. Although Aten was relegated to a more general position within the Egyptian pantheon during the reign of Tutankhamun, Aten worship was not banned by the young pharaoh. This is confirmed by the colorful gold and inlaid back panel of his throne, which depicts him and his wife, Ankhesenpaaten, together with the Aten disc. Tutankhamun did, however, move the royal capital from Akhetaten to Memphis.

28 Osman, Ahmed, *Moses, Pharaoh of Egypt*, p. 105.

29　Prior to his initial departure, Akhenaten (the Moses) had been persuaded by his mother, Tiye, to move from Thebes – and this he did, establishing his newly-built center of Akhetaten (Horizon of the Aten), the site of modern Tell el-Amarna. *See* Clayton, Peter A., *Chronicle of the Pharaohs*, p. 122. However, a fact which reference books generally fail to explain is that Akhenaten did not invent the god Aten. Even before Akhenaten's birth, the boat used by his father, Amenhotep III, on the lake at Zaru was called *Tehen Aten* (Aten Gleams). *See* Baikie, James, *The Amarna Age*, A. & C. Black, London, 1926, p. 91. There was also an Aten temple at Zaru before Akhenaten built his own Aten temples at Karnak and Luxor. *See* Osman, Ahmed, *Moses, Pharaoh of Egypt*, ch. 12, p. 121.

30　Osman, Ahmed, *Moses, Pharaoh of Egypt*, ch. 6, pp. 63–4.

31　Clayton, Peter A., *Chronicle of the Pharaohs*, pp. 128–34.

32　*Ibid.*, p. 124.

33　Osman, Ahmed, *Moses, Pharaoh of Egypt*, ch. 18, pp. 178–9.

34　Clayton, Peter A., *Chronicle of the Pharaohs*, p. 120.

35　Budge, Sir Ernest A. Wallis (trans.), *The Book of the Dead*, p. 201.

36　Manetho's *Egyptian King List* records Smenkhkare by the name Achencheres, He is also recorded as Akenkheres. (*See* Carpenter, Clive, *The Guinness Book of Kings, Rulers and Statesmen*, Guinness Superlatives, Enfield, 1978, p. 68.) This was later corrupted by the Christian Church Father, Eusebius, to Cencheres. (*See* Velikovsky, Immanuel, *Ages in Chaos*, p. 5.) By the name Cencheres (further varied to Cinciris in the Gaelic annals), pharaoh Smenkhkare was of particular significance to the histories of Ireland and Scotland, for he was the father of the princess historically known as Scota, from whom the original Scots Gaels were descended. Her husband was Niul, the Governor of Capacyront by the Red Sea. (*See* Keating, Geoffrey, *The History of Ireland*, trans. David Comyn and Rev. P.S. Dinneen, 1640; reprinted by Irish Texts Society, London 1902–14, vol. II, pp. 20–21.) Niul was, by birth, a Black Sea prince of Scythia, and according to the 17th-century *History of Ireland*, "Niul and Aaron entered into an alliance of friendship with one another" (*Ibid.*, vol. II, p. 17). The Gaelic text further states that Gaedheal (Gael), the son of Niul and Princess Scota, was born in Egypt "at the time when Moses began to act as leader of the children of Israel" (*Ibid.*, vol. I, p. 233). The name Scota (Scythian: "ruler of people") was gained by the princess on marrying Niul.

37 Clayton, Peter A., *Chronicle of the Pharaohs*, pp. 140–1.

38 Osman, Ahmed, *Moses, Pharaoh of Egypt*, p. 64.

39 *Ibid.*, p. 43.

40 Clayton, Peter A., *Chronicle of the Pharaohs*, p. 142.

41 Osman, Ahmed, *Moses, Pharaoh of Egypt*, pp. 48–9. Also
    Velikovsky, Immanuel, *Ages in Chaos*, p. 7. The Hebrews (*Habiru*)
    of Canaan had been documented long before the Israelite exodus
    from Egypt; they feature in letters from the reigns of Amenhotep
    III and Akhenaten. In 1887, a peasant woman, searching among
    the ruins of Amarna, unearthed a large number of inscribed clay
    tablets which proved to be diplomatic correspondence between
    various Canaanite rulers and the pharaohs of the 18th dynasty.
    From these (known as the *Amarna Letters*) it has now been
    deduced that the Egyptian Empire was in serious decline by the
    time of Akhenaten, with the Hittites invading Syria, while Abda-
    khiba, the Mitannian Governor of Jerusalem, appealed for
    Akhenaten's help against an invasion by the Hebrews (Peet, T.
    Eric, *Egypt and the Old Testament*, Liverpool University Press,
    Liverpool, 1922, p. 115).

42 *Ibid.*, p. 109. Also Osman, Ahmed, *Moses, Pharaoh of Egypt*, p. 47.

43 Clayton, Peter A., *Chronicle of the Pharaohs*, p. 157.

44 In studying the Old Testament account of the exodus, and the
    dramatic crossing of the Red Sea, whose waters parted to become
    "a wall unto them on their right hand, and on their left" (Exodus
    14:22), we find there was actually no sea for the Israelites to cross.
    We are told that Moses led the people from Avaris (Pi-Rameses)
    in the Nile delta plain of Goshen, from where they traveled into
    Sinai (Exodus 16:1) on a route towards Midian (Exodus 18:1). But
    this route traversed the desert wilderness north of the Red Sea
    where the 103-mile (165 km) artificial Suez Canal (opened in
    1869) is now located. This, of course, places the story of Moses
    parting the waters in the same mythical realm as the early tale of
    the ark of bulrushes.

45 Osman, Ahmed, *The House of the Messiah*, HarperCollins, London,
    1992, p. 159.

46 Baikie, James, *The Amarna Age*, p. 241.

47 Osman, Ahmed, *The House of the Messiah*, p. 159.

48 Aldred, Cyril, *Akhenaten, King of Egypt*, Thames & Hudson,
    London, 1988, pp. 203–4.

49 *Ibid.*, p. 286.

50 Aldred, Cyril, *Akhenaten, King of Egypt*, p. 234.

51 Josephus, Flavius, *The Antiquities of the Jews*, II, 10:2.

52 Other pre-biblical Hebrew texts mentioned, but not included, in the Old Testament are the *Book of the Wars of the Lord* (Numbers 21:14), the *Book of the Acts of Solomon* (1 Kings 11:41), the *Book of the Records* (Ezra 4:15), and the *Book of the Lord* (Isaiah 34:16).

53 Alcuin, Flaccus Albinus, Abbot of Canterbury (trans.), *The Book of Jasher*, Longman, London, rep. 1929, section, "Testimonies and Notes."

54 In the 14th century, the British reformer and Bible translator John Wyckliffe (1320–84) wrote, "I have read the book of Jasher twice over, and I much approve of it as a work of great antiquity." It is generally reckoned that Jasher's position in the Bible should be between the books of Deuteronomy and Joshua, but it was sidelined because it sheds a very different light on the sequence of events at Mount Horeb.

55 Jasher 6:10. The name Jethro (*Ithra*) means "abundance."

56 Jasher 14:9–33.

57 Jasher 15:1–12.

58 Jasher 15:15–17.

59 *See* more detailed information in Gardner, Laurence, *Genesis of the Grail Kings*, ch. 17, pp. 178–81, "Four Centuries of Silence."

Chapter 5: The Ark of the Covenant

1 Hastings, James, *Dictionary of the Bible*.

2 Joshua 3:3–17, 6:6–13.

3 Leviticus 10:1–2, 2 Samuel 6:6–7.

4 1 Samuel 5.

5 Deuteronomy 9:17.

6 Ginsberg, Louis, *Legends of the Jews*, John Hopkins University Press, Baltimore, MD, 1998, vol. 3, p. 158.

7 Translation: Budge, Sir E.A. Wallis, *Kebra Nagast* (a.k.a. *The Queen of Sheba and her only son Menyelek*), Oxford University Press, Oxford, 1932.

8 A full account of the Ethiopian tradition is given in Hancock, Graham, *The Sign and the Seal*, Heinemann, London, 1992.

9 *See* note 15 below re cubits.

10 Exodus 31:2–11.

11 Porter, J.R., *The Illustrated Guide to the Bible*, p. 26.

12 Discovered in the excavations of G. Lankester Harding and Fr. Ronald de Vaux.

13 *See* Hastings, James, *Dictionary of the Bible*, under "Tabernacle, 1 & 9."

14 The Tabernacle is detailed intermittently from Exodus chapters 26–40.

15 The Bible gives all its related measurements in cubits – a loose standard based upon a forearm's length from elbow to fingertip. The measurement was therefore a variable, ranging from 18 inches to 22 inches. Within this range, there were differences between Egyptian, Hebrew, and Sumerian cubits. Other variables were Royal, Sacred, and Angelic cubits. For our purposes, the minimum 18-inch cubit has been used throughout (*c.* 46 cms).

16 *See* Hastings, James, *Dictionary of the Bible*, under "Tabernacle, 5c."

17 *See* note 15 above.

18 Acacia trees still flourish in the Serâbît valley: Cerny, Jaroslav (ed.), *The Inscriptions of Sinai*, vol. 2, p.5. Isaiah 4:19 refers to the shittah tree as the singular of shittim. The place called Abel-shittim (Meadow of the acacias), mentioned in Numbers 33:49, was identified by Josephus as Abila, about six miles east of Jordan, near Jericho. *See* Hastings, James, *Dictionary of the Bible*, under "Shittim."

19 Robinson, James, and the Coptic Gnostic Project, *The Nag Hammadi Library*, E.J. Brill, Leiden, 1977.

20 *The Catholic Encyclopedia*, Robert Appleton Co., New York, NY, 1908.

21 The books of 1 and 2 Chronicles were originally known in Greek as the *Paralipomenon* (Things passed Over), and in old Hebrew as *Dibhere Hayyamim* (Acts of the Days). *See* in *The Catholic Encyclopedia*, under "Paralipomenon."

22 Josephus, Flavius, *The Antiquities of the Jews*, VI, 2:5.

23 Patai, Raphael, *The Hebrew Goddess*, ch. 3, pp. 75–6.

24 As per the *Concise Oxford English Dictionary*.

25 A subject discussed in Chapter 1. The vowels are switched here, just as from Yahweh to Jehovah.

26 Psalm 99:1.

27 Numbers 7:89.

28 1 Samuel 4:4, 2 Samuel 6:2, 1 Chronicles 13:6, Psalm 80:1, Psalm 99:1, Isaiah 37:16.

29 Ginsberg, Louis, *Legends of the Jews*, vol. 3, p. 228.

30 *Ibid.*, pp. 157, 210.

31 *Ibid.*, p. 170.

32 Petrie, Sir W.M. Flinders, *Researches in Sinai*, p. 145.

33 The complete transcript is to be found in Ezekiel 10:8–22.

34 Narrative extracted from Ezekiel 1.

35 The subject is well covered in Däniken, Erich von, *Chariots of the Gods*, Souvenir, London, 1969.

36 *See* Gardner, Laurence, *Bloodline of the Holy Grail*, HarperCollins, London, 2002, ch. 4, section "Priests and Angels."

37 Ginsberg, Louis, *Legends of the Jews*, vol. 3, p. 243.

38 *Concise Oxford English Dictionary*.

39 Ginsberg, Louis, *Legends of the Jews*, vol. 3, p. 187.

40 *Ibid.*, p. 229.

41 All as per the *Oxford Concise English Dictionary*.

42 Strong, James, *The Exhaustive Concordance of the Bible*, Abingdon Press, New York, NY, 1890. Also *see* Ziegler, Jerry L., *YHWH*, Star Publications, Morton, IL, 1977, ch. 4, p. 24.

43 The term was used later in Greece to distinguish the high judges of Athens.

44 Robinson, James, *The Nag Hammadi Library*. "Hypostasis" = Foundation.

Chapter 6: The Power of Gold

1 1 cubit = 18 inches. Ark lid was 2.5 cubits x 1.5 cubits – *see* Chapter 5.

2 As given in Chapter 8, under "Masters of the Fire-stone," there are seven nouns in the Bible which have the meaning "gold": *zahav, paz, ketem, harus, s'gor, ophir, baser*. Among the adjectival references *zahav tahor* referred to "pure gold," as applicable to the lid of the Ark. The Midrash defines "pure gold" as gold which does not diminish on melting. *See* Patai, Raphael, *The Jewish Alchemists*, Princeton University Press, Princeton, NJ, 1994, ch. 3, pp. 41–6.

3 Levine, Moshe, *The Tabernacle: Its Structure and Utensils*, Soncino Press, Tel Aviv. 1969, p. 88.

4 A non-profit association of gold producers worldwide, headquartered in London, with offices in all major markets.

5 1 ton = 2,240 pounds/1,016.05 kgs.

6 All information in this section is obtained from the World Gold Council, 45 Pall Mall, London SW1Y 5JG.

7 Herodotus, *The Histories*, (trans. Robin Waterfield), Oxford University Press, Oxford, 1998.

8 The finest book on this subject is Ramage, Andrew, and Craddock, Paul, *King Croesus' Gold: Excavations at Sardis*, British Museum, London, 2000.

9 The *Golden Fleece* legend has been credited to Apollonius of Alexandria in about 250 BC.

10 Patai, Raphael, *The Jewish Alchemists*, ch. 20, p. 268.

11 Faivre, Antoine, *The Golden Fleece and Alchemy*, State University of New York Press, New York, NY, 1993, ch. 2, p. 53.

12 Jung, Carl Gustav, *Psychology and Alchemy*, Routledge, London, 1980, part 2, ch. 3, pp. 158–9, and part 3, ch. 5. p. 370. A commentary concerning Jung and Jason is given in Joscelyn Godwin's Foreword to Faivre, Antoine, *The Golden Fleece and Alchemy*, pp. 1–6.

13 Faivre, Antoine, *The Golden Fleece and Alchemy*, ch. 1, p.15.

14 *Ibid.*, ch. 2, p. 37.

15 For more explicit details *see* Patai, Raphael, *The Jewish Alchemists*, ch. 2, pp. 30–40.

16 *Ibid.*, ch 12, p. 163. The Old Testament's book of Job is one of the Bible's most intriguing works in terms of its esoteric content. As a text whose message lies far beneath its superficial story, Job was cited in the works of many visionary philosophers and writers. Among such works are the *Mosaical Philosophy* of the English hermeticist Robert Fludd (1574–1637), *Faust* by the German poet Johann Wolfgang Goethe (1749–1832) and *The Marriage of Heaven and Hell* by the English visionary poet and artist William Blake (1757–1827).

17 Breasted, James H., *The Dawn of Consciousness*, ch. 17, p. 371.

18 *Ibid.*, ch. 17, pp. 377–8.

19 Catalogued as Additional MS 23,198.

20 Josephus, Flavius, *The Antiquities of the Jews*, I, 2:3.

21 Hastings, James, *Dictionary of the Bible*, under "Pillars."

22 Hall, Manly P., *The Secret Teachings of All Ages*, p. CLXXIII.

23 Neoplatonism emerged in about 250 AD.

24 Watterson, Barbara, *Gods of Ancient Egypt*, Sutton, Stroud, 1996, pp. 182–8.

25 Although not discovered at Nag Hammadi, this Treatise is included within Robinson, James, *The Nag Hammadi Library*.

26 Hall, Manly P., *The Secret Teachings of All Ages*, p. XXXVII.

27 1 Enoch 8:1. *See* Charles, R.H. (trans.), *The Book of Enoch*, (revised from Dillmann's edition of the Ethiopic text, 1893), Oxford University Press, Oxford, 1906 and 1912.

28 Tyana was in Asia Minor (modern Turkey).

Chapter 7: Electrikus

1 Ziegler, Jerry L., *YHWH*, ch. 1, p. 8.

2 For example, 2 Samuel 22:15, Psalm 18;14.

3 Exodus 6:25.

4 Osman, Ahmed, *Moses, Pharaoh of Egypt*, ch. 19, p. 185.

5 Weigall, Arthur, *The Life and Times of Akhenaten*, Thornton Butterworth, London, 1910, pp. 138–9.

6 Petrie, Sir W.M. Flinders, *Ancient Egypt and Ancient Israel*, (1910), Ares Publishers, Chicago, IL, 1980, ch. 4, p. 61. This portrayal of Ma'at appears as two similar images to the left and right of the entrance to the 19th-dynasty pharaoh Siptah's tomb (KV 47) in the Valley of the Kings.

7 Carlyon, Richard, *A Guide to the Gods*, Heinemann/Quixote, London, 1981, pp. 278–9, under "Hu." In Egyptian lore, Hu was the attendant of the sun-god Ra.

8 About 99% of the visible Universe is plasma.

9 Alternatively known as Erasmus.

10 Leviticus 26:30, Numbers 21:28. 22:41, 23:3, 33:52, etc.

11 Ziegler, Jerry L., *YHWH*, ch. 3, p. 17.

12 Graves, Robert, *The White Goddess*, Faber & Faber, London, 1961, ch. 16, p. 287. Also, according to the Coptic *Holy Book of the Great Invisible Spirit* (Nag Hammadi Library), the pronunciation is: iiiiiiiiiiiiiiiiiiiiiii–eeeeeeeeeeeeeeeeeeeeeee–ooooooooooooooooooooo oo–uuuuuuuuuuuuuuuuuuuuuu–eeeeeeeeeeeeeeeeeeeeee–aaaaa aaaaaaaaaaaaaaaaa–ooooooooooooooooooooooo (22 of each letter in each vowel section).

13 O'Brien, Christian and Barbara Joy, *The Shining Ones*, Dianthus, Cirencester, 1997, Prol. I, pp. 33–4. Also *see* the associated Golden Age Project Web site of the Patrick Foundation at <http://www.goldenageproject.org.uk/> which features the fascinating work of Christian and Barbara Joy O'Brien.

14 Ziegler, Jerry L., *YHWH*, ch. 1, p. 10.

15 Schwalb, Harry M. in *Science Digest*, 41:17–19.

16 Childress, David Hatcher, *Technology of the Gods*, Adventures
    Unlimited, Kempton, IL, 2000, ch. 4, p. 118.

17 Watterson, Barbara, *Gods of Ancient Egypt*, p. 125.

18 A title also confirmed in *Ibid.*, p. 122.

19 Clayton, Peter A., *Chronicle of the Pharaohs*, pp. 17–18.

20 Childress, David Hatcher, *Technology of the Gods*, ch. 4, pp. 124–5.

21 A device consisting of a sealed enclosure in which electrons flow
    between electrodes, separated either by a vacuum or an ionized
    gas at low pressure. The two principal electrodes of an electron
    tube are the cathode and the anode. They have been widely used
    in the fields of transmission and television, but are now replaced
    in many instances, apart from high-voltage, by solid-state devices
    such as transistors.

22 Subsequent to Faraday's discovery, the physicist Johann Hittorf
    observed that in some glass tubes glowing rays extended from
    the negative electrode and produced a florescent glow where
    they struck the walls of the tube. In 1876 these were named
    Cathode Rays by the scientist Eugene Goldstein. A few years
    later William Crookes used tubes which he designed to
    demonstrate that cathode rays would cast shadows of objects and
    turn a small metal wheel in their path, and could be deflected by
    a magnet.

23 Chassinat, Emile, *Le Temple de Dendera*, Institut français
    d'archaeologie orientale, Paris, 1934.

24 Cauville, Sylvie, *Le Temple de Dendera: Guide Archaeologique*,
    Institut français d'archaeologie orientale du Caire, 1990. Volume
    IV of the translations is currently due for imminent publication.

25 *See* note 22 above.

26 Good reference material may be found in Kaiser, Cletus J., *The
    Capacitor Handbook*, Van Nostrand Reinhold, New York, NY, 1993.

Chapter 8: The Orbit of Light

1 Ramage, Andrew, and Craddock, Paul, *King Croesus' Gold:
   Excavations at Sardis*, British Museum, London, 2000.

2 *Concise Oxford English Dictionary.*

3 Ramage, Andrew, and Craddock, Paul, *King Croesus' Gold:
   Excavations at Sardis*, Appendix 4, pp. 238–43.

4 *Ibid.*, ch. 2, p. 31.

5 Patai, Raphael, *The Jewish Alchemists*, Princeton University Press, Princeton, NJ, 1994, ch. 3, pp. 41–6.

6 Ramage, Andrew, and Craddock, Paul, *King Croesus' Gold: Excavations at Sardis*, ch. 2, p. 32.

7 *Ibid.*, ch. 2, p. 31.

8 *Ibid.*, Prologue, p. 31.

9 BBC2 TV documentary, *Cosmic Bullets*, 1997, citing Gubbio, Northern Italy, in particular.

10 *Nexus*, October/November 1996, David Hudson lecture, Part 2, p. 39.

11 The subject of high-spin metallic elements is expanded upon in Chapters 11 and 12.

12 *Nexus*, August/September 1996, David Hudson lecture, Part 1, p. 30.

13 Patterson, David. "Electric Genes," in *Scientific American*, May 1995, pp. 33–4. Superconductors are used for brain scanning and can even measure thoughts. A superconductor is sensitive to magnetic fields of minute proportion. Unlike electric conductivity, superconductivity does not require physical contacts.

14 A quarterly publication of Johnson Matthey plc, 40–42 Hatton Garden, London EC1N 8EE.

15 For example: "Anti-tumour Platinum Coordination Complexes," in *Platinum Metals Review*, volume 34, no. 4, 1990, p. 235.

16 Bristol-Myers Squibb, 345 Park Avenue, New York, NY 10154 0037. The first and the largest corporate research grants program of its kind in the world is marking two major milestones: 25 years and $100 million. Since its inception in 1977, the Bristol-Myers Squibb Unrestricted Biomedical Research Grants Program has given $100 million in "no strings attached" funding to major research institutions worldwide in the areas of cancer, cardiovascular, infectious diseases, metabolics, neurosciences, and nutrition research. The program has resulted in significant medical discoveries and continues as a cherished source of biomedical research funding for scientists worldwide.

17 Breasted, James H., *The Dawn of Consciousness*, p. 49; and Gardiner, A., *Egyptian Grammar*, Griffith Institute, Ashmolean Museum, Oxford, 1957, Excursion A, ch. 4, p. 72.

18 Budge, E.A.W., *The Book of the Dead: Papyrus of Ani*, p. 75.
19 Utiger, Robert D., "Melatonin, the Hormone of Darkness," in *The New England Journal of Medicine*, vol. 327, no. 19, November 1992.
20 Becker, Robert O., and Selden, Gary, *The Body Electric*, William Morrow, New York, NY, 1985, pp. 42–3.
21 Hardland, R., Reiter, R. J., Poeggeler, B. and Dan, D. X., "The Significance of the Metabolism of the Neurohormone Melatonin: Antioxidative Protection of Bioactive Substances," in the *Neuroscience and Biobehavioral Review*, vol. 17, 1993, pp. 347–57.
22 Roney-Dougal, Serena, *Where Science and Magic Meet*, Element Books, Shaftesbury, 1993, ch. 4 p. 91.
23 Hall, Manly P., *The Secret Teachings of All Ages*, p. LXXIX.
24 In Sitchin, Zecharia, *The 12th Planet*, ch. 6, p. 175, it is similarly given as "Great one who points the way."
25 In Anunnaki times there had been seven Apkallu appointed by the Sumerian god Enki. They were: U-an adapa, U-an-dugga, En-me-duga, En-megalanna, En-me-buluga, An-enlilda, and Utu-abzu.
26 The pine cones were called *mullilû* (purifiers), *see* Black, Jeremy, and Green, Anthony, *Gods, Demons and Symbols of Ancient Mesopotamia*, p.46.
27 *Ibid.*, p.115.
28 Excavated in 1845 by the English diplomat Sir Austen Henry Layard. Subsequently, Britain's foremost Assyriologist, Sir Henry Creswicke Rawlinson, also unearthed the great library of King Ashurbanipal a little north of Nimrud at Nineveh. Nimrud (once called Kalhu or Calah, as mentioned in the book of Genesis) was the biblical city of Nimrod the mighty hunter.
29 Jacobsen, Thorkild, *The Sumerian King List*, (Assyrialogical Studies No.11), University of Chicago Press, Chicago, IL, 1939.
30 Wilson, Colin, and Grant, John, *The Directory of Possibilities*, Webb & Bower, Exeter, 1981, p. 37. The concept of the Grail existed long before Christian times.
31 Scholem, Gershom G., *On the Kabbalah and its Symbolism*, Schocken Books, New York, 1965, p. 192. The Semitic word *da'ath* means "gnosis" or "true knowledge."
32 Shapiro, Debbie, *The Body Mind Workbook*, Element Books, Shaftesbury, 1990, p. 49.

33 Roney-Dougal, Serena, *Where Science and Magic Meet*, ch. 4, p. 106.
34 Grant, Kenneth, *The Magical Revival*, Skoob Books, London, 1991., p. 73 note.
35 Yatri, *Unknown Man*, Sidgwick & Jackson, London, 1988, p. 80.
36 Weinberg, Steven Lee (ed.), *Ramtha*, Sovereignty Inc., Eastbound, WA, 1986, pp. 173, 189.
37 Grant, Kenneth, *The Magical Revival*, p. 36.
38 Yatri, *Unknown Man*, p. 86.
39 Hall, Manly P., *The Secret Teachings of All Ages*, pp. XXXII and LXXXIX. The Swan is a symbol of the initiates of the ancient mysteries, and of incarnate wisdom.
40 The human spine contains 24 individual vertebrae (7 cervical, 12 thoracic, and 5 lumbar), plus the separately fused sections of the sacrum and the coccyx, which contain 5 and 4 vertebrae, respectively. These total 33 in all.
41 Hall, Manly P., *The Secret Teachings of All Ages*, p. LXXIX.
42 *Physical Review A*, vol. 39, no. 5, 1 March 1989, "Gravity as a zero-point fluctuation force," by H.E. Puthoff.
43 *Nexus*, November 1996, p. 38.
44 The Great Pyramid has been reliably estimated to consist of some 2.3 million blocks. *See* also Hancock, Graham, *Fingerprints of the Gods*, William Heinemann, London, 1995, ch. 4, p. 284.
45 Hodges, Peter, *How the Pyramids were Built*, (ed. Julian Keable), Element Books, Shaftesbury, 1989, p. 123.
46 Jennings, Hargrave, *The Rosicrucians: Their Rites and Mysteries*, Routledge, London, 1887, pp. 4, 108, and 225.
47 Hancock, Graham, *Fingerprints of the Gods*, ch. 35, p. 298.
48 Edwards, I. E. S., *The Pyramids of Egypt*, Viking, New York, NY, 1986, p. 115.
49 Hancock, Graham, *Fingerprints of the Gods*, ch. 38, p. 330.

Chapter 9: King Solomon's Secret

1 For example, Numbers 14:33, 14:34, 32:13, Deuteronomy 2:7, 8:2, 8:4, 29:5.
2 For example, Exodus 15:24, 16:2, 16:7, 16:8, 16:9, 17:3, Numbers 14:2, 14:27, 14:29, 14:36, 16:11, 16:14, 17:5, 17:10, Deuteronomy 1:27, Joshua 9:18.
3 Judges 13:1.
4 Genesis, Exodus, Leviticus, Numbers, and Deuteronomy.

5 Chase, Mary Ellen, *Life and Language in the Old Testament*, Collins, London, 1956, ch. 3, pp. 32–9.

6 Thiering, Barbara, *Jesus the Man*, Transworld, London, 1992, Appendix I, pp. 177, 196.

7 Genesis 17:19.

8 Genesis 25:20–21.

9 Genesis 26:34.

10 Genesis 28:19, and as discussed in Chapter 4 under "Israelites and Hebrews."

11 The full story of this generational descent from Esau is given in Gardner, Laurence, *Genesis of the Grail Kings*, ch. 16, pp. 167–84.

12 Matthew 1:1–16.

13 Luke 3:23–32.

14 Genesis 22.

15 Genesis 17:16.

16 Numbers 10:33–36.

17 Numbers 11:1.

18 Numbers 14:44–45.

19 Jericho is the oldest continuously inhabited city on earth, first settled in about 8500 BC as a salt trading center.

20 Deuteronomy 32: 48–34:12.

21 Keller, Werner, *The Bible as History*, ch. 15, pp. 157–58.

22 Joshua 3:3–4.

23 Keller, Werner, *The Bible as History*, ch. 15, pp. 157–58.

24 Joshua 6:21–25.

25 Keller, Werner, *The Bible as History*, ch. 15, pp. 159–60.

26 *Lifelines Magazine*, Lifelines Trust, Honiton, July 1997.

27 The first excavations were those of the German–Austrian expedition led by professors Ernst Sellin and Karl Watzinger from 1907. British excavations commenced in 1930 under Prof. John Garstang, followed by those of Dr. Kathleen Kenyon in 1953.

28 As determined in Chapter 7 under "Into the Ark-light."

29 Herzog, Chiam, and Gichon, Mordechai, *Battles of the Bible*, Greenhill Books, London, 1997, ch. 2, p. 51.

30 Jeremias, Alfred, *The Old Testament in the Light of the Ancient Near East*, Williams & Norgate, London, 1911, ch. 22, p. 152.

31 Joshua 24.

32 As cited, for example, in Judges 2:13 and 3:7.

33 Judges 21:19–25.
34 Judges 11:30–39.
35 Judges 4.
36 Keller, Werner, *The Bible as History*, ch. 16, p. 167.
37 A good account of the military tactics used in this confrontation is given in Herzog, Chiam, and Gichon, Mordechai, *Battles of the Bible*, ch. 3, pp. 66–71.
38 Judges 6:5.
39 Isserlin, B.S.J., *The Israelites*, Thames & Hudson, London 1998, ch. 3, p. 68.
40 Keller, Werner, *The Bible as History*, ch. 16, p. 168.
41 Judges 7:16–22.
42 Hastings, James, *Dictionary of the Bible*, under "Philistines" and "Caphtor." *See* also Keller, Werner, *The Bible as History*, ch. 17, p. 174.
43 The great battle between Rameses III and the Philistines is depicted as a stone relief in the Egyptian temple of Medinet Habu. It was the greatest victory in all the history of the Nile.
44 Herzog, Chiam, and Gichon, Mordechai, *Battles of the Bible*, ch. 4, p. 80.
45 Genesis 11:28. Sumer was a southern Mesopotamian region by the Persian Gulf.
46 Hastings, James, *Dictionary of the Bible*.
47 Rohl, David M., *A Test of Time*, ch. 9, p.200.
48 Amos 9:7 and Jeremiah 47:4.
49 Hastings, James, *Dictionary of the Bible*.
50 Roux, Georges, *Ancient Iraq*, ch. 14, pp. 190–1.
51 Judges 15:15.
52 Judges 14:6.
53 Keller, Werner, *The Bible as History*, ch. 18, p. 177.
54 1 Samuel 4:17.
55 1 Samuel 5:1–6:16.
56 1 Samuel 22:18–19.
57 1 Samuel 17.
58 2 Samuel 13.
59 2 Samuel 6:6–7.
60 Keller, Werner, *The Bible as History*, ch. 19, pp. 189–90.
61 2 Samuel 18:33.
62 1 Kings 2:13–25.

63 2 Samuel 12:24–25. Also *The Oxford Concordance to the Bible* and Hastings, James, *Dictionary of the Bible*.

64 Keller, Werner, *The Bible as History*, ch. 19, pp. 191.

65 1 Kings 10:14. This is about 30 tons: today's value *c.* $250 million. For more on gold weights and values, *see* "The Abundance," page 76. One talent of gold = 108 pounds *avoirdupois*: Hastings, James, *Dictionary of the Bible*, under "Money." One ton = 2,240 pounds.

66 1 Kings 10:21.

67 1 Kings 10:16.

68 1 Kings 10:17.

69 1 Kings 10:18.

70 1 Kings 4:26.

71 Charpentier, Louis, *The Mysteries of Chartres Cathedral*, ch. 7, p. 55–6.

72 1 Kings 7.13–14.

73 The name Abif does not appear in the 1399 *Regius Manuscript* of Masonic Constitution, but does appear in the 1550 *Downland Manuscript*.

74 1 Kings 6:20–30.

75 1 Kings 8:6–7.

76 Yadin, Yigael, *The Temple Scroll*, Weidenfeld & Nicolson, London, 1985, ch. 13, p. 130.

77 Re. the location of Ophir, *see* Hastings, James, *Dictionary of the Bible*.

78 i.e. *shem-an-na*.

Chapter 10: Into The Darkness

1 For good reading on the history of the rival Churches, *see* Martin, Malachi, *The Decline and Fall of the Roman Church*, Secker & Warburg, London, 1982.

2 Notwithstanding the practicalities of the break between Rome and Constantinople, the fact that it resulted in two separate and independent Churches was not formalized by the Catholic and Orthodox denominations until 1945.

3 Malan, Rev. S.C. (trans.), *The Book of Adam and Eve*, (from the Ethiopic text), Williams & Norgate, London, 1882, pp. v–vi.

4 Budge, Sir Ernest A. Wallis (trans.), *The Book of the Cave of Treasures*, The Religious Tract Society, London, 1927, p. xi.

5 Budge, Sir Ernest A. Wallis (trans.), *The Book of the Bee*, (from the Syriac text), Clarendon Press, Oxford, 1886, ch. 13.

6 For further details *see* Grierson, Roderick, and Munro-Hay, Stuart, *The Ark of the Covenant*, Weidenfeld & Nicolson, London, 1999.

7 *Ibid.*, ch. 16, pp. 250–1 for a full translation from Abu Salih.

8 Hastings, James, *Dictionary of the Bible*, under "Sheba" and "Sheba, Queen of." Location also confirmed in BBC 2 TV documentary, *Queen of Sheba: Behind the Myth*, 18th May 2002.

9 *See* Chapter 9, note 67.

10 Cruden, Alexander, *Complete Concordance to the Old and New Testaments and the Apocrypha*, Frederick Warne, London 1891.

11 Genesis 10:7.

12 Genesis 10:28.

13 2 Samuel 20:1.

14 Genesis 26:33.

15 *Ibid.*, ch. 8, pp. 106–27 is very explanatory concerning the variously depicted hiding places.

16 1 Kings 14:25.

17 Clayton, Peter A., *Chronicle of the Pharaohs*, pp. 185–6.

18 Unterman, Alan, *Dictionary of Jewish Lore and Legend*, Thames & Hudson, London, 1997, under "Ark of the Covenant."

19 2 Kings 23:29–30.

20 2 Kings 23:31–34.

21 2 Kings 25:1–7 and Jeremiah 39:6–7, 52:10–11.

22 Sinclair, Andrew, *The Sword and the Grail*, Crown, New York, NY, 1992, ch. 7, p. 73, and Notes pp. 216–17. Also *see* Gerber, Pat, *Stone of Destiny*, Cannongate, Edinburgh, 1997, ch. 5, pp. 45–6.

23 2 Kings 21:3.

24 2 Kings 23:12.

25 2 Kings 21:14–15.

26 2 Kings 24:3.

27 Roux, Georges, *Ancient Iraq*, ch. 23, p. 310.

28 *The Catholic Encyclopedia*, under "Paralipomenon."

29 Albany, HRH Prince Michael of, *The Forgotten Monarchy of Scotland*, Chrysalis/Vega, London, 2002, ch. 5, pp. 62–3. The author is the prevailing Grand Master of the Knights Templars of St. Anthony and Sovereign Grand Master of all Jacobite lodges worldwide.

30 The Hasmonaeans were a distinguished and priestly family, prominent in Jerusalem in the 2nd century BC. At the time of Antiochus IV, the head of the household was the high priest Mattathias, who initiated the Jewish Revolt. Before he died, he nominated his third son Judas (nicknamed Maccabaeus or Maccabee: "the appointed") to be the movement's military commander. Judas was in turn succeeded by his brothers Jonathan and Simeon who, along with all their followers, were thereafter known as Maccabees.

Chapter 11: A Parallel Dimension

1 Information about the Hudson research in this chapter are derived from a series of lectures given by David Hudson from 1994 to 1996, along with newsletters and communiqués from his related organization, Science of the Spirit Foundation, Tempe, Arizona, from 1995 to 2001. Along with talks in Phoenix, Arizona; San Diego, California; Salem, Massachusetts; Meza, Arizona; Ashland, Oregon; Tampa, Florida; Charlotte, North Carolina; Los Angeles, California; Pasadena, California, and Vancouver, British Columbia, the principal lectures were given at Global Sciences, Denver, Colorado; Northwest Service Center, Portland, Oregon; The Eclectic Viewpoint, Dallas, Texas; Ramtha's School of Enlightenment, Yelm, Washington; Mt. Hood Community College, Gresham, Oregon; Maharishi University of Management, Fairfield, Iowa; US Psychotronics Association, Columbus, Ohio, and The Ritz Carlton, Santa Barbara, California.

2 Neutron activation analysis (NAA) is a sensitive analytical technique for performing both qualitative and quantitative multi-element analysis of major, minor, and trace elements in samples from almost every conceivable field of scientific or technical interest. For many elements and applications, NAA offers sensitivities that are superior to those attainable by other methods, on the order of parts per billion or better. Because of its accuracy and reliability, NAA is generally recognized as the referee method of choice when new procedures are being developed or when other methods yield results that do not agree. The basic essentials required to carry out an analysis of samples by NAA are a source of neutrons, instrumentation suitable for

detecting gamma rays, and a detailed knowledge of the reactions that occur when neutrons interact with target nuclei.

3 The most important single institution in Russian and Soviet science has been the Academy of Sciences, founded in 1725 according to a plan worked out by Tsar Peter the Great. Since the Academy has traditionally encompassed all fields of knowledge, including both the natural and social sciences, histories of the Academy are generally histories of science in Russia. A work that provides much information on the Soviet period is Vucinich, Alexander, *Empire of Knowledge: The Academy of Sciences of the USSR (1917–1970)*, University of California Press, Berkeley, CA, 1984.

4 Russian scientists refer to this process as "fractional vaporization."

5 *Platinum Metals Review*, volume 44, no. 1, January 2000.

6 These include patents numbered as follows: Great Britain GB2219995; France FR2632974; Sweden SE8902258; Germany DE3920144; Switzerland CH680136; Belgium BE1003134; Australia AU3662489.

7 Varian Associates Inc., Hansen Way, Palo Alto, CA. Varian, Inc. is a global technology company that builds leading-edge tools and solutions for diversified high-growth applications in life science and industry. With over 50 years of technical experience, they respond to customer requirements for scientific instruments, vacuum technologies, and electronics manufacturing.

8 This breakthrough discovery was made by Alex Müller and Georg Bednorz at the Rüschlikon Laboratory, Switzerland. The original article was published in *Zeitschrift für Physick Condensed Matter*, April 1986.

9 Giner Inc., 14 Spring Street, Waltham MA. Giner, Inc. and Giner Electrochemical Systems, LLC (GES) are now world-class research and development firms, specializing in the development of proton-exchange membrane (PEM) based electrochemical technologies. GES applies membrane technology to fuel-cells for power generation, high-pressure electrolyzers for regenerative power, hydrogen fuel production, and oxygen production for life support. Giner, Inc. focuses PEM technology on electrochemical sensors and biomedical devices such as self-contained transdermal alcohol sensors and environmental gas sensors.

10 Dr. Harold E. Puthoff is Director of the Institute for Advanced
    Studies at Austin. A theoretical and experimental physicist
    specializing in fundamental electrodynamics, his research ranges
    from theoretical studies of quantum vacuum states as they apply
    to the stability of matter, gravitation, cosmology, and energy
    research, to laboratory studies of innovative approaches to
    energy generation. A graduate of Stanford University in 1967, he
    has published over 30 technical papers in the areas of electron-
    beam devices, lasers, and quantum zero-point energy effects, has
    patents issued and pending in the laser, communications, and
    energy fields, and is co-author of the textbook *Fundamentals of
    Quantum Electronics*, John Wiley, New York, NY, 1969.

11 *Physical Review A*, vol. 39, no. 5, 1 March 1989, "Gravity as a zero-
    point fluctuation force," by H.E. Puthoff.

12 In addition to those otherwise cited, related science press
    articles of this period included: "Microclusters," *Scientific
    American*, December 1989, Michael A. Duncan, Dennis H.
    Rouvray, pp. 110–15; "New Radioactivities," *Scientific American*,
    March 1990, Walter Greiner, Aurel Sandulescu, pp. 58–67;
    "Possible discontinuity in the octupole behavior in the Pt-Hg
    Region," *Physical Review C*, vol. 39 # 3, March 1989, C.S. Lim,
    R.H. Spear, W.J. Vermeer, M.P. Fewell, pp. 1142–4; "Collective
    and single particle structure in 103Rh," *Physical Review C*, vol.
    37 # 2, February, H. Dejbakhsh, R.P. Schmitt, G. Mouchaty, pp.
    621–35; "Structure of Os and Pt Isotopes," *Physical Review C*,
    vol. 38 # 2, August 1988, A. Ansari, pp. 953–9;
    "Superdeformation in 104, 105Pd," *Physical Review C*, vol. 38 #
    2, August 1988, A.O. Macchiavelli, J. Burde, R.M. Diamond,
    C.W. Beausang, M.A. Deleplanque, R.J. McDonald, F.S.
    Stephens, J.E. Draper, pp. 1088–91; "Direct Mapping of
    Adatom/Adatom Interactions," *Physical Review Letters*, vol. 62 #
    10, March 1989, Fumiya Watanabe and Gert Ehrlich, pp. 1146–4;
    "Inertias of superdeformed bands," *Physical Review C*, vol. 41 #
    4, April 1990 Y.R. Shimizu, E. Vigezzi, R.A. Broglia, pp. 1861–64;
    "Bound States, Cooper Pairing, and Bose Condensation in Two
    Dimensions," *Physical Review Letters*, vol. 62 # 9, February 1989,
    Mohit Randeria, Ji-Min Duan, Lih-Yir Shieh, pp. 981–84;
    "Quantum size effects in rapidly rotating nuclei," *Physical
    Review C*, vol. 41 # 4, April 1990 Y.R. Shimizu, R.A. Broglia, pp.

1865–8; "The Classical Vacuum," *Scientific American*, Timothy H. Boyer, pp. 70–8; "Beyond E=mc²," *The Sciences*, November/December 1994, Bernhard Haisch, Alfonso Rueda, H.E. Puthoff, pp. 26–31; "Everything for Nothing," *New Scientist*, 28 July 1990, H.E. Puthoff. "Inertia as a zero-point field Lorentz Force," *Physical Review A*, vol. 49 # 2, February 1994, Bernhard Haisch, Alfonso Rueda, H.E. Puthoff, pp. 678–94; "Spin Cycle: The Spectra of Super Deformed Nuclei," *Scientific American*, October 1991, Philip Yam, p. 26; "Evidence from Activation Energies for Superconductive Tunneling in Biological Systems at Physiological Temperatures," *Physiological Chemistry and Physics 3*, 1971, pp. 403–10; "Magnetic Flux Quantization and Josephson Behavior in Living Systems," *Physica Scripta*, vol. 40, 1989, E. Del Giudice, S. Doglia, M. Milani, C.W. Smith, G. Vitiello, pp. 786–91; "Biological Sensitivity to Weak Magnetic Fields Due to Biological Superconductive Josephson Junctions," *Physiological Chemistry and Physics 5*, 1973, pp. 173–6; "Biophysical Studies of the Modification of DNA by Antitumour Platinum Coordination Complexes," *Platinum Metals Review*, vol. 34, # 4, 1990, p. 235.

13 The Niels Bohr Institute for Astronomy, Physics and Geophysics, Blegdamsvej, 17 DK-2100 Copenhagen, Denmark. NBIfAFG was formed in January 1993. All physics activity at the University of Copenhagen was then joined in one Institute instead of the previous four departments. The Institute is responsible for all the teaching of physics at the University. Undergraduate study and master's programs are organized by the Teaching Committee. The graduate Ph.D. school and admissions hereto are under the preview of the Ph.D. Committee. The research program of the Institute is the responsibility of the Director, the four departments and the Research Committee.

14 Argonne National Laboratory, 9700 S. Cass Avenue, Argonne, IL 60439. A USA Department of Energy laboratory operated by the University of Chicago, it is the nation's first national laboratory, chartered in 1946. Argonne is a direct descendant of the University of Chicago's Metallurgical Laboratory, part of the World War II Manhattan Project to build the atomic bomb before the Germans. It was at the Met Lab where, on 2 December 1942, Enrico Fermi and his band of about 50 colleagues created the

world's first controlled nuclear chain reaction in a squash court at the University of Chicago. After the war, Argonne was given the mission of developing nuclear reactors for peaceful purposes. Over the years, Argonne's research expanded to include many other areas of science, engineering, and technology, but is not now a part of the weapons industry.

15 Oak Ridge National Laboratory, Bethel Valley Road, Oak Ridge, TN 37831. ORNL is a multi-program science and technology laboratory managed for the US Department of Energy. Scientists and engineers at ORNL conduct basic and applied research and development to create scientific knowledge and technological solutions that strengthen the nation's leadership in key areas of science; increase the availability of clean, abundant energy; restore and protect the environment; and contribute to national security. ORNL also performs other work for the Department of Energy, including isotope production, information management, and technical program management, and provides research and technical assistance to other organizations.

16 *Classical and Quantum Gravity*, volume 11, May 1994, University of Wales, Cardiff. Article entitled "The Warp Drive: hyperfast travel within general relativity."

17 "Space-time Hypersurfing," in *American Scientist*, volume 82, pp. 422–3, October 1994.

18 SOSF then at PO Box 25709, Tempe, Arizona 85285. SOSF *Newsletter* # 1 was issued 13th October 1995.

19 5,000 members at individual subscriptions of $500 each.

20 SOSF *Newsletters* # 14 and 15, November/December 1996.

21 SOSF *Newsletters* # 18 and 19, March/April 1997.

Chapter 12: The Quantum Protocol

1 Chemically they are more than 4 angstroms apart. An *angstrom* is a unit of length equal to 0.00000001 centimeters. Named after the Swedish physicist Anders Jonas Angstrom, who died in 1874.

2 The Brown University, Rhode Island, physicist Leon Cooper and his colleagues John Bardeen and Robert Schrieffer won the Nobel Prize in 1972 for explaining why superconductors superconduct. Another significant advancement came from Cambridge graduate Brian Josephson. He predicted and confirmed that electrical current would flow between two superconducting materials even

when they are separated by a non-superconducting insulator. This tunneling phenomenon, now known as the "Josephson Effect" won him the Nobel Prize in physics in 1973.

3   In 1933 Walter Meissner and Robert Ochsenfeld discovered that a superconducting material will repel a magnetic field. A magnet moving by a conductor induces currents in the conductor (the principle on which the electric generator operates). However, in a superconductor the induced currents precisely mirror the field that would otherwise have penetrated the superconducting material, causing the magnet to be repulsed. This phenomenon is known as diamagnetism and is referred to as the Meissner Effect.

4   Hawking, Stephen, *The Illustrated A Brief History of Time*, Bantam, London, 1996. ch. 5, pp. 89–90.

5   On 14th April 1999.

6   <http://newton.dep.anl.gov/archive.htm>. Direct questions may be asked of Argonne scientists through this online facility. Another good web link for questions is: <http://imagine.gsfc.nasa.gov/docs/ask_astro/ask_an_astronomer.html> hosted by the Laboratory for High Energy Astrophysics at NASA/Goddard Space Flight Center.

7   The process is currently featured on website: <http://science.nasa.gov/ headlines/y2002/27mar_stoplight.htm>.

8   *Physical Review Letters*, vol. 88, article 05401.

9   *Nature*, vol. 413, p. 400. Also featured by *New Scientist* News Service, <http://www.newscientist.com/news/news.jsp?id=ns99991346> entry 26, September 2001.

10 For a full explanation of the lotus in the ancient Star Fire ritual of Mesopotamia, *see* Gardner, Laurence, *Realm of the Ring Lords*, ch. 10, pp. 116–20.

11 Hawking, Stephen, *The Illustrated A Brief History of Time*, ch. 11, p. 227. Since 1979 Professor Hawking has held the post of Lucasian Professor of Mathematics in the Department of Applied Mathematics and Theoretical Physics at Cambridge University – the same chair held by Isaac Newton in 1663.

Chapter 13: Fire In The Desert

1   Matthew 26:26–28, Mark 14: 22–24, Luke 22:19–20.

2   Allegro, John M., *The Dead Sea Scrolls*, Penguin, Harmondsworth, 1964, ch. 7, p. 131; ch. 12, p. 164; and ch. 13, p. 168.

3 *Scroll of The Rule*, Annex II, 17–22.

4 The Jewish festival of lights, which commemorates this event in 165 BC.

5 Josephus, Flavius, *Wars of the Jews*, Book I and *Antiquities of the Jews*, Book XV.

6 Dupont-Sommer, André, *The Jewish Sect of Qumrân and the Essenes*, Vallentine Mitchell, London, 1954, Postscript p. 169.

7 Josephus, Flavius, *Antiquities of the Jews*, XV, 5:2.

8 Milik, J.T., *Ten Years of Discovery in the Wilderness of Judaea* (trans. J. Strugnell), SCM Press, London, 1959, ch. 3, pp. 51–3.

9 Josephus, Flavius, *The Wars of the Jews*, II, 8:6.

10 Allegro, John, *The Dead Sea Scrolls*, ch. 5, p. 94.

11 *Ibid.*, ch. 5, p. 93.

12 Thiering, Barbara, *Jesus the Man*, ch. 7, p. 34.

13 Perowne, S., *The Life and Times of Herod the Great*, Hodder & Stoughton, London, 1956, ch. 17, pp. 135–6.

14 Josephus, Flavius, *Antiquities of the Jews*, XV, 9:1–2.

15 Ritmeyer, Leen and Kathleen, *Secrets of Jerusalem's Temple Mount*, Biblical Archaeological Society, Washington, DC, 1998, ch. 3, pp. 47, 49.

16 Her name in Greek was Cypros.

17 Ritmeyer, Leen and Kathleen, *Secrets of Jerusalem's Temple Mount*, ch. 1, pp. 24–5.

18 Allegro, John, *The Dead Sea Scrolls*, ch. 7, p. 110.

19 Ahmed Osman, *The House of The Messiah*, HarperCollins, London, 1992, ch. 5, p. 31.

20 Allegro, John, *The Dead Sea Scrolls*, ch. 5, p. 99.

21 As currently detailed on the *ORMUS* website <http://www.subtleenergies. com/ormus/ormus/ormus4.htm>.

22 Josephus, Flavius, *The Wars of the Jews*, II, 8:6.

23 Genesis 18–19.

24 For a good reference concerning the sects at Qumrân, *see* Eisenman, Robert, *Maccabees, Zadokites. Christians and Qumrân*, E.J. Brill, Leiden, 1983.

25 Ezekiel 44:15, 48:11.

Chapter 14: The Desposyni

1 Smith, Dr. William, *Smith's Bible Dictionary*.

2 Wilson, A.N., *Jesus*, ch. 4, p. 80.

3 There is minor element of debate here since although Ezra 3:2 and Haggai 1:1 confirm that Zerubbabel was born into Shealtiel's family, there could have been a generation between the two. Possibly Shealtiel had a son named Pedaiah, who would have been Zerubbabel's father. The account in 1 Chronicles 3:19 is confusing in this regard.

4 Eusebius of Caesarea, *Ecclesiastical History* (trans. C. F. Crusé), George Bell, London, 1874, book I:7. Some extant writings of Julius Africanus can be found in Roberts, Rev. Alexander, and Donaldson, James (eds.), *Ante-Nicene Fathers No.6*, Continuum International and T. & T. Clark, Edinburgh, 1980.

5 Thiering, Barbara, *Jesus the Man*, ch. 5, p. 29.

6 Josephus, Flavius, *The Antiquities of the Jews*, XVII, 13:5; XVIII, 1:1.

7 Perowne, Stewart, *The Later Herods*, Hodder & Stoughton, London, 1958, ch. 5, pp. 26–9.

8 Thiering, Barbara, *Jesus the Man*, ch. 8, p. 48 and ch. 11, p. 61.

9 *Ibid.*, ch. 12, p. 64.

10 Wilson, A.N. *Jesus*, ch. 4, p. 83.

11 *Ibid.*, ch. 4, p. 79.

12 Qualls-Corbett, Nancy, *The Sacred Prostitute*, Inner City Books, Toronto, 1988, ch. 2, p. 58.

13 *Panarion* 78:8:1 and 78:9:6; *Ancoratus* 60:1.

14 *Protevangelion* 19:3–20:3.

15 Philip 59:10–11.

16 Mark 15:47, Mark 16:1, Matthew 27:56, Matthew 27:61, Matthew 28:1, and Luke 24:10. The only exception is a 7th entry in John 19:25 which, in introducing Jesus' mother, lists the women by a ranking of age seniority.

17 The italicized "*the mother*" insert in Luke 24:10 is spurious and not part of the original text.

18 Taylor, J.W., *The Coming of the Saints*, Covenant Books, London, 1969, ch. 6, p. 105.

19 She is discussed in her own context in Gardner, Laurence, *Realm of the Ring Lords*, ch. 4, pp. 47–8.

20 Edessa (now Urfa) in Turkey, as opposed to Edessa in Greece.

21 Abdias is recorded as one of the 70 disciples of Jesus – as per Luke 10:1. He was the first Bishop of Babylon, consecrated by Simon and Jude, the brothers of Jesus.

22 Eusebius of Caesarea, *Ecclesiastical History*, book I:7.

23 Martin, Malachi, *The Decline and Fall of the Roman Church*, p. 43.
24 Eusebius of Caesarea, *Ecclesiastical History*, book I:7. Also *see* Schonfield, Hugh J., *The Passover Plot*, Element Books, Shaftesbury, 1985, ch. 5, p. 245–6.
25 Eusebius of Caesarea, *Ecclesiastical History*, book III:11.
26 Martin, Malachi, *The Decline and Fall of the Roman Church*, p. 44.
27 This is also confirmed by Eusebius (*c.* AD 260–340), *Ecclesiastical History*, book 3:17.
28 Martin, Malachi, *The Decline and Fall of the Roman Church*, pp. 42–4.
29 *See* Robinson, James, *The Nag Hammadi Library*.
30 For the full story of Mary Magdalene and her marriage to Jesus, *see* Gardner, Laurence, *Bloodline of the Holy Grail*, ch. 5, pp. 53–60 and ch. 9, pp. 97–112.
31 For the full story of Joseph of Arimathea, with all relevant source notes and references *see* Gardner, Laurence, *Bloodline of the Holy Grail*, ch. 10, pp. 113–25.
32 This subject is covered more fully as the primary subject of Gardner, Laurence, *Genesis of the Grail Kings*.

Chapter 15: Hermetic Renaissance

1 "Aelia" in honor of the Emperor Hadrian, whose full name was Publius Aelius Hadrianus. "Capitolina" after the Capitoline triad, Jupiter, Juno, and Minerva, who were to be the patrons of the new city. The triad was worshipped on the Capitoline Hill in Rome.
2 The Dome of the Rock was not always golden as it is today. The 80 kilos of gold plating was a recent undertaking by the late King Hussein of Jordan, who sold one of his London houses to help fund the project.
3 *Sultan* = Ruler of Power.
4 Although Suni Muslims consider Jerusalem as their third holy city, the Shi'ite Muslims place it fourth after Karabala in Southern Iraq.
5 The original *Ordre de Sion* was established so that eligible Muslims, Jews, and others could be allied to the Christian Order that became the Knights Templars.
6 Gibson, Shimon, and Jacobsen, David M., *Below the Temple Mount in Jerusalem*, Tempus Reparatum, Oxford, 1996, Pref., p. vii.

7 Cistercian ideals were far removed from the concerns of the curia at the Vatican; they pertained to education, agriculture, and the sacred arts.

8 After the fall of Acre, which ended the Crusades in 1291, the Hospitallers were forced to leave Palestine. They went to Rhodes and Cyprus, adding secular and military ventures to their activities, and from 1530 they were established as the Knights of Malta. A Hospitallers' offshoot, chartered in 1888, created Britain's St. John Ambulance Association, which still uses the same badge.

9 Tacitus, *The Histories* (trans. Kenneth Wellesley), Penguin, London, 1994, p. 285.

10 *Ibid.*, ch. 8, p. 69. Other selected works on the subject of the Templars and the Crusades are: Andressohn, John C., *The Ancestry and Life of Godfrey of Bouillon*, University of Indiana Press, Bloomington, IN, 1947; Baigent, Michael and Leigh, Richard, *The Temple and the Lodge*, Jonathan Cape, London, 1989; Seward, Desmond, *The Monks of War*, Paladin/Granada, St. Albans, 1974; Addison, Charles G., *The History of the Knights Templars*, Adventures Unlimited, Kempton, IL, 1997; and Runciman, Steven, *A History of the Crusades*, Cambridge University Press, Cambridge, 1951.

11 Begg, Ean C.M., *The Cult of the Black Virgin*, Arkana, London, 1985, ch. 4, p. 103.

12 Sworder, Mary (ed.), *Fulcanelli: Master Alchemist: Le Mystère des Cathédrales*, Brotherhood of Life, Albuquerque, NM, 1986, ch. 3, p. 42.

13 Brewer, Rev. E. Cobham, *The Reader's Handbook of Famous Names in Fiction*, J.B. Lippincott, Philadelphia, PA, 1899.

14 Charpentier, Louis, *The Mysteries of Chartres Cathedral*, ch. 2, p. 29. Also *see* ground-plan diagram in Gardner, Laurence, *Bloodline of the Holy Grail*, ch. 17, p. 219.

15 A dolmen usually comprises two upright stones with a horizontal capstone across the top, as at Stonehenge. From prehistoric times, dolmens were used as gigantic resonators (much like sound boxes used to amplify acoustic musical instruments) to boost the properties of the Earth's telluric current.

16 The School of Practical High Sciences.

17 This subject is also referenced in Faivre, Antoine, *The Golden Fleece and Alchemy*, Foreword, p. 2 and ch. 2, p. 41.

18 The most comprehensive account to date of the Septimanian kingdom is in Zuckerman, Arthur J., *A Jewish Princedom in Feudal France*, Columbia University Press, New York, NY, 1972.

19 The Jewish faith is represented here by the collective term Torah for the first five scriptural books of the Hebrew Bible. The Masoretic Hebrew Bible had not long been compiled, and the oldest extant copy (written in about 1010) is currently held in the Russian National Library, St. Petersburg, where it is known as the *Leningrad Codex*.

20 The subject is well covered in Baigent, Michael, with Leigh, Richard, and Lincoln, Henry, *The Holy Blood and the Holy Grail*, ch. 2, pp. 19–34.

21 A concise overview of Provence as a cradle of awakening is given in Starbird, Margaret, *The Woman With the Alabaster Jar*, Bear, Santa Fe, 1993, ch. 4, pp. 67–78.

22 Eleanor of Aquitaine (1122–1204) is a good example of female equality in the region. Her importance and influence were a constant embarrassment to the Roman Church bishops.

23 Recommended on the subject of the Albigensian Crusade is Oldenbourg, Zoé, *Massacre at Montségur* (trans. Peter Green), Pantheon, New York, NY, 1961.

Chapter 16: The Hidden Scroll

1 *Archives des Frères Aînés de la Rose Croix*, Bibliothèque Nationale, Paris.

2 Baigent, Michael and Leigh, Richard, *The Temple and the Lodge*, Jonathan Cape, London, 1989, ch. 3, pp. 51–62 and ch. 4, pp. 63–76, is additionally informative on the Inquisition of the Templars and the Templar Fleet.

3 Albany, HRH Prince Michael of, *The Forgotten Monarchy of Scotland*, ch. 5, pp. 62–4.

4 The excommunication of Scotland as a nation was not repealed until 1323. This followed Robert the Bruce's defeat of Edward II at Bannockburn in 1314 and the drawing up of the Scottish Constitution (the *Declaration of Arbroath*) in 1320. Subsequently, in 1328, the Treaty of Northampton confirmed Scotland's independence under King Robert I.

5 The Franco-Scots *Auld Alliance* was one of the longest-standing arrangements in the history of Europe, whereby (until 1906) Scots entered France as French citizens, and vice-versa.

6 De Molay was executed on 18th March 1314.

7 Albany, HRH Prince Michael of, *The Forgotten Monarchy of Scotland*, ch. 5, p. 65.

8 *Ibid.*, ch. 8, pp. 125–6.

9 *The Mail on Sunday*, 20 June 1997.

10 Charpentier, Louis, *The Mysteries of Chartres Cathedral*, ch. 18, pp. 144–51.

11 Howard, Michael, *The Occult Conspiracy*, Rider/Century Hutchinson, London, 1989, ch. 1, pp. 9–10.

12 The system of measurement that is much to be preferred is that which counts in feet and inches, rather than in meters. Indeed, adepts in sacred geometry and metrology regard the meter as nothing more than a "fashionable folly" because of its determined adherence to tens and hundreds. The decimal base of 10 leads to inevitable inaccuracies and such nonsenses as recurring decimals. Universal measurement is much more accurately founded on a base of 12, which is divisible by five of the first six numbers and provides a more flexible foundation for any numerical calculation. Similarly, geometry that is founded upon a decagon is inherently unstable. The cardinal factors in sacred mathematics are 3, 4, and 12. *See* Michell, John, *The Dimensions of Paradise*, Thames & Hudson, London, 1988.

13 *Hera*, numero 27, Marzo 2002: *Templari: Assolti Con Formula Piena*, di Adriano Forgione e Francesco Garufi.

14 *The Times*, London, 30th March 2002.

Chapter 17: Rise Of The Phoenix

1 Vermes, Geza, *The Complete Dead Sea Scrolls in English*, p. 130.

2 Ritmeyer, Leen and Kathleen, *Secrets of Jerusalem's Temple Mount*, ch. 6, p. 108.

3 Talmud, Yoma 54a.

4 Ritmeyer, Leen and Kathleen, *Secrets of Jerusalem's Temple Mount*, ch. 6, pp. 109–10.

5 Seleucid I to Seleucid VI: Kings of Syria from 301 to 93 BC. Seleucid IV (also called Soter, 187–176 BC) sent his chancellor, Heliodorus, to plunder the Temple of Jerusalem (2 Maccabees

3:1–40). However, as the result of an apparition, he was prevented from fulfilling the task and murdered Seleucus instead.

6 Ritmeyer, Leen and Kathleen, *Secrets of Jerusalem's Temple Mount*, ch. 5, p. 57.

7 Gibson, Shimon, and Jacobsen, David M., *Below the Temple Mount in Jerusalem*, Pref., p. vii.

8 Josephus, Flavius, *The Antiquities of the Jews*, XV, 11:5.

9 Tacitus, *The Histories*, V:12., p. 287.

10 *Middoth* 5:5.

11 Palestine Exploration Fund, 2 Hinde Mews, Marylebone Lane, London, W1U 2AA.

12 Ritmeyer, Leen and Kathleen, *Secrets of Jerusalem's Temple Mount*, ch. 5, pp. 71-7.

13 *Ibid.*, ch. 5, p. 83.

14 These artifacts are now held by the Scottish Templar archivist, Robert Brydon, at Roslin, near Edinburgh. *See* Knight, Christopher, and Lomas, Robert, *The Hiram Key*, Century, London, 1996, ch. 13, p. 267.

15 Horne, Alex, *King Solomon's Temple in the Masonic Tradition*, ch. 2, p. 32.

16 For further reading in this regard, *see* Jones, Bernard E., *Freemasons' Book of the Royal Arch*, ch. 3, p. 20 ff.

17 St. Anthony, *c.* AD 300, was the founder of Christian monasticism in Egypt.

18 The *Privy Seal Register* of Scotland.

19 The story of Sir Robert Moray is well told in Lomas, Robert, *The Invisible College*, Headline, London, 2002.

20 Recommended books concerning Robert Boyle, Isaac Newton, Christopher Wren and the Royal Society in general are: Wojcik, Jan W., *Robert Boyle and the Limits of Reason*, Cambridge University Press, Cambridge, 1997; White, Michael, *Isaac Newton*, Fourth Estate, London, 1997; Tinniswood, Adrian, *His Invention so Fertile: A Life of Christopher Wren*, Jonathan Cape, London, 2001; and Hunter, Michael, *Science and Society in Restoration England*, Cambridge University Press, Cambridge, 1981.

21 Ward, J.S.M., *Freemasonry and the Ancient Gods*, Baskerville, London, 1926, p. 300.

22 Further reading on this can be found in Horne, Alex, *King Solomon's Temple in the Masonic Tradition*, ch. 1, p. 44.

23 This famous Jacobite era Count of St. Germain was the son of Juan Tomazo Enriquez de Cabrera, Conte de Melgar of Castille, and Maria Anna, dowager Queen of Spain and widow of King Carlos II.

24 Jones, Bernard E., *Freemasons' Book of the Royal Arch*, ch. 3, p. 36.

25 *Ibid.*, ch. 11, p. 132.

26 Graphic depictions of the main elements of each Degree, pictorially displayed on ceremonial panels.

27 Jones, Bernard E., *Freemasons' Book of the Royal Arch*, ch. 3, p. 36.

28 The father of Queen Victoria.

29 Having resigned his sovereign rights in 1793, Augustus was actually Grand Master of the English branch of the French Templars. For the full story, *see* Albany, HRH Prince Michael of, *The Forgotten Monarchy of Scotland*, ch. 16, pp. 241–7.

30 In Scotland the Templar standard bearer was called the *Beaucennifer*.

31 Knight, Christopher, and Lomas, Robert, *The Hiram Key*, ch. 13, pp. 264–5.

32 From the *Aldersgate Ritual of the Royal Arch*, published by Lewis Masonic, Hersham, 1999.

33 *Jah* is the root of *Hallelujah*: Praise the Lord.

34 Lewis, H. Spencer, *The Mystical Life of Jesus*, pp. 191–2.

Chapter 18: The Resting Place

1 MS Fergusson 210: *De Alchemia Opuscula complura veterum philosophorum*, Frankfurt, 1550.

2 Albany, HRH Prince Michael of, *The Forgotten Monarchy of Scotland*, ch. 10, p. 150–1. The Templars had been given asylum in Scotland by King Robert the Bruce, and 432 Knights had fought at Bannockburn under the command of Chevalier Hugues de Crecy. Thereafter, the Order was justifiably honored in the Kingdom of the Scots, and successive heirs to the Stewart crown were Knights of the Temple from birth.

3 Excellent research concerning the Heidelberg/Royal Society connection is to be found in Yates, Frances A., *The Rosicrucian Enlightenment*, Routledge, London, 1972.

4 Curtis, John (ed.), *Art and Empire: Treasures from Assyria in the British Museum*, Metropolitan Museum of Art, New York, NY, 1995, Item 9, p. 59.

5 Yadin, Yigael, *The Temple Scroll*, ch. 13, p. 128.

6 Some years ago, an early translation was thought to have been "Here things take their course. You are to work through the Ark" – as in Charpentier, Louis, *The Mysteries of Chartres Cathedral*, ch. 9, p. 70.

7 These translations, which are now generally confirmed, were first proposed in Hancock, Graham, *The Sign and the Seal*, ch 3, pp. 54–5.

8 Miller, Malcolm, *Chartres Cathedral*, Pitkin Guides, Andover, 1996, p. 18.

9 Catalogue shelf number: MS Lat. 1104. His accompanying manuscript notes are numbered MS. Fr. 19093.

10 There is good coverage of Villard de Honnecourt in French literature. In the English language, he may be found referenced in Bucher, François, *Architector: The Lodge Books and Sketchbooks of Medieval Architects*, Abaris Books, New York, NY, 1979 and in Gimpel, Jean, *The Medieval Machine: The Industrial Revolution of the Middle Ages*, Pimlico, London, 1976.

11 The labyrinth circumference is 12.85 meters.

12 Miller, Malcolm, *Chartres Cathedral*, p. 18.

13 Chevalier, Jean, and Gheerbrant, *Dictionnaire des Symboles*, Robert Laffont, Paris 1997.

14 Freitas, Lima de, *The Encyclopedia of Religion* (ed. Mercia Eliade), Macmillan, New York, NY, 1987, under "Labyrinth."

15 Miller, Malcolm, *Chartres Cathedral*, p. 18.

16 This sequence is also confirmed in Knight, Christopher, and Lomas, Robert, *The Hiram Key*, ch. 13, p. 270.

17 Miller, Malcolm, *Chartres Cathedral*, p. 18.

18 Knight, Christopher, and Lomas, Robert, *The Hiram Key*, ch. 15, pp. 306–21.

19 Wallace-Murphy, Tim, and Hopkins, Marilyn, *Rosslyn*, Element Books, Shaftesbury, 1999, ch. 14, p. 213.

20 Adrian, Frank J. and Cowan, Dwaine O., "The New Superconductors," in *Chemical and Engineering News*, 21st December 1992.

21 Genesis 28:12.

22 2 Kings 2:11.

23 Lister, Martin, *A Journey to Paris in the Year 1698*, Jacob Tonson, London 1699, p. 80 ff.

24 Gerber, Pat, *Stone of Destiny*, ch. 5, pp. 41–2.
25 Temple, Robert, *The Crystal Sun*, Century, London, 2000, ch. 8, p. 283.
26 *Ibid.*, ch. 9, pp. 388–9, 420–1.
27 Budge, E.A. Wallis, *Cleopatra's Needle and Other Egyptian Obelisks* (1926), rep. Dover Publications, New York, NY, 1990, pp. 26–38.
28 In Superstring Theory, the premise is that although particles occupy single points in time, they are not the ultimate objects by which to determine universal gravity. Instead, it is now perceived that the basic objects of existence are not point-like but string-like. They might be open-ended or looped (closed strings), and the average size of a string is around the Planck Length of a millionth of a billionth of a billionth of a billionth of a centimeter, as determined as a base constant by the German Scientist Max Planck in 1900. Superstrings are featured in Hawking, Stephen, *The Illustrated A Brief History of Time*, ch. 11, pp. 212–27. For more comprehensive reading, *see* Greene, Brian, *The Elegant Universe*, Vintage, New York, NY, 2000; also Gribbin, John, *The Search for Superstrings*, Little, Brown, New York, NY, 1999; and Kaku, Michio, *Beyond Einstein*, Anchor/Doubleday, New York, NY, 1995.
29 Charpentier, Louis, *The Mysteries of Chartres Cathedral*, ch. 9., p. 72.
30 Ravenscroft, Trevor, and Wallace-Murphy, Tim, *The Mark of the Beast*, Samuel Weiser, York Beach, ME, 1997, ch. 5, p. 52. *See also* Wallace-Murphy, Tim, and Hopkins, Marilyn, *Rosslyn*, ch. 12, pp. 265–6.

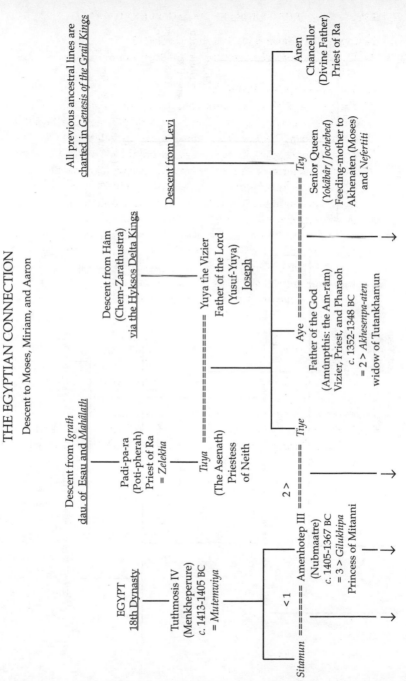

THE EGYPTIAN CONNECTION
Descent to Moses, Miriam, and Aaron

All previous ancestral lines are
charted in *Genesis of the Grail Kings*

Descent from Levi

Descent from Hám
(Chem-Zarathustra)
via the Hyksos Delta Kings

Descent from *Igrath*
dau. of Esau and *Mahálath*

EGYPT
18th Dynasty

Tuthmosis IV
(Menkheperure)
c. 1413-1405 BC
= *Mutemwiya*

Padi-pa-ra
(Poti-pherah)
Priest of Ra
= *Zelekha*

Yuya the Vizier
Father of the Lord
(Yusuf-Yuya)
Joseph

Tuya ==========
(The Asenath)
Priestess
of Neith

Sitamun ========= Amenhotep III
(Nubmaatre)
c. 1405-1367 BC
= 3 > *Gilukhipa*
Princess of Mitanni

2 > ==========

Tiye

Aye ==========
Father of the God
(Amûnpthis: the Am-râm)
Vizier, Priest, and Pharaoh
c. 1352-1348 BC
= 2 > *Akhesenpa-aten*
widow of Tutankhamun

Tey ==========
Senior Queen
(*Yokábár / Jochebed*)
Feeding-mother to
Akhenaten (Moses) and
Nefertiti

Anen
Chancellor
(Divine Father)
Priest of Ra

<1

331

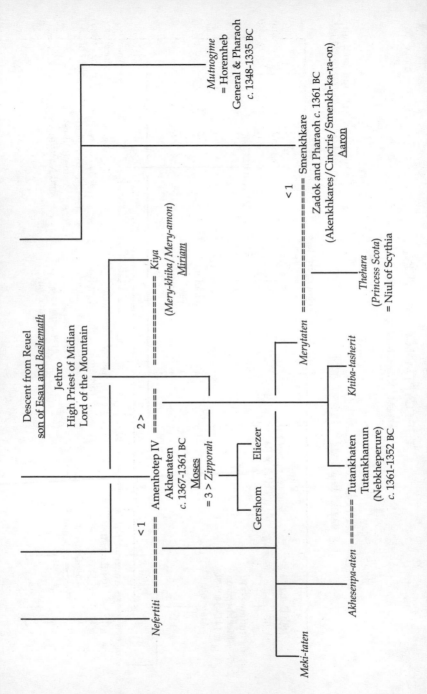

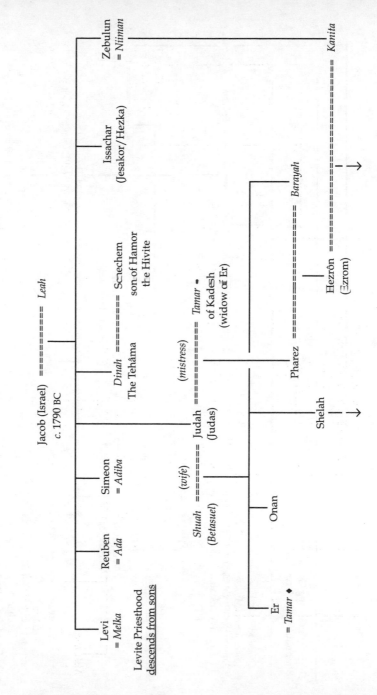

OUT OF EGYPT

Descent from Miriam to King David

Jacob (Israel) ========= *Leah*
c. 1790 BC

Levi
= *Melka*

Levite Priesthood
descends from sons

Reuben
= *Ada*

Simeon
= *Adiba*

Judah
(Judas)

Dinah ========= Schechem
The Tehâma   son of Hamor
                the Hivite

Issachar
(Jesakor/Hezka)

Zebulun
= *Niiman*

Shuah ======== (wife)
(Betasuel)

(mistress)

Tamar ========= of Kadesh
(widow of Er)

Er
= *Tamar* ◆

Onan

Shelah →

Pharez

Kanita

Barayah

Hezrôn ============
(Ezrom)

→

333

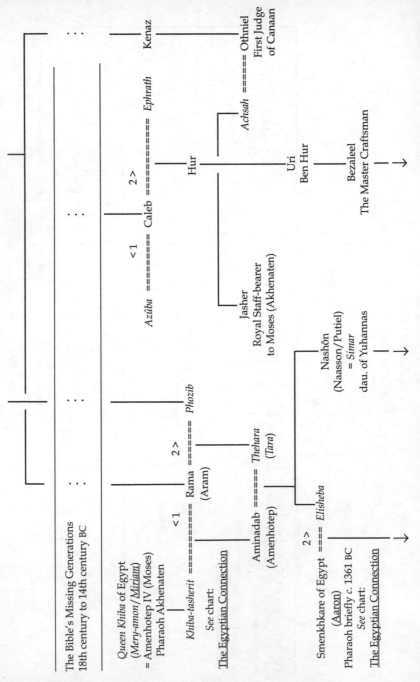

The Bible's Missing Generations
18th century to 14th century BC

*Queen Khiba of Egypt
(Mery-amon / Miriam)
= Amenhotep IV (Moses)
Pharaoh Akhenaten*

Khiba-tasherit =========== Rama
                                (Aram)
                        <1   2> ======== *Phozib*

See chart:
The Egyptian Connection

Aminadab ====== *Thehara*
(Amenhotep)   *(Tara)*

Smenkhkare of Egypt ==== *Elisheba*
(Aaron)
Pharaoh briefly c. 1361 BC
                        2>
See chart:
The Egyptian Connection

Nashón
(Naasson/Putiel)
= *Simar*
dau. of Yuhannas

Azúba ========= Caleb ============ *Ephrath*
        <1   2>

Jasher
Royal Staff-bearer
to Moses (Akhenaten)

Hur

Kenaz

Achsah ===== Othniel
              First Judge
              of Canaan

Uri
Ben Hur

Bezaleel
The Master Craftsman

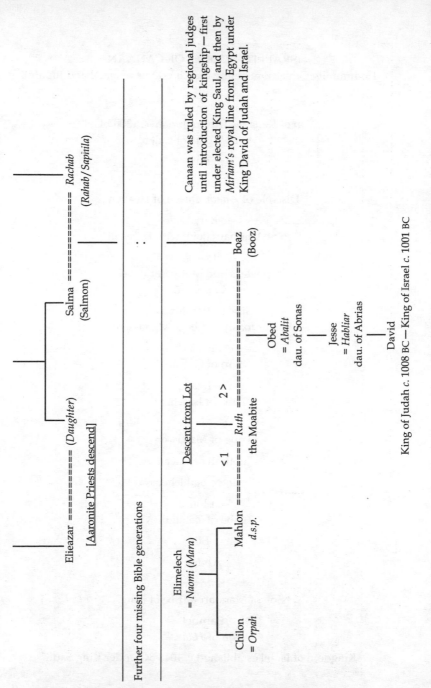

Elieazar ========= (Daughter)
[Aaronite Priests descend]

Salma ============ Rachab
(Salmon)   (Rahab / Sapitila)

Further four missing Bible generations

. .

Canaan was ruled by regional judges
until introduction of kingship — first
under elected King Saul, and then by
Miriam's royal line from Egypt under
King David of Judah and Israel.

Elimelech
= Naomi (Mara)

Chilon   Mahlon ========= Ruth ========= Boaz
= Orpah   d.s.p.   the Moabite   (Booz)

                        <1   2>
                Descent from Lot

                                Obed
                                = Abalit
                                dau. of Sonas

                                Jesse
                                = Habliar
                                dau. of Abrias

                                David

King of Judah c. 1008 BC — King of Israel c. 1001 BC

ISRAELITE JUDGES OF CANAAN
Community Governors before the Kingdoms of Israel and Judah

Othniel
Son of Kenaz — Tribe of Judah, *c.* 1300 BC
= *Ashsah*, dau. of Caleb

Ehud

Shamgar
Disciple of *Anath*, Queen of Heaven

Barak
Son of Abinoam (joint with *Deborah*)

Deborah
Prophetess and Mother of Israel
= Lappidoth

Gideon (Jerubbaal)
Son of Joash — Tribe of Manasseh

Abimelech
Son of Gideon

Tola
Tribe of Issachar

Jair
Tribe of Manasseh

Jepthah of Gilead

Ibzan of Bethlehem

Elon
Tribe of Zebulun

Eli

Abdon

Samson
Son of Manoah — Tribe of Dan

Samuel
Son of *Hannah*

Kingdom of Israel established *c.* 1048 BC under King Saul

RAMESSIDE DYNASTIES OF EGYPT
Contemporary with Bible period from Miriam to David

19th Dynasty

Rameses I 1335-1333 BC

Seti I 1333-1304 BC

Rameses II — The Great 1304-1236 BC

Merneptah 1236-1202 BC

Amenmeses 1202-1199 BC

Seti II 1199-1193 BC

Siptah 1193-1187 BC

Queen Twosret (Tausert) 1187-1185 BC

20th Dynasty

Setnakhte 1185-1182 BC

Rameses III 1182-1151 BC

Rameses IV 1151-1145 BC

Rameses V 1145-1141 BC

Rameses VI 1141-1133 BC

Rameses VII 1133-1129 BC

Rameses VIII 1129-1126 BC

Rameses IX 1126-1108 BC

Rameses X 1108-1098 BC

Rameses XI 1098-1070 BC

THE ROYAL HOUSE OF JUDAH

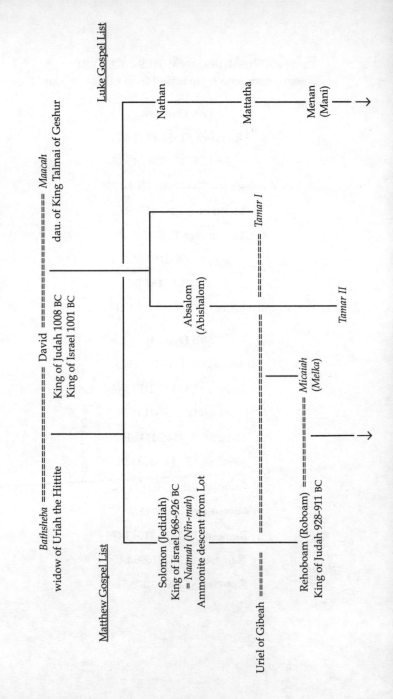

Melea

Eliakim

Jonan

Joseph

Juda

Simei
(Simeon)

→

Abijah (Abia)
King of Judah 911-908 BC
= *Maachah (Malkit)*, dau. of Abisholom of Jerusalem

Asa (Asaph)
King of Judah 908-868 BC
= *Azubah (Azobha)*, dau. of Shilhi (Sala)

Jehoshaphat (Josaphat)
King of Judah 868-851 BC
= *Malkiya*, dau. of Abiud

Jehoram (Joram)
King of Judah 851-843 BC
= *Athalia (Phitalia)*, dau. of Ahab, King of Israel, and *Queen Jezebel*
Athaliah was Queen of Judah 843-839 BC, succeeding her son

Ahaziah
King of Judah 843 BC
= *Zibiah (Subha)*, dau. of Habralias of Beersheba

Joash
King of Judah 839-799 BC
= *Jehoaddan (Joadan)* of Jerusalem

→

Levi

Matthat

Jorim

Eliezer

Jose

Amaziah
King of Judah 799-785 BC
= Jecoliah (Ikhalya) of Jerusalem

Uzziah (Oziah)
King of Judah 785-742 BC
= Jerusha (Irusha), dau. of Sadoc the High Priest

Jotham (Joatham)
King of Judah 742-735 BC
= Hadast, dau. of Elkanah

Ahaz (Achaz)
King of Judah 735-715 BC
= Abijah (Abhi), dau. of Zechariah

Hezekiah (Hezekias)
King of Judah 715-687 BC
= Hephzibah (Basyar), dau. of Bartenas

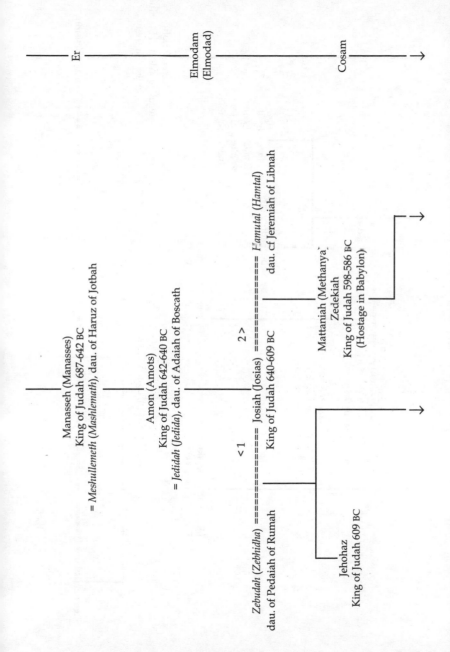

Er

Elmodam
(Elmodad)

Cosam

Manasseh (Manasses)
King of Judah 687-642 BC
= *Meshullemeth (Mashlemath)*, dau. of Haruz of Jotbah

Amon (Amots)
King of Judah 642-640 BC
= *Jedidah (Jedida)*, dau. of Adaiah of Boscath

<1   2>

Zebudah (Zebhidha) ========== Josiah (Josias) ========== *Hamutal (Hamtal)*
dau. of Pedaiah of Rumah   King of Judah 640-609 BC   dau. of Jeremiah of Libnah

Jehohaz
King of Judah 609 BC

Mattaniah (Methanya`)
Zedekiah
King of Judah 598-586 BC
(Hostage in Babylon)

341

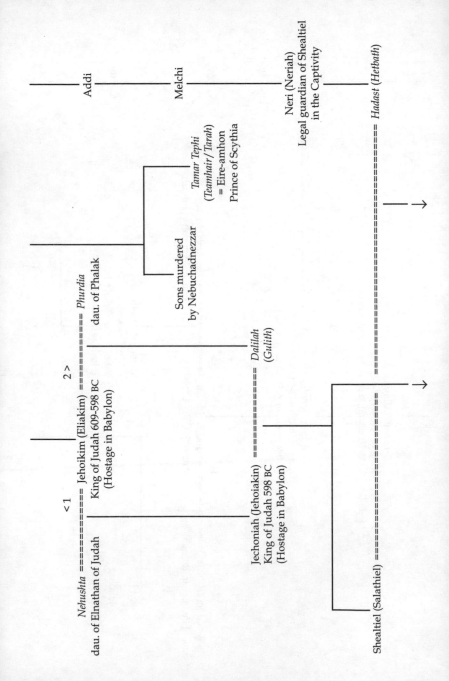

Addi

Melchi

Neri (Neriah)
Legal guardian of Shealtiel
in the Captivity

Nehushta ============= Jehoikim (Eliakim) ============= *Phurdia*
dau. of Elnathan of Judah   King of Judah 609-598 BC   dau. of Phalak
                              (Hostage in Babylon)

<1   2>

                                                    Tamar Tephi
                                                    (Teamhair / Tarah)
                          Sons murdered   = Eire-amhon
                          by Nebuchadnezzar   Prince of Scythia

Jechoniah (Jehoiakin) ============= *Dalilah*
King of Judah 598 BC   *(Gulith)*
(Hostage in Babylon)

Shealtiel (Salathiel) ============= *Hadast (Hetbath)*

342

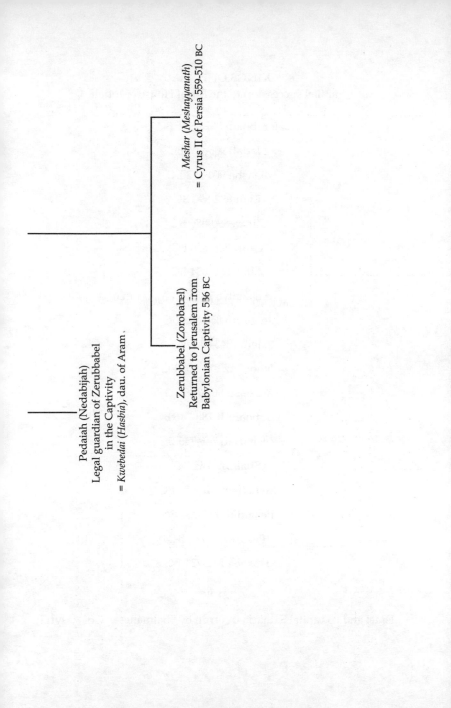

Pedaiah (Nedabijah)
Legal guardian of Zerubbabel
in the Captivity
= *Kwebedai (Hasbia)*, dau. of Aram.

Zerubbabel (Zorobabel)
Returned to Jerusalem from
Babylonian Captivity 536 BC

Meshar (Meshayyanath)
= Cyrus II of Persia 559-510 BC

KINGS OF ISRAEL
Parallel succession to the Royal House of Judah

Jeroboam I 928-906 BC

Nadab 906-904 BC

Baasha 904-892 BC

Elah 892-890 BC

Zimri 890-886 BC

Omri 886-878 BC

Ahab 878-854 BC

Ahaziah 854-852 BC

Jehoram 852-843 BC

Jehu 843-815 BC

Jehoahaz 815-801 BC

Jehoash 801-786 BC

Jeroboam II 786-746 BC

Zechariah 746-745 BC

Shallum 745 BC

Menahem 745-738 BC

Pekahiah 738-737 BC

Pekah 737-732 BC

Hoshea 732-721 BC

721 BC

Israel and its capital Samaria overrun by Shalmaneser V of Assyria

THE PRIESTLY HOUSE OF AARON
And the Old Testament Prophets

Smenkhkare ========================= *Elisheba*
2 >   dau. of Aminadab (Amenhotep)
Pharaoh of Egypt c. 1361 BC
(Akenkhkares/Cinciris/Smenkh-ka-ra-on)

Aaron
= 1 > *Merytaten of Egypt*

Eleazar
= *Daughter* of Nashôn/Putiel

Merytaten   Phinehas
Princess Scota II of Scythia
= Prince Niul of Scythia   Abishua

                                         Bukki

                                         Uzzi

                                         Zerahiah

                                         Meraioth

                                         Amariah
                                         →

345

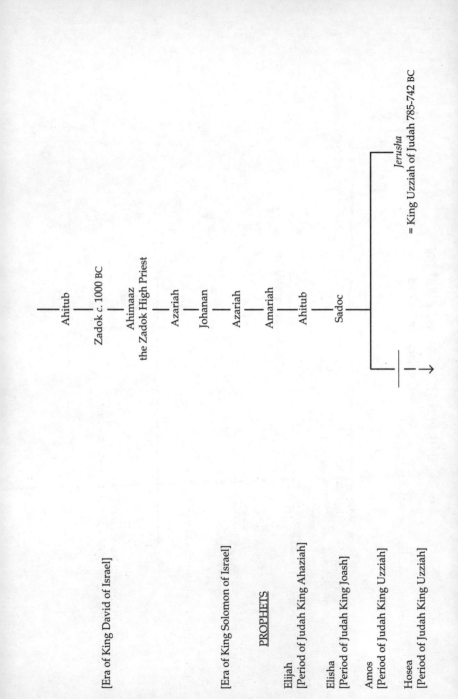

Ahitub

Zadok c. 1000 BC

Ahimaaz
the Zadok High Priest

Azariah

Johanan

Azariah

Amariah

Ahitub

Sadoc

Jerusha

= King Uzziah of Judah 785-742 BC

[Era of King David of Israel]

[Era of King Solomon of Israel]

<u>PROPHETS</u>

Elijah
[Period of Judah King Ahaziah]

Elisha
[Period of Judah King Joash]

Amos
[Period of Judah King Uzziah]

Hosea
[Period of Judah King Uzziah]

Isaiah
[Period of Judah Kings Jotham, Ahaz, and Hezekiah]

Micah
[Period of Judah Kings Hezekiah, and Manasseh]

Nahum
[Period of Judah Kings Manasseh, Amon, and Josiah]

Zephaniah
[Period of Judah Kings Amon and Josiah]

Habakkuk
[Period of Judah Kings Josiah and Jehoahaz]

Shallum

Hilkiahok
The Zadok

Azariah

Jeremiah, Prophet and
Captain of the Temple Guard
[Period of Judah Kings Jehoiakim, Jechoniah, and Zedekiah]

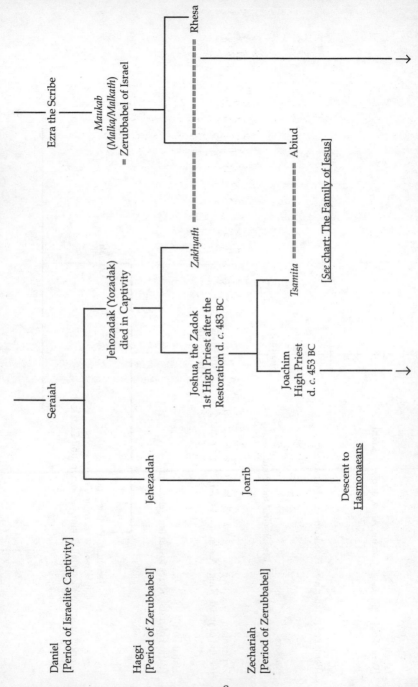

Ezra the Scribe

Maukab
(Malka/Malkath)
= Zerubbabel of Israel

Rhesa

Abiud

[See chart: The Family of Jesus]

Daniel
[Period of Israelite Captivity]

Seraiah

Jehozadak (Yozadak)
died in Captivity

Zakhyath

Joshua, the Zadok
1st High Priest after the
Restoration d. c. 483 BC

Tsamita

Joachim
High Priest
d. c. 453 BC

Haggi
[Period of Zerubbabel]

Jehezadah

Joarib

Descent to
Hasmonaeans

Zechariah
[Period of Zerubbabel]

348

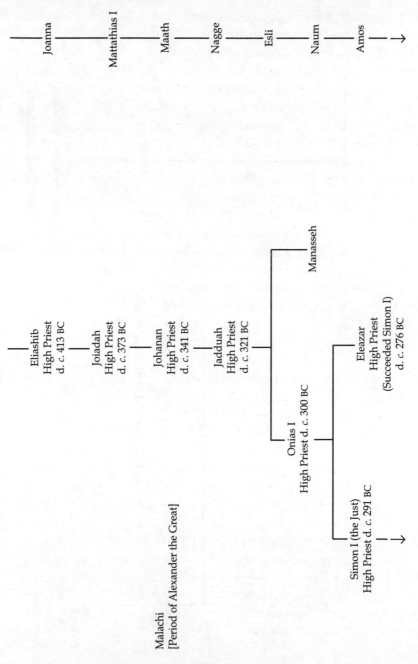

Joanna — Mattathias I — Maath — Nagge — Esli — Naum — Amos →

Eliashib
High Priest
d. c. 413 BC

Joiadah
High Priest
d. c. 373 BC

Johanan
High Priest
d. c. 341 BC

Jadduah
High Priest
d. c. 321 BC

Manasseh

Onias I
High Priest d. c. 300 BC

Eleazar
High Priest
(Succeeded Simon I)
d. c. 276 BC

Simon I (the Just)
High Priest d. c. 291 BC →

Malachi
[Period of Alexander the Great]

349

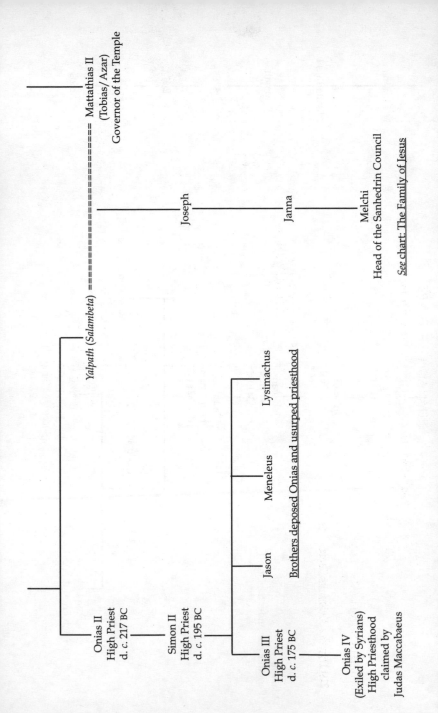

Mattathias II
(Tobias/Azar)
Governor of the Temple

Yalpath (Salambeta) ==========

Joseph

Janna

Melchi
Head of the Sanhedrin Council

See chart: The Family of Jesus

Onias II
High Priest
d. *c.* 217 BC

Simon II
High Priest
d. *c.* 195 BC

Onias III
High Priest
d. *c.* 175 BC

Onias IV
(Exiled by Syrians)
High Priesthood
claimed by
Judas Maccabaeus

Jason   Meneleus   Lysimachus

Brothers deposed Onias and usurped priesthood

PHARAOHS OF EGYPT

21st to 26th Dynasties — Contemporary with the Kings of Judah

THIRD INTERMEDIATE PERIOD

21st Dynasty: Rule from Tanis

Smendes I 1069-1043 BC ========= *Daughter* of Rameses XI
Son of High Priest   (20th dynasty)
Menkheperre

Amenemnisu 1043-1039 BC
Son of High Priest Herihor

Psusennes I 1039-991 BC
= *Mutnodjmet*

Amenemope 993-984 BC

Orsorkon the Elder 984-978 BC
Previous High Priest at Tanis

Siamun 978-959 BC   ⟶

22nd Dynasty: Rule from Tanis

Psusennes II 959-945 BC

Sheshonq I 945-924 BC =============== *Maatkare*

(*Junior Queen*) =========== Orsorkon I 924-889 BC ========================= (*Senior Queen*)

Takelot I 889-874 BC

Sheshonq II 889 BC
co-Regent with father,
but predeceased him

Orsorkon II 874-850 BC
= *Karomama I*

Harsiese 870-860 BC
Simultaneous rule from Thebes

Takelot II 850-825 BC

Shehonq III 825-773 BC - - →

23rd Dynasty: Breakaway rule from Leontopolis

Pedibastet 818-793 BC - - →

352

Sheshonq IV 793-787 BC

Orsorkon III 787-759 BC

Takelot III 764-757 BC

Rudamon 757-754 BC

Iuput 754-715 BC

Nubian Rule from Napata
25th Dynasty: The Kushites

Piankhi
(King of Nubia)
Pharaoh 747-716 BC

Orsorkon IV
730-715 BC

24th Dynasty: Rule from Sais — 2nd Breakaway

Pami 773-767 BC
(Indirect succession)

Sheshonq V 769-730 BC

Shabaka 716-702 BC

Tefnakht
727-720 BC

Bakenrenef
720-715 BC

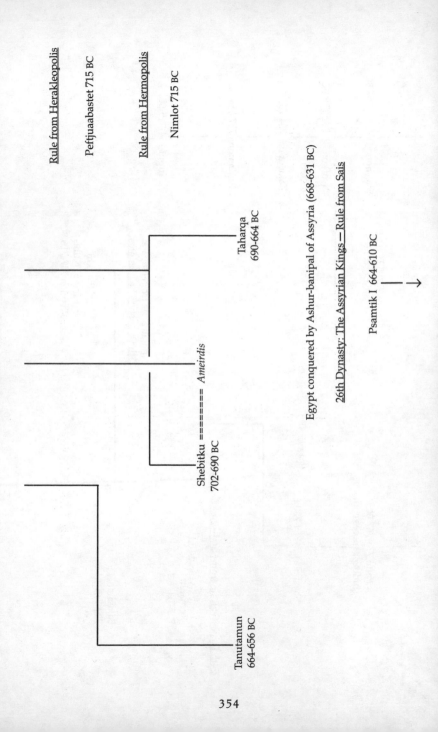

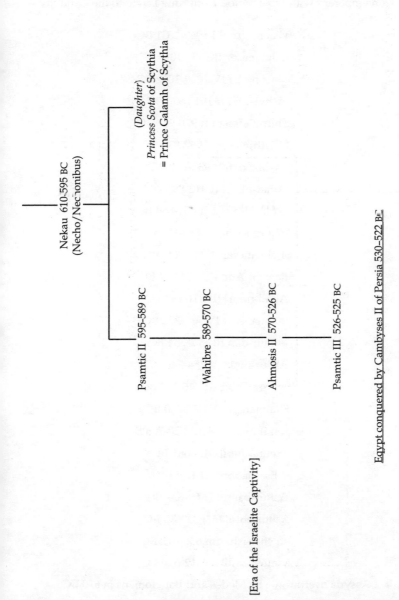

Nekau 610–595 BC
(Necho/Necnonibus)

(*Daughter*)
Princess Scota of Scythia
= Prince Galamh of Scythia

Psamtic II 595–589 BC

Wahibre 589–570 BC

Ahmosis II 570–526 BC

Psamtic III 526–525 BC

[Era of the Israelite Captivity]

Egypt conquered by Cambyses II of Persia 530–522 BC

MESOPOTAMIAN KINGS OF ASSYRIA
Contemporary with Bible period from King David to the Captivity

Ashurnasirpal I 1049-1031 BC

Shalmanaser II 1031-1019 BC

Ashur-nirâri IV 1019-1012 BC

Ashur-râbi II 1012-970 BC

Ashur-rêsh-ishi II 970-967 BC

Tiglathpileser II 967-935 BC

Ashur-dân II 935-912 BC

Adad-nirâri II 912-891 BC

Tukulti-Ninurta II 891-884 BC

Ashurnasirpal II 884-859 BC

Shalmaneser III 859-824 BC

Shamshi-Adad V 824-811 BC

Adad-nirâri III 811-783 BC

Shalmaneser IV 783-772 BC

Ashur-dân III 772-754 BC

Ashur-nirâri V 754-746 BC

Tiglathpileser III 746-727 BC

Shalmaneser V 727-720 BC

Sargon II (Sharru-kîn) 720-705 BC

Sennacherib 705-681 BC

Esarhadon 681-669 BC

Ashur-banipal 669-631 BC

Ashur-etil-ilâni 631-630 BC

Sin-shar-ishkum 630-612 BC

Ashur-uballit II 612-610 BC

Assyria overthrown by Medes and Babylonians in 610 BC

KINGS OF BABYLON
Contemporary with Bible period from King David to the Captivity

Adad-apal-iddina 1067-1046 BC

[Interregnum]

Shimmash-shipak 1038-1032 BC

[Interregnum]

Nabû-mukin-apli 990-955 BC

Ninurt-akud-urusu II 955-953 BC

Mar-bîti-ahhê-iddin 953-942 BC

Shamash-mudammiq 942-901 BC

Nabû-shumi-shkun I 901-885 BC

Nabû-apal-idinna 885-852 BC

Marduk-zakir-shumi I 852-828 BC

Nabû-mukinzeri

Marduk-balatsu-iqbi

Marduk-apal-iddina II

Eriba-Marduk 782-763 BC

Nabû-shum-ishkun 763-747 BC

Nabû-nâsir 747-733 BC

Ukîn-zêr 733-730 BC

Marduk-zakir-shumi II 730-721 BC

Marduk-apal-iddina III 721-711 BC

[Interregnum]

Bêl-ibni 702-700 BC

Ashur-nadim-shum 700-694 BC

Nergalu-shezib 694-693 BC

Mushezib-Marduk 693-669 BC

Shamash-shum-ukin 669-648 BC

Kandalanu 648-627 BC

Nabopolassar 627-605 BC

Nebuchadrezzar II 605-562 BC
(Nebuchadnezzar)

Awêl-Marduk

Neriglissar

Labâshi-Marduk

Nabu-na-id 556-545 BC

Belsharusur 545-539 BC

(Belshazzar)

539 BC
Babylon ruled by Cyrus II of Persia

KINGS OF PERSIA AND PHARAOHS OF EGYPT

To the period of Alexander the Great of Macedonia

Teispes 675-640 BC
|
Cyrus I (Kurash) 640-600 BC
|
Cambyses I (Kambujia) 600-559 BC
|
Cyrus II (Kurash) 559-530 BC

= (*wife*) *Meshar,* sister of Zerubbabel   = (*mistress*) *Nitetis,* dau. of
who led the Israelites from   Pharaoh Wahibre 589-570 BC
Captivity in 536 BC

Persian Kings also become
<u>27th dynasty Pharaohs of Egypt</u>

Cambyses II (Kambujia) 530-522 BC
Pharaoh

Darius I (Darayavaush) 522-485 BC
Pharaoh
|
Xerxes I 485-465 BC
Pharaoh
|
Artaxerxes I (Artakhshathra) 465-425 BC
Pharaoh
|
Xerxes II 425-424 BC
Pharaoh
|
Darius II (Darayavaush) 424-404 BC
Pharaoh
|
↓

<u>Parallel 28th dynasty of Egypt</u>

Amyrtaeus of Sais
404-399 BC

Artaxerxes II
(Artakhshathra)
404-358 BC
Pharaoh

<u>29th dynasty</u>

Nefaarud I of Mendes
399-393 BC

Hakor (Achoris)
393-380 BC

<u>30th dynasty</u>

Nakhtnebef of Sebennytos
380-362 BC (Nectanebo I)

Nakhthoreb
360-343 BC (Nectanebo II)

2nd Persian Period
<u>31st dynasty</u>

Djedhar (Teos)
362-360 BC

Artaxerxes III (Artakhshathra) 358-338 BC
Pharaoh

Arses 338-336 BC
Pharaoh

Darius III (Darayavaush) 335-330 BC
Great-nephew of Artaxerxes II
Pharaoh

Persia and Egypt ruled by Alexander's Macedonians from 330 BC

Persia integrated into Seleucid Empire 312-250 BC

KINGS OF SPARTA AND MACEDONIA
Including part of period between the Old and New Testaments

Sparta	Macedonia
Dual kingship in two family lines: Agiadai and Eurypontidai	
Anaxandridas (A) 560-520 BC	
Ariston (E) 560-520 BC	
Demaratos (E) 520-491 BC	Perdiccas 500-498 BC
Kleomenes I (A) 520-487 BC	
Leotychidas (E) 491-476 BC	Alexandros I 498-450 BC
Leonidas I (A) 487-480 BC	
Pleistarchos (A) 480-458 BC	
Archidamos II (E) 476-427 BC	
Pleistoanax (A) 458-400 BC	Perdiccas II 450-413 BC
Agis I (E) 427-401 BC	Archelaus 413-399 BC
Agesilaos II (E) 401-361 BC	
Agesipolis I (A) 400-380 BC	[Interregnum]
Kleombrotos II (A) 380-371 BC	Amyntas III 393-370 BC
Agesipolis II (A) 371-370 BC	Alexandros II 370-367 BC
	Perdiccas III 367-359 BC
Kleomenes II (A) 370-309 BC	Amyntas IV 359 BC
Archidamos III (E) 361-338 BC	Philippos II 359-336 BC
Agis II (E) 338-331 BC	Alexandros III 336-323 BC
	Alexander the Great
	= *Roxane* of Persia
Eudamidas I (E) 331-309 BC	Philippos III (co-ruler) 323-317 BC
Areus I (A) 309-265 BC	Alexandros IV (co-ruler) 323-316 BC

Cassander 316-297 BC

Archidamos IV (E) 309-265 BC

Philippos IV (co-ruler) 297 BC

Antipater I (co-ruler) 297-296 BC

Alexandros V (co-ruler) 297-295 BC

Demetrios I (Poliorcetes of Asia)
295-288 BC

[Interregnum]

Lysimachus 285-281 BC
also King of Thrace 305-281 BC

Seleucus 281-280 BC
First of the Seleucids

Ptolemaios (Keraunos) 280-279 BC

Acrotatus (A) 265-263 BC

Meleager 279 BC

Eudamidas II (E) 265-245 BC

Antipater II 279-278 BC

Areus II (A) 263-256 BC

Leonidas II (A) 256-252 BC

Antigonus II (Gonatus of Asia)
278-239 BC

Agis IV (E) 245-241 BC

Kleombrotos III (A) 252-237 BC

Euridamidas (E) 241-236 BC

Demetrios II 239-229 BC

Kleomenes III (A) 237-229 BC

Archidamos V (E) 236-220 BC

Philippos V 229 BC and 221-179 BC

Agesipolis III (A) 229-210 BC

Lykurgos (E) 220-210 BC

Pelops (E)

Mahanidas (E)

Perseus 179-168 BC

Nabis (E)

Sparta fell to Rome 146 BC

MACEDONIAN EGYPT AND THE PTOLEMIES

Alexander III, the Great
of Macedon 332–323 BC
= *Roxane of Persia*

Philip Arrhidaeus
323–317 BC

Alexander IV
317–305 BC

Pharaohs of Egypt – Ptolemaic Dynasty and the Cleopatras

Daughter of Pharaoh
Nectanebo II

<1

Ptolemy I (Soter I) 305–282 BC
(Macedonian general of Alexander III)
= (*mistress*) *Berenice*
Lady-in-waiting to *Eurydice*

2 >

= *Eurydyce*, dau. of Antipater
Regent of Macedon

Ptolemy II (Philadelphus) 285–246 BC
= *Arsinoe*, dau. of General
Lysimachus of Thrace

→

→

Berenice
= Antiochus II of Syria

Ptolemy III 246-222 BC
(Euergetes I)
= *Berenice*, dau. of Magnus of Cyrenaica

Arsinoe ============================ Ptolemy IV (Philopator)
222-205 BC

Ptolemy V (Epiphanes) 205-180 BC
Cleopatra I, dau. of Antiochus III of Syria

Ptolemy VI (Philometor)   <1   2 >   Ptolemy VIII (Euergetes II)
180-164 and 163-145 BC   === *Cleopatra II* ===   170-163 and 145-116 BC
Ruled from Memphis   Ruled from Alexandria

Ptolemy VII ================= *Cleopatra III*
Neos-Philopator 145 BC

Cleopatra Thea
= 1 >Alexander Balas (Seleucid)
= 2 > Demetrius II (Seleucid)
= 3 > Antiochus VII (Seleucid)

→

364

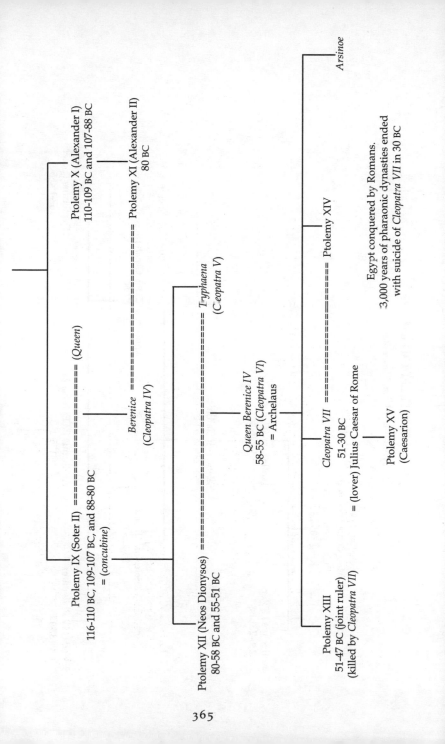

Ptolemy IX (Soter II)
116-110 BC, 109-107 BC, and 88-80 BC
= (concubine)

(Queen)

Ptolemy X (Alexander I)
110-109 BC and 107-88 BC

Ptolemy XI (Alexander II)
80 BC

Berenice
(Cleopatra IV)

Tryphaena
(Cleopatra V)

Ptolemy XII (Neos Dionysos)
80-58 BC and 55-51 BC

Queen Berenice IV (Cleopatra VI)
58-55 BC
= Archelaus

Cleopatra VII
51-30 BC
= (lover) Julius Caesar of Rome

Ptolemy XIII
51-47 BC (joint ruler)
(killed by Cleopatra VII)

Ptolemy XV
(Caesarion)

Ptolemy XIV

Arsinoe

Egypt conquered by Romans.
3,000 years of pharaonic dynasties ended
with suicide of Cleopatra VII in 30 BC

365

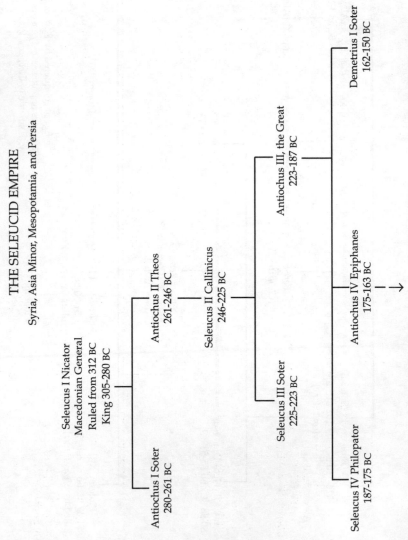

THE SELEUCID EMPIRE

Syria, Asia Minor, Mesopotamia, and Persia

Seleucus I Nicator
Macedonian General
Ruled from 312 BC
King 305–280 BC

Antiochus I Soter
280–261 BC

Antiochus II Theos
261–246 BC

Seleucus II Callinicus
246–225 BC

Seleucus III Soter
225–223 BC

Antiochus III, the Great
223–187 BC

Demetrius I Soter
162–150 BC

Antiochus IV Epiphanes
175–163 BC

Seleucus IV Philopator
187–175 BC

→

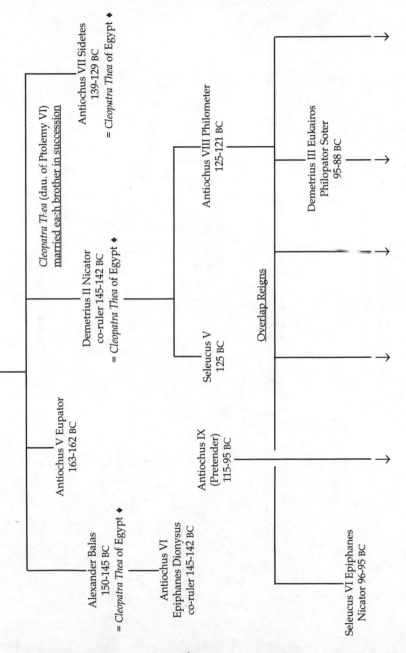

Antiochus VII Sidetes
139-129 BC
= *Cleopatra Thea of Egypt* ◆

Cleopatra Thea (dau. of Ptolemy VI) married each brother in succession

Antiochus VIII Philometer
125-121 BC

Demetrius III Eukairos
Philopator Soter
95-88 BC

Demetrius II Nicator
co-ruler 145-142 BC
= *Cleopatra Thea of Egypt* ◆

Seleucus V
125 BC

Overlap Reigns

Antiochus V Eupator
163-162 BC

Alexander Balas
150-145 BC
= *Cleopatra Thea of Egypt* ◆

Antiochus VI
Epiphanes Dionysus
co-ruler 145-142 BC

Antiochus IX
(Pretender)
115-95 BC

Seleucus VI Epiphanes
Nicator 96-95 BC

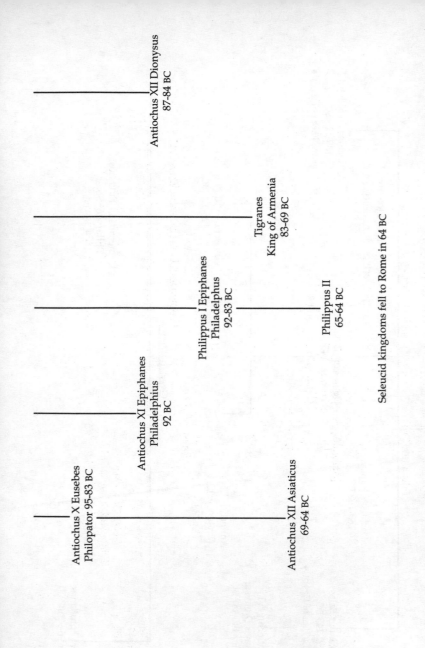

Antiochus X Eusebes Philopator 95-83 BC

Antiochus XI Epiphanes Philadelphius 92 BC

Philippus I Epiphanes Philadelphius 92-83 BC

Antiochus XII Dionysus 87-84 BC

Tigranes King of Armenia 83-69 BC

Philippus II 65-64 BC

Antiochus XII Asiaticus 69-64 BC

Seleucid kingdoms fell to Rome in 64 BC

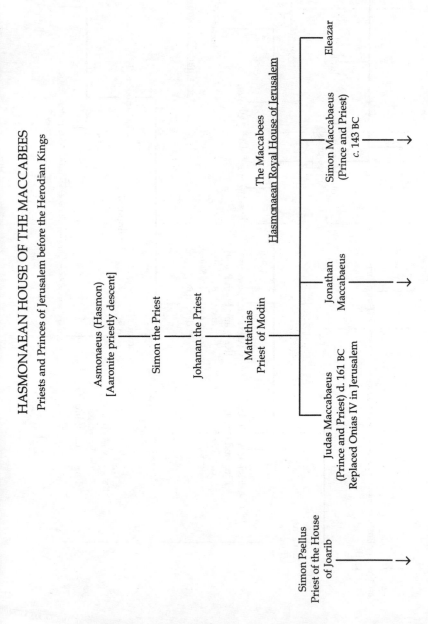

HASMONAEAN HOUSE OF THE MACCABEES
Priests and Princes of Jerusalem before the Herodian Kings

Asmonaeus (Hasmon)
[Aaronite priestly descent]

Simon the Priest

Johanan the Priest

Mattathias
Priest of Modin

The Maccabees
Hasmonaean Royal House of Jerusalem

Judas Maccabaeus
(Prince and Priest) d. 161 BC
Replaced Onias IV in Jerusalem

Jonathan
Maccabaeus

Simon Maccabaeus
(Prince and Priest)
c. 143 BC

Eleazar

Simon Psellus
Priest of the House
of Joarib

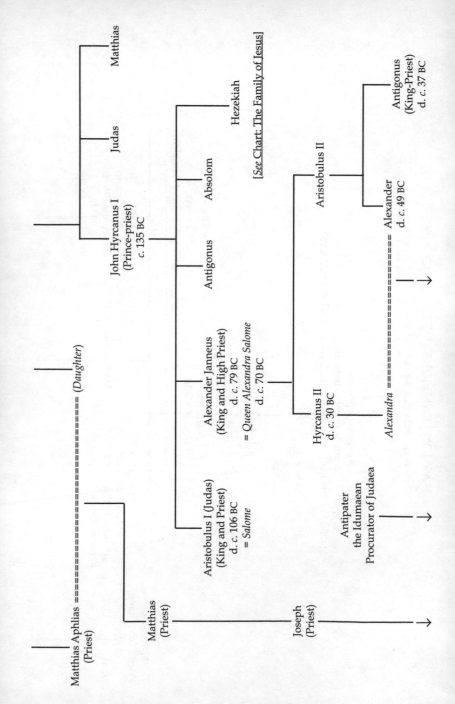

Matthias Aphlias ================== (Daughter)
(Priest)

Matthias
(Priest)

Aristobulus I (Judas)
(King and Priest)
d. c. 106 BC
= Salome

Alexander Janneus
(King and High Priest)
d. c. 79 BC
= Queen Alexandra Salome
d. c. 70 BC

John Hyrcanus I
(Prince-priest)
c. 135 BC

Antigonus   Absolom

Hezekiah

[See Chart: The Family of Jesus]

Judas   Matthias

Hyrcanus II
d. c. 30 BC

Aristobulus II

Alexandra ================

Alexander
d. c. 49 BC

Antigonus
(King-Priest)
d. c. 37 BC

Joseph
(Priest)

Antipater
the Idumaean
Procurator of Judaea

370

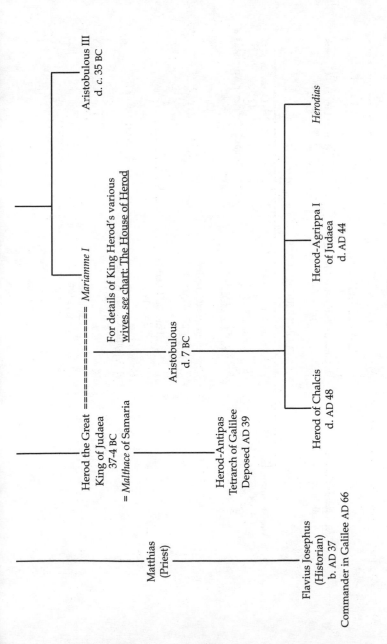

Matthias
(Priest)

Herod the Great ================ *Mariamme I*
King of Judaea
37-4 BC
= *Malthace* of Samaria

For details of King Herod's various
wives, *see* chart: The House of Herod

Aristobulous III
d. *c.* 35 BC

Herod-Antipas
Tetrarch of Galilee
Deposed AD 39

Aristobulous
d. 7 BC

Flavius Josephus
(Historian)
b. AD 37
Commander in Galilee AD 66

Herod of Chalcis
d. AD 48

Herod-Agrippa I
of Judaea
d. AD 44

Herodias

ROMAN REPUBLIC AND EARLY EMPIRE

From Julius Caesar to Nero

Gaius Julius Caesar
60–44 BC

FIRST TRIUMVIRATE

Gnaeus Pompeius Magnus
60–48 BC

Marcus Licinius Crassus
60–53 BC

Marcus Antonius
42–30 BC

SECOND TRIUMVIRATE

Marcus Aemilius Lepidus
42–13 BC

Gaius Octavius
42 BC
Became Emperor Augustus ◄

ROMAN EMPERORS

Augustus (Octavian) ◄
27 BC–AD 14

Claudius Tiberius
AD 14–37

Gaius Caesar (Caligula)
AD 37–41

Claudius I
AD 41–54

Lucius Domitius Nero
AD 54–68

THE HOUSE OF HEROD

New Testament Kings and Governors of Judaea (37 BC to AD 99)

Antipater the Idumaean
d. 48 BC
= Cypros (Arabian)

Herod the Great
King of Judaea from 37 BC
d. 4 BC

< = *Ten wives (some simultaneous) including* = >

1	2	3	4	5	6	7
= *Doris* (Idumaean)	= *Mariamme I* dau. of Alexander the Hasmonean (Jewess)	= *Pallas*	= *Phaedra*	= *Mariamme II* dau. of Simon Boethus High Priest (Jewess)	= *Malthace* of Samaria d. 4 BC (Samaritan)	= *Cleopatra* of Jerusalem (Jewess)

1
Antipater
d. 4 BC

2
Aristobulous
d. 7 BC
= *Berenice*
niece of
Herod the Great →

Alexander
d. 7 BC
= *Glaphyra*

4
Herod-Philip
(Thomas)
= Herodias ◆

Salome ◆

5
Archelaus
Ethnarch
of Judaea
deposed AD 6
[exile in Gaul]

6
Herod-Antipas
Tetrarch of
Galilee
depcsed AD 39
[exile in Gaul]
= Herodias ◆
(see below)

7
Herod-Philip
Tetrarch of
Trachonitis
d. AD 34
= Salome ◆
d.s.p.

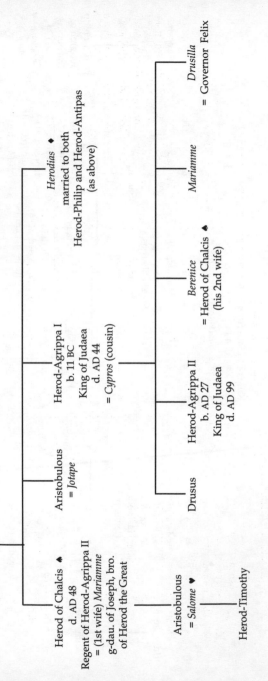

THE FAMILY OF JESUS

Ancestors of the Messiah and the Magdalene

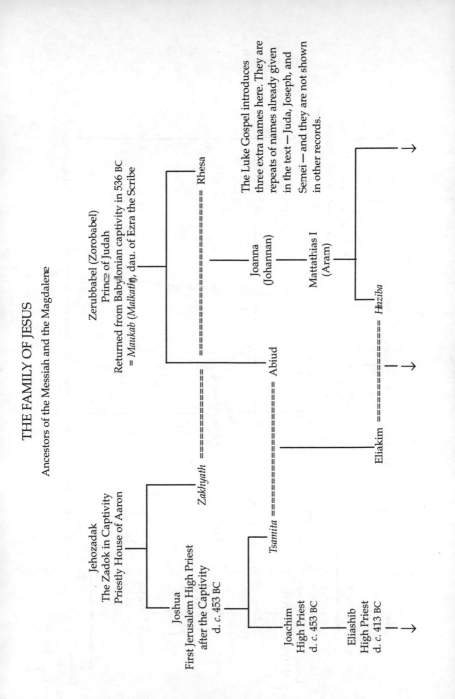

Jehozadak
The Zadok in Captivity
Priestly House of Aaron

Joshua
First Jerusalem High Priest
after the Captivity
d. c. 453 BC

Zakhyath ================

Joachim
High Priest
d. c. 453 BC

Tsamita =====================

Abiud

Eliashib
High Priest
d. c. 413 BC

Eliakim ================= *Haziba*

Zerubbabel (Zorobabel)
Prince of Judah
Returned from Babylonian captivity in 536 BC
= *Maukab* (*Malkath*), dau. of Ezra the Scribe

Rhesa

================

Joanna
(Johannan)

Mattathias I
(Aram)

The Luke Gospel introduces
three extra names here. They are
repeats of names already given
in the text — Juda, Joseph, and
Semei — and they are not shown
in other records.

375

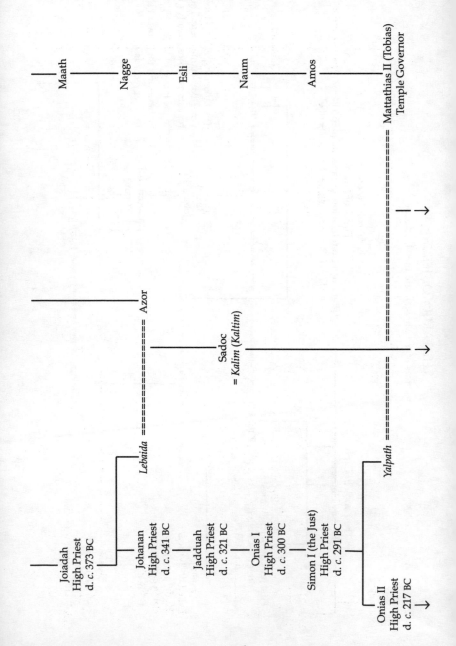

Maath

Nagge

Esli

Naum

Amos

Mattathias II (Tobias)
Temple Governor

Azor

Sadoc
= *Kalim (Kaltim)*

Lebaida ==================

Yalpath ==================

Joiadah
High Priest
d. *c.* 373 BC

Johanan
High Priest
d. *c.* 341 BC

Jadduah
High Priest
d. *c.* 321 BC

Onias I
High Priest
d. *c.* 300 BC

Simon I (the Just)
High Priest
d. *c.* 291 BC

Onias II
High Priest
d. *c.* 217 BC

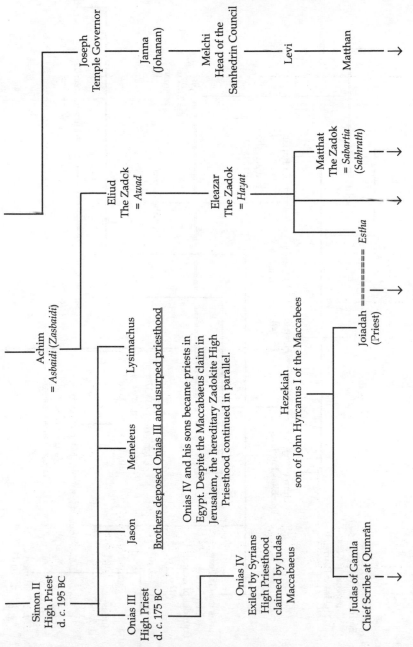

Simon II
High Priest
d. c. 195 BC

Onias III
High Priest
d. c. 175 BC

Onias IV
Exiled by Syrians
High Priesthood
claimed by Judas
Maccabaeus

Jason   Meneleus   Lysimachus

Brothers deposed Onias III and usurped priesthood

Onias IV and his sons became priests in
Egypt. Despite the Maccabaeus claim in
Jerusalem, the hereditary Zadokite High
Priesthood continued in parallel.

Achim
= *Asbaidi* (*Zasbaidi*)

Eliud
The Zadck
= *Avad*

Eleazar
The Zadok
= *Hazat*

Matthat
The Zadok
= *Sabartia*
(*Sabhrath*)

Joseph
Temple Governor

Janna
(Johanan)

Melchi
Head of the
Sanhedrin Council

Levi

Matthan

→

→

Hezekiah
son of John Hyrcanus I of the Maccabees

Joiadah ========= *Estha*
(Priest)

Judas of Gamla
Chief Scribe at Qumrân

→

→

377

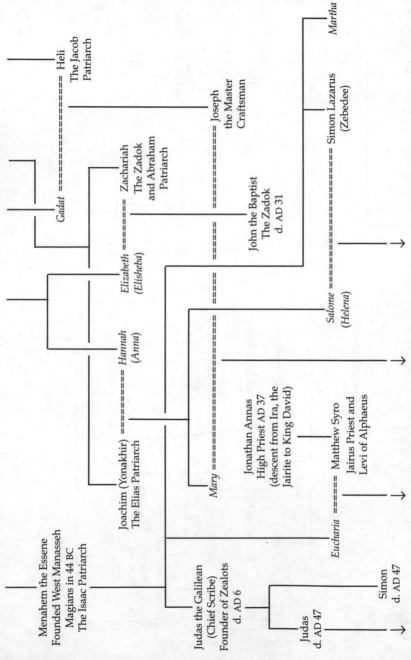

Heli
The Jacob Patriarch

Gadat

Joseph
the Master Craftsman

Zachariah
The Zadok
and Abraham Patriarch

Elizabeth
(Elisheba)

John the Baptist
The Zadok
d. AD 31

Simon Lazarus
(Zebedee)

Martha

Hannah
(Anna)

Salome
(Helena)

Joachim (Yonakhir)
The Elias Patriarch

Mary

Jonathan Annas
High Priest AD 37
(descent from Ira, the
Jairite to King David)

Matthew Syro
Jairus Priest and
Levi of Alphaeus

Menahem the Essene
Founded West Manasseh
Magians in 44 BC
The Isaac Patriarch

Eucharia

Judas the Galilean
(Chief Scribe)
Founder of Zealots
d. AD 6

Judas
d. AD 47

Simon
d. AD 47

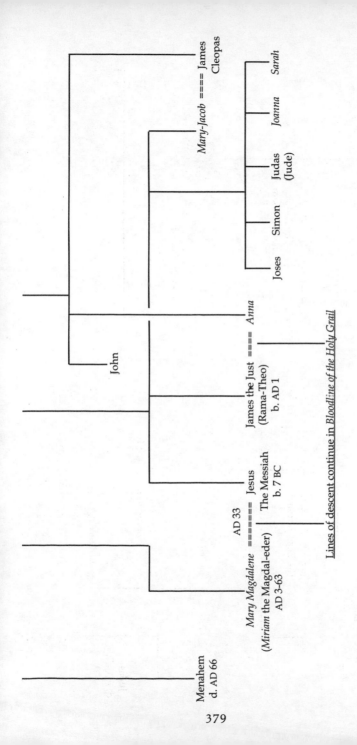

379

APPENDICES

Enigma of the Tombs

In the *Journal of Near Eastern Studies*[1] it is reported that since Nefertiti was the designated Great Royal Wife of Akhenaten, she was doubtless of superior royal blood. Akhenaten achieved his kingly status by marrying her as the senior heiress in the pharaonic tradition but, undeterred by this, many Egyptologists (in a continued attempt to decry the Amarna Kings) make light of Nefertiti's heritage. They prefer to suggest that she was not necessarily the daughter of Amenhotep III and Sitamun, and take little notice of the fact that a boundary stela of Akhenaten specifically denotes her as the heiress, calling her Mistress of Upper and Lower Egypt; Lady of the Two Lands.[2] In fact, through some 3,000 years of dynastic history, the face of Nefertiti has emerged as the best known of all the queens of Egypt, and her great importance is emphasized by the astonishing frequency of her name on discovered cartouches: sixty-seven mentions in contrast with only three for her husband Akhenaten.[3]

With regard to the Sinai exile of Akhenaten, it can be said that there is not a shred of evidence concerning his death: he simply disappeared from Egypt.[4] While speculation continues over Smenkhkare, there is no Egyptian record of his death either. A tomb over which controversy now rages in respect of

Smenkhkare and Akhenaten is not at Amarna, but that numbered Tomb KV 55 in the Theban Valley of Kings. This tomb was discovered, unfinished and water-damaged, in January 1907. It has only one burial chamber and the body within was identified as a female. At first it was thought that it was probably Akhenaten's mother, Queen Tiye, but this was only a guess since there were no cartouches to indicate the occupant's name. There were, nevertheless, some remnants of Tiye's gold-overlaid sarcophagus. Subsequently, another unidentified female body was found nearby in Tomb KV 35 (the tomb of Amenhotep II) and this is now thought to be the body of Queen Tiye.[5]

In the wake of this discovery, the body from Tomb KV 55 (which is just a badly preserved skeleton) seems mysteriously to have changed sex, and was then claimed to be the remains of Akhenaten.[6] The reason for this revised theory was that some contemporary depictions of Akhenaten show him with an unusually rounded pelvic structure. But Amarna Art, as it has become known, was unique in Egypt and incorporated many physical eccentricities, such as the exceptionally long neck on the famous bust of Nefertiti. To endeavor to match real figures against this revolutionary artistic style is rather like looking for the distorted characters who modeled for Picasso. Recognizing this, and conceding that the body was female, some Egyptologists (in order to sustain their Akhenaten theory) even suggest that perhaps Akhenaten was really a woman masquerading as a man – completely disregarding the fact that he and Nefertiti are known to have had six daughters. Others, who also pursue the idea that the body is an unusually shaped male, reckon it is perhaps the remains of Smenkhkare[7] – but this notion is quite unsupported and there is not one textual fragment which even suggests his name.

Four alabaster canopic jars (used for the entrails of an embalmed body), with finely carved female heads, were also found in the tomb, but they are not inscribed. In spite of the ongoing debate over whether the skeletal remains could perhaps be those of Akhenaten (Moses) or Smenkhkare (Aaron), the only extant textual fragments indicate that the tomb was prepared for a royal female and, although the inscriptions are badly damaged, the occupant's name certainly has a feminine ending.

As far as Akhenaten is concerned, his correctly planned tomb site has been separately located at Amarna, where it appears to have been cut from the rock in about year six of his seventeen-year reign. Also found is the outer of his three destined mummy casings (the main sarcophagus), but there are none of the inner casings that would have been used to house his mummy. Similarly, there are no items of funerary furniture, which indicates that the tomb was never used. Akhenaten's alabaster canopic chest (with four compartments for the jars) has also been found, but this too was empty, unstained, and quite unused; it had simply been placed in the tomb in readiness to receive the jars, as was the preparatory custom.[8]

1 Vol. 14, 1955, pp. 168–80. Item: Seele, *King Aye and the Close of the Amarna Age*.

2 Aldred, Cyril, *Akhenaten, King of Egypt*, Thames & Hudson, London, 1988, p. 222.

3 Smith, Ray Winfield, *The Akhenaten Temple Project*, Aris & Phillips, Warminster, 1976, p. 22.

4 Osman, Ahmed, *Moses, Pharaoh of Egypt*, Grafton/Collins, London, 1990, p. 134.

5 Rohl, David M., *A Test of Time: The Bible from Myth to History*, Century, London, 1995, p. 397.

6 Clayton, Peter A., *Chronicle of the Pharaohs*, Thames & Hudson, London, 1994, p. 126.

7 *Ibid.*, p. 127.

8 Osman, Ahmed, *Moses, Pharaoh of Egypt*, pp. 138–47. The subject of Tomb KV 55 is also well covered in Watterson, Barbara, *Amarna: Ancient Egypt's Age of Revolution*, Tempus, Stroud, 1999. ch. 6, pp. 108–120.

The Exodus

Having identified that the Israelite exodus from Egypt took place in about 1335 BC, it is necessary to consider the statement in the book of 1 Kings (6:1) which claims that the Temple of King Solomon was built 480 years after the exodus. Solomon's reign can be determined fairly accurately from the astronomically dated Assyrian record of the Battle of Karkar in 853 BC. King Ahab of Israel was present at this battle in alliance with Hadad-idri of Damascus, and it was the 21st year of Ahab's reign. By working back through the regnal years of the kings of Judah and Israel, we arrive at Solomon in 968 BC, with the Jerusalem Temple begun around 966 BC.[1] Adding back 480 years to this date produces an exodus date of 1446 BC, which is considerably earlier than has been calculated. However, there is another important factor to consider when reading the 1 Kings entry.

At the very earliest, the Old Testament was begun during the Israelites' Babylonian captivity from 586 BC, by which time all the kings of Judah in the Davidic succession from Solomon had reigned. During the course of this, a figurative dynastic standard had been established in the royal line – a symbolic standard of "40 years" for each generation,[2] which is why the reigns of David and Solomon are given at precisely 40 years each (2 Samuel 5:4, 1 Kings 11:42). The Bible lists a total of 12 generations from Jacob (who took the Israelites into Egypt) down to Solomon, and the resultant calculation of 12 x 40 produces 480 years.

On account of this, the original estimate was made from the time the Israelites first arrived in Egypt, not from the later time of the exodus as stated. The problem confronting the scribes who made the calculation was that some four centuries of history are completely ignored between the books of Genesis and Exodus, and so the 40-year dynastic standard could not be applied back to Jacob. It was, therefore, strategically applied to the period between the exodus and King Solomon, even though it did not conform to the generation standard. As pointed out by Professor of Egyptology T. Eric Peet, back in 1923, the 480 years as given in 1 Kings "is a figure open to the utmost suspicion."[3]

1 Peet, T. Eric, *Egypt and the Old Testament*, Liverpool University Press, Liverpool, 1922, pp. 111–12.
2 Thiering, Barbara, *Jesus the Man*, Transworld, London, 1992, pp. 177 and 196.
3 Peet, T. Eric, *Egypt and the Old Testament*, p. 28.

Gold for Sale

From the 1700s, gold has been the key bullion reserve against national currencies, but few have ever understood why. Gold is bulky, heavy, and not especially rare when compared, for example, with certain gemstones. It has nevertheless taken prime position as a financially underpinning substance. The reason is because, from the most ancient of times, gold has had a perceived value beyond that of currency wealth – a meta-physical and scientific value, the secrets of which had been lost but were destined one day to return. This has now happened with the rediscovered science of monatomic high-spin metallurgy – the ability to transmute noble metallic elements into a single-atom, superconductive, anti-gravitational state. Now the stockpiles are being "swapped" (to use the official terminology) for fickle currencies – especially for the controversial Euro.

In 1999, the International Monetary Fund announced that it was to sell large quantities of gold bullion, at which time it became clear that gold was purposely to be devalued. In an attempt to justify their proposal, IMF representatives announced that it was part of a scheme to aid the Heavily Indebted Poor Countries (the HIPCs as they were dubbed). But, as the World Gold Council pointed out, some 41 countries on the HIPC list were actually gold producers whose own national economies would be crippled, if not completely destroyed, by the plan. Notwithstanding this, the price of gold duly fell to its lowest level for 20 years in preparation for cheap selling.[1]

In April 1999 the IMF proposal came under the scrutiny of the US House of Representatives Congressional Sub-committee, whose spokesman stated, "It would be a cruel irony if the assistance that is being offered to the world's poorest countries in fact did further damage to these already troubled economies and deterred investment in gold mining." Apparently, despite all the supposedly benevolent waffle, the HIPCs were the very least of IMF concerns in this regard.

On 6 July 1999 the first tranche of 25 tons of Britain's gold reserves was sold – bringing the price down to another new low. It was stated, however, that the total of proposed auction sales would amount to some 415 tons from an overall UK reserve of 715 tons. The World Gold Council called this "The economics of a madhouse," and the WGC Chief Executive asserted that, even if the gold price fell no lower, the cash receipts will "shortchange the people of Britain by £450 million ($600 million)!" Meanwhile, no less than 15 European Central Banks announced their plans to sell 2,000 tons of gold between the years 2000 and 2005.

In September 1999, despite considerable public opposition and further warnings from the World Gold Council, the UK Treasury sold a further 25 tons of gold at an even lower price, receiving some £2.83 million less than in the July sale. At that point, the cash deficit potential increased to £540 million and three more auctions were planned for that fiscal year, with HM Treasury confirming plans for further sales of 150 tons at six auctions to the end of 2001.

Eventually, after continuing regular auctions and a total of 395 tons of Britain's original 715 tons sold, Haruka Fukuda, the World Gold Council Chief Executive, criticized the program yet again. On 6 March 2002,[2] he stated that in making these sales "the move had seen the Treasury fail to exploit fully rises in gold's price seen in the past two years." What he referred to here was that, in general terms, gold prices had been buoyant enough since July 1999, but that the regular high price points had constantly been at dates between the regular auction sales. Very conveniently for the buyers, the price had always dropped significantly before each sale date, only to regain its true level again soon afterwards. The UK Treasury's response was that it was all a matter of "long-term restructuring of the reserves portfolio, not a short-term chasing of the market." The fact that the nation had been short-changed by hundreds of millions of pounds did not seem to enter the equation. What has happened, nevertheless, is that certain approved buyers (whose identities are not being disclosed by the Bank of England) are now well stocked with cheaply bought gold. In fact, to date they have acquired some 55% of the original British Treasury holding. It appears that the current round of auctions has now ceased for the time being, and coincidentally we discover that the gold price has "risen to its highest level in over two years!"[3]

Quite apart from the superconductive fire-stone qualities of monatomic gold, there are numerous other lately developed uses for metallic gold, which make it a necessary requirement for industrial and manufacturing markets. The rocket engines of USA space shuttles are lined with gold alloys to reflect heat. Touch-tone telephones include up to 33% gold-plated contacts.

In addition to all this, there has been a significant parallel increase of Western interest in South Africa's platinum group mines. This began in 1997, when Amplats (Anglo-American Platinum Corporation) was formed by a merger of four independent companies.[4] This put the corporation in control of some 70% of world platinum supply. By virtue of this great upsurge in PGM interest, Britain's *Sunday Telegraph* investigated the matter in October 2000,[5] at which point it was finally revealed by those concerned that the noble metals markets were being restructured with new ownerships to satisfy and sustain the new incoming fuel-cell technology.[6]

1 All information in this section is obtained from the World Gold Council, 45 Pall Mall, London SW1Y 5JG. Website: <http://www.gold.org/>.
2 *The Times*, Business section, p. 25, Tuesday 6 March 2002.
3 *The Times*, Money section, p. 8, Saturday 1 June 2002.
4 Anglo Platinum, Rustenburg Platinum Mines (RPM), Potgietersrust Platiniums (PPRust) and Lebowa Platinum Mines (Leplats).
5 *The Daily Telegraph*, Business Section article "The Most Precious of Metals," by Edward Simpkins, 1 October 2000.
6 See details of article in Chapter 11 under "Stealth Atoms and Space-time."

Amenemope and the Book of Proverbs

EXAMPLES OF EGYPTIAN WISDOM LITERATURE
USED IN THE BIBLE

**From The Wisdom
of Amenemope**

Incline thine ears to hear my
sayings,
And apply thine heart to their
comprehension.
For it is a profitable thing to put
them in thy heart.
(Amenemope 1:6)

Remove not the landmark on the
boundary of the fields …
And trespass not on the
boundary of the widow.
(Amenemope 7:12–15)

They have made themselves
wings like geese,
And they have flown to heaven.

(Amenemope 10:5)

**From The Proverbs
of Solomon**

Bow down thine ear, and hear
the words of the wise,
And apply thine heart unto my
knowledge.
For it is a pleasant thing if thou
keep them within thee.
(Proverbs 22:17–18)

Remove not the old landmark,

And enter not into the fields of
the fatherless.
(Proverbs 23:10)

Riches certainly make
themselves wings.
They fly away as an eagle
towards heaven.
(Proverbs 23:4–5)

Better is poverty in the hand
of God,
Than the riches in the storehouse.

Better are loaves when the heart
is joyous.
(Amenemope 9:5–8)

Better is little with fear of the
Lord,
Than great treasure and trouble
therewith.

Better is a dinner of herbs where
love is.
(Proverbs 15:16–17)

Fraternise not with the hot-
tempered man.
And press not on him for
conversation.
(Amenemope 11:13–14)

Make no friendship with an
angry man.
And with a furious man thou
shalt not go.
(Proverbs 22:24)

Towards the Vanishing Point

During the course of David Hudson's research concerning Orbitally Rearranged Monatomic Elements in the latter 1990s (as discussed in Chapter 11), the medical fraternity began to take a keen interest in the potential use of ORMEs for cancer treatment. Those involved in the early research were the Roswell Park Cancer Institute, the National Cancer Institute, Merck & Co., Rutgers University, the University of Illinois, Wayne State University, the University of Wisconsin-Madison, and the Institute of Biotechnology.[1] Journals such as the *Platinum Metals Review* and *Scientific American* had reported how monatomic platinum group metals will resonate with deformed body cells, causing the DNA to relax and become corrected.[2] Instead of destroying tissue with radiation, or killing the immune system with chemotherapy drugs, here was a prospective remedy which actually rectified altered cells. It was not so much "anti-cancer," but more "pro-life." The National Institute of Health implemented a variety of tests on independent cells for all manner of cancer types. From some 58 early studies, it was concluded that ORME application caused a dramatic reduction or cessation in cancer activity.[3] Other analytical centers reported similar results.

The researchers were amazed and, to quote from the Science of the Spirit Foundation *Newsletter* of March/April

1996: "They had previously seen materials which would kill cancer cells ... But they had never before seen a material that literally changes the nature of cancer cells and made them act normal."[4] After a number of successful tests on individual volunteers, whom the doctors had previously classified as terminal, specific ORMEs treatment of leukemia, AIDS, and cancer patients was commenced at designated clinics. In New York State, 30 patients entered the test-bed scheme, with the doctor in charge reporting directly to the Alternative Medical Division of the National Institute of Health (NIH). A similar program was begun for 10 patients in Portland, Oregon, while doctors in nearby Ashland agreed to participate in associated brainwave monitoring. Immune system and body tissue protocol was prepared in North Carolina, and a cell engineering facility was established to research thoroughly the precise effects of the monatomic substances on DNA.

As all this progressed and expanded to clinical research centers in different regions, certain facts became increasingly apparent. In the first place, there was no doubt that this was a cancer treatment to end them all – not a cancer killer but a malformed cell corrector. However, there was no drug involved. The ORME materials are noble metals in a monatomic form, but cannot be classified as metal. In the world of science, Hal Puthoff had called them "exotic matter," while in the world of physical benefit, Hudson had classified them as "sacramental material." The emergent problem was that the USA Food and Drugs Administration (FDA) does not have a Department of Sacramental Material. Neither is there a government department designed to oversee exotic substances. This led to a major dilemma in the pharmaceutical world. Chemotherapy compounds produce voluminous income for the drug industry, but here was a more efficient alternative that was not a drug. Moreover, Hudson had lodged the patents and was about to move into production and supply.

David Hudson's main point of contention in this was that, although the dictionary description of "medicine" relates to the treatment of a condition by methods other than surgical procedure, the official interpretation is that medicine is about drugs. Products and treatments which do not fall into a drug classification are designated as "complementary" therapy. This can include all manner of reliefs, cures, and counter-measures from ingested herbal substances to physically applied techniques such as acupuncture. In this respect, however, David was not about to produce or manufacture a drug or even a medicine – simply to supply a product which could be used for curative purposes, but which was equally suited to fuel cells, heat-resistant ceramics, and the like. Copper bracelets are used to alleviate rheumatism; a warmed gold ring will combat a sty – but such things are never classified as medicines or drugs. ORME materials are no different except that, unlike copper and gold, they cannot even be classified as metal.

To quote David in this specific regard, he stated: "I'm not a doctor, so I can't practice medicine. Anything that is administered to someone for the purpose of curing a disease is medicine ... My purpose in this was not to cure diseases and illness, but I did want to know: Does it work? ... I can tell you, it's been used on Lou Gehrig's disease; it's been used on MS; it's been used on MD; it's been used on arthritis ... I can tell you that at 2mg. a day it totally has gotten rid of Karposi Sarcomas (KS) on AIDS patients (there's 32,000mg. in an ounce, 2mg. is nothing). And it gets rid of KS. I can tell you that for people who have taken it at 2mg. injections, within 2 hours their white blood cell count goes from 2,500 to 6,500. I can tell you that Stage-4 cancer patients have taken it orally, and after 45 days have no cancer any place in their body."

The mighty drug corporations must have been reeling at the prospect and, by virtue of the Hudson team's confidentiality agreements, there was no way in which his finalization process could be successfully replicated. What the industry would have recognized was that, once the Phoenix product hit the cancer treatment market, the days of extortionate profits from semi-effective drugs with harmful side effects (requiring yet more compensatory drugs) would be over. However, there would be a way to keep profits high if Hudson was gone from the scene. Instead of an outsider perfecting products from a naturally monatomic substance to sell at reasonable prices, ORMEs in their various forms could be directly made from gold and platinum group metals.

Precisely the same scenario would have been applicable to the oil companies. If ORME-based fuel cells were to become the fuel of the future, then they too could be expensively manufactured from traditionally mined metals. (Indeed the motor components industry was already using palladium for its catalytic converters.) This would not only ensure a continuation of high market prices and high profits, but governmental tax percentages could also be maintained in respect of pharmaceutical and fuel revenues.

It was not long after the collapse of the Hudson enterprise that information concerning PGMs and fuel cells moved into the public domain. In October 2000, Britain's *Daily Telegraph* newspaper reported on the substantially growing industrial demand for PGMs, citing the world's largest producer and supplier as the Anglo-American Platinum Corporation (Amplats), with annual revenues of $2.8 billion. "The long term demand," said the chief executive Barry Davison, "is expected to come from fuel-cell technology."[5] The article continues with a statement that the oil companies, "having seen the writing on the wall," are also looking to a future involvement in fuel cells. Also, "most of the big car manufacturers, including Daimler–Chrysler, Opel, BMW, and Ford, are experimenting with fuel-cell powered cars." To this, Graham Titcomb, group managing director of Johnson Matthey, added that "fuel cells are the only real alternative to the internal combustion engine. The potential demand from this new sector is huge."

As we have seen (under "The Plane of Shar-On," pages 120–4) the May 1995 issue of *Scientific American* confirmed that when single ruthenium atoms are placed at each end of a short strand of DNA, it becomes a superconductor. Also, when a DNA state is altered, as in the case of a cancer, the application of a platinum compound will resonate with the deformed cell, causing the DNA to relax and become corrected. But how is it possible for surgeons to work on such an infinitely small scale?

In the world of physics, the more expansive science gets, the more compact it gets. Scientists have recently announced that they have now invented a transistor from a single atom[6]. This advances the prospect of building powerful computers small enough to fit within the full stop at the end of this sentence. It seemingly opens up a new era in the science of nanotechnology – the construction of machines on a scale of millionths of a millimeter. These include devices which literally can be guided through a body by minute on-board computers to effect precisely the type of DNA corrections discussed in relation to ruthenium atoms and cancer cells. The first such atomic components have now been developed at both Cornell University[7] and Harvard University,[8] and they are just one nanometer (a millionth of a millimeter) across – that is 100,000 times thinner than a human hair.

To put this into perspective: Intel's 1993 microprocessor of less than ten years ago, had 3.1 million transistors on a single silicon chip. The latest powerful microprocessors can hold 40 million transistors. The new discovery, however, can multiply even this by 100 times to an astonishing 4,000 million transistors per chip. This, says *The Times* science correspondent,[9] is the ultimate road to the vanishing point. In "nano" terms, everything is now headed towards realms within the previously unknown hyper-dimensions, and from that point all things will become possible.

1 As detailed in Science of the Spirit Foundation *Newsletters* # 8 & 9, May/June 1996.
2 For example: "Anti-tumour Platinum Coordination Complexes," in *Platinum Metals Review*, volume 34, no. 4, 1990, p. 235.
3 SOSF *Newsletters* # 12 & 13, September/October 1996.
4 SOSF *Newsletters* # 6 & 7, March/April 1996.
5 1st October 2000, *The Daily Telegraph*, Business Section article "The Most Precious of Metals," by Edward Simpkins.
6 *The Times*, News section, p. 12, 13th June 2002. Also in *Nature*, 13th June 2002, article by Leo Kouwenhoven, Department of Applied Physics professor of the Delft University of Technology.
7 Led by Paul McEuen, professor of physics, and Héctor Abruña, professor of chemistry.
8 Led by Hongkun Park, assistant professor of chemistry and physics.
9 *See* date of *The Times* issue in Note 6 above.

Theseus and the Minotaur

Theseus and his mother, Aethra, lived at the foot of a great mountain in a place called Troezen. When Theseus was young, his father, Aegeus, had lifted a huge rock amid the mountain pines, burying his sword and sandals beneath. He told Aethra that, when Theseus was strong enough to lift the rock, she must let him take the sword and sandals, and go to him in Athens, where he was the King of Attica.

When Theseus had grown, he retrieved the sword and the sandals, and set out for Athens. The country was wild, and behind the rocks lurked giants and robbers, but Theseus bade his farewell and began his adventure. He had not gone far when he was attacked by Periphetes the "club-bearer." He looked terrible indeed with his great iron club, but Theseus went bravely forward and soon left Periphetes dead in the road. Taking the club, he then progressed his journey.

Next he met with Sinus the "pine-bender." He would rip travelers apart by bending down the tops of two pines, letting them spring back with his captives tied between. Sinis carried a young pine tree for a club, but it was not so strong as the iron club which Theseus now wielded, and that day it was he who was ripped between the pines. Having traveled a little further, Theseus met with the robber Sciron. He would compel wayfarers to wash his feet, and would then kick them off the cliff into the sea. On this occasion, however, it was Sciron who met the same sorry fate. Not far away lived another robber, Procrustes, who would pretend to entertain strangers at his hut. If they were too long for his bed, he would cut off their heads or feet. If they were too short, he would stretch them to fit. Procrustes too was slain by Theseus, as were other giants and robbers along the road to Athens.

At that time, the beautiful sorceress, Medea, was living in the King's palace. She had a son whom she wished to place on the throne after King Aegeus, and so she mixed a cup of poisonous herbs for Theseus. She told the King that the young visitor was a traitor who plotted against his life, and persuaded Aegeus to hand the cup to Theseus. With no thought of Medea's treachery, Theseus raised the cup to his lips, but at that moment Aegeus noticed the sword and recognized his own son, casting the cup aside.

Medea used all her enchantments to get safely away. First, she summoned a thick mist to rise from the river. Then she called her winged dragons, jumped into her chariot, and departed from Athens, never daring to return. The people lost no time in telling the King of all the brave deeds Theseus had performed on his journey from Troezen. Aegeus was so pleased that he granted three days of rejoicing and feasting. In the midst of this, however, a messenger came to announce that the tribute collectors had arrived from Crete.

A long time before, the eldest son of King Minos of Crete had been slain in Athens. To avenge his death, King Minos brought a great army and compelled the Athenians to pay him, every ninth year, a tribute of seven young noblemen and seven maidens. It was said that the "children of the tribute" were devoured by the Minotaur. This bloodthirsty creature, with the body of a man and the head of a bull, lurked in a labyrinth near the Cretan palace. None who entered the labyrinth had ever returned.

Theseus duly resolved to kill the Minotaur, and to make an end of the tributes. And so, before the lots were drawn, he offered himself as one of the seven young men. This pleased the Athenians, and made Theseus very popular. The other six other young men and the seven maidens were drawn by lot, and everything was made ready for the voyage. It was traditional that the ship which carried the "children of the tribute" should be rigged with black sails, but King Aegeus gave Theseus a white sail to hoist on his return, if he succeeded in his mission.

When the "children of the tribute" arrived in Crete, Theseus informed King Minos that he meant to kill the Minotaur. Minos told the prince that if he could perform this task, then he and all his companions would go free, and never more would the tribute prevail. Nevertheless, he would not permit Theseus to go armed to meet the creature.

Directly over the captives' dungeon were the rooms of King Minos' daughters, Ariadne and Phaedra, who decided to help Theseus slay the Minotaur. Ariadne released Theseus when the others were asleep, and she and Phaedra showed him the famous labyrinth, with its white marble walls gleaming in the moonlight. "This is the best time to attack the Minotaur – while he is sleeping," whispered Ariadne. "Do not wait until the morning. His den is at the very heart of the labyrinth, and you must follow the sound of his breathing. Here is a sword and a ball of thread, by means of which you can find your way back." With these words she held tight to the loose end of the thread, and Theseus entered the labyrinth, sword in hand.

The interior was cut into narrow paths, bordered by high walls. Many of the paths were dead ends and Theseus often had to retrace his steps. There never was a labyrinth so intricate as this, which was made by the famous Daedalus. Back and forth, in and out, Theseus went. He could hear the heavy breathing and knew when he was near to the Minotaur's den. Meanwhile Ariadne and Phaedra stood at the gate, Ariadne still holding her end of the thread. At length they heard a great roar that shook the walls, after which all was silent again. Ariadne did not know if Theseus might be lying dead, or if he might have dropped the ball of thread, but then she felt the thread tighten, and before long the victorious prince emerged.

The galley which had brought Theseus and his companions to Crete was lying on the shore. The sleeping youths and maidens were roused, and were soon on their way back to Athens. Having good reason to fear their father's reprisals, Ariadne and Phaedra went with them. On the voyage, they stopped at the island of Naxos and camped on the rocks for the night. Early next morning they set sail again, but Ariadne remained asleep and was left behind. Not only did Theseus forget Ariadne; he also forgot to hoist the white sail. Thus it was that, when the ship returned to Athens with the ominous black sail flying, King Aegeus (believing that his son was dead) threw himself into the sea.

Back on the island, Ariadne had watched in despair as the galley sailed clear out of sight, but then she heard strange music – the sound of tambourines, pipes, and the clash of cymbals. Behind her, from the pine wood, came a chariot drawn by two panthers. In the chariot, surrounded by nymphs and satyrs, sat Bacchus, god of the vine, with a pine-cone speared upon his lance. When he heard Ariadne's sad story, he said, "Theseus should certainly have taken you to Athens for his queen. But you shall have a better crown than he can offer." With that, he placed a crown of nine bright stars on Ariadne's head. Afterwards, the other gods took her up into the northern sky, where her crown still shines to this day.

Bibliography

Addison, Charles G., *The History of the Knights Templars*, Adventures Unlimited, Kempton, IL, 1997.

Albany, HRH Prince Michael of, *The Forgotten Monarchy of Scotland*, Chrysalis/Vega, London, 2002.

Albright, William F., *Yahweh and the Gods of Canaan*, Athlone Press, London, 1968.

Alcuin, Flaccus Albinus, Abbot of Canterbury (trans.), *The Book of Jasher*, Longman, London, 1929.

Aldred, Cyril, *Akhenaten, King of Egypt*, Thames & Hudson, London, 1988.

— *Egypt to the End of the Old Kingdom*, Thames & Hudson, London, 1992.

Alexander, David and Pat (eds.), *Handbook to the Bible*, Lion Publishing, Oxford, 1983.

Allegro, John M., *The Dead Sea Scrolls*, Penguin, Harmondsworth, 1964.

Allyn, Avery, *A Ritual of Freemasonry*, John Marsh, Boston, MA, 1831.

Alter, Robert, and Kermode, Frank, *The Literary Guide to the Bible*, Fontana, London, 1989.

Anati, Emmanuel, *Palestine Before the Hebrews*, Jonathan Cape, London, 1963.

Anderson, George Wishart, *A Critical Introduction to the Old Testament*, G. Duckworth, London, 1959.

Andressohn, John C., *The Ancestry and Life of Godfrey of Bouillon*, University of Indiana Press, Bloomington, IN, 1947.

Armstrong, Karen, *A History of God*, Ballantine, New York, NY, 1994.

Baigent, Michael and Leigh, Richard, *The Temple and the Lodge*, Jonathan Cape, London, 1989.

Baigent, Michael, with Leigh, Richard, and Lincoln, Henry, *The Holy Blood and the Holy Grail*, Jonathan Cape, London 1982.

Baikie, James, *The Amarna Age*, A. & C. Black, London, 1926.

Barnstone, Willis (ed.), *The Other Bible*, HarperSanFrancisco, San Francisco, CA, 1984.

Bauckham. Richard J., *Jude and the Relatives of Jesus in the Early Church*, T. & T. Clark, Edinburgh,1990.

Baumgartel, E.J., *The Cultures of Prehistoric Egypt*, Oxford University Press, Oxford, 1955.

Baumgartner, W., *The Wisdom Literature: The Old Testament and Modern Study*, (H.H. Rowley, ed.), Clarendon Press, Oxford, 1951.

Bayoumi, Tamim, with Eichengreen, Barry, and Taylor, Mark P. (eds.), *Modern Perspectives of the Gold Standard*, Cambridge University Press, Cambridge, 1997.

Becker, Robert O., and Selden, Gary, *The Body Electric*, William Morrow, New York, NY, 1985.

Begg, Ean C.M., *The Cult of the Black Virgin*, Arkana, London, 1985.

Bernstein, Peter L., *The Power of Gold*, John Wiley & Sons, New York, NY, 2000.

Bertholet, Alfred, *A History of Hebrew Civilization*, (trans. A.K. Dallas), G.G. Harrap, London, 1926.

Besant, Annie, and Leadbetter, Charles, *Occult Chemistry*, Theosophical Publishing, London, 1919.

Bible, The Authorized King James Version with Apocrypha, Oxford University Press, Oxford, 1998.

Bible, The Revised Version, Cambridge University Press, Cambridge, 1885.

Black, Jeremy, and Green, Anthony, *Gods, Demons and Symbols of Ancient Mesopotamia*, British Museum Press, London, 1992.

Bleeker, C., *Hathor and Thoth*, E.J. Brill, Leiden, 1973.

Bordo, Michael, and Schwartz, Anna J., *The Gold Standard and Related Regimes*, Cambridge University Press, Cambridge, 1999.

Box, G.H., *Judaism in the Greek Period*, Oxford University Press, Oxford, 1932.

Branner, Robert, *Chartres Cathedral*, W.W. Norton, London, 1996.

Breasted, James H., *The Dawn of Consciousness*, Charles Scribner's
    Sons, New York, NY, 1934.
Brenton, Sir Lancelot C.L. (trans.), *The Septuagint*, Samuel Bagster,
    London, 1851.
Brewer, Rev. E. Cobham, *The Reader's Handbook of Famous Names in
    Fiction*, J.B. Lippincott, Philadelphia, PA, 1899.
Bright, John, *Early Israel in Recent History Writing*, SCM Press,
    London, 1956.
British Museum, *Hieroglyphic Texts from Egyptian Stelae*, British
    Museum, London, 1911.
Browne, Lewis (ed.), *The Wisdom of Israel*, Michael Joseph, London,
    1948.
Bucher, François, *Architector: The Lodge Books and Sketchbooks of
    Medieval Architects*, Abaris Books, New York, NY, 1979.
Budge, Sir Ernest A. Wallis (trans.), *The Book of the Bee* (from the
    Syriac text), Clarendon Press, Oxford, 1886.
— *The Book of the Cave of Treasures* (from the Syriac text), The
    Religious Tract Society, London, 1927.
— *The Book of the Dead: Papyrus of Ani*, University Books, New York,
    1960.
— *Cleopatra's Needle and Other Egyptian Obelisks* (1926), rep. Dover
    Publications, New York, NY, 1990.
— *Kebra Nagast: Glory of the Kings*, Oxford University Press, Oxford,
    1932.
Bull, Norman J., *The Rise of the Church*, Heinemann , London, 1967.
Burchardt, Titus, *Chartres and the Birth of a Cathedral*, Golgonooza
    Press, Ipswich, 1995.
Burney, C.F., *The Book of Judges*, Rivingtons, London, 1930.
— *Israel's Settlement in Canaan*, Oxford University Press, Oxford,
    1919.
— *Notes on the Hebrew Texts of the Books of Kings*, Clarendon Press,
    Oxford, 1903.

Carlyon, Richard, *A Guide to the Gods*, Heinemann/Quixote, London,
    1981.
Carpenter, Clive, *The Guinness Book of Kings, Rulers and Statesmen*,
    Guinness Superlatives, Enfield, 1978.
Carter, Howard, *The Discovery of Tutankhamun's Tomb*, Metropolitan
    Museum of Art, New York, NY, 1978.

Catholic Encyclopedia, The, Robert Appleton Co., New York, NY, 1908.

Cauville, Sylvie, *Le Temple de Dendera: Guide Archaeologique*, Institut Francais d'Archaeologie Orientale, Paris, 1990.

Cerny, Jaroslav, *The Inscriptions of Sinai*, Egypt Exploration Society, London, 1955.

Challine, Charles, *Recherches sur Chartres*, Société Archéologique d'Eure & Loir, Chartres, rep. 1994.

Charles, R.H. (trans.), *The Book of Enoch*, (revised from Dillmann's edition of the Ethiopic text, 1893), Oxford University Press, Oxford, 1906 and 1912.

Charpentier, Louis, *The Mysteries of Chartres Cathedral*, Research Into Lost Knowledge Organization and Thorsons, Wellingborough, 1972.

Chase, Mary Ellen, *Life and Language in the Old Testament*, Collins, London, 1956.

Chassinat, Emile, *Le Temple de Dendera*, Institut Francais d'Archaeologie Orientale, Paris, 1934.

Chevalier, Jean, and Gheerbrant, *Dictionnaire des Symboles*, Robert Laffont, Paris 1997.

Childress, David Hatcher, *Anti-Gravity & The World Grid*, Adventures Unlimited, Kempton, IL, 2001.

— *Technology of the Gods*, Adventures Unlimited, Kempton, IL, 2000.

Childs, Brevard S., *Myth and Reality in the Old Testament*, SCM Press, London, 1960.

Church, Rev. Leslie F. (ed.), *Matthew Henry's Commentary on the Whole Bible*, Marshall Pickering, London, 1960.

Ciba Foundation, *Telomeres and Telomerase*, John Wiley, New York, NY, 1997.

Clayton, Peter A., *Chronicle of the Pharaohs*, Thames & Hudson, London, 1994.

Clébert, Jean-Paul, *The Gypsies*, Vista Books, London, 1963.

Cohen, A., *Joshua and Judges*, Soncino Press, London, 1950.

Cohn-Sherbok, Lavinia and Dan, *A Short Reader in Judaism*, Oneworld, Oxford, 1997.

Collins, Andrew, *From the Ashes of Angels*, Michael Joseph, London, 1996.

Cook, Nick, *The Hunt for Zero Point*, Century, London, 2001.

Cook, Stanley A., *The Religion of Ancient Palestine in the Light of Archaeology*, (from the 1925 Schweich Lectures of the British Academy), Oxford University Press, Oxford, 1930.

Corteggiani, Jean Pierre, *The Egypt of the Pharaohs at the Cairo Museum*, Scala, London, 1987.

Covey-Crump, Rev. W.W., *The Hiramic Tradition*, R.A. Kessinger, Kila, MT, 1998.

Crowfoot, John W. and Grace M., *Early Ivories from Samaria*, Palestine Exploration Fund, London, 1938.

Cruden, Alexander, *Complete Concordance to the Old and New Testaments and the Apocrypha*, Frederick Warne, London 1891.

Curtis, John (ed.), *Art and Empire: Treasures from Assyria in the British Museum*, Metropolitan Museum of Art, New York, NY, 1995.

Danby, Herbert (trans.), *The Mishnah*, Oxford University Press, Oxford, 1933.

Däniken, Erich von, *Chariots of the Gods*, Souvenir, London, 1969.

Daube, David, *The Exodus Pattern in the Bible*, Faber and Faber, London, 1963.

David, Rosalie, and Antony E., *A Biographical Dictionary of Ancient Egypt*, Seaby, London, 1992.

Davidson, Robert F., *The Old Testament*, Hodder & Stoughton, London, 1964.

Davies, Norman De Garis, *The Rock Tombs of El-Amarna*, Egypt Exploration Society, London, 1906.

Day, David, *Tolkien's Ring*, HarperCollins, London, 1994.

De Lubicz, R.A. Schwaller, *Sacred Science*, Inner Traditions, Rochester, VT, 1988.

Dobbs, Betty J.T., *The Foundations of Newton's Alchemy*, Cambridge University Press, Cambridge, 1975.

Doresse, Jean, *The Secret Books of the Egyptian Gnostics*, Hollis & Carter, London, 1960.

Driver, G.R., *Canaanite Myths and Legends*, T. & T. Clark, Edinburgh, 1956.

Dummelow, J.R., ed., *A Commentary on the Holy Bible*, Macmillan, London, 1909.

Dupont-Sommer, André, *The Essene Writings from Qumrân* (trans. G. Vermes), Basil Blackwell, Oxford, 1961.

– *The Jewish Sect of Qumrân and the Essenes*, Vallentine Mitchell, London, 1954.

Edwards, I.E.S., *The Pyramids of Egypt*, Viking, New York, NY, 1986.

Ehler, Sidney Z., and Morral, John B. (eds.), *Church and State through the Centuries*, Burns & Oates, London, 1954.

Eichengreen, Barry, and Flandreau, Marc, *Gold Standard in Theory and History*, Routledge/Taylor & Francis, London, 1997.

Eisenman, Robert, *The Dead Sea Scrolls and the First Christians*, Element Books, Shaftesbury, 1996.

– *Maccabees, Zadokites, Christians and Qumrân*, E.J. Brill, Leiden, 1983.

Elliot-Binns, L., *The Book of Numbers*, (Westminster Commentaries), Methuen, London, 1926.

Encyclopaedia Judaica Decennial, Keter Publishing, London, 1997.

Engnell, Ivan, *Studies in Divine Kingship in the Ancient Near East*, Basil Blackwell, Oxford, 1967.

Epstein, Perle, *The Way of the Jewish Mystic*, Shambhala, Boston, MA, 1988.

Eusebius of Caesarea, *Ecclesiastical History* (trans. C.F. Crusé), George Bell, London, 1874.

Fagan, Brian M., *Kingdoms of Gold, Kingdoms of Jade*, Thames & Hudson, London, 1991.

Faivre, Antoine, *The Golden Fleece and Alchemy*, State University of New York Press, New York, NY, 1993.

Faulkner, R.O., *The Ancient Egyptian Pyramid Texts*, Oxford University Press, Oxford, 1969.

Forbes, R.J., *Studies in Ancient Technology: No. 8, Metallurgy in Antiquity* – Part 1: *Early Metallurgy*, E.J. Brill, Leiden, 1971.

Frankfort, Henri, *Kingship and the Gods*, University of Chicago Press, Chicago, 1948.

Gadd, C. J., *The Fall of Nineveh*, British Academy & Oxford University Press, Oxford, 1932.

– *The Stones of Assyria*, Chatto & Windus, London, 1936.

Gahlin, Lucia, *Ancient Egypt: Gods, Myths and Religion*, Lorenz Books, New York, NY, 2001.

Gardiner, Alan, *Egyptian Grammar*, Griffith Institute, Ashmolean Museum, Oxford, 1957.

Gardner, Laurence, *Bloodline of the Holy Grail*, HarperCollins, London, 2002.

– *Genesis of the Grail Kings*, Bantam Press, London, 1999.

— *Realm of the Ring Lords*, HarperCollins, London, 2003.

Garstang, John, *The Foundations of Bible History: Joshua and Judges*, Constable, London, 1931.

Geden, Alfred D., *Studies in the Religions of the East*, Charles H. Kelly, London, 1913.

Gerber, Pat, *Stone of Destiny*, Cannongate, Edinburgh, 1997.

Gherman, Beverly, *The Mysterious Rays of Dr. Roentgen*, Atheneum, New York, NY, 1994.

Gibson, Shimon, and Jacobsen, David M., *Below the Temple Mount in Jerusalem*, Tempus Reparatum, Oxford, 1996.

Gimpel, Jean, *The Medieval Machine: The Industrial Revolution of the Middle Ages*, Pimlico, London, 1976.

Ginsberg, Louis, *Legends of the Jews*, John Hopkins University Press, Baltimore, MD, 1998.

Glasser, Otto, *Dr. W.C.R. Röntgen*, Charles C. Thomas, Springfield, IL, 1972.

Gould, R.F., *Gould's History of Freemasonry*, Caxton, London, 1933.

Grant, Kenneth, *The Magical Revival*, Skoob Books, London, 1991.

Graves, Robert, *The White Goddess*, Faber & Faber, London, 1961.

Gray, John, *The Canaanites*, Thames & Hudson, London, 1964.

Greene, Brian, *The Elegant Universe*, Vintage, New York, NY, 2000.

Gribbin, John, *The Search for Superstrings*, Little, Brown, New York, NY, 1999.

Grierson, Roderick, and Munro-Hay, Stuart, *The Ark of the Covenant*, Weidenfeld & Nicolson, London, 1999.

Guirand, Felix, *Greek Mythology*, (trans. Delano Ames), Paul Hamlyn, London, 1965.

Guthrie, H.H., *God and History in the Old Testament*, SPCK, London, 1961.

Hall, Manly P., *The Lost Keys of Freemasonry*, Macoy Publishing and Masonic Supply, Richmond, VA, 1976.

— *The Secret Teachings of All Ages*, Philosophical Research Society, Los Angeles, CA, 1989.

Hamill, J., *The Craft: A History of English Freemasonry*, Crucible/Thorsons, London, 1986.

Hancock, Graham, *Fingerprints of the Gods*, William Heinemann, London, 1995.

— *The Sign and the Seal*, William Heinemann, London, 1992.

Harden, Donald, *The Phoenicians: Ancient People and Places*, Thames & Hudson, London, 1963.

Hasse, A, Landwehr, G., and Umbach, E., *Rontgen Centennial: X-Rays Today in Natural Life Sciences*, World Scientific Publishing, London, 1997.

Hastings, James, *Dictionary of the Bible*, T. & T. Clark, Edinburgh, 1909.

Hawking, Stephen, *The Illustrated A Brief History of Time*, Bantam, London, 1996.

Heard, Richard, *An Introduction to the New Testament*, Adam & Charles Black, London, 1950.

Hebert, Arthur Gabriel, *The Authority of the Old Testament*, Faber and Faber, London, 1947.

Heidel, Alexander, *The Babylonian Genesis*, University of Chicago Press, Chicago, IL, 1942.

Herodotus, *The Histories*, (trans. Robin Waterfield), Oxford University Press, Oxford, 1998.

Herzog, Chiam, and Gichon, Mordechai, *Battles of the Bible*, Greenhill Books, London, 1997.

Hill, Mary, *Gold*, University of California Press, Berkeley, CA, 2000.

Hocart, A.M., *Kingship*, Oxford University Press, Oxford, 1927.

Hodges, Henry, *Technology in the Ancient World*, Allen Lane, The Penguin Press, London, 1970.

Hooke, S.H., *The Labyrinth*, SPCK, London, 1935.

– *Myth, Ritual, and Kingship*, Clarendon Press, Oxford, 1958.

– *The Siege Perilous*, SCM Press, London, 1956.

Horne, Alex, *King Solomon's Temple in the Masonic Tradition*, Aquarian Press, London, 1971.

Howard, Michael, *The Occult Conspiracy*, Rider/Century Hutchinson, London, 1989.

Hunter, Michael, *Science and Society in Restoration England*, Cambridge University Press, Cambridge, 1981.

Isserlin, B.S.J., *The Israelites*, Thames & Hudson, London, 1998.

Jack, J.W., *The Ras Shamra Tablets: Their Bearing on the Old Testament*, T. & T. Clark, Edinburgh, 1935.

Jacobsen, Thorkild, *The Sumerian King List*, (Assyrialogical Studies No.11), University of Chicago Press, Chicago, IL, 1939.

— *The Treasures of Darkness: A History of Mesopotamian Religion*, Yale University Press, New Haven, CT, 1976.

James, E.O., *The Ancient Gods*, Weidenfeld & Nicolson, London, 1960.

— *The Nature and Function of the Priesthood*, Thames & Hudson, London, 1955.

James, John, *The Master Masons of Chartres*, West Grinstead Publishing, Leura, NSW, 1990.

Jennings, Hargrave, *The Rosicrucians: Their Rites and Mysteries*, Routledge, London, 1887.

Jeremias, Alfred, *The Old Testament in the Light of the Ancient Near East*, Williams & Norgate, London, 1911.

Jerusalem Bible, The, Darton, Longman & Todd, London, 1996.

Jones, A H.M., *The Herods of Judaea*, Clarendon Press, Oxford, 1938.

Jones, Bernard E., *Freemasons' Book of the Royal Arch*, George G. Harrap, London, 1980.

— *Freemasons' Guide and Compendium*, Harrap, London, 1956.

Jones, Steve, *In the Blood: God, Genes and Destiny*, HarperCollins, London, 1996.

Josephus, Flavius, *The Works of Flavius Josephus*, including *The Antiquities of the Jews, The Wars of the Jews* and *Against Apion*, (trans. William Whiston), Milner & Sowerby, London, 1870.

Jung, Carl Gustav, *Psychology and Alchemy*, Routledge, London, 1980.

Kaiser, Cletus J., *The Capacitor Handbook*, Van Nostrand Reinhold, New York, NY, 1993.

Kaku, Michio, *Beyond Einstein*, Anchor Books, New York, NY, 1995.

Keating, Geoffrey, *The History of Ireland*, (trans. David Comyn and Rev. P.S. Dinneen), 1640; reprinted by Irish Texts Society, London, 1902–14.

Keil, K.F., *Manual of Biblical Archaeology*, (trans. Peter Christie), T. & T. Clark, Edinburgh, 1888.

Keller, Werner, *The Bible as History*, (trans. William Neil), Hodder & Stoughton, London, 1956.

Kennett, R.H., *Deuteronomy and the Decalogue*, Cambridge University Press, Cambridge, 1920.

Kenney, James F., *The Sources for the Early History of Ireland*, Four Courts Press, Dublin, 1966.

Kenyon, Kathleen, *Amorites and Canaanites*, (The Schweich Lectures, 1963), Oxford University Press, Oxford, 1966.

King, Karen L. (ed.), *Images of the Feminine in Gnosticism*, Fortress Press, Philadelphia, PA, 1988.

Kingsland, William, *The Gnosis or Ancient Wisdom in the Christian Scriptures*, Allen & Unwin, London, 1937.

Kipling, David, *The Telomere*, Oxford University Press, Oxford, 1995.

Kitchen, Kenneth Anderson, *Ramesside Inscriptions*, B.H. Blackwell, Oxford, 1975.

Kjellson, Henry, *Forvunen Teknik*, Nihil, Copenhagen, 1974.

Knappert, Jan, *The Encyclopedia of Middle Eastern Religion and Mythology*, Element Books, Shaftesbury, 1993.

Knight, Christopher, and Lomas, Robert, *The Hiram Key*, Century, London, 1996.

Knight, S., *The Brotherhood: The Secret World of the Freemasons*, Granada, St. Albans, 1984.

Kostjuk, Olga G., *Gold of the Tsars*, Arnoldsche Verlagsanstalt, Stuttgart, 1996.

Kramer, Samuel Noah, *History Begins at Sumer*, Thames & Hudson, London, 1958.

– *Sumerian Mythology*, Harper Bros., New York, NY, 1961.

Kuhl, C., *The Prophets of Israel*, Oliver and Boyd, London, 1960.

Lambert, W.G., *Babylonian Wisdom Literature*, Clarendon Press, Oxford, 1960.

Lapidus, *In Pursuit of Gold: Alchemy in Theory and Practice*, (ed. Stephen Skinner), Neville Spearman, London, 1976.

Leick, Gwendolyn, *Mesopotamia*, Allen Lane/Penguin, London, 2001.

Lemesurier, Peter, *The Great Pyramid Decoded*, Element, Shaftesbury, 1997.

Levine, Moshe, *The Tabernacle: Its Structure and Utensils*, Soncino Press, Tel Aviv, 1969.

Levine, Sue A., *The Northern Foreportal Column Figures of Chartres Cathedral*, Verlag Peter Lang, Frankfurt, 1984.

Lewis, H. Spencer, *The Mystical Life of Jesus*, Ancient and Mystical Order Rosae Crucis, San Jose, CA, 1982.

Lindblom, J., *Prophecy in Ancient Israel*, Basil Blackwell, Oxford, 1962.

Lister, Martin, *A Journey to Paris in the Year 1698*, Jacob Tonson, London 1699.

Lloyd, Seton, *The Art of the Ancient Near East*, Thames & Hudson, London, 1961.

Lohmeyer, E., *Lord of the Temple*, (trans. S. Todd), Oliver and Boyd, London, 1961.

Lomas, Robert, *The Invisible College*, Headline, London, 2002.

Loomis, Roger Sherman, *The Grail: From Celtic Myth to Christian Symbolism*, University of Wales Press, Cardiff, 1963.

Luckert, Karl W., *Egyptian Light and Hebrew Fire*, State University of New York Press, New York, NY, 1991.

Maiman, Theodore, *The Laser Odyssey*, Laser Press, Blaine, WA, 2000.

Malan, Rev. S.C. (trans.), *The Book of Adam and Eve*, (from the Ethiopic text), Williams & Norgate, London, 1882.

Manley, M.A., *The Book of the Law: Studies in the Date of Deuteronomy*, Tyndale Press, London, 1957.

Marazov, Ivan, Fol, Alexander, Tacheva, Margarita, and Venedikov, Ivan, *Ancient Gold: The Wealth of the Thracians*, Harry N. Abrams, New York, NY, 1998.

Marshall, Peter, *The Philosopher's Stone*, Macmillan, London, 2001.

Martin, G.T., *The Royal Tomb at El-Amarna*, Egypt Exploration Society, London, 1974.

Martin, Malachi, *The Decline and Fall of the Roman Church*, Secker & Warburg, London, 1982.

Matthews, W.H., *Mazes and Labyrinths*, Dover Publications, New York, NY, 1970.

May, Herbert G., *Oxford Bible Atlas*, Oxford University Press, Oxford, 1964.

McCalman, Iain, with Cook, Alexander, and Reeves, Andrew (eds.), *Gold*, Cambridge University Press, Cambridge, 2001.

McEwan, John, *Pre-Columbian Gold*, Fitzroy Dearborn, Chicago, IL, 2001.

McNeile, A.H., *The Book of Exodus*, (Westminster Commentaries), Methuen, London, 1917.

McTaggart, Lynne, *The Field*, HarperCollins, London, 2001.

Michell, John, *The Dimensions of Paradise*, Thames & Hudson, London, 1988.

Miles, Jack, *God: A Biography*, Vintage, New York, NY, 1996.

Milik, J.T., *Ten Years of Discovery in the Wilderness of Judaea* (trans. J. Strugnell), SCM Press, London, 1959.

Miller, Malcolm, *Chartres Cathedral*, Pitkin Guides, Andover, 1996.

Mills, Watson E. (ed.), *Lutterworth Dictionary of the Bible*, Lutterworth Press, Cambridge, 1994.

Montet, Pierre, *Eternal Egypt*, (trans. Doreen Weightman), Weidenfeld & Nicolson, London, 1964.

Muller, Hans Wolfgang, and Thiem, Eberhard, *The Royal Gold of Ancient Egypt*, I.B. Tauris, London, 1999.

North, Christopher R., *The Old Testament Interpretation of History*, Epworth Press, London, 1946.

Noth, Martin, *The History of Israel*, (trans. S. Godman), Adam & Charles Black, London, 1960.

O'Brien, Christian and Barbara Joy, *The Genius of the Few*, Dianthus, Cirencester, 1999.

– *The Shining Ones*, Dianthus, Cirencester, 1997.

Oesterley, W.O.E., and Robinson, T.H., *Hebrew Religion, Its Origin and Development*, SPCK, London, 1937/Macmillan, New York, 1937.

Oldenbourg, Zoé, *Massacre at Montségur*, (trans. Peter Green), Pantheon, New York, NY, 1961.

Osman, Ahmed, *Moses, Pharaoh of Egypt*, Grafton/Collins, London, 1990.

– *The House of the Messiah*, HarperCollins, London, 1992.

– *Stranger in the Valley of Kings*, Souvenir Press, London, 1987.

Patai, Raphael, *The Hebrew Goddess*, Wayne State University Press, Detroit, MI, 1967.

– *The Jewish Alchemists*, Princeton University Press, Princeton, NJ, 1994.

– *The Jewish Mind*, Charles Scribner's Sons, New York, NY, 1977.

Peet, T. Eric, *Egypt and the Old Testament*, Liverpool University Press, Liverpool, 1922.

Perowne, S., *The Later Herods*, Hodder & Stoughton, London, 1958.

– *The Life and Times of Herod the Great*, Hodder & Stoughton, London, 1956.

Petrie, W.M. Flinders, *Ancient Egypt and Ancient Israel*, (1910), Ares Publishers, Chicago, IL, 1980.

– *Researches in Sinai*, John Murray, London, 1906.

Philalethes, Eirenaeus, *Introitus apertus ad occulusum regis palatium* – *Open entrance to the closed palace of the King: Secrets Revealed*, Musaeum Hermeticum, Amsterdam, 1667.
– *Tres tractatus de metallorum transmutatione* – *Brief Guide to the Celestial Ruby*, Musaeum Hermeticum, Amsterdam, 1668.
Porter, J.R., *The Illustrated Guide to the Bible*, Duncan Baird, London, 1995.
Presley, Reg, *Wild Things They Don't Want Us to Know*, Blake/Metro, London, 2002.
Pritchard, James B., *The Ancient Near East In Pictures: Relating to the Old Testament*, Princeton University Press, Princeton, NJ, 1954.

Qualls-Corbett, Nancy, *The Sacred Prostitute*, Inner City Books, Toronto, 1988.

Rad, G. von, *Studies in Deuteronomy*, SCM Press, London, 1953.
Ramage, Andrew, and Craddock, Paul, *King Croesus' Gold: Excavations at Sardis*, British Museum, London, 2000.
Rankin, O.S., *Israel's Wisdom Literature*, T. & T. Clark, Edinburgh, 1936.
Ravenscroft, Trevor, and Wallace-Murphy, Tim, *The Mark of the Beast*, Samuel Weiser, York Beach, ME, 1997.
Read, John, *Prelude to Chemistry*, Bell, London, 1936.
Reade, Julian, *Assyrian Sculpture*, British Museum, London, 1983.
– *Mesopotamia*, British Museum, London, 1991.
Reader's Digest, *The World's Last Mysteries*, Reader's Digest, London, 1978.
Recht, Rolland, *Les Bâtisseurs des Cathédrales Gothiques*, Éditions les Musées de la Ville de Strasbourg, Strasbourg, 1989.
Redford, Donald B., *Akhenaten, the Heretic King*, Princeton University Press, Princeton, NJ, 1984.
– *Egypt, Canaan and Israel in Ancient Times*, Princeton University Press, Princeton, NJ, 1992.
Reed, William L., *The Asherah in the Old Testament*, Texan Christian University Press, Fort Worth, TX, 1949.
Reeder, Ellen (ed.), *Scythian Gold*, Harry N. Abrams, New York, NY, 1999.
Reeves, Nicholas, *The Complete Tutankhamun*, Thames & Hudson, London, 1990.

— *Ancient Egypt: The Great Discoveries*, Thames & Hudson, London, 2000.

Reiter, Russel J., and Robinson, Jo, *Melatonin*, Bantam Books, New York, NY, 1996.

Ritmeyer, Leen and Kathleen, *Secrets of Jerusalem's Temple Mount*, Biblical Archaeological Society, Washington, DC, 1998.

Roaf, Michael, *Cultural Atlas of Mesopotamia and the Ancient Near East*, Equinox, Oxford, 1990.

Roberts, Rev. Alexander, and Donaldson, James (eds.), *Ante-Nicene Fathers No.6*, Continuum International/T. & T. Clark, Edinburgh, 1980.

Robinson, H.W., *Inspiration and Revelation in the Old Testament*, Clarendon Press, Oxford, 1956.

— *The Religious Ideas of the Old Testament*, G. Duckworth, London, 1959.

Robinson, James, *The Nag Hammadi Library*, The Coptic Gnostic Project, E.J. Brill, Leiden, 1977.

Rohl, David M., *A Test of Time: The Bible from Myth to History*, Century, London, 1995.

Rola, Stanislas Klossowski de, *Alchemy*, Thames & Hudson, London, 1977.

Roney-Dougal, Serena, *Where Science and Magic Meet*, Element Books, Shaftesbury, 1993.

Roux, Georges, *Ancient Iraq*, George Allen & Unwin, London, 1964.

Rowley, H.H., *From Moses to Qumrân*, Lutterworth Press, 1963.

— *The Rediscovery of the Old Testament*, James Clarke & Co., London, 1945.

— *Royal Arch: Aldersgate Ritual*, Lewis Masonic, Hersham, 1999.

Runciman, Steven, *A History of the Crusades*, Cambridge University Press, Cambridge, 1951.

Sanderson, Ivan T., *Investigating the Unexplained*, Prentice Hall, Englewood Cliffs, NJ, 1972.

Sarna, Nahum M., *The Origins of the Biblical Israel*, Schocken Books, New York, NY, 1996.

Sassoon, John, *From Sumer to Jerusalem*, Intellect Books, Oxford, 1993.

Schonfield, Hugh J., *The Essene Odyssey*, Element Books, Shaftesbury, 1984.

— *The Passover Plot*, Element Books, Shaftesbury, 1985.

Scholem, Gershom G., *Major Trends in Jewish Mysticism*, Thames & Hudson, London, 1955.

— *On the Kabbalah and its Symbolism*, Schocken Books, New York, 1965.

— *Zohar: The Book of Splendour*, Schocken Books, New York, NY, 1963.

Schrödter, Willy, *A Rosicrucian Notebook*, Samuel Weiser, York Beach, Maine, 1992.

Segal, J.B., *The Hebrew Passover: From the Earliest Times to AD 70*, Oxford University Press, Oxford, 1963.

Seward, Desmond, *The Monks of War*, Paladin/Granada, St. Albans, 1974.

Shafer, Byron E., *Temples of Ancient Egypt*, Cornell University Press, Ithaca, NY, 1999.

Shapiro, Debbie, *The Body Mind Workbook*, Element Books, Shaftesbury, 1990.

Simpson, Cuthbert A., *Composition of the Book of Judges*, Basil Blackwell, Oxford, 1957.

— *The Early Traditions of Israel*, Basil Blackwell, Oxford, 1948.

Sinclair, Andrew, *The Sword and the Grail*, Crown, New York, NY, 1992.

Sitchin, Zecharia, *Divine Encounters*, Avon Books, New York, NY, 1990.

— *Genesis Revisited*, Avon Books, New York, NY, 1995.

— *The 12th Planet*, Avon Books, New York, 1978.

Smith, Dr. William, *Smith's Bible Dictionary*, (1868 revised), Hendrickson, Peabody, MA, 1998.

Smith, Ray Winfield, and Redford, Donald B., *The Akhenaten Temple Project*, Aris & Phillips, Warminster, 1976.

Smith, Sidney, *Early History of Assyria*, Chatto & Windus, London, 1928.

Smith, W. Robertson, *The Religion of the Semites*, Adam & Charles Black, London, 1894.

Snape, Steven, *Egyptian Temples*, Shire Publications, Risborough, 1996.

Spahn, Heinz-Peter, *From Gold to Euro*, Springer Verlag, Heidelberg, 2001.

Sparks, H.F.D. (ed.), *Apocryphal Old Testament*, Clarendon Press, Oxford, 1984.

Spong, John Selby, *Born of a Woman*, HarperSanFrancisco, San Francisco, CA, 1994.

Stierlin, Henri, *The Gold of the Pharaohs*, Pierre Terail, Paris, 1997.

Stoyanov, Yuri, *The Hidden Tradition in Europe*, Arkana/Penguin, London, 1995.

Strong, James, *The Exhaustive Concordance of the Bible*, Abingdon Press, New York, NY, 1890.

Suarès, Carlo, *The Cipher of Genesis*, Samuel Weiser, Maine, 1992.

Sworder, Mary (ed.), *Fulcanelli, Master Alchemist – Le Mystère des Cathédrales*, Brotherhood of Life, Albuquerque, NM, 1986.

Tacitus, *The Annals of Imperial Rome*, (trans. Michael Grant), Penguin, London, 1956.

– *The Histories*, (trans. Kenneth Wellesley), Penguin, London, 1995.

Taylor, F. Sherwood, *The Alchemists*, Heinemann, London, 1952.

Taylor, J.W., *The Coming of the Saints*, Covenant Books, London, 1969.

Taylor, Nick, *Laser: The Inventor, the Noble Laureate, and the Thirty-year Patent War*, Simon & Schuster, New York, NY, 2000.

Temple, Robert, *The Crystal Sun*, Century, London, 2000.

Thiele, Edwin R., *The Mysterious Numbers of the Hebrew Kings*, Zondervan, Grand Rapids, MI, 1983.

Thiering, Barbara, *Jesus the Man*, Transworld, London, 1992.

Thomas, D. Winton (ed.), *Documents From Old Testament Times*, HarperCollins, New York, NY, 1961.

Times Atlas of Archaeology, The, Times Books, London, 1988.

Times Atlas of the Bible, The, Times Books, London, 1987.

Tinniswood, Adrian, *His Invention So Fertile: A Life of Christopher Wren*, Jonathan Cape, London, 2001.

Tiradritti, Francesco (ed.), *Ancient Egypt*, British Museum, London, 2002.

– *The Cairo Museum*, Thames & Hudson, London, 1999.

Torjesen, Karen Jo, *When Women Were Priests*, HarperSanFrancisco, San Francisco, CA, 1995.

Unterman, Alan, *Dictionary of Jewish Lore and Legend*, Thames & Hudson, London, 1997.

Van der Leeuw, G., *Religion in Essence and Manifestation*, (trans J.E. Turner), Allen & Unwin, 1938.

Vaux, Roland de, *The Early History of Israel to the Period of the Judges*, Darton, Longman & Todd, London, 1978.

Velikovsky, Immanuel, *Ages in Chaos*, Sidgwick & Jackson, London, 1952.

– *Worlds in Collision*, Victor Gollancz, London, 1973.

Vermes, Geza, *The Complete Dead Sea Scrolls in English*, Penguin, London, 1998.

– *Jesus the Jew*, SCM Press, London, 1983.

Vernus, Pascal, and Lessing, Erich, *The Gods of Ancient Egypt*, Tauris Parke, London, 1998.

Vilar, Pierre (trans. Judith White), *A History of Gold and Money*, 1450–1920, Verso Books, London, 1984.

Voragine, Jacobus de, *The Golden Legend*, (trans. William Caxton), Cambridge University Press, Cambridge, 1972.

Vriezen, Thomas C., *An Outline of Old Testament Theology*, (trans. S. Neuijen), Basil Blackwell, Oxford, 1958.

Waite, Arthur Edward, *Alchemists Through the Ages*, Steinerbooks, New York, NY, 1988.

– *The Brotherhood of the Rosy Cross*, William Rider, London, 1924.

– *The Hidden Church of the Holy Grail*, Rebman, London, 1909.

– *The New Encyclopedia of Freemasonry*, Weathervane, New York, 1970.

Wallace-Murphy, Tim, and Hopkins, Marilyn, *Rosslyn*, Element Books, Shaftesbury, 1999.

Ward, J.S.M., *Freemasonry and the Ancient Gods*, Baskerville, London, 1926.

– *Who Was Hiram Abiff?*, Baskerville, London, 1925.

Watterson, Barbara, *Amarna: Ancient Egypt's Age of Revolution*, Tempus, Stroud, 1999.

– *Gods of Ancient Egypt*, Sutton, Stroud, 1996.

Weigall, Arthur, *The Life and Times of Akhenaten*, Thornton Butterworth, London, 1910.

Weinberg, Steven Lee (ed.), *Ramtha*, Sovereignty Inc., Eastbound, WA, 1986.

Welch, A.C., *The Work of the Chronicler*, (Schweich Lectures, 1938), The British Academy, London, 1939.

White, Michael, *Isaac Newton*, Fourth Estate, London, 1997.

Wilkinson, John T., *Principles of Biblical Interpretation*, Epworth Press, London, 1960.

Wilkinson, Richard H., *The Complete Temples of Ancient Egypt*, Thames & Hudson, London, 2000.

Williams, Dyfri, and Ogden, Jack, *Greek Gold*, British Museum Press, London, 1994.

Wilson, A.N., *Jesus*, Sinclair Stevenson, London, 1992.

Wilson, Colin, and Grant, John, *The Directory of Possibilities*, Webb & Bower, Exeter, 1981.

Witt, Reginald Eldred, *Isis in the Greco – Roman World*, Thames & Hudson, London, 1971.

Wojcik, Jan W., *Robert Boyle and the Limits of Reason*, Cambridge University Press, Cambridge, 1997.

Wolters, Al, *The Copper Scroll*, Sheffield Academic Press, Sheffield, 1996.

Wood, David, *Genisis: The First Book of Revelations*, Baton Press, Tunbridge Wells, 1985.

Wright, G. Ernest, *The Old Testament Against its Environment*, SCM Press, London, 1950.

Yadin, Yigael, *The Art of Warfare in Biblical Lands*, Weidenfeld & Nicolson, London, 1963.

– *The Temple Scroll*, Weidenfeld & Nicolson, London, 1985.

Yates, Frances A., *The Rosicrucian Enlightenment*, Routledge, London, 1972.

Yatri, *Unknown Man*, Sidgwick & Jackson, London, 1988.

Young, Edward J., *An Introduction to the Old Testament*, Tyndale Press, London, 1960.

Ziegler, Jerry L., *YHWH*, Star Publications, Morton, IL, 1977.

Zuckerman, Arthur J., *A Jewish Princedom in Feudal France*, Columbia University Press, New York, NY, 1972.

Picture Credits

Thanks must go to those below in respect of the following photographic illustrations and copyright images:

10, 18, 25, Bridgeman Art Library, London; 9, Fitzwilliam Museum, Cambridge; 15, British Museum, London; 11, 12, 14, 16, 19, 20, Private Collection; 5, 6, 21, Peter Robson Studio <http://www.entropic-art.com/> and Entropic Fine Art Inc; 23, Andrew Jones Studio; 1, 2, 17, 24, The Cleminson Collection; 3, Nancy Vann; 4, Michael Gerrish; 7, 13, The Patrick Foundation; 22, Sonia Halliday Photographs; 8, Hera Magazine, Rome.

While every effort has been made to secure permissions, if there are any errors or oversights regarding copyright material, we apologise and will make suitable acknowledgement in any future edition.

Index